HURSTPIERPOINT COLLEGE

1849-1995

The School by the Downs

Hurstpierpoint College in 1979.

HURSTPIERPOINT COLLEGE
1849-1995

The School by the Downs

Peter King

Phillimore

1997

Published by
PHILLIMORE & CO. LTD.,
Shopwyke Manor Barn, Chichester, West Sussex

ISBN 1 86077 043 6

Printed and bound in Great Britain by
BUTLER AND TANNER LTD.
London and Frome

Contents

List of Illustrations

Frontispiece: Hurstpierpoint College, 1979

Acknowledgements

The author was at Hurst for 17 years, and accumulated far too many debts of help while studying College history to list them in full. However, this book could not have been written without the help of the following: the School Council of Hurstpierpoint College, and particularly, Sir Derek Day, the Chairman; two former headmasters, Roger Griffiths and Simon Watson; two bursars, David Williamson and Martin Sherwin, who in difficult economic times did all they could to ensure the book's success; Hugh Dillon, formerly Woodard Archivist; Timothy Ganz, for an excellent pamphlet on the chapel; Martin Williams, who founded the Archives; Roger Moulton, the compiler of the new Register; former members of the Common Room including Kenneth Mason, George Lambert, William Alban, Reginald Ruddock, George Hill, John Peters, Hugh Thomas, and Christopher Dean; Mrs. Margaret Gregory.

An addition has been made to the archives. This is a collection of some forty letters or memoirs covering the period 1924 to 1956. I should particularly like to thank F.R. Whitbourn, Brigadier Francis H.B. Ingall, R. Bestre, J.E. Robins, A.H. Franks, R.G. Allwood, I.M. Dadley, C.H. Simmons, A.H. Clarke, T.D. Walshaw, J.W.H. Watts, A.B. Henwood, D. Coles, D.O. Norman and J.A. Turner for their contributions.

The main source for Hurst's archival material outside the College is at Lancing College. I should like to thank Janet Pennington, the Archivist, for her help and support. Hurst owes her a debt of gratitude. I should also like to thank the following individuals and academic institutions who over a number of years have provided information, or where I have worked: Dorothy M. Owen, Keeper of the University Archives, Cambridge; Kerry York, Resources Centre Librarian, King Edward VI School Birmingham; J.M. Morris, Archivist, Emmanuel College, Cambridge; A. Tilke, Head of Library, Oakham School, Rutland; David West, Honorary Archivist, Marlborough College; A. Monney, Archivist, Radley College; V.H.H. Green, Sub-Rector, Lincoln College, Oxford; Helen Powell, Assistant Librarian, The Queen's College, Oxford; A.G. Lee, Librarian, St. John's College, Cambridge; J. Scovill, Librarian, Magdalen College, Oxford; P. Hare, Archivist, Magdalen College School, Oxford; The Department of Printed Books, The Bodleian Library, Oxford; The Record Office, The House of Lords; The British Library; The London Library, St James's Square; The Woodard Corporation Registry, The Sanctuary, Westminster; The County Record Office, Chichester; Brighton and Burgess Hill Libraries. In the publication of local history few firms can equal the excellent record of Phillimore and Co. Ltd. I should like to thank all those involved in publication, and particularly the Managing Director, Noel Osborne, for scholarly and sympathetic support throughout, Nicola Willmott, the Production Manager and Christine Hanson, Production Assistant. I should like to thank the following for permission to use materials or quote from their work: Lancing College Archives; Radley College Archives; David Newsome, *A History of Wellington College*, John Murray, 1959; Jonathan Gathorne-Hardy, *The Public School Phenomenon 1597-1977*, The Viking Press, New York, 1978 edition; J.R. de S. Honey, *Tom Brown's Universe, The Development of the English Public School*, Millington Books Ltd., 1977; Martin Williams for allowing me to consult and use his work on Edward Lowe; Charles Mitchell, photographer.

This is the first history of Hurstpierpoint, and it is based almost entirely on primary sources, printed and unprinted. I am not so sanguine as to imagine that there are not some factual errors in spite of every care being taken, and I would be pleased if these were pointed out by any readers who may notice them. I wish to point out that books have finite numbers of pages, and limitations of space often prevents full justice being done to events and persons. Not everything is here, but I believe everything of importance has at least received some mention.

Preface

In 1914 the first register of Hurstpierpoint College was published, edited by H.L. Johnson, a former master at the School. By then Hurst had been in existence for 65 years, and yet this was the first attempt to provide some information about its past. Already the sources for this register were thin on the ground, and as a result it contained many mistakes and omissions. Although some attempts were made to update it, most notably by Robert Bury after 1971, it is only now that Roger Moulton is preparing the first authoritative register of the College.

Many independent schools have extensive archives collected over many years looked after by an archivist. It was not until Martin Williams became Head of History in 1971 that any effort was made at Hurst to collect materials and sources, and this was continued by his successor, the present writer. Unfortunately, by this time there were some considerable gaps in surviving material; one of the most serious of which was a lack of primary unprinted sources between 1902 and 1923—the headmastership of Canon Arthur Coombes. What survived was catalogued by Hugh Dillon, Woodard Archivist for a time, and the archives are now housed in their own room opened in 1992.

Lack of a detailed register, and immediately available original sources no doubt played their part in preventing any earlier attempt to write a history. From May 1858 *The Hurst Johnian* school magazine provided an official, but surprisingly detailed and informative source, for those who wished to read the nine hundred or more editions. This magazine contains obituary articles, and from 1888 reminiscences were published from time to time. There were a small number of specifically historical articles, and in the 1949 centenary number there was an historical supplement. In recent years *The Hurst Johnian Newsletter* has also provided some useful information.

But the need for a full history grew increasingly obvious as the years passed, and Hurst became one of the few public schools without one. It was Canon Coombes who first drew attention to this omission when he was editing the magazine during the First World War. His wife, Isabel, collected the existing photographs into albums, and Arthur Coombes printed a number of useful articles including an attempt to provide lists of housemasters. But no action followed his suggestion of a history apart from an annual lecture on the history of the chapel given by H. Bedford Pym. Roger Griffiths, headmaster from 1964 to 1986, was interested in the idea of a history, and it was Simon Watson, headmaster from 1986 to 1995, who brought the project to fruition in 1992 when the present writer retired as Head of History and began his task.

This book has been written with two purposes in mind. The first has been to give an account of the main developments in the School's history based as far as possible on primary printed and manuscript sources. The second has been to make this account interesting, not only to readers who have been associated in some way with the College, but also to others who enjoy educational and local history. The approach has been broadly chronological, but it is not a dull recital of facts. Each chapter seeks to give a picture 'in the round' of school life under the nine headmasters between 1849 and 1995. Of necessity school histories are much concerned with administration, appointments, buildings, finance and changing patterns of educational and school organisation. But they should also be about the pupils themselves. Every effort has been made to describe school life, and highlight boys who, just as much as masters, personified their generation, or contributed substantially to school life.

There are also three points about a history of Hurst which give it added significance as a work on educational history. This is the first history, so far at least, to tell the complete story of a boys' boarding school from foundation to the start of co-education. Hurst is a member of the Woodard Corporation. This is why the first chapter begins devoting some time to Nathaniel Woodard, the Founder, and the aims of his large school organisation. Hurst was the biggest school he founded, and it lay at the centre of his plans for providing Church, middle-class, and reasonably priced education first of all for Sussex and then in a national network of schools.

The first headmaster, and second founder of Hurst, Edward Lowe, was an important figure in 19th-century education all too often overshadowed by Woodard. It was Lowe who put Woodard's educational plans into practical shape, and made them a success in Sussex and then in the Midlands. He also made what started as a middle grammar school into a well-known public school, and because no biography of this man exists the early chapters are devoted, in some detail, to his life and work at Hurst and in the Southern Chapter of the Woodard Society as it was then known.

Thirdly, although Hurst like all independent schools, has always drawn its masters and boys from the whole country, and many parts of the world, it is situated in Sussex. Lowe once remarked that 'the Diocese of Chichester, and the County of Sussex owe many a debt to the Woodard Schools'. Similarly school life at every level from the bishop's palace at Chichester and receptions at Danny Park, to farmers providing fields for a steeple-chase, and a stream for swimming, intermingled with Sussex life. Quite often events at the School illustrate local history from the bitter battles over the appearance of High Churchmen in Sussex in the 1850s to the Home Guard and firewatchers of the 1940s.

For most of its history Hurst has been a boys' school with common rooms staffed by masters. This was not completely true. Girls from other schools were involved in College activities and there were day girls in the sixth form for a time. There were mistresses in the junior house and school and in the senior school as a result of wartime emergency and changing attitudes in the 1960s. But from September 1995 Hurst became fully co-educational and this made a suitable stopping point for the book. At the same time Stephen Meek arrived from Sherborne School to be Hurst's tenth headmaster and to lead the College into a new era as the School by the Downs approaches its 150th Jubilee celebrations.

A Note of Some Terms and Words Used

Any work dealing with a specific institution is bound to contain a number of words special to that institution. This note gives details of some which may cause confusion.

Hurstpierpoint	Refers to the village
Hurst	Refers to the School or College
The Johnian	*The Hurst Johnian*, the school magazine
Johnians	Members of the School
Old Johnians (OJs)	Members of The Hurst Johnian Club, the old boys of the College. Johnian is pronounced with a long 'o' as in R<u>o</u>me
Council	Firstly called the School Committee, the school governors
Division	First called a chapter this is one of the five administrative regions of the Woodard Corporation
Corporation	Firstly called Society this is the Woodard Corporation
Provost	Until 1946 the provost of the Southern chapter was also provost of the Corporation. Thereafter he is Provost of the Southern Division
The Rooker	The house prefects, or the house prefects' room
P.G.C.	The Playground Committee
Danny	The slang term used for Wolstonbury Hill. Danny Park is the house close to it
Boar's Head	A ceremony carried out in December
Etheldreda Day	The old boys' day (and from 1902 to 1937 also Prize or Speech Day)
Form names	Shell, thirteen years, Remove, fourteen years; Fifth, fifteen; Lower, Middle and Upper Sixth, sixteen to eighteen years.

ONE

FOUNDERS AND FOUNDATIONS
1849-1853

Nathaniel Woodard and the Village School at Shoreham and Hurstpierpoint

Dr Bloxam came out [from Oxford] accompanied by some friends including a Mr Woodard who is trying to establish a school for the middle classes on the Church system at New Shoreham. He seems to have a good deal of energy and boldness, which essential qualities are not likely to be embarrassed by over-refinement! I dare say he is just the man for the work. Thus are sound principles of education making rapid progress.

> Diary of Rev. Robert Singleton,
> 5 September 1848,
> Radley College Archives

I have this day taken a house for six months here, large enough to hold ten or twelve boys of the second class—so that now the School is begun, and on Thursday [16 August 1849] four or five boarders will come to make an opening ...

> Rev. Nathaniel Woodard to Rev. Julius Hare, from Shoreham,
> 14 August 1849
> Lancing College Archives

Hurstpierpoint near Brighton. Mr Creasy has to let on lease unfurnished a most desirable freehold house called the Mansion House, situate in the pleasant and healthy village of Hurstpierpoint ... About one mile from the Hassocks Gate first-class station of the Brighton Railway, and near the parish church.

> Advertisement, *The Sussex Advertiser*, 1849

The ceremony of opening S. John's College—an institution, as our readers are aware, devoted to the education of the middle classes on Church of England principles, took place yesterday with a solemnity befitting the great cause which has thus made so important a step in advance ... the grey flint of which it is constructed, relieved by Caen stone copings ... harmonises delightfully with the verdure which surrounds it, and although remarkable for the simplicity of its construction, its magnitude renders it by no means an unimposing feature of the landscape.

> *The Morning Post*, 22 June 1853

In early Victorian Sussex the chief port of the county was Shoreham with a population of nearly four thousand sustained by trade in coal, corn, and timber, by fishing, harbour work, ship repairs, and industries like cement and rope manufacture. It was by the standards of the day a progressive sort of place, lit by gas, with a new union workhouse, and a new iron suspension bridge over the Adur. Like any seaport, however, it had its poorer tenements where there was cholera in 1849, and its many inns like the *Fountain*, the *Dolphin* on the quay looking up Star Lane, and the principal coaching inn itself, the *Star*. In 1840 the first railway line in Sussex opened between Brighton and Shoreham. Either by coach to the *Star*, or in the black and yellow carriages of the railway, a poor curate came in 1846 to take up a post in the town bringing with him from London his wife, Elizabeth, and the first five of their seven surviving children.

There were two parish churches in the town: St Nicolas at Old Shoreham, and St Mary de Haura at New Shoreham. Both churches dated back to Norman times, and recently Magdalen College, holder of the title to the two parishes, had arranged to have St Nicolas restored under the eye of John Neale. St Mary's was in a less fortunate state because it had lost its nave in the great storm of 1703, and still remained in a truncated condition. Magdalen College, Oxford, then in the hands of its redoubtable Tory and Old High Church President, Dr. Routh, had appointed to both titles in 1843 William Wheeler, a High Churchman, later to be a Roman Catholic. As he prepared to welcome his new curate, Wheeler could have had no idea that the curate, Nathaniel Woodard, would found a great educational institution in the rectory, and in various houses surrounding the quadrangular churchyard, and stretching down Star Lane. During the rest of his life he would control or found 14 schools. Four of them including Hurstpierpoint College would start their life at Shoreham between 1847 and 1858.

Hurst's founder, Nathaniel Woodard, like Edward Lowe, Hurst's first headmaster, and Woodard's right-hand man, came from the middle class for whom they intended to provide a national network of schools. Woodard was the member of a family of lesser gentry at Basildon in Essex where he was born on 21 March 1811 as the ninth child of 12 children. His elder brothers farmed the land while Nathaniel was educated by tutors locally, and at Boughton in Norfolk before he took a similar position for himself. Had it not been for the fortuitous death of an uncle who left him some money he would not have been able to enter university. As it was he had to enter one of the poor men's colleges, Magdalen Hall, in October 1833. When he married Elizabeth Brill in 1836 he could not afford two establishments and moved with his wife to Great Parndon near Harlow in Essex. He took a pass degree in 1840, and was ordained by Bishop Charles Blomfield of London in 1842, taking up his first post as curate in the slum parish of Bethnal Green. Due to opposition to some of his views, Blomfield was forced to threaten to dismiss him unless he resigned which he did in December 1843. Blomfield sympathised with Woodard, and sent him next to a parish run by High Church clergy; St James, at Clapton. Woodard had started teaching the poor in Bethnal Green, and at Clapton met Joshua Watson, an important figure in the National Society promoting Anglican primary education. There, too, Woodard came into contact with those interested in education and prepared to give financial backing to new schemes, particularly Henry Tritton of Barclay's Bank, and Sir Alexander Beresford Hope. Charles Miller, rector of Harlow, had been much impressed by Woodard and it was he who had recommended him to the more congenial surroundings of a High Church parish like Shoreham.

It did not take Woodard long to realise that Shoreham lacked adequate educational facilities: indeed all there was in the town was a ladies' seminary and a single church primary school. He began to write to others involved in church education to seek advice, and before long he was in contact with William Sewell, founder of Radley College in 1847, and Charles Wordsworth, second master of Winchester College. Others wrote to him including a Devonshire curate, Edward Lowe, who was thinking of starting a similar school for the farming and trading classes. All those who met Woodard described him as a forceful personality with tremendous energy, and not at all like the reticent cleric he has been portrayed as by some past writers. Two future Prime Ministers, Lord Robert Cecil (later Lord Salisbury), and William Gladstone, who were among his earliest financial backers and public supporters, spoke of his constructive power, his administrative and financial skills, and within a short time Shoreham saw evidence of his plans.

His first school was founded on 11 January 1847, and another followed next year when on 1 August 1848 Lancing College started. On that day Woodard appointed the first scholar of his new organisation. It was called the Society of St Mary and St Nicolas College, Shoreham, which was simultaneously the start of a national organisation and of the Southern Chapter or division of that organisation. Woodard became Provost from 1848 to his death in April 1891, and he was succeeded by Edward Lowe until 1898. In time four other chapters or divisions followed, although only one, the Midland, during his life time, based at Denstone, and with Edward Lowe as Provost from 1873 to 1891.

Woodard ruled his Society as an absolutist. Although there were chapter meetings at Shoreham there was no formal constitution. All that was done was the enrolling of a Trust Deed in the Court of Chancery in April 1855. Although he drew up a constitution it was not published until after his death, and during his lifetime he maintained complete control over the day-to-day affairs of his schools, and every aspect of the Society's work for many years. Not until 1863 was a finance committee set up, and a Society bursar, Edmund Blackmore (OJ), was not appointed until 1871. When he became too infirm to manage everything he handed the rôle of custos and steward of the lands and property to his son, William, in 1868. He resisted any attempt to interfere in the running of his organisation. When the government appointed a commission under Lord Taunton to investigate endowed and grammar schools, Woodard refused either to divulge accounts or to appear before it. You are, Lowe told him, 'acting differently from the authorities of all other schools'. But Woodard did not appear, leaving Lowe to do that, and in the end secured exemption for his schools from the Endowed Schools Act (1869) through his old friend Gladstone, then the Prime Minister.

His single-mindedness, hard work, and strong will bore fruit. By the time he died the Society controlled a thousand acres of land on which some of the most distinguished school buildings of the century had been purpose built by Richard Carpenter and his son, Richard. He had been involved in founding or taking over 14 schools, and only two of them had failed. Within a few years of his death another three had been added to the Society. In Sussex, Lancing, Hurstpierpoint, Ardingly, a girls' school at Bognor and a preparatory school at Ditchling were flourishing, and throughout the country his schools contained about a thousand boys and girls and a hundred staff. During his lifetime he had raised at least £500,000 by ceaseless correspondence with individuals, publishing leaflets, holding large public meetings, and the creation of a network of committees of which those at Brighton (1854), London (1855), Oxford (1861), and Cambridge (1864) were the most important.

He resigned as curate at Shoreham in 1850 and, although continuing to rent a small house there, lived at 12 Cannon Place in Brighton until in 1862 he bought and moved into a large country house, Martyn Lodge, at Henfield. He became a wealthy man with his salary as Provost drawn from all the schools, and in 1870 Gladstone secured him a canonry at Manchester to which he added the rectory of St Philip's in Salford. The pass degree man was honoured with a DCL at Oxford the same year in the Sheldonian, presented to him by Lord Salisbury, the Chancellor, with boys from his schools, including Hurst, in the galleries to watch. When he died he was laid to rest in medieval state in his own chantry in the great central minster of his Society at Lancing looking down on Shoreham where it had all begun.

Woodard first put his ideas on education in a privately printed and circulated pamphlet *Plea to the Middle Classes* (1848) developed four years later in *Public Schools for the Middle Classes*. In early Victorian England there was a serious educational problem brought about by the failure of the small number of existing secondary schools, both public and grammar, to keep pace with the immense demand for education created by a rising population and particularly a rising middle class which could afford to pay for one, and was anxious to acquire it. The small number of great schools then recognised as 'the public schools' were exclusively for the aristocratic and rich, and did not have an enviable reputation for behaviour, learning, or religious practice. The thousand or so grammar schools had largely ceased to provide a proper service, and the funds once allocated to pay for education in them had gone into the hands of trustees and schoolmasters. In Sussex, for example, by the 1850s some grammar schools like Cuckfield and Horsham were virtually primary schools, the schoolmaster at Horsham taking his salary to coach Oxbridge candidates privately. Chichester's Prebendal School, and Steyning and Lewes Grammar Schools fell to less than twenty boys and the grammar schools at Hastings, Midhurst and Rye had virtually disappeared.

Something was being done to correct this situation. Proprietary schools like Marlborough (1843) were coming into existence. Headmasters like Welldon at Tonbridge, Thring at Uppingham, Harper at Sherborne or Pears at Repton were to revive grammar schools, raising them to public school status. Woodard was concerned about two aspects of the problem. He was worried that the middle class could not afford the secondary education on offer, and certainly not those who were poorer, and he was even more worried that the middle class were turning from the Church of England and not coming forward as clergy and schoolmasters. Instead they were inclined to be Dissenters. As a young man Woodard himself had experienced the difficulties he set out to address, as did his right-hand man, Lowe, and as an Anglican High Tory Woodard was quite ready to associate dissent with political dissent, a message not lost on Sussex churchmen and landowners in the age of the Chartists and the Year of Revolutions. There were plenty in the county who agreed with him, and had already stressed similar views. Archdeacon Henry Manning of Chichester in his 1846 visitation charge referred to farmers and tradesmen who 'fill the pews of meeting houses', and the expense of ordination which deprived the middle class of a 'chance of entering the church'. Archdeacon Julius Hare of Lewes repeated similar views in his 1850 visitation charge. And the local gentry were of the same mind. Nathaniel Borrer of Pakyns near Hurstpierpoint lamented that farmers and shopkeepers who, in his view, were the backbone of the country were those amongst whom 'there was most dissent'.

Woodard's solution to the lack of Church of England, affordable, middle- and lower-class education was the largest ever proposed by a single individual, complex and far reaching. There were two main features. At first he intended to provide every diocese or county with an Anglican secondary boarding school, but by the time he set out his plans in some detail in a pamphlet published in 1869 in the form of a letter to Lord Salisbury, this had changed to creating five provinces. The Southern Chapter founded at Shoreham of course became the Southern Division based on Lancing: the Midland (1873), Western (1897), Northern (1903), and Eastern (1968) provinces or divisions followed in due time, and during their history at least fifty schools in England and Wales were involved with Woodard's organisation.

Between his schools, Woodard said, 'it shall be understood that there is a federal structure'. The second key feature was that each province would provide a variety of schools, and within many of the schools, a variety of departments, so that pupils might move from school to school according to the courses desired, the fees that could be paid, and as a result of taking competitive exams for scholarships. Woodard also envisaged the masters similarly moving between the schools for promotion. And beyond schools Woodard wanted to provide for teacher training, ordination, and missionary training: a comprehensive plan for the education of all classes in Anglican foundations. Woodard believed in promotion by merit, and putting 'in the way of everyone an opening for advancement' so that all classes might benefit from church education and church and state in turn benefit from such a system. It was not designed to end class but so that, in Lowe's words, 'class distinctions are modified and made subordinate to merit'. As we shall see, what is particularly interesting about Hurst is that it was the first school to start operating this scheme on a large scale. It lay in the fulcrum of the ladder of advancement among Sussex boys' schools, and contained under its roof no less than four different schools for more than twenty of its first years.

The extent of this scheme clearly shows Woodard's skills to have been in administration just as its success shows they lay also in financial and publicity activities, but he was not an educationalist; nor did he have educational experience of the public school world into which he wished to introduce his middle-class pupils. At Shoreham he could certainly rely on backing from Magdalen College who provided £100 and books for his schools. Woodard met two fellows of Magdalen, John Bloxam (who had a Sussex cure at Upper Beeding), and James Mozley, who succeeded Wheeler at Shoreham from 1856 to 1878, and preached at Hurst on occasion. Through Bloxam, Woodard met William Sewell, visited Radley, and adopted some of his ideas at Hurst and Ardingly. But he needed practical information on running schools, and for this, as Lowe said, 'we naturally turned our eyes towards the best models of our public schools': meaning Winchester College.

The Winchester connection which so influenced particularly Lancing and Hurst is extremely important. All too often public school reform is placed at the feet of Thomas Arnold of Rugby. Arnold was a Low Churchman and a friend of Whig governments. While admitting there was reform in the 1830s and 1840s Charles Wordsworth, Winchester's second master, pointed out that in his school this reform 'partook decidedly of a Church character such as Arnold's teaching and example ... had little or no tendency to create'. Winchester had certainly been in an appalling state in Regency times: it was reformed by George Moberly, headmaster from 1835 to 1866. He was a High Churchman, who confessed to John Keble at neighbouring Hursley, and Woodard was warned Winchester had been 'half ruined by Puseyism'; but it was to Moberly's Winchester that Woodard turned. Firstly, because he was a High Churchman himself and saw his schools as part of a movement which set on foot Radley, St Edward's, Bradfield and Bloxham, schools where Oxford and Winchester influence was powerful.

Secondly, because, in Lowe's words, Woodard was 'building in the country of William of Wykeham'. Lowe and Woodard saw Hurst recreating the conditions that had given rise to Winchester in the 1390s. Then it had been a church foundation given magnificent buildings and a collegiate structure with warden and fellows, but it was for poor boys with only a few places for the rich. All that had changed, but in his account of his work published in 1861 Lowe was clear he saw Hurst recreating those same conditions for a new generation: it was 'an essential element' in the school. There were several features of Hurst life, and terms used directly borrowed from Winchester. Prize day from 1852 was Port Latin Day from the Winchester *Ad Portas*. Climbing Wolstonbury Hill as a Hurst ceremony in part echoes climbing St Catharine's Hill at

Winchester. The scholars' gown was of the long Winchester pattern. At prize giving at Christmas 1851 it was reported that the 'Winchester holiday song *Dulce Domum* was given in admirable style', and it was used for the rest of the century. Another paper commented on the reciting of the Winchester Ode on prize days which was 'rather hard upon Reformers and Puritans'.

Winchester certainly helped both Lancing and Hurst to acquire the status of public schools. Charles Wordsworth preached at the opening of Lancing in 1848 in St Mary's, Shoreham. George Moberly gave £5 to the Hurst Building Fund. He preached in the same place at Hurst's opening a year later, and on subsequent occasions at the school. Charles Moberly was an unsuccessful head of Lancing. Leonard Moberly taught at Hurst. Most significantly from Hurst's point of view Woodard used Winchester's second master to help him find a successor to Lowe, and ended up unwisely making him Hurst's second headmaster.

Considering Woodard's administrative and educational work it is all too easy to forget he was a priest, and that, in Brian Heeney's words, 'all Woodard's work was inspired by religious belief'. Woodard himself would have put it more narrowly. He was building schools to help the Church of England maintain its position against what he called 'Whigs and state bishops'. He was worried that the Anglican Church's largely monopolistic position in education was being undermined by state trained teachers, and non-denominational schools. Both Woodard and Lowe were at Oxford when a movement came into being designed to make the church independent of government, restore the centrality of the sacraments, and the priesthood, and make worship more Catholic. Called the Oxford Movement because it derived much of its intellectual force from a group of Oxford academics and clergy in the 1830s and 1840s, it was, in fact, a much wider reforming movement which divided the Church between High Churchmen emphasising the Catholic elements in Anglicanism, and Low Churchmen who saw the movement as a threat to Protestantism and the Reformation Settlement. Someone once wrote to Woodard saying, 'you drink down every cup of doctrine or duty which the Oxford Movement puts in your head'. This was not true. Woodard was a High Churchman of an older school; the one he found at Magdalen and Winchester Colleges. The Trust Deed setting up his Society made it plain he supported the existing Church by law established, and he said he would not defend anything 'that is not plainly and palpably Anglican'. He told Lowe he was concerned 'to reduce our ceremonial to as simple a ritual as is compatible with reverence', and the Chapter Minute Book makes it plain he was concerned about frequent and reverent religious services rather than incense and vestments.

Clearly Woodard derived strength from the Oxford Movement. East Sussex was the more Protestant part of the county as the Bonfire Riots at Lewes in 1847 would have quickly reminded him, but High Churchmen were at work in Brighton, Lewes and East Grinstead, and naturally there was a mutual pooling of support. John Neale at East Grinstead was one example. The Wagners at Brighton were another. Arthur Wagner contributed to the Hurst Building Fund. The choir from his church, St Paul's, was at the opening of the College in 1853. Lowe preached there on one occasion. Nationally, too, Oxford Movement leaders backed the schools. Edward Pusey gave books to Hurst Library. John Keble, Charles Marriott, James Mozley, and Henry Liddon visited or preached at the school. There could be no real doubt as to where Woodard stood. Both his senior chaplains, Rev. John Knott (1850), and Rev. Edmund Field (1857), who was chaplain of Hurst from 1854, were High Church. Knott went off to work for Pusey at St Saviour's in Leeds. Field fervently backed Wagner, preaching frequently at St Paul's, and also other High churches in London, going too far on occasion even for Woodard.

On the other hand Woodard and Lowe's position affected the chances of success for the Society and particularly the first major school to start functioning. Hurst's early years, as we shall see later in this chapter, were bedeviled by religious criticism which could have affected its chances of success. Starting in March 1850 a campaign by Protestant-minded clergy and local press accused the school of Puseyism, the offensive word for High Churchism, and corrupting boys into becoming Papists. The situation boiled over in the early 1850s because the Roman Catholic Church restored its episcopal order in Britain in 1850, and over a hundred Anglicans were to go over to Rome including many close to Woodard like Manning, Wheeler, Hewett and Bampfield, and much as he deplored these moves they added fuel to the flames of Protestant indignation.

It was, therefore, of supreme importance to Woodard, and to the success of Hurst, that the bishop of the diocese, and the leading clergy, were on his side. Ashley Gilbert (1785-1870) who became Bishop of Chichester in 1842 was like Woodard a Tory High Churchman. He certainly had considerable doubts about some of Woodard's activities as his letters show, but in public he backed him. In March 1848 he became Visitor of the Society, and from then on he was actively involved. Nationally he travelled to London, Oxford and Cambridge to back Woodard. In the diocese he became a frequent visitor to Hurst, being at both opening ceremonies in 1851 and 1853, often at speech day (Port Latin Day), and services. He confirmed boys from the school until 1868, and he accepted for ordination those from the school who had undertaken a special course at Hurst. He gave £400 to the Hurst Building Fund. Where the bishop led, the clergy by and large followed. Manning and Hare, the archdeacons, Chandler and Hook, the deans, were Woodard supporters, and although the opposition proved an annoyance in Hurst's early years it failed, and came to an end after a stormy meeting in Brighton Town Hall heckled Gilbert in December 1856. There were far more clergy who gave support to the Society, and at Hurst's opening ceremonies the papers had to report 'substantial' numbers of clergy present. Neither Woodard nor Lowe was ever Puseyite or Ritualist, and the opposition to them was never as widespread as some past writers have suggested. As we shall see, Lowe was able to ride the storm in the College's early years with success.

II

The founding of Woodard's third school, known as St John's Middle Grammar School, and soon to be Hurstpierpoint College, was announced at a service held in St Mary de Haura Church on 1 August 1849. The Devonshire curate, Edward Lowe, had come to Shoreham in January that year to teach in St Nicolas Grammar School (later, of course, Lancing College), and had impressed Woodard sufficiently to make him headmaster. The school opened its doors for business on 16 August in a single-storey cottage at 20 Star Lane where, according to Lowe, the school room was in the former stable, and the dining room was the old brew house of the house next door. Lowe, a servant, and two boys, soon joined by two others, were the residents, and the new school grew steadily enough. In October four more boys appeared, and by the end of the year the school was outgrowing its humble house and Woodard had to look for new premises. Among the first boys were George Butler and William Pratt who transferred from St Mary's Grammar School.

In the Chapter Minute Book it is recorded that Lowe was told to enforce discipline strictly and attention to the duties of religion, and each day began with a service in St Mary's. From the start Hurst had a modern, wide curriculum compared with the older grammar schools. Latin, English and French were taught with Greek as an extra if required. There was history, geography, mathematics, and natural philosophy (elementary science) and, perhaps more surprisingly still, singing, book-keeping and handwriting lessons. The fees were 18 guineas a year (£18 18s.), and parents also made a contribution to the rent of the building. Life was frugal, and the College's first account book records a total domestic expenditure on food, lighting,

1 Nos. 24, 22, and 20 Church Street (formerly Star Lane), Shoreham. In its first term Hurst was housed in No. 20 and used the facilities at the rear of No. 22. Lancing and Ardingly Colleges subsequently occupied 24, and 22 and possibly 20 as well. The original house was owned by Captain John Butler, and the premises were leased or sold to Nathaniel Woodard by Richard and George Butler in 1849.

heating, bed linen and so forth of £38 3s. 11d. at Shoreham. In their free time the boys exercised on gymnastic poles set up in the dining room, ran on the Downs, or swam in the Adur.

As curate at Shoreham, Nathaniel Woodard was involved in helping the sick during the 1849 cholera outbreak, and went to recuperate in the countryside while he was looking for a site for his new school. He started to look at several properties in the village of Hurstpierpoint like Stroods when he saw an advertisement for the Mansion House, a rambling building with a large garden, whose 18th-century frontage faced the High Street a short distance from the *New Inn*. Woodard saw at once this house had two advantages. The London to Brighton railway line had opened in 1841 and there was a nearby station at Hassocks Gate: the school was thus in direct contact with the two main centres of population in the south. Secondly, in 1845 a large new church designed by Sir Charles Barry had been opened. Holy Trinity provided the necessary church accommodation and, even more valuably, the rector was sympathetic to Woodard's educational and church views.

25 January 1850 was a chilly, wet day when the move from Shoreham was made. It cost £6 19s. 6d. to bring the school on the train, and then in dog carts and flies piled high with boys and luggage up from the station. The move was assisted by the well-built presence of Frederick Arnold, second master at Lancing, and soon to be a headmaster elsewhere, and Lowe now had an assistant second master, Charles Lomax, who had been teaching at St Mary's. On Tuesday 29 January 34 boys walked to Holy Trinity Church where 'a large party of clergymen' and 'a great many ladies and principal tradesmen' awaited a sermon by Bishop Ashley Gilbert. In the congregation were some distinguished faces including Hare and Moberly, and the three leading local squires. A collection of £50 was taken, and the congregation then adjourned for their lunch to the assembly room at the *New Inn* where all major village meetings took place.

Hurstpierpoint was a village somewhat smaller than the town of Shoreham, having a population of two and a half thousand. It contained businesses and shops dependent on the local agricultural community including a number of corn mills. There were corn and fat stock markets, and the local farms yielded apples, beans, walnuts and wheat. If the school was to succeed it needed the support of the village traders, and the neighbouring farmers whom Lowe seems to have managed very well. He and other members of his staff like Lomax and Pennell were frequent guests at village dinners in the *New Inn*. In December 1850 Lowe and Lomax were at the annual dinner of the recently formed Trade Association. In 1852 Lowe and Pennell joined the local friendly society and were at their annual dinner in May. The rector remarked in his diary in June the next year on a *New Inn* dinner where Lowe was present and all 'went off admirably'. Lowe continued to attend these functions for some years: he was at the Fatstock Dinner in July 1859, for example, to pay tribute to Henry Beeching, a retiring local butcher who supplied the College. Some ten per cent of the Mansion House boys came from the local community, and over the school's first ten years the register includes tradesmens' sons like Marchant, Anscombe, Wadey, Beeching and Stevens, and farmers' boys like Broad, Packham, Catt, King and Mitchell. Lowe's down-to-earth view of teaching saying he wanted to educate 'plain born boys' to be 'plain bred men' no doubt had its effect.

Quite as important was the backing of the local gentry in days of deference. Brian Heeney was wrong to say Woodard's scheme did not attract much support in this direction. The new school received strong backing from at least seven local landowning families. The most important of these were the Campions who lived at Danny Park in the shadow of Wolstonbury Hill. William Campion opened his grounds for the boys to climb Wolstonbury Hill, and for cricket matches. He donated prizes for history, general knowledge and the sports, and contributed to the Building Fund. Above all Danny House became vital to Lowe's social life as a suitable setting for entertaining bishops like Gilbert and Wilberforce, and putting up distinguished guests who came as preachers or speakers.

Nathaniel Borrer of Pakyns, who died in 1863, lent the College fields to play cricket, gave a prize and sports day prizes, and an annual Christmas tree. It was from him Woodard bought the land on which the College building would soon stand, and it was from J.G. Dodson of North End House, Member for Rye, that he bought more land later. Robert Blencowe of Chailey, Robert Loder of Wakehurst Place, Francis Barchard of Horsted Place, and the Hanningtons of Little Park were all supporters, and the presence of these dignitaries at prize givings and ceremonies duly noted in the press was of great benefit to the new school which later took some of their sons as pupils. Edward Lowe adopted a Palmerstonian tone in his political pronouncements, and was firmly patriotic. As early as November 1852 a supper costing £4 8s. 11d. was given at the Mansion House to commemorate the Prince of Wales's birthday and this annual ceremony grew in size over the years. During the coming Crimean War and the French invasion scare leading to the Volunteer Movement Lowe had every opportunity to bang the patriotic drum in his new school as we shall see in a later chapter.

The third place in the village where Lowe looked for support and found it was at the rectory where Carey Hampton Borrer was rector from 1841 to 1898. He was not High Church and relations with Lowe in later years when the school had its own chapel were not always friendly, but Borrer's diary shows how from the earliest days Lowe, Lomax and Pennell were rectory guests. Borrer granted them permission to hold their daily service in the church, and to use a choir and preach in surplices; both then considered dangerous Puseyism by Protestants. The Hurst choir sang carols in the neighbourhood at the rectory and Pakyns. Borrer gave a divinity prize, and contributed £30 to the Hurst Building Fund, and on a sadder note in 1853 he permitted the setting aside of the south-west corner of his churchyard as a special burial area for the College: a place sadly requiring two extensions as the years passed, and many small coffins were lowered into the ground by the old thorn tree.

All this local support was vital when Lowe faced his most serious problem in the Mansion House years—religious opposition from outside the school. From the start Julius Hare warned him to be careful, tactfully suggesting the removal of John Henry Newman's picture from the mantelpiece, but the opposition started within two months of Lowe's arrival with the *Brighton Herald*'s article on events in Shoreham. Protestants brandished bibles at the Mansion House as they passed. Gilbert came to see Woodard and Lowe privately at the school, and he was given assurances that there were no non-Prayer Book activities. The reality was that Hurst was doing something controversial and new in a rural community. Divinity lessons, the daily service, the surplices, and sung Sunday services, the use of plainsong from Helmore's Psalter, and preparing boys for confirmation were not then everyday events in grammar schools. They were bound to arouse suspicion that boys were being made 'the easy victims of Romish subtlety and superstition'.

In January 1851 two boys including one at Hurst, Frederick Woodhouse, were withdrawn by parents who claimed they had been forced to attend confession. There were mutterings from a meeting of rural deans next month, and in April John Hewett, a master at Lancing, resigned with dark tales of confession. The shadow hung over the school until early in 1853. Then Hewett told a parent that boys had been the subject of 'habitual confession', and Bishop Gilbert was forced to act. On 12 March he set up a commission of enquiry which met in the uncompleted new building of the College in what was to be the fellows' library. Woodard, the diocesan registrar, the chancellor, the archdeacon of Chichester, and the vicar of Burwash standing in for Hare who was ill, were required by Gilbert to investigate the matter. Their report was published on 14 June, and Gilbert made use of it at the opening of the College buildings a week later, repeating twice that Woodard 'had in no respect departed from the strict principles of the Church'.

The commission concluded that confession was occasional and voluntary, linked only to preparation for confirmation, and never used without parental permission. In fact, Lowe and Woodard had a lucky escape: careful readers of the report would have seen Gilbert firmly telling them to stick to the letter of the law. Woodard and Lowe acted as chaplains in the various schools, and practised confession. No letters from parents giving permission have ever been found, and there was, in fact, fairly frequent opportunity for confession throughout the year. Lowe admitted as much later, saying it was available before Communion, and on specific occasions. Returns submitted to Gilbert four years later showed it was by no means infrequent. However, the main charge that Puseyism was 'the animating principle of the institution' still in the papers in 1855 was untrue, and the report and Gilbert's public support did much to clear the air.

It was perfectly usual for schools to start in private houses—Marlborough and St Edward's Oxford to name but two did so—but it was soon apparent that the Mansion House was not big enough. On the top floor were the school servants and masters' bedrooms. On the first floor Lowe slept in the small room over the main door, and the boys in the rooms on each side of the long passage used for evening prayers. Teaching took place on the ground floor, Thomas Sharp (OJ) recalling, 'I remember almost every inch of that room with its wall of books, and wooden wainscot, tall chimney piece and windows to the ground'. At the end of 1850 Lowe told Woodard, 'I cannot say we are comfortable and we lack almost everything a school needs'. The school started to expand, renting other village properties until the High Street was like a rabbit warren of boys. In 1851 Black Lion House and Middle House were rented. In 1852 a cottage for use as an infirmary, and a house called Luscombes were rented.

2   The Mansion House, Hurstpierpoint. Home of the College from January 1850 until July 1853.

In 1853 houses were rented from Mr. Broad and Mr. Beeching. The house had a garden—and a gardener, Edward Neale, whose wife was the laundry woman, but this was used by Lowe and the masters. For playground the boys went to a field behind the *White Horse* rented at £1 10s. 0d. a quarter from Mr. Spratley. To play cricket a better surface was needed and in 1851 they used the village ground next to the rectory, and next year began renting fields from Ham Farm and Latchetts House.

In one sense over-crowding was a good problem to have: it meant Hurst was succeeding and income was rising. In April 1850 the first substantial intake of 29 boys occurred, and by the end of the first year there were at least sixty members of the school. Numbers rose each year, and about one hundred and fifty boys moved from the Mansion House into the new school buildings. No more than approximate numbers can be given because the register based on Lowe's own record is not complete. For example, Edward Richardson left Lancing for Hurst, and Studholme Hodson left St George's for Hurst, and neither is listed as arriving. The number of boys crammed into the buildings seems excessive by any standards, but it must be remembered that the register did not mention day boys. In 1851 the Society Calendar shows 12 day boys at the school. Most of the boys were small, young boys—indeed the youngest was one Pidding, aged six. In 1851 there were only three boys over 16 so it is feasible that so many were accommodated in so small a space.

In another sense large numbers caused the most serious internal problem of the new school, controlling illness, a problem which was to damage Hurst's reputation for much of the

19th century as it got far worse in the permanent buildings later. A letter in a local paper said that 'fever has worked well for the doctors both at Shoreham and Hurst', and it was certainly true that in 1851 and 1852 there was scarlet fever at the Mansion House in spite of building improvements like a new cess pool costing £10: crowded together it was inevitable it would spread, and without permanent medical isolation or staff, that some cases would take a fatal turn. Hurst had already lost C.B. Field, aged 11, who came in January and died in May 1851. That summer, although a nurse was hired, and a cottage rented with an isolation room, Charles Curtis, aged 15, died on 24 August. Lowe was incorrect to say later, 'we lost none of our boys'. Indeed early in 1853 there was a third loss when S.B. Ford, aged 14, died.

Life for boys in the early school was spartan because Woodard had to save every penny: any development was to come out of current income because he had decided against endowment, linked as that was to corruption in the older grammar schools. Household expenditure in the first year in the Mansion House was £632 and this had risen after two years to £1,450 out of which all running expenses, except for teaching and salaries, had to be met. These included, as the newspaper complainant said, heavy medical expenditure rising to £82 15s. 6d. for the boys in 1852. In his early years Lowe was also establishing his reputation as a wielder of the birch—a bundle of twigs tied together and administered on the bare back. Among a good many cases reported to Woodard during the first year two boys were flogged for lewd talk and two prefects for rebellion. A mother who complained in September that her son was to be flogged for stealing pencils got short shrift: he was flogged and stayed. Lowe no doubt thought that the class of boy he had to deal with required sharp treatment, writing to Woodard on one occasion 'the sailor boy is very rough', and 'I have had to threaten him with the cat [o'nine tails]'.

It is important not to exaggerate the down side of life in earlier times. Reports of prize days commented favourably on the boys: that in 1851 said they were 'rosy cheeked and happy looking', and their treatment has to be seen in the context of living conditions and treatment of young people in mid-Victorian times. Lowe's letter to Woodard in December 1851 when he talked of carol singing and how 'the boys have decorated the dining room with more zeal than taste' shows that life was not all misery and woe. In 1850 on Ascension Day the first climb of Wolstonbury Hill was made. There on the top the choir sang *Te Deum Patrem Colimus*, Lowe gave a gift or dole to them, and the boys then chased biscuits and coconuts and other foodstuffs rolled down the slope to the wood at the bottom where Campion and Blencowe brewed up tea. This is certainly Hurst's oldest ceremony, and illustrates very well how Magdalen and Winchester Colleges affected Hurst's customs. While at Oxford, Lowe had seen John Bloxam's revival of the Magdalen custom of singing this hymn from the top of the tower on May morning, and knew Bloxam gave Magdalen College School a dole. At Winchester and Eton there was a custom of going *ad montem*, and Lowe combined the two to provide a tradition that has lasted a hundred and fifty years.

There were school trips in 1852. The newly opened railway line to Newhaven enabled a sea-side trip costing £6 15s. 3d. to be made to Seaford, and even more remarkably a school party went by rail to Polegate, visited Pevensey Castle, and then were taken by horse brake to Julius Hare's rectory at Herstmonceux and entertained with fruit tarts in the garden. The accounts make it clear that there were outside lectures from time to time. There was also sport. Matches were played with the Shoreham boys at cricket from 1850, and in 1852 there was a game with the village XI which was lost, but took place in a more relaxed atmosphere than in later years with cider being drunk by all, and the winning team being given a cricket ball. There was swimming, too, after a two-mile walk across the fields to Pond Leigh (or Lye) which lies still today just beyond the *Sportsman Inn*. The accounts show that from at least 1852 Henry Alford (at £27 a year) was employed to teach drilling and fencing.

Lowe himself taught Latin, Divinity and English on an irregular basis. He began with only one assistant master, Charles 'Carrots' Lomax, whose main responsibility was mathematics. He was joined during the first year by the Rev. Richard Lewin Pennell from Cheriton Bishop in Devon, teaching history and geography, a man much loved and respected over many years to come, Hurst's first long serving master, and first great common room eccentric. The register published in 1914 gives an inaccurate list of the early masters: reference to the account book shows who was paid. It shows Charles Mallard arrived later in 1850. During 1851 Charles Turner came from St Mary's in Shoreham, and four associates started teaching: Sayer Warmoll, Albert Verrall, Herbert Hurst who came on from Lancing, all of whom left in 1854, and the Rev. Edwin Marten (or Martin) who left in 1856, and was to make an important contribution to Hurst music, and the play. Henry Alford was drilling master, and Frederick Earp taught drawing from 1851. The accounts show that by June 1852 Lowe had seven masters in the school, and they remained the same a year later when the move took place. No-one apart from Lowe, whose salary reached £200 a year in 1853, earned very much money. The total masters' salary bill was £125 10s. 10d. in June 1853.

The School continued to provide its broad syllabus, and several of the boys soon demonstrated that Woodard's plan could work. Francis Williams was the school's first successful Oxbridge candidate, going to Lowe's old college, Lincoln, at Oxford. Both he and Joseph White went on to be headmasters. Among those who were associates or pupils in the Mansion House were George Ling, Herbert Hurst, William Pratt, and Joseph Eaton who all taught at Hurst. William Pratt became school secretary. John Dayson not only taught at Hurst but became first bursar of King's, Taunton, and Edmund Blackmore, as we have seen, was bursar of the Southern Chapter. According to the sparse information on careers in the 1914 register, four Mansion House boys entered the Civil Service, four teaching, three the church, three law, nine the medical profession, one the army, and one the navy, so that a narrow ladder of advancement had been opened into the professional world.

Lowe was a convinced believer in exams and prizes, and as early as 1851 asked Woodard to appoint external examiners, although this took some years to arrange. The first prize day took place on 21 June 1850, and there was a second annual prize distribution in December each year. That year the summer prizes were followed by a buffet meal in the garden of the Mansion House while the Christmas prizes were distributed in the *New Inn* assembly room and the choir performed. By 1852 Lowe had moved towards the idea of prize day being as near as possible to 6 May, Port Latin Day, and that year the *Brighton Guardian* reported favourably on a programme including a service in the church when Lowe preached, and a prize giving during which the choir sang, there were declamations, and Nathaniel Borrer spoke to the boys. No expense was spared (that year it cost £22) to make this a grand occasion, well reported in the press, and within a few years the cost had doubled and the accounts included a wine merchant's bill, special preserves, and pigeons for a pie.

Lowe had clearly made a great success of the new school. Not only were numbers rising, but the reputation of the College was spreading. Lowe's own register recorded place of birth, and it was inevitable that many came from the locality. Hurst village had a scholarship for a free place for a day boy, and Cuckfield was given one in 1854 after subscribing more than any other parish to the Building Fund. No doubt they were missing their closed grammar school—there were six boys from there in Lowe's register. Eleven came from Shoreham, and 37 from Brighton. But what was most significant was that boys were coming from further afield, from London, and no

3 Richard C. Carpenter's design for the College buildings with its high chapel tower, complete inner cloister, approach directly from the south, and headmaster's house to the north-west.

less than 13 counties by 1853. By 1860 this had risen to eighteen. So Woodard could almost immediately start planning a permanent site for the College. At the first anniversary of the opening Woodard told his congregation in St Mary's that land was to be acquired, and early in 1851 he bought 12½ acres of Copthall Farm from Nathaniel Borrer for £800. In March 1851 the Building Fund was opened with £500 from the Society. On 24 June 1851 the village was full of excitement, shops closed, windows crammed with people as the school marched to Holy Trinity for a service at which Julius Hare preached. Lowe and his party waited on the steps of the Mansion House for Bishop Gilbert, and as the time passed and he did not arrive they began to wonder if he had decided not to come because of the confession row. Then a light carriage driven at speed dashed up the High Street, passed the Mansion House, and drew up at the church. Gilbert had got down at the wrong station and had to hire a carriage. After the service the party made their way across the fields to lay the foundation stone.

Nathaniel Woodard had met Richard Carpenter in London, and recognised his quality as an architect. Among his works in Sussex are the churches of St Paul in Brighton and St Giles at Burwash, and restoration work at St Nicholas, Sompting and St Peter's, Chichester. Sadly he died young in 1855, but his partner William Slater, and later his son, Richard, carried on his work and, in the case of the Woodard schools, the same basic plans he had prepared for Lancing and

Hurstpierpoint. Carpenter was a Camden Society member, obviously an early enthusiast for the Gothic revival, and Hurst and Lancing were remarkably lucky in their architect. Instead of red brick there was knapped flint. Instead of elaborate detail there were clear lines and, most important of all, instead of buildings ill-adapted to their purpose his schools were purpose-built. It is true that the economy demanded by Woodard may well have restrained him, but this did not affect the attractiveness of the buildings.

Hurst College was a building in Early English Gothic designed around two quadrangles. The building was sited on a fairly low ridge but, by pitching the roofs steeply and adding high chimneys, Carpenter gave an illusion of greater height. It must be remembered that he originally intended the main approach to be directly from the south to the main entrance across the south field which then sloped gently upwards. The knapped flint gave a lustrous shine to the walls in contrast to the dull surface produced by the more usual red brick of its day. The mouldings of corners, doors and windows were in Caen stone, and the blending of blackish flint and white stone against the green foliage was pleasantly harmonious.

Looking at the buildings Carpenter designed from the front, as they were to be used in Lowe's time, on the left was upper school (later the ground floor of Red Cross) in which most of the teaching took place, a fellows' library and accommodation for associates (later the ground floor of Fleur de Lys). Beyond lay the kitchens and servants' quarters, and above them the servitors' rooms. It was intended later to build a headmaster's house to the north west. On the right there was a science laboratory and accommodation for the special school (later the ground floor of Shield). Above these facilities over the main entrance were the headmaster's and provost's rooms and accommodation for the chaplain, while the buildings to the west and east contained four dormitories each designed for 50 boys; additional dormitory accommodation could be fitted in to the ground floor on the eastern side, thus making provision for 300 pupils. The transepts sticking out westwards and eastwards were for masters' and probationers' accommodation. The school hall had been built, but as yet there was no chapel, and so the crypt beneath this was to be the chapel. The inner quadrangle had a wide cloister running round three sides.

Unfortunately, if the College was privileged to have buildings designed by a great architect, it can only be said that everything else concerned with their construction left much to be desired, producing a building with substantial faults which were to plague all the Victorian headmasters. Construction was in the hands of George Cheeseman and Company of Brighton. The original contract was to cost £11,953 and the completion date promised was June 1852. The final cost was £16,463 10s. 3d. and completion was announced on 9 April 1853. Woodard was partly to blame because he insisted on absolute economy, but the structure he obtained was by no means as solid as it looked, and with high chimneys and roofs was actually unstable. Later Lowe told Woodard that in a high wind 'the College itself vibrated and rocked', and Woodard honestly admitted in reply, 'I know the construction of Hurst is not satisfactory'.

The internal fittings of this building were to be handled by two firms: Grimsells for the living and teaching accommodation, and Jeakes for the kitchens and services dependent on a water supply. Woodard was worried by the ever spiralling costs, and insisted on the most rigid economies. Lowe said that, when they moved in, the buildings were, therefore, in a badly unfinished state, 'unglazed, unfloored and unfurnished altogether'. The construction of doors, fireplaces and other internal fitting was imperfect. As an early pupil, Charles Churton, remarked, 'we learnt by necessity to endure hardness' in buildings with no gas for lighting nor hot pipes for heating. Most seriously of all, the high praise lavished at the time on Jeakes' work proved misplaced. It was said in 1853 that by means of a steam pump and six water tanks a supply flowed all over the College 'in a most complete, convenient and durable manner' when the reality in a short time was to be defects in drainage, sewage, and water supply not finally tackled until the next century. Not until 1857 was the basic fitting out of the College completed, and by then the total cost had risen to £22,063 10s. 3d., and even then in the pamphlet announcing relative completion Woodard asked for another two thousand pounds for 'extra drains and a cesspool'. Gas and heating pipes did not appear until the 1860s, and until then the buildings were lit by candles and oil lamps, and heated only by single open fires in dormitories and other open spaces like the hall and upper school.

These design faults and difficulties were, of course, hidden from those who contemplated with amazement and pride the construction of such an impressive looking building, and Woodard was probably correct to say it was the largest school building for several hundred years. On Tuesday 21 June 1853 the first of many magnificent Woodard ceremonies took place when Hurstpierpoint College was opened and dedicated by Bishop Gilbert in his capacity as Visitor. To Carey Borrer writing in his diary it was a 'glorious day', sunny and warm, but with thunder clouds threatening, and a shower of rain at one point. It began with early morning Communion, and then at a service in Holy Trinity Church when the sermon was preached by the scholarly and by no means High Church Bishop, Connop Thirlwall of St David's, who had been persuaded to come by Julius Hare, somewhat against his better judgement. On foot or in various carriages the crowds then made their way across the fields and down the lanes to the new building where a grand procession formed in the outer quadrangle.

Bishop Gilbert was to bless the upper school, a dormitory and finally the crypt. The procession was led by the combined choirs of Hurst and St Paul's, Brighton, and throughout the proceedings they sang in plainsong a number of psalms. Behind them in turn were the scholars, probationers and associates. Then came Gilbert and Woodard with their chaplains, and a group of clergy including not only Thirlwall, but Henry Phillpotts, Bishop of Exeter, who had ordained Lowe and knew him well. Lastly came the masters and boys. Each group was divided from another by tasselled banners of crimson and blue, and the College banner itself, and as the river of black and white, crimson and blue, flowed in through the main entrance Hurst was truly open.

As with all such Woodard festivities there followed luncheon in the hall into which crammed about four hundred guests, the newspapers disagreeing on whether the meal that followed was eaten in comfort or chaos. The company included Sewell of Radley, Liddon, soon to be principal of Cuddesdon College, Julius Hare, Connop Thirlwall, Henry Phillpotts, and Lord Robert Cecil, and speeches were made by Hare, Woodard, and Gilbert. It was the latter's speech firmly rebutting accusations of Puseyism, praising Woodard and Lowe, and the educational plan they were starting, that set the seal on the proceedings. At the end of term Lowe returned to Devon, and in September married 24-year-old Henrietta Coleridge, to whom he had been engaged for some two years. He and his wife moved into their rooms above the main entrance with her sister, a maid, and a footman, and young Edward Lowe, only 26 at the time, looked out from his study window for the first time, and contemplated how he would make a great school within the newly opened buildings, and fulfil Nathaniel Woodard's ambitious plans for middle-class education in Sussex.

TWO

FOREMOST CAPTAIN OF HIS TIME
1853-1872

Edward Clarke Lowe and the Making of a School

Of the groups of schools that are under St Nicolas College the most interesting and the most difficult to manage is the Middle School at Hurst. The bulk of the boys are sons of tradesmen, the others being recruited from the agricultural and humbler professional classes ... It has been a trying task to plant the public school method in this soil.

Report of the Schools Inquiry Commission, 1864-1868

Public schools enable boys to study not only in the school of books, but in that of men, where they learn how to play their part in life.

Edward Lowe speaking on Port Latin Day, 1859
The Hurst Johnian 12/79, June 1859

The Provost laid the stone. The singing was excellent, the arrangements were good. The only drawback ... was the marching of the boys of the three schools in front of the surpliced procession. All went out of step, half were giggling, others talking, and when they reached the platform set apart for them, the clatter of boots, the pushings, squabblings, and cool behaviour of these parties was insufferable.

Sam Brook's Journal, The Diary of a Lancing Schoolboy, 1860-1865,
printed privately, 1953, p.97, 17 September 1861

I have thought we might begin on a small scale in the first instance, a magazine among the boys, past and present, of the School once a month. I would undertake the general editorship for a year ... I think of *The Hurst Johnian* as a title ...

Edward Lowe to Nathaniel Woodard, 11 March 1858,
Lancing Archives

It is really difficult to exaggerate the services he has rendered to the cause of education in that branch in which he has been engaged ...

Sir John Taylor Coleridge to William Gladstone,
14 January 1869

Edward Lowe was Hurst's first headmaster, and second founder. He was headmaster for 23 years, and involved in school affairs for 56 years to 1905. The provisions of his will continued to produce money for chapel improvements until 1926. He made Hurst into a public school, developed features of its educational programme still in use, and started customs still observed. Lowe was also Woodard's right-hand man in the development of the Southern Chapter, and the creation of the Midland one where he was acting head of Denstone College for a time. Woodard may have been autocratic in his way of running his Society, but in Lowe's case he made an exception. In 1854 Lowe was empowered to 'act in the general business of the Society', and in 1867 to act in Woodard's name without first consulting him if Woodard was ill. Lowe was the educationalist who developed Woodard's somewhat back-ward looking and limited educational ideas, and he was known nationally as a prominent figure in the world of education whose advice was sought, and who spoke frequently at conferences particularly on topics like the teaching of modern languages, the provision of girls' education, and ways to open universities to poorer students. Lowe's character and life are of central importance to Hurst, and of considerable significance to education in general, and an account of the man and his work is long overdue.

His life began in the same way as Woodard's, experiencing difficulties in education, only in his case as the son of a professional family. His father, Samuel, was a solicitor who moved his practice from Whitchurch in Shropshire to Liverpool where he lived in Everton Crescent in the middle-class suburb of that name. There at Number One on 15 December 1823 Edward was born, one of a family of 10 children. The main occupations of the Lowe family were in law, medicine and teaching. His sister Eliza ran schools in Whitchurch and then at Mayfield House, Southgate in Edmonton helped by two other sisters, Mary and Charlotte. A niece took over Mayfield House when Eliza died in 1872, but following her death a year later the school closed. Edward's brother, John, was vicar of Abbot's Bromley, where Lowe as Midlands Provost was to establish two girls' schools. Charlotte taught at Abbot's Bromley. A niece became first headmistress of St Winifrid's School for girls near Bangor, and a nephew was the last headmaster of St Augustine's School at Dewsbury—both Woodard foundations.

In the same way as Woodard's family, the Lowes benefited from the Woodard Society. Seven of them went to Lancing, and Lowe wrote to Woodard urging the claims of his widowed sister-in-law's children or his brother's children to places at the school. One relative came to Hurst although Lowe made no mention at the time of the family link. William Mosley was the son of his widowed sister, Maria. He went to Lancing from 1849 to 1856, and then transferred to Hurst's special school to prepare for army entrance. He was killed at Umbeyla in India in 1863, a death reported in the *Hurst Johnian* without reference to Lowe.

Edward was educated privately and, like Woodard, entered Oxford going up to Magdalen Hall in October 1842, but obtaining a scholarship he moved next year to Lincoln College from which he went on to obtain a third-class degree in *Litterae Humaniores* in 1846. Oxford deeply impressed Lowe. He was to adapt ceremonies from Magdalen and Queen's Colleges for use at Hurst. He made friends with his tutor at Lincoln, Mark Pattison, later rector of the College, and an educational reformer, who visited Hurst and helped Lowe to organise external exams for the school. Lowe was closely involved in the Oxford Movement. Edward Pusey was a friend, and heard his confession, and Pusey gave books to Hurst while Lowe visited his church in Leeds. Lowe knew John Keble, who visited Hurst but declined to preach there. Edwin Bunce, one of Lowe's servants at Hurst, came from Keble's parish of Hursley. At Lincoln College, Lowe was a founder member of a religious society, and attended such meetings in other colleges particularly Oriel. Like Woodard, however, Lowe was no ritualist. The famous writer, Sabine Baring-Gould, who taught at Hurst, was sharply reprimanded for wearing vestments, and on one occasion told he was 'talking nonsense' by Lowe when he considered joining a monastic order: the same year Lowe told Woodard that one Bond who was reading Romish books 'wants a good overhauling'.

At Oriel College, Lowe met Henry Coleridge, one of the Devonshire Coleridges, and in April 1847 left Oxford for Ottery St Mary in Devon where on the recommendation of Henry's father he became a curate, and taught in the grammar school. He was ordained by Henry Phillpotts, Bishop of Exeter, on 23 September 1848, after which, he told Pattison, he spent 'very pleasant holidays, part of them in touring this country'. But he also told Pattison he was concerned about the condition of the people, and about education: ' I am full of thoughts about setting up a commercial school'. He was advised by the Coleridges to contact Woodard and, as we saw in the last chapter, did so and came to Shoreham. He married F.G. Coleridge's daughter Henrietta, known as Harriet, who accompanied him to Hurst, bringing with her a much younger sister, Alice Mary, who was seven years old. As she grew up at Hurst she was taught by probationers like J.C. Rowlatt, and was the first girl taught in the school. Later she became Lady Warden of one of the schools at Abbot's Bromley from 1878 to 1899, and on her death in 1907 left her library to Hurst.

In 1853 Lowe's position as an employee of Woodard's was regularised. He was required to make a declaration 'to form no cabals', or 'suffer such to be formed' against the Provost, and admit 'the right of the Society' to interfere in the operation of the College. He was required to keep the accounts himself and render quarterly returns to Woodard. The declaration was no more than a legal formality because Lowe and Woodard were close friends. 'In him I find great delight', wrote Lowe to Pattison and, although there were times when they clashed and Lowe told Woodard 'I feel the weight of your reprimand' or apologised for 'any warmth of manner', their partnership was the essential key to the Society's success. Brian Heeney in an odd passage said Lowe was 'impetuous, lacking in judgement', and that Woodard 'obviously preferred not to leave too much to him'. On the contrary, Lowe held office as vice-provost most years while he was head of Hurst and added the posts of librarian and chief examiner. He prepared the annual Calendar. He was put in charge of the Benefit Fund, and appeared on Woodard's behalf before the Taunton Commission. Woodard actually first proposed that Lowe should remain at Hurst, and be Midlands Provost as well as telling him in 1871 how much he valued his opinions on practical matters.

Hard working and valued though Lowe was as a colleague, it cannot be said he enjoyed a salary in any way comparable to other Victorian headmasters: Marlborough got £2,000 and Winchester £3,000 a year. Lowe started at Hurst on £200 a year, and only in 1859 was his salary improved on a 'payments by results' method. He was to get a pound a year for every boy in the school over a hundred, and two pounds a year for those in his two dormitories—Blue and Red Shield—with an additional sum of £6 2s. for each special school member. This increase came after complaints from Lowe from 1854 to 1859 that he was in debt, and needed to borrow money to pay his wife's medical bills. His salary rose to its maximum in 1869 of £435 16s. 8d., and thereafter actually fell again with a slight fall in numbers. Lowe was no doubt therefore interested in the phrase in his declaration about 'perquisites and provisions'. His household expenditure was included in the general housekeeping expenses, and the school provided two servants. Lowe had to pay for his own footman-valet and a lady's maid. He was provided with a carriage and horse. To the south west of Red Cross a pleasant garden was made with rhododendrons and trees, a croquet lawn, and a summer house. Lowe used to watch cricket on West field from this garden.

An Outline of the Lowe Family Tree

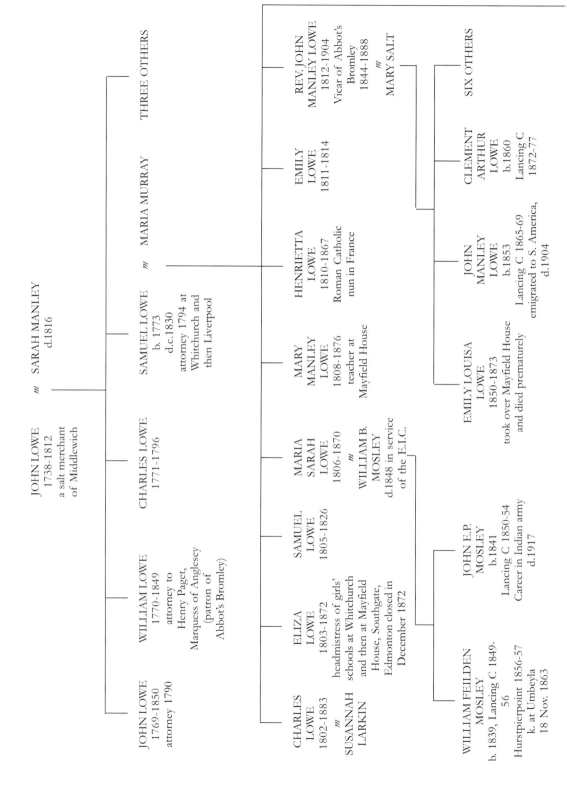

GEORGE
LOWE
1813-1892
FRCS doctor at
Burton-on-Trent
_m_
CECILIA
LANDOR

WILLIAM
HENRY
LOWE
1815-1900
MD Edinburgh 1840,
Fellow(1846), and
President (1873) of
Edinburgh Royal College
of Surgeons
_m_
MARIA BOYELL

JAMES HENRY
LOWE
b.1849
Lancing 1864-65
surgeon

EMILY
LOUISA
LOWE
1816-1849

ALFRED
LOWE
1817-18

CHARLOTTE
LOWE
1819-1897
mistress at Mayfield
House, and then at
St Anne's,
Abbot's Bromley

EDWARD
CLARKE
LOWE
b. 15 December 1823
m. 27 September   d. 30 March
1853   1912
D.D. 1860,
Canon 1870

_m_

HENRIETTA
DUKE
COLERIDGE
b. 12 September 1828
d. 21 April1918
daughter of
F.G. Coleridge
of Ottery St Mary

ALICE MARY
COLERIDGE
1846-1907
lived at Hurst, later
Lady Warden
of St Anne's,
Abbot's Bromley
1878-1899

EMILY LANDOR
LOWE
1852-1929
headmistress of St
Winifrid's School,
Bangor, 1887

ALFRED
LOWE
1854-1934
Lancing C 1868-73
Lancing master 1877-81
Prebend of Lichfield,
1919

HENRY
WILLIAM LOWE
1859-1932
Lancing C 1872-77
clergyman, headmaster of
St Augustine's, Dewsbury
1896-99

GEORGE EDWARD
LOWE
1861-1932
Lancing C 1873-78
solicitor

_m_

DIANA MARY
LITLER

EDWARD
LITLER LOWE
1900-1972
Lancing c.1914-1918

EIGHT OTHERS

But when it came to accommodation the Lowes suffered greatly. Their rooms at the front of the College bore the full blast of the wind, and were cold and wet. In 1859 Lowe told Woodard 'our drawing room is flooded again—the water literally across the room, and this is the third time'. In 1864 plans for a new house were started, but it was not until 1867 that they were in Lowe's hands. He was delighted, telling Woodard, 'they will give us some comfort which one has waited long for', and Woodard replied, 'we must soon begin your new house'. In October 1868 its foundation stone was laid by Robert Blencowe. The choirs of the three boys schools combined, ending with *All People That on Earth do Dwell*. The Chapter heads including St Michael's were present and a supper was given to the guests and prefects in the crypt tastefully decorated with evergreens. Lowe never occupied the new house as expenditure on Ardingly and Lancing got in the way, and it was Lowe's successor, Awdry, who in September 1873 was the first occupant. It is hardly surprising that Lowe made a major issue out of obtaining good quality accommodation for the Provost at Denstone!

Lowe was a healthy young man in the prime of life during his headship, and apart from references to influenza and quinsy (throat inflammation) suffered no illness. He remained a great walker and in 1856, for example, while staying with Mrs. Hare at Herstmonceux, thought nothing of walking with an associate, Joseph Eaton, to Hastings 12 miles away. In 1867, when Lowe was at Chamonix, Woodard was told, 'I have done a great deal of walking and a little climbing'. Unfortunately it was his wife, Harriet, who suffered from the less than perfect living conditions.

It was perhaps Lowe's cross to bear in life that a vigorous man married a wife who became a semi-invalid and bore him no children, and a measure of his kindness that he looked after her most carefully—indeed she survived him by six years! The first signs of illness came in 1856 with visits to Harley Street, and by March 1857 she was described as 'quite an invalid'. Next year the press commented on her absence from ceremonies, and Harriet went for the first of endless cures to spa towns—in this case to Malvern. Victorian medical descriptions are notoriously vague, but it seems that her illness was some form of rheumatoid arthritis. In the winter of 1864 Lowe told Woodard 'she is almost doubled with pain', and next year that she had suffered for two months in the winter. She became too ill to attend chapel, and for this reason William Barrett (OJ) writing to his parents in 1869 said 'Mrs. Lowe does not seem to have anything to do with the school'.

This was untrue because, in spite of her disability, she did a good deal for the College. She designed the school cap badge, and the badge for the First Eleven. She gave away sports day prizes and laid the foundation stone of the gymnasium in 1872. Above all she was engaged in raising money for the chapel. Harriet had become interested in church architecture at Ottery St Mary when the church was restored, and was particularly interested in the reredos. At Hurst from December 1865 to December 1872 she raised not only the £1,800 for the reredos, but another £110 for a super-altar decorated with precious stones chosen by her. Lowe told the Old Johnians that the money was raised by her without assistance from him, and in one letter to Woodard urged that 'Mrs Lowe's wishes' regarding the reredos design should be considered. Incidentally it was a visit by her father that gave Hurst the figures of St Jerome and St Catharine at the entrance porch because he thought it a little plain. Sabine Baring-Gould was asked to design them, and many years later Harriet Lowe had them restored.

Harriet did her best to keep up with her husband's activities, particularly his European holidays from which Lowe returned with engravings of European pictures and albums of architectural photographs for the fellows library. The Lowes were in Paris in 1854, 1856, and 1869—incidentally visiting one of Lowe's sisters who was a Roman Catholic nun—and on the last trip Harriet suffered so badly on the Channel crossing that they had to let her recuperate in a Dover hotel. Visits were made to Belgium and Baden in 1871 when Harriet in common with many others over the years was overcome with exhaustion during the Oberammergau play.

Speaking to the Taunton Commissioners Lowe said 'we are quite in the country and there is hardly anyone except a few peasantry around us'; a view of his neighbours which presumably did not include the tradesmen and gentry he had got to know so well at the Mansion House. Good relations with both groups continued. In 1859 'most of the leading farmers and tradesmen' were at a performance of *Macbeth*, and a farce was added at the end of the Shakespeare plays to amuse the local visitors. On Shrove Tuesdays there was a concert with conjuring and amusing skits followed by an annual dinner for College tradesmen and their apprentices. In the same year 'many of the gentry of Sussex' attended the first Old Johnian dinner, and in their early years Edward and Harriet were often at Danny Park at balls and weddings, and in the early 1860s returned the compliment by holding balls in the school hall.

Above all it was Campion's support which helped the College. 'The squire of Hurst', said Francis Barchard when William Campion died in 1869, 'has been the best friend of the College in its early days of difficulty.' Boys from the school lined his funeral route, and the first chapel window to be dedicated was to his name. The advantage access to Danny gave Lowe is well illustrated by an extract from Henry Liddon's diary when he came to preach at the opening of the chapel and recorded alighting at Hassocks Gate:

> there met the Bishop of Chichester and Mrs Gilbert. They took me in their carriage to Danny Park—Mr W.J. C[ampion's]. At Danny I found James Mozley, and Mrs M[ozley], Mr and Mrs B[archard], Mr and Mrs Tower. A large party at dinner—Lowe and Mrs Lowe.

Lowe was always delighted to secure children of the gentry for the school; one of the Campions was at Hurst in the mid-1850s paying £10 for a special room and extra meat while preparing for his army exam, and Lowe wrote at once to express his pleasure to Woodard in 1861 when 'Mr Marshall, the large farmer at Bolney' entered his three sons (two of whom became prefects) in the school. Good relations helped the school in practical ways. The gentry supplied sports day prizes and the annual Christmas tree. Mr. Broad allowed them to swim in his mill stream, and Mr. Mitchell allowed steeplechases to be run over his land.

By and large good relations continued with Carey Borrer although as early as 1855 his diary records that he thought Lowe was trying to 'subvert his influence in the parish'. The Hurst services were attractive and different, and local people started attending particularly when the chapel was opened. During 1867 there was a sharp dispute between Lowe and Borrer, but as the bishop had licensed the chapel for public worship there was little Borrer could do. The Hurst choir encouraged good relations, singing in local churches at Cuckfield, Keymer, and at the opening of Horsham's new church in 1865. Above all Lowe was never happier than when amidst a flutter of lawn sleeves with Gilbert's pre-eminent amongst them. It was no coincidence that the chapel's second memorial window was to him and, on Lowe's last visit to the palace at Chichester, Gilbert said 'remember me to your boys, and tell them I send them my blessing'.

Lowe had mixed motives for courting bishops. They were the leaders of his Church and he wished them to preach. Their support gave the lie to mutterings about Popery. Bishops' visits, said Lowe, are events 'highly valued within these walls' because they brought middle-class boys into contact with leading churchmen, and over fifteen different bishops came to Hurst in Lowe's headship. When Gilbert died Lowe wrote to Woodard expressing concern for the future. He need not have worried for a remarkable appointment was made. A canon of Manchester, Richard Durnford, aged 70, was given the bishopric and lasted until his 96th year!

4 The Rev. Canon Edward C. Lowe, seated in the middle, and some masters, *c*.1860. Seated on the left of him is Rev. Edmund Field, and on the right, Rev. Charles Lomax. Standing, on the left is Rev. Richard L. Pennell.

In March 1870 the new Visitor was received by the fellows and masters in the front quad when he came to his first confirmation service. He stayed overnight, breakfasted with the masters and prefects, and later received an address from the school read by the school captain. He remained a steady friend of Hurst which was perhaps still necessary. William Barrett, who had recently arrived at Hurst, was told by a friend in a letter, 'I expect you will be turning Roman Catholic soon'; the old prejudices lingered on.

Because Lowe's life has not been studied his character has been subject to more than the usual patina of legend. In much that he did he was a typical headmaster of his day, and his forceful personality meant that he runs truer to a Benson or a Warre rather than a Wilkinson or Mitchinson. He was an imperial kind of headmaster preceded into chapel by a verger with a tipstaff, and looked after by a butler and a footman. Each evening he dined in Hall in full academicals, and must have been an impressive sight with the scarlet of his DD robes contrasting with his jet black hair and ruddy face. Round him the fellows and masters dined in evening dress, and before them on fine napery were china and silver, and choice wines. Lowe was ever one for amusing after-dinner speeches and toast giving, and drank himself from a grey horn goblet rimmed with silver.

Robert Hill (OJ) has given perhaps the most dramatic description of Lowe whose 'glaring eye was the terror of every poor boy', and whose rasping voice 'took the skin off your face'. When Robert Bennett (OJ) came to write an article on Lowe he said he was 'an iron disciplinarian and terrible in his wrath', and Bertram Mitford (OJ) in his novel about school life in Lowe's time said the head was 'absolutely and entirely despotic'. Members of his staff spoke in similar terms. Joseph Fowler, his second chaplain, said 'we all rather feared than loved him'. 'Sometimes,' he said, 'his outbreaks of temper were terrible', and his life-long friend, master at Hurst and later founding head of Denstone, David Edwardes, said 'a more complete control of his temper would have been desirable'. Lowe himself admitted to Woodard in May 1863 'how impatient I am of criticism and misconstruction', although he did little to curb his faults, refusing to give a scholarship to a boy who smiled during the installation in 1872. Plenty of stories exist to confirm these impressions. A party of prefects fled from his drawing room one evening when inadvertently, while he was out of the room, they drank the last of the port. When attending a dinner in London William Millward (OJ) said that he 'had thought the Doctor stern, perhaps excessively stern, in the performance of his duties'. Lowe rose to reply to the 'subdued acrimony of that gentleman's remarks' recalling 'a striking and stinging interview' he had once had with Millward, and said he was delighted to have had the effects which 'the eloquent speech they had heard from Mr Millward proved they had been in his case!'

When Lowe was questioned about discipline by the Taunton Commission, he said 'both cane and [birch] rod' were used. Canes were carried by masters and used on the hands. Birching took place in the room at the South end of upper school. Lowe said he birched about two boys a term and 'the fact of its being available' was what mattered. Although on one occasion in 1859 he was pleased to tell Old Johnians that a term had passed for the first time when he had not birched, he firmly defended its use. Firstly, he said Hurst should have the same 'standard of punishment such as Shrewsbury [and] Rugby employed', if it was to be a public school—a shrewd hit since Moss of Shrewsbury was a notorious flogger. Secondly, he believed the conditions at Hurst required him to be strict, and the commissioners agreed that 'the elements of discontent are numerous and potent enough' in a school with so many boys crowded together and many from poorer homes. It does come as something of a shock to read of cases like that in 1854 when Albert Tilley, a tradesman's son at the College, struck

Lomax, the second master, in class. Lowe had him publicly flogged and turned out of the school, and when we look at school life in more detail we shall see that this was not an isolated incident.

Lowe the disciplinarian is, however, but one facet of a multi-faceted man. Robert Hill also spoke of his 'profound reverence' for Lowe, and this respect followed him all his days. At the 1859 OJ Dinner Edward De la Hooke spoke of his 'many excellent qualities'. Hill referred to his skill at organisation and his effective teaching. Although some more academically minded boys admired his preaching, few others did: his sermons to boys were not a strong point, but his speeches on Port Latin Day or at the end of term were often laced with humour and received extremely well. In 1860 Lowe was given his DD by Oxford, and the money for his robes was collected by boys and masters. When Lowe spoke on Port Latin Day of 'affection subsisting between himself and his old pupils' there was great cheering.

As early as 1851 Lowe began sending an Easter letter to Old Johnians with news and advice. The school magazine he started was partly for them. Port Latin Day was preceded and followed by Old Johnian football and cricket matches and in the interval they stayed in College, and were entertained by Lowe and his wife. Lowe was in charge of the Woodard Benefit Fund and saw this as another opportunity for good relations with OJs—in his letters to Woodard there are several cases where he helped former pupils. It was Lowe who in December 1859 told Old Johnians, 'I am ready to dine with you', and presided at the first OJ dinner on 21 December that year. Although it was not followed up, Lowe believed 'the bonds of love and fraternity in a Hurst Johnian were as great as those of the Freemasons'. Later he urged leavers 'to put their names down on the Old Johnians list', adding that when he left his would go there also. The Old Johnians gave him a dinner in January 1873 after he left. Good relations and frequent visits by old boys are the result of long-term respect for a headmaster, and Lowe clearly earned this from them.

Study of Lowe's letters to Woodard show him to have been a compassionate and liberal minded man dedicated to benefiting the poorer classes with education, concerned about individual boys, and also with all those in his school. In a surprisingly modern speech at Port Latin Day in 1859 Lowe said the school had its 'non-literary boys', but 'they are not stupid'. He said the following year that 'every encouragement will be given to manly games', and pointed out that games players who joined the services were serving their country just as much as clergy or doctors. Lowe often complained to Woodard about the rough conditions in the school, asking for more heating, a proper infirmary, and more playing fields with great persistence—it was Woodard who turned him down advocating harsh (and cheap) conditions. Lowe was deeply saddened by the number of pupil deaths, writing to Woodard in August 1858, 'you will hate the sight of my handwriting so often does it convey ill news'.

His concern was for the highest and lowest in his school. When wretched Charles Lomax was 'ill, poor and in debt' in 1859 Lowe got permission to pay his medical fees from school funds. When William Smith, the engineer, died suddenly in April 1860 Lowe wrote to Woodard, 'I have just come from burying poor Smith', and secured a pension of half-a-crown (12½p) a week for his widow and five children. A relation of the Daveys, among the most loyal of school servants, was given a pension of two shillings a week in 1871. When he left Lowe was given 'their heartiest thanks for all the kindnesses which we have enjoyed'.

There are many cases of his concern for individual boys in his letters. A boy called Montagu Goffe had re-offended, and Woodard wanted him removed. Lowe wrote that he did not wish this because he sympathised with his godmother, and because 'we ought not to cast him off because he is bad'. In 1856 he was concerned about a 'poor boy of low rank' whose father was 'one of those wife-beating monsters'. In 1857 he told Woodard of a 'real case of distress'. 'A good little boy' was likely to have to leave because his father, a Dorset farmer, had dropped dead on the way to Blandford Fair leaving a pregnant wife and six children. Lowe did not wear his heart on his sleeve. He knew that fear of the Lord is also love of the Lord, and while he was as firm as he believed necessary in public he was as kind as possible in private. Newspaper reports of Hurst ceremonies referred to the boys having a 'healthy, cheerful air', 'under no fear or undue restraint', and 'quite at ease and at home'. Edwin Fisher's diary (OJ) gives a rare glimpse of an Old Johnian returning to the school in April 1867. He met Edward and Harriet in their drawing room, and examined the plans for the new head's house. Then they walked across to see the new bathing place in the mill stream, and Lowe 'talked and joked with nearly all the boys he met'. This gives substance to Robert Bennett's view in his obituary article that Lowe 'was as popular as a schoolmaster can afford to be'.

Speaking to Old Johnians in 1859 Lowe maintained 'the genuine, manly spirit of a public school has now fully and permanently taken up its abode within the College walls'. The Society Calendar referred to Hurst as a public school for the first time in 1862, and speaking on Port Latin Day in 1867 Francis Barchard told Lowe, 'you are one of the very best headmasters of any public school in the kingdom'. In spite of its few years, George Thomson wrote, when Lowe left, that he had succeeded in giving the College the air of a 'well-established public school' combining older traditions with the fulfilment of his complicated task in running Hurst and operating its various schools, and Woodard's ladder of advancement within its walls.

II

The opening of a building designed for 300 boys with just 135 was the decisive moment for the failure or success of Woodard's scheme. The subscription list had fallen well short of the cost of the building and fittings, and debt had been incurred which had to be repaid. Woodard wrote to Lowe saying, 'you must begin to look up boys', and by late 1854 he could feel reassured. Lowe told him 'a great number are unable to get in' because the dormitory accommodation was not ready: this was the limiting factor on early growth not lack of applicants. Mid-Victorian prosperity would last for all of Lowe's headship, affecting the rural community during the years of 'High Farming' as well as the commercial middle classes. Population was rising, the school was already linked by railway to two large population centres, and railway extensions increased this market. 'Fifty or a hundred miles by rail is not a serious matter', said Lowe a few years later. Hurst was first in the field offering moderately priced education for the middle class, and was able to draw on a national market. In 1859 Lowe spoke of boys 'from distant Glamorgan' and others 'from the far North', and eventually over thirty counties were represented on the school list as well as those with expatriate parents abroad.

Between 1848 and 1872 Lancing Register gives 740 entrants: Hurst between 1849 and 1872 gives 2,329 and, as we shall see, this figure underestimates numbers in the school considerably. The total in the school as a whole reached 203 in 1858, and 341 in 1862: the rise in four years due to the completion of the dormitory programme by 1861. This provided for 300 boys, but numbers continued to rise to a maximum of 364 in 1869. Grammar school numbers rose from 135 in 1853 to 202 in 1859, and a peak of 309 in 1869. In that year the total population of the school—which then still consisted only of the central block—including 17 masters and 20 resident servants approached four hundred. Neither headmaster's house nor sanatorium had been built, and Lowe urged Woodard to build and acquire more land. 'I hoped you would find yourself able to go on with the dormitories', he wrote.

The rise in numbers was the most important fact about Lowe's Hurst. The debt was cleared by 1861 and a profit made, some of which went towards other Society schools. The experiment had worked, and it was a matter of pride for Lowe to tell the Taunton Commissioners that the school had no debts and 'I have always a list standing over' of potential applicants. Such numbers were not seen again in the school as a whole until 1953 and in the senior school until 1960. On the other hand this success brought problems of discipline and health, and overcrowded facilities, from dormitories with beds pressed side by side to lack of playing field space. In Lowe's last years a fall in numbers started: the total was down to 341 by 1872, and Lowe wrote about 'the falling numbers this year' which he was convinced were caused by bad living conditions.

That this was true is even more likely when the true number of boys in the school is calculated. For many years Hurst has suffered in its history because of a seriously defective register produced in 1914. The writer did not use the limited materials available ignoring, for example, the Society Calendars, and he was anxious to exclude mention of three of the four departments in Lowe's Hurst—the servitors, the special school for engineers, and the probationary associates or trainee teachers—because mention of them did not accord with the image of a public school in Edwardian England. A glance at the magazine soon shows the difficulty. A. Guidotti, swimming champion in 1858, A. Chisholm, junior chorister in 1860, and G. Farajellah, probably the school's first coloured boy, here in 1868, are not in the register.

The preparatory school, Little St John's at Ditchling, is ignored altogether, and its pupils' names can only be found in lists of school teams. They are not even in the Society Calendar. The register ignored the servitors completely—except for one of them, George Cory, who was one of the school's most distinguished scholars later and was therefore included. Servitors' names are given in the Society Calendar, and in partial lists in the school magazine although it is noticeable there are gaps here—Percy Roberts, in a swimming list in 1874, is not in an official list. Guidotti and Farajellah turn out to have been servitors, and between 1854 and 1891 about two hundred and fifty of their names can be traced. The total in the special school from 1857 to 1874 will never be known because the register arbitrarily selects those it lists, or does not designate them as special school members. The Society Calendar provides a fuller list. So, for example, James Davis who came to Hurst in July 1858 and entered the special school in 1861 is not in the register while a Samuel Davis is given twice; or George Clode is referred to in the register when a William Clode, who was in the special school in 1863, is omitted.

There are other problems with this particular school's numbers. It is clear that those like Campion's relative were admitted before the school officially came into being in 1856. Secondly, the register does not chronicle boys from the grammar school who transferred to the special school. Leaving dates are wrong. This means that calculations of the number of older boys in the school are going to be difficult. For example, both Henry and Arthur Radford entered the special school in 1856 and 1859. Thomas Dearnden listed as leaving in 1864, entered the special school in 1866, and there are many such examples—William Birmingham, Charles Moore, and Sydney Smith—who actually stayed on for another four years! Edwin Dean(e) who was nearly drowned in a dramatic accident in 1865 was in the special school, and is not in the register. Lastly, there are gaps in the list of probationers: William Pooley, who came in 1861 and died in 1863, and Henry Wearing, at Hurst from June to October 1867 when he died, are not in the register.

The consequences of this deficit in information, now irreparable, are great. It is clear that numbers need to be revised upwards—I suggest a figure of 2,550. The revised figures for servitors and special school housed in cramped conditions re-emphasise the problem of over-crowding. Calculations of general statistics, such as the average age of the boys or the number of deaths in the school, need to be altered. The two most serious consequences will be dealt with later. It is very difficult to assess how effective Woodard's ladder of advancement was if we do not know who was in the various schools and how they transferred—between departments in Hurst, and between Hurst and the other two boys' schools. A new calculation of these transfers will be made showing the scheme worked much better than earlier writers like Brian Heeney believed. The other problem is that, without the names or details of their subsequent careers, the destination of those leaving Hurst is unknown in a very large number of cases, making any full calculation of the number of boys who became upwardly mobile as a result of being at the school virtually impossible.

Calculations of the financial success of Hurst in Lowe's time are fraught with similar hazards arising from incomplete figures. In this case the three main difficulties preventing a full assessment of the economic position were inherent in Woodard's scheme and his method of handling its finances. Both he and Lowe firmly maintained in public that each school was 'completely self-supporting'. This, said the Commissioners, 'is an integral feature of the system'. The truth emerged to some extent when the Hurst masters put in a salary claim in April 1869. Woodard rejected their claim which was based on the obvious profits in the School's best year. He pointed out Hurst needed to be 'more than just solvent' because it was affected by Society plans as a whole. The three schools, he said 'stand or fall together'. Joseph Fowler, the chaplain, replied saying they were greatly surprised to find the school 'was heavily taxed for the general purposes of the College [Society]'. Of this there was no doubt. Hurst had given Ardingly a subsidy of £500 in 1868, and the same year Woodard announced that all future pupils would contribute to the building of Lancing chapel as a 'central minister'. Five shillings a year was asked for. It brought in £55 4s. 4d., enough to pay two masters' salaries for a year.

Indeed it would have been remarkable if the schools had not been financially interlocked in an organisation designed to link them educationally. Hurst under Lowe was undoubtedly the most profitable school in numerical terms, but lost part of its profits to the Society. Payments were made for great Woodard occasions. Hurst paid £52 5s. 5d. towards the induction of the Lady Warden of St Michael's in 1866, and £30 19s. 8d. towards the Lancing chapel opening ceremony, and no doubt received some help back for its own ceremonies. The expenses of the Chapter included two Octave meetings a year, a summer retreat to discuss religious matters, public meetings, publicity, and grants to Anglican causes like missionaries and primary schools. Then there were the salaries of officials—Lowe himself got £25 a year as vice-provost. When Edmund Blackmore became bursar Hurst paid him £33 6s. 8d. which was a third of his salary. Woodard himself did well from his schools. By 1870 Hurst's contribution to his salary was £290 6s. 8d., giving the Provost an income of at least £900 a year.

The second problem in calculating the school's financial position came from the fee structure. By 1870 the schools of the Southern Chapter charged 27 different basic fees, and levied at least 45 different extra charges, and these were changed without formal notification. Although the total of boys with named scholarships is known—18 in 1870 obtained reduced fees, the precise number of other groups like Sussex boys on reduced fees, or boys in Lowe's dormitories on higher fees is unknown. Servitors were given their clothes, but did menial work thereby reducing the domestic bill. Probationers had to buy their gown and surplice, but did some limited teaching, reducing costs again. Lowe pointed out that, although masters' salaries were low in comparison with other public schools, their perks were not and they 'lived in the society of gentlemen'. They had free coal, candles, gas, food and some drink, and the use of their rooms and the school servants. Fellows were allowed to reside throughout the year.

Lastly, the accounts themselves were in a muddle until 1870. Lowe, it will be recalled, was required to do them himself, and his calculations with Lomax's help were irregular in form. Woodard apparently kept no central accounts, and there was no Chapter finance committee until 1863. Lowe pointed out that in one year his petty cash box had handled £3,816 15s. 0d., and this was bound to lead to mistakes. He asked Woodard for a secretary [bursar today] and three years later in 1860 William Taylor was appointed. This proved a great mistake. Economies in food led to the College pudding being called 'Freddie' pudding after his son, and the son was expelled in February 1862 for theft. Taylor demanded a salary rise to £50 a year and, as Woodard thought this 'very disproportionate', he left in 1862. More wisely William Pratt became school secretary, and in 1870 began an elegant series of balance sheets. By the mid-1860s the accounts were certainly in trouble. Unpaid debts from parents were £776 1s. 6d. and unpaid bills to tradesmen were £260 17s. 3d. With the aid of the mathematics master, John Gorham, these were sorted out. Arrears were cut to £40 0s. 11d.

Methods of calculating the accounts, which switched from quarterly returns to twice or sometimes three times a year, make absolute accuracy impossible. In its first year in the main buildings Hurst's income was £1,464 12s. 0d. It rose only slowly during the 1850s, and the debt stayed until 1861, because revenue had to go out to pay for four dormitories. By 1860 revenue had reached £5,860 2s. 3d. Then in five years it doubled to £10,380 5s. 8d. in 1865, and reached its maximum in 1869 at £12,121 15s. 1d., a figure not reached again until 1918. In Lowe's last years revenue was falling, and it was £10,139 17s. 6d. when he left. Throughout Lowe's years, of course, domestic and scholastic spending rose rapidly with the numbers, and there was scarcely any surplus for long-term development. Although three important buildings were started under Lowe they were not completed, and the money for the most spectacular of them—the first Woodard chapel—was raised by voluntary contributions.

Lowe later said it was 'a labour of love' for him to write an account of Hurst's buildings. At the time it seemed more like the labours of Hercules to look after them because, while their beauty was obvious, the defects were less so until the building was fully in use. It had been built on the basis of 'stern economy and simplicity', and as we have seen was in an unfinished and unfurnished state in 1853. As late as 1857 Woodard asked for another £2,000 for the buildings, but it was not forthcoming. He was busy with the costs of building Lancing, and therefore the basic requirements were not completed until 1861 when six dormitories were in use. The nave of the chapel was built from 1861 to 1865. The headmaster's house was built between 1868 and 1873. The gymnasium was built between 1872 and 1873. The promised sanatorium did not appear. Lowe began complaining in 1855, and for the rest of his headship there is far more in his letters to Woodard about drains than discipline, down to his very last letter from Hurst in January 1873.

Woodard admitted that things were wrong as early as 1856, and sent back Mr. Cordy, Clerk of the Works during building, so that Lowe could point out 'all the work that failed as soon as finished'. Thomas Wadey, the village builder, was a frequent visitor, but matters did not really improve. In 1861 Woodard came with William Slater, an architect, to 'hear from you any hints about the construction' of future schools to be learned from mistakes made at Hurst. The reality was that it was lack of funds caused by Woodard's own rigid control that caused the faults to become perennial, and conditions so atrocious. Lowe's requests for a sanatorium, more dormitories, or playing fields fell on deaf ears and, when William Woodard became custos in charge of the buildings, Nathaniel told Lowe 'his orders must be absolutely obeyed'. William Woodard and Edmund Blackmore were the Empson and Dudley of Hurst finances for nearly forty years. Because there was inadequate room in dormitories, boys slept in laundry rooms and even in the lofts directly under the tiles. Because of the delay in building the chapel which Lowe had optimistically told Old Johnians in 1856 would start that year, the crypt remained in use. Its smelly charcoal brazier, hard forms, and overcrowded nature were unpleasant. Lowe told Woodard in April 1861 that 'our chapel today was full and the savour was not of holiness alone'. The introduction of a small organ and pews for guests made it even more cramped, and the atmosphere with the charcoal burning and the gas flaring and the whole school present for lengthy services must have been atrocious. The crypt was not available for teaching for the lower school until 1865, so teaching facilities were crowded as well. Dormitories without curtains or carpets were like barracks. Indeed Lowe remarked to Woodard that the military privations of 'the army in the Crimea reconcile me to a good deal'!

There was only one room in the whole school which was warm and well furnished—the fellows library (the room today nearest the main notice board). This room was fitted with trellised iron bookcases designed by Sabine Baring-Gould, and display cases planned by John Gorham. In them were books donated by Pusey, Hare, and others, Lowe's albums of foreign travel, and the first parts of a collection of Sussex flora, fauna and geology. £10 a year grant was given to this room, and it acted as a masters' common room, meeting room, and dining room for important guests. On the walls there was the start of a collection of paintings, including portraits of Keble, Pusey, Gilbert and Phillpotts.

The buildings lacked every main service in a satisfactory state. The only heating for six years was by open braziers in hall and chapel, and single fireplaces in upper school and the dormitories monopolised by senior boys. Lowe admitted 'we shall not soon forget the cold dormitories in the early morning' when the ice on water basins had to be broken. In 1855 Lowe complained to Woodard that the cold in the hall for boys sitting still eating was so bad the school was losing boys. One of them, Joseph Eaton, who came from the West Indies, wrote direct to Woodard saying the cold 'has nearly incapacitated me for work'. In 1859 hot pipes were provided for the hall, crypt and upper school corridor, but nowhere else—pipes did not reach dormitories until the 1890s! The new chapel obtained them after a year in 1866.

Lowe maintained that the dormitories were 'quite open and well ventilated'. They were certainly open, but the penetrating cold forced boys to shut windows, adding to health risks. There was another trouble because opening windows caused chimney problems. In 1858 Lowe told Woodard 'every chimney through the place is smoking the wrong way'. Dormitory ventilation remained unsatisfactory until Tower's day.

At first lighting was by candles and oil lamps, and supplies of both were kept to the minimum. In 1854 probationers stole chapel candles to read by, and the gloomy buildings had their problems. In 1857 Lowe told Woodard that 'someone is prowling about the place at night', and a master had woken to find someone in his room. He asked for more candles to be kept alight at night, and later told Woodard, 'I am going tomorrow to look for a dog'. Gas was installed at a cost of £243 16s. 4d. in December 1862, and the new chapel lit by spectacularly designed gas chandeliers or 'serpents'. A poem in the *Hurst Johnian* beginning, 'Hail Deity bright-beaming gas', reflected the relief at its arrival. It remained in place until 1926!

The two most serious defects in the building led directly to Hurst's mid-Victorian reputation as an unhealthy school, and will be dealt with in detail when examining the health issue in the

5 The choir in the early 1860s. Back row, standing, third from left is Rev. Sabine Baring-Gould.

next chapter. The first was that the medical room and dispensary were next to the kitchens, and close to the servitors' quarters. Once the whole space available was filled with dormitories there was no possibility of isolation and, although a cottage was taken later in the lane for seriously ill cases, quarantine and antisepsis were not properly understood, and the buildings remained to a degree a death trap until numbers fell, and the old Crescent House was used as an infirmary until 1890. The real reason why the illnesses appeared in the first place was the state of the drains, sewage and water supplies for drinking and washing in overcrowded buildings. They were inadequate with one basin and one outside tap per dormitory, and one toilet from which the night soil had to be removed. There was one tin bath per house, and the lack of water meant that the boys bathed in turn in re-used water starting with the seniors. The trouble was that providing these services in rural Sussex was not easy—mains service did not come until early in Edwardian times. It was expensive, and the clay soil and absence of deep foundations made it difficult. Lack of knowledge and Woodard's meanness meant that the problems, although constantly addressed, were not solved and from the 1850s to the mid-1880s Hurst suffered as a result.

It is a relief to turn to the one magnificent building of the period. Many early public school chapels like Marlborough's and Tonbridge's first efforts in 1848 and 1859 were small affairs. *The Builder* and *The Ecclesiologist* among commentators on Hurst's chapel, incomplete though it was, remarked that it was the first successful large public school chapel to be built at that time. Unlike the rest of the building it was larger than required for a school of 300 boys, and was in fact large enough to take a congregation of up to five hundred. Richard Carpenter had included a chapel with a high tower linked to the rest of the buildings by a cloister along the north side of the inner quadrangle. Economy precluded this being realised in full by William Slater who was the chapel's main architect joined by Richard the Younger as a partner in 1863. Slater died in 1872 and Richard, who himself died in 1893, took on Benjamin Ingelow as partner, and he became the principal architect for the relative completion of the chapel between 1892 and 1914.

Carpenter's design was in the Early Decorated style of late 13th-century Gothic architecture, a little more flamboyant than the design base of the rest of the College. It clearly owed much to Oxbridge chapels and has been compared particularly with that at Merton College, Oxford. Under a high braced oak roof the seats were arranged facing each other, and the choir and organ were to be centrally placed (the blowing room was in the wall abutting into Chevron). This cleared the east end for an altar loftily placed on 14 steps, doing away with a separate choir or sept. The design of this area was to tell in glass and stone the story of Christ's life by means of the stained glass windows and a reredos, the whole completed with seating and panelling in oak.

A meeting to start the chapel was held on 17 February 1861, and the subscription list opened on 20 March to raise £6,000. This was a vast sum equal to a quarter of the cost of the whole building, and it was not all raised, the result being yet another unfinished interior. Foundations were put in by Jackson and Shaw, two bricks were laid by William Pratt and George Thomson on 20 August, and on 17 September 1861 the angle stone (not foundation) was placed on the NW/NE angle of the second buttress from the east end on the north side by Nathaniel Woodard with the mallet used in 1851 and a silver trowel given by the probationers. This day was Hurst's third great ceremony. Bishop Gilbert took the service, and Bishop Wilberforce preached. A collection of £100 was raised before the 400 guests crowded the hall to hear 12 speeches! Four years' work by the Brighton firm of Fabian and their clerk of the works, Knight, now began, and Lowe was often to be seen ascending the scaffolding as the building grew.

The delays were worse than those of Cheeseman on the main building. Lowe later said that what should have been a pleasure had been a tale which 'had made the heart well nigh sick during the interval'. By the summer of 1864 Woodard asked, 'Shall we go to law?'. Blencowe said they should, describing Fabian as a 'coarse, unmanageable man', but in the end they struggled on, and the Rev. J.H. Edmonds has left a description of the last feverish night before the opening service, when everyone in the College stayed up until three in the morning to put the finishing touches to the preparations, and help instal the gas fittings. Lowe had wanted Charles Longley, Archbishop of Canterbury, but when this was not possible he had to look elsewhere for a preacher. He obtained the distinguished scholar, Henry Liddon, and 17 October 1865 was the only day he could manage. This happened to be the day in the church calendar when St Etheldreda (630-679), first Abbess of Ely, and one of the first women saints, was commemorated: it was actually the day in 695 when her body had been translated to its shrine in Ely Cathedral. Contrary to legend, the day had nothing to do with Woodard's daughter's name being the modern version of Etheldreda namely Audrey. Old Johnians returned in considerable numbers, and hence this became Old Johnians day thereafter.

The organ was revoiced. There was a row between Woodard and the Hurst music master, John Dayson, over the choice of service music, resolved by inviting Tapsfield and Boyd, two distinguished former musicians, who had been at the College as master and boy to take the service. It lasted from 11.00 to 2.30. Fowler and Field took the service and Liddon preached for an hour. The offertory was £200, but it cost £106 14s. 3d. to put on the fourth of Hurst's great ceremonies, which was not equalled again until 1877. The boys had missed lunch, but in the evening a fine supper was served, and punch distributed, and there was much hilarity, singing and toasting until their voices 'were becoming hoarse if not disorderly'.

The chapel was still little more than a shell. It had a temporary wooden altar, and a plain deal pulpit. There were deal benches, the central aisle was earth still, and the west end was to be bricked up. A committee on furnishing the chapel met in March 1865. The job was finished in 1926! Heating and paving came first in 1866. Then a start was made on the windows. John Clayton and Arthur Bell, among the best Victorian glass designers later used at Truro Cathedral, designed the glass, and by the time Lowe left three windows—the great east one, the Campion and Gilbert Memorial ones—were in place. The east window alone cost £1,000. William Slater designed the reredos (he also did one for Chichester), and it was cast by Forsyth at a cost of £1,800. Contributions to the east end included a panel of the reredos given by William Campion, the statues given as a memorial to a master who died in 1866, and the pelican at the apex given as a memorial by Richard Pennell when he left in 1867. Much remained to be done, and the chapel was the focus for fund raising over sixty years until its completion in 1930.

The wooded site of the College was an attractive one, but the acreage inadequate. Until 1862 all games had to take place on the South field which sloped and had several trees on it. The cricketers had to seek fairly unsuitable rented fields. To the west of the College was a large vegetable patch of an acre, Lowe's garden, and the fellows' garden. The space was let to farmers, or the hay crop kept and sold by the College. But in 1861 it was decided to use part of the West field for cricket, uneven though it was, and a grim accident followed two years later in February 1863. The College had a large horse roller usually pulled by the boys: on this occasion John Clothier, son of a Haslemere doctor, slipped and 'the heavy instrument passed over the poor boy who never spoke again'. In 1861 when the debt on the building was cleared Woodard was persuaded to buy another ten acres. This was two fields to the north of the buildings and, although the boys grubbed up the hedge between the fields and the North field came into use in 1864, it was many years before it was a proper playing surface. Lowe constantly drew Woodard's attention to other good land purchases—indeed at one point rumour of a railway line close to the village created alarm—but nothing was done, and no more land acquired until Coombes' headship in Edwardian times.

Besides selling hay and vegetables for a profit, the College kept pigs for dripping, pork and tallow, and sometimes sold them as well. Income from agricultural produce was £90 12s. 3d. in 1872. The piggery was next to the stable and both abutted onto Thomas Davey's cottage standing at the north-east corner next to the east end of the chapel. Thomas Davey with his white ruffle of whiskers was a true Sussex worthy who came to Hurst in 1853 and retired in 1915. His son, Amos Davey, also served the school for many years. They looked after the horses, including a pony owned by Sabine Baring-Gould, and the College donkey used for pulling the luggage cart. David Edwardes, a master, in his memoirs referred to this area, saying it was rat infested, and in other memoirs occurs the story of Harry King (OJ) who was bitten and nearly died as a result. Davey's main contribution as gardener from 1857 was a shrub- and tree-planting programme to west and east of the College, and gradually the austere surroundings began to mellow. A terrace was made fronting South field with steps, a sundial carved by Baring-Gould, and a Stevenson Screen manned by John Gorham. A masters' bowling green appeared north of the hall, and by 1879 a bank and planted trees surrounded the North field.

III

The Chapter Calendar mentions a 'preparatory school for little boys' situated at West End House in Ditchling which came under the supervision of Lowe, although it was run by Miss H. Nickoll, called Lady Principal, daughter of the vicar. No other information about membership is given, but the names of some of those at the school can be traced in team lists, showing that it acted as a feeder school to Hurst. According to John Honey, there were only about twenty preparatory schools in the 1850s so Lowe's proposal to Woodard in May 1857 to set one up is further evidence of his educational awareness. It took years to persuade Woodard, but by May 1863 Lowe was able to tell him that the school would have a successful base, and it opened in 1864. Lowe wanted it to take boys under ten years old, and it continued to do so until at least 1892, after which there is no further mention of the school.

Fees of £31 11s. 0d. a year were high, but the curriculum besides the basic subjects offered drawing, Greek, music and even dancing. The school had close relations with Hurst and Miss Nickoll attended Hurst functions. In June 1866 a cricket match with the youngest at Hurst took place, and this seems to have been an annual event. On 26 June 1868 what must surely have been one of the first ever preparatory school sports days took place with 10 events. John Nickoll, who won the high jump, was later a member of the special school at Hurst. Prizes awarded included a paint box, cricket belt, telescope and, rather surprisingly, a tankard. The school in fact took some older boys, as George Moore passed directly from it to the Navy as a cadet in 1875, and Ernest Beck who came second in the same exam went on to Hurst.

The majority of boys at Hurst were boarders, but there were up to ten day boys a year paying £3 3s. 0d. and having a free midday meal. Lowe told the Taunton Commission 'we do not care for day boys', but as we have seen there were some at the Mansion House, and presumably in the years between, until their number was listed separately from 1860. The scholarships to Hurst in the hands of the Hurstpierpoint and Cuckfield vestries provided that candidates who were day boys would receive a free education if they were deserving cases like John Albery, the first Cuckfield scholar, described as 'a clever lad' whose widowed mother was struggling to bring up her family. Day boys would have found full participation in school life difficult as they were required to be in school from seven in the morning until nine at night. Reginald Turner (OJ) recalled the hard time he had some years later even with the aid of an early bicycle in fulfilling this demand.

Hurst's servitors were ignored in the register with one exception, but to Lowe and Woodard they were of great importance because they were proof that the school gave a step up the ladder of advancement in life to 'the lowest and meanest'. It is clear from many of their names like Job Scrivens, Reuben Gregory, Moses Butler, or Hiram Elliott that they were sons of servants or farm labourers although there were some foreign names in their ranks including Antonio Guidotti, Werner Stauffen and George Farajellah. Provision was made for eight a year at £5 and eight more at £10 a year although in six years under Lowe the maximum number was exceeded. In 1872 the income from servitors was £127 10s. 0d. but they reduced the domestic bill by cleaning knives and shoes, clearing tables, scrubbing and sweeping. Lowe told the commissioners 'one is a carpenter', and 'one minds the steam engine'. The Chapter Minute Book in 1854 gave details of the dress provided for them: 'tunics of grey serge or other woollen stuff with a leathern belt and a leathern apron for domestic work, and a brown cap with a blue border.'

They were housed at the top of the hall stairs. Their dining room, where they were taught, was on the left, and they lived above in a dormitory next to the butler's bedroom. It is not entirely clear who was in charge of these boys. Clearly the butler supervised their domestic work, but in 1860 William Pratt became master of the servitors at £20 a year, and was perhaps responsible for organising their education. In 1861 there is a record of a primary schoolmaster engaged to teach them for a guinea. Although most of them were no doubt destined to working-class life it was Lowe's intention they should receive a good education and rise in the world if at all possible. They had three hours teaching a day in Divinity, English, arithmetic, and limited geography, history and singing. Servitors' prizes in English and Divinity started in 1858—William Diskett won both in 1874. Lowe was proud to point out to the commissioners that a servitor, Richard Cunnington, was now a personal servant—he became secretary (bursar) of Ardingly in 1870, and later Edwin Bunce, another of Lowe's servants, became secretary of Denstone in 1876. Because they are not in the register, tracing their careers is virtually impossible—the one exception was George Cory, a servitor from 1879 to 1881, who was to be a professor of chemistry at Rhodes University and a distinguished South African historian.

The servitors lived in rough conditions, but better in all probability than they would have experienced at home. Only two deaths, of James Dallison in December 1872 and Garibaldi Raishbrook in February 1873 are recorded, and no cause is given. Servitors attended chapel and were confirmed, and raised a sad little seven and sixpence for the chapel building fund. They took part in sport. Guidotti won the first swimming prize in 1858, and William Diskett, for example, the same prize in 1874. In 1860 a servitors' race on Sports Day began with small prizes given to all the competitors, and in later years there were occasional cricket matches with the Ardingly servitors.

Lowe seems to have been less happy with the second 'school' within the buildings, first called the engineering and military, and later the special school. From at least December 1852 the accounts make it clear that a small number of boys, whose parents wished them to have a private room and 'be pushed on for some special commercial purposes', were admitted to the College. We saw a Campion among them. When St George's, a Woodard school providing a similar curriculum, collapsed, Hurst took over its function in 1856, and the special school survived until 1874 when Lancing College began a Modern department fulfilling some of its rôle. Although Lowe criticised it as being a concession to 'the weakness of parental nature', and Robert Hill (OJ) called them 'parlour boarders' the special school was of some importance and value.

From two members listed in 1856 numbers rose to double figures by 1861, and to a peak of 20 boys in 1870, although the usual number under Lowe was fifteen or sixteen. Their fees at £47 5s. a year were high, they paid a higher entrance fee, and an additional fee for their laboratory of five shillings a year. A sum of £700 for 15 boys was well worth having. It has been pointed out that numbers in the school and their length of stay have been underestimated: in fact, the special school provided the school with more older boys for teams and to act as prefects, and added to the school's academic success. The first two listed in 1856 were Lowe's nephew, who went on to Addiscombe College, which trained entrants for the Indian army until 1861, and Henry Radford. In 1860 Robert Beeston obtained entrance to Addiscombe, and in 1862 John Blurton became the first Hurst Johnian to go to Sandhurst where competitive entry had started four years previously.

The special school provided expert tuition for military, naval, and other professional examinations like accountancy and engineering. It was situated at the south end of the ground floor of Shield House where there was a laboratory, and a common room. The boys had their own table in hall, but slept in Lowe's Red Shield dormitory at extra cost. They attended ordinary lessons when necessary, and took part in the school sports—their presence in teams showing that they stayed on longer than the register states. They were also allowed to employ tutors for special subjects, and this is why Hurst was able to offer such remarkable subjects as Hindustani, naval architecture, and military surveying if required. Because their careers were not detailed in the register the success of the school remains unknown, although the suspicion must be that there were many others, like Thomas Dearden, who became engineers in later life as a result of the specialist training provided in this school.

Like the servitors the Training School for Probationary Schoolmasters, soon known as the Probationary Associates, served three purposes to provide revenue, reduce expenses, and add rungs to Woodard's ladder of advancement. Considerable confusion surrounds the first appointments to this school. The term 'associates' and another one, 'exhibitioners', were in use at Hurst from 1850. Francis Williams and Sayer Warmoll were exhibitioners, and Eaton, Turner and Verrall, associates at the Mansion House. However, it is clear from the Minute Book that discussions on the probationers took place in June 1852, and the scheme came into operation when Hurst opened in 1853. The first four probationers were Herbert Hurst (not in register), Edmund Blackmore, George Ling, and James Woodward. During 1856 there was further discussion of an appropriate exam for the end of the course. Lowe devised one taken in December that year, and as a result four A.S.N.C.s were on the staff in 1857—Edmund Blackmore, George Ling, James Woodward and James Morris.

The purpose of the school was for it to be a teacher training and theological college, which would help the middle and poorer classes to be clergy and schoolmasters and attend university, while providing Hurst and indeed the Chapter with cheaply paid teachers, both before and after graduation, and clergy sympathetic to High Church teaching. Woodard in 1856 was talking in terms of 30 members, and proposed a fund to provide prizes, books, maps, and models for teaching. This was too sanguine. The number of probationers reached ten in 1859, and a maximum of fourteen in 1869. The average number under Lowe was between ten and twelve, and by the time the last one left in 1908 one or two a year was the norm. Entrance to the school was at 16 or over after an exam which Lowe said was of 'low standard', although it covered seven subjects from Latin to handwriting. If a young man entered the school directly there was a three guinea admission, and it cost £27 6s. 0d. a year for three years. If he entered from the College there was no entrance fee, and costs were reduced to £17 17s. 0d. a year. The probationers had their own common room next to the fellows library, two separate tables in hall, and slept in 'rookeries'—the bedrooms on the top floor of the west and east transepts of the building. They had to provide their gown and surplice, but did not pay school dues, although taking part fully in school life in teams or as prefects. Although we have no precise details, we know they also could teach up to three hours a week and be paid £10 a term.

The probationers caused Lowe much trouble. The same age as the sixth form, they were both being taught and teaching, and this confused disciplinary situation taxed Lowe's powers. In 1854 all but two of the probationers and exhibitioners were involved in trouble. While Lowe was away attending his father-in-law's funeral Lomax lost control. Probationers cut chapel, came late to meals, drank and smoked, invited sixth formers to their rooms, and stayed up late. When Lowe returned in October Williams, Turner and Marriott were expelled.

Trouble re-occurred. In 1860 Lowe complained about 'absurd flirtings' with village girls after the Shrove Tuesday tradesmen's dinner, and a probationer was expelled for smoking. In 1862 Thomas Blackman was expelled for going to Redhill and staying there overnight. James Rowlatt was reported to Woodard for drinking and smoking and displaying 'awful temper' to Pennell, although he managed to survive. As late as 1871 Lowe laid down in his headmaster's book that probationers had no right to use corporal punishment, were to be punctual to chapel and meals, not entertain, and put their gas out at 11 o'clock. In spite of these problems Lowe was generally satisfied with the probationers, and told the commissioners of their efficiency, their high tone and bearing, their general usefulness.

At the end of three years they took an exam to become A.S.N.C.s and obtained the right to wear a grey gown. They then performed up to twelve hours a week teaching for a salary rising from £20 to £50 a year. Although they were not permanent residents, and could be required to teach at other Chapter schools, the A.S.N.C.s also had leave of absence to attend university. In return for this help for three years they were honour bound to teach three more years in a Woodard school after getting a degree. There were 18 A.S.N.C. degrees awarded from 1856 to 1864. There were never less than four listed on the staff, and in 1867 there were as many as eight. At least twenty-four A.S.N.C.s taught in Victorian Hurst, and many stayed in Woodard schools—in 1888 there were 23 teaching in the Midland chapter. Some of course gave up teaching or taught outside Woodard's scheme in unknown numbers.

It was also true that A.S.N.C. masters, being inexperienced, provided Lowe with more trouble. James Jackman (A.S.N.C. 1860) ran the corps band and was organist. In April 1865 Lowe found he had secretly married Margaret Wadey from the village and he was asked to leave. Suffering from tuberculosis, he died in December 1868 (and not 1864 as the register says!). George Ling taught mathematics and writing. In 1867 the mother of two boys accused Ling of striking them on the head and face with his clenched fist, and told Lowe she had 'for a long time heard of Mr Ling's cruelty'. The boys were withdrawn, and Ling admonished. Edward Hewett was later to be an important priest involved in slum mission work in Glasgow, but from 1863 to 1870 he was at Hurst and an A.S.N.C. by 1869. He hit the brother of the school's leading athlete, George Clapp, in hall, and Thomson had to separate them. The boys were again withdrawn.

There was one further extension of career possible to A.S.N.C.s. In 1857 Lowe and Woodard devised a course leading to ordination which Bishop Gilbert was prepared to accept. Blackmore and Woodward began work on this course, and in December 1861 passed. In 1862 they were ordained, and they were followed by at least 65 in the Southern, and 27 in the Midland division. The last candidate who entered the ministry by this method did so in 1919.

With the help of probationers and A.S.N.C.s teaching, Lowe was able to have a much smaller common room than one might think necessary to teach so many boys so diverse a range of subjects. The common room consisted of masters and fellows (a distinction ignored in the register). The fellows were appointed by Woodard, and were meant to be the governing body of the Society. In fact, they never met as such, and it became an honorary title carrying with it certain privileges including full-time College residence. Twice a year, however, there were Octave meetings. In December there was a sermon and a dinner. Sam Brooke, a relative of Mertens, head of Ardingly, was close to the staff of the schools. He heard Lowe preach 'a very good Octave sermon indeed' at Lancing. Issues including scholarships and exam results were discussed. From 1855 to 1865, mainly at Hurst, a second Octave was held for a week. At this academic issues were considered and current religious topics discussed. There were special services, meditations, and prayers. Brooke described the fellows walking in the countryside, playing bowls, or being entertained in Harriet Lowe's 'pretty and hospitable drawing room'.

Field and Fowler, Lowe's two chaplains, were fellows, and six members of the common room—Pennell, Thomson, Gorham, Edwardes, Bennett and Washbourn. Their presence was clearly part of the collegiate atmosphere that Lowe and Woodard wanted to encourage. Their ideal was a common room of bachelor ordained Oxbridge men or, as Lowe put it referring to a new master in 1864, 'he was the better sort of Oxford High Churchman we remember in days gone by'. In fact, this was not achieved. John Honey calculated that in mid-Victorian England about 54 per cent of masters were ordained, and this was true of Hurst. Similarly the percentage fell to 13 per cent by the early 1900s, and even lower at Hurst. Of about seventy-five appointments made by Lowe, 22 were ordained and 14 were later ordained, although the main posts were in clerical hands with the exception of one dormitory master. They were certainly all bachelors and, although A.S.N.C.s like Dayson married and lived in the village, it seems David Edwardes who married his wife Ann in June 1869 was the first married resident, although sadly his wife died in December 1871. Academically Lowe's staff were poorly qualified. Twenty-four had A.S.N.C. degrees, and 29 of them had degrees from the four English universities, including 16 Oxford and 10 Cambridge ones.

The teaching profession was then in process of formation. Lowe's masters had no contracts, no pensions, and were removed at a term's notice according to fluctuations in numbers. According to Martin Williams's figures only 11 stayed more than 10 years, and half stayed less than two years, although as former Johnians and probationers their residence was for longer. Alford the drilling master and Pratt the writing master had the longest service records of Lowe's appointees, and only one, Richard Pennell, was a truly long-serving master of the sort Hurst was to produce so good a crop of in the next century. The main masters appointed were Charles Lomax, John Gorham and Richard Pennell in the 1850s, John Dayton, David Edwardes, Frederick Bennett, George Thomson, and George Willes in the 1860s, and Robert Wix and John Edmonds in the early 1870s. Even dormitory masters' appointments had no real element of stability, and only George Thomson (Red Shield 1867-1880) and Frederick Bennett (Crescent 1865-1879) served for long periods, although John Dayson, Robert Wix and George Willes managed more than five years.

6   George O.L. Thomson the first School Captain, 1858-1861. He later became a master from 1866 to 1880.

About ten of Lowe's masters stand out for both achievements and characters that became part of school legend as well as history. Charles Lomax was second master for 10 years from 1850. 'Carrots', with his wispy hair and whiskers, was a good administrator and a poor disciplinarian. One reason for this was his health. In 1855 Lowe reported him 'still very seedy' at the start of the school year, and by 1859 he was 'quite unfit for work'. Lowe urged he be found a quiet parish which did the trick. Lomax's health recovered and he died aged eighty-eight! For a time he had no successor until George Thomson (OJ) returned, and a year later in September 1867 became second master until the end of 1879. He taught classics and history, relying on sarcasm as his main weapon, and was the author manqué of the common room, editing and contributing considerably to the *Hurst Johnian*, and active in the play. George Willes (OJ), a friend of his, returned to Hurst the same year and stayed until 1879. This Falstaffian character who often nodded to sleep in afternoon lessons was later to achieve fame as 'the Padre' in Rudyard Kipling's *Stalky and Co.*

Richard Lewin Pennell from the West Country was at the College from 1850 to 1867 teaching a wide variety of subjects to the younger forms. His sister married Frederick Mertens, first headmaster of Ardingly, and five of his family went to Lancing. Although he had a cataract operation in 1864, Pennell was excessively short sighted, and stories abound of his actions. He was said to have hit a loaf thinking it was a boy's head, poured milk into a clergyman's collar thinking it was a jug, and stabbed a frog placed on his desk instead of an inkwell. But he was respected as a deeply involved and pious schoolmaster, and Lowe was horrified when Pennell said he had receive the call to be a missionary. His death not long afterwards in East Africa will be described in the next chapter. He was lower master from 1860, and he was succeeded by an able science master, Oliver Churchyard, who left in 1870. The last lower master appointed was Frederick Fryer, who had been head of St Edward's, Oxford, which nearly collapsed under his rule. He stayed at Hurst as dormitory master, too, of Chevron until 1873.

Sabine Baring-Gould was at Hurst from 1856 to 1864 (not 1855 as the register claims, or 1857-65 as his memoirs did). As one of the most important writers of the century—he produced at least one hundred and twenty books—he is still well-known: indeed there is a Baring-Gould Society. He was a flamboyant and pushy master known as 'Snout', and caused considerable annoyance to Lowe with demands to be appointed precentor, for higher wages, for his gown to be bought for him, and above all by his interest in church vestments. However, he was a marvellous all-rounder. Dormitory master of Red Shield, he taught chemistry, music, Latin, French and German, was an actor and play producer and contributed handsomely to the *Hurst Johnian*. It is said he designed its cover, the saints at the front entrance, the sundial for the terrace, and the fellows library bookcases.

Opposite Red Shield in Blue Shield was John Gorham from 1858 to 1866. A Sussex man from West Wittering (who had been to sea), six foot tall, with a stentorian voice, Gorham was a man to be reckoned with. He taught mathematics, helped Lowe as an unofficial bursar, and encouraged the boys in a range of interests including geology and meteorology. He was an active sportsman at football and cricket, responsible for starting dormitory matches in 1864. This made his swift death in April 1866 all the more tragic when a chill turned to fever. He received the Last Rites in his dormitory master's bedroom in the company of Lowe, Fowler, Pennell, Mrs. Marchant, and Walter Hand, his dormitory prefect.

John Dayson taught at Hurst for 20 years from 1860, and was the first major producer of the Shakespeare play, and the first major choir master and organist. He was also church organist in the village and managed to fit in all the services on a Sunday. 'Bluff old Dayson' was well thought of, and he went on to be the first bursar of King's College, Taunton. William Pratt established the long service record on the staff which he joined in 1859, dying in harness in 1908. The boys admired him as a cricket coach who had occasionally played for Sussex, and played regularly in the village. He was secretary (bursar), master of the servitors, writing master, and in charge of stationery.

The old register is more defective in its list of masters prior to 1880 than anywhere else. It included those like Frederick Arnold, Sir Frederick Gore Ouseley, and the Rev. T. Oakley who did not teach at Hurst. It included part-time outsiders like William Gates, Brighton bandmaster, or Alexander White, head of the Sussex School of Art. No mention is made of C.F. Hill or W.F. Stevens who joined the staff in 1861, or Alfred Whipham who taught at Hurst from 1865 to 1868. Henry Alford, the drilling master, is ignored. The amount of time spent teaching by probationers and associates is unknown, and therefore it is not easy to say how many were on the staff, how much work they had to do, or even precisely how much they were paid although the accounts and Lowe's letters help a good deal. The number of full-time masters and fellows was six in 1853, and rose to 10 in 1864 and 11 in 1868 falling back to 8 in 1872. Including the A.S.N.C.s the teaching staff was 10 in 1853, reached a maximum of 20 in 1868, and fell back slightly to 17 in 1872.

They were poorly paid: the total salary bill in 1869 came to only £1,800 excluding part-time masters, and payments to probationers. When Lowe was asked by the commissioners about low salaries he pointed out that the masters had extra commons like fuel and food, but when he was asked how this affected individuals he said, 'I have never considered the question'. In fact in 1867 extra commons only amounted to £99 14s. 7d. in addition to normal house-hold expenditure. Dedicated churchmen were willing to accept low salaries; Field, for instance, saying he was 'content to work for less'. They were paid better than many parish clergy, but less than masters in the great or proprietory schools. By the 1860s staffing became difficult. Lowe's letters show that Hurst lost Robert Quick, a distinguished educationalist, in 1866, and the mathematician, Septimus Phillpotts, in 1869 on financial grounds. Lowe was anxious to keep Oliver Churchyard, and told Woodard he had 'screwed up his pay to £100', but he left in 1870. The masters knew Hurst was expanding and earning a profit, and could not see why their salaries were so low. Led by the chaplain, Fowler, in April 1869 they wrote to Woodard asking for a rise to 'smooth down the asperities inseparable from the life of a schoolmaster'. They got short shrift, as we know, from Woodard who pointed out that the profits went elsewhere. So did the masters. Fowler and Washbourn left soon after the rejection of this request, and it was clear by the 1870s that salaries were too low to attract many Oxbridge first-class men, or even a new headmaster of distinction.

The Victorian timetable was an arduous one, and the Victorian curriculum at Hurst wider than it was to be again until over a hundred years later. There were only two holidays a year: in 1867 from 23 December to 29 January, and from 30 July to 17 September, and for some a short break was possible after Port Latin Day from 8 to 18 May. So they spent 40 weeks in school, and overseas boys remained perhaps for their whole school life, boarding with the headmaster in the holidays. Fortunately this was leavened by easier rules on leisure time, wide bounds for seniors, and a range of half-holidays for regular traditions, special occasions, and celebration of success.

One of William Barrett's letters gives the daily timetable. The bell sounded at 6.15 a.m., chapel was at 7.00 a.m., and divinity at 7.30 a.m. Breakfast was at 8.00 a.m., and lessons began with a period of preparation at 9.15 a.m. and continued without break until 12.15. There was an hour for sport, and then lunch, school resuming at 3.15 p.m. and going on until 5.30 p.m. Then came chapel, tea at 6.00 and, starting at 7.00 p.m., prep for two hours. Dormitory prayers and bed followed at 9.15 p.m. In forms 'they place you', said Barrett, 'according to what Latin you know'. The top forms were the upper and lower sixth, changed for a time to sixth and division in 1870. Below came upper and lower fifths, upper and lower fourths, lower third, remove, upper and lower second, and first forms ranging in age from nine to nineteen. The eleven forms were grouped into five departments: divinity, grammar, (Latin, Greek, English), mathematics, history (including ancient history and geography), and modern languages. There was more science than Lowe was keen to admit under the title natural philosophy.

Lowe like any other Victorian educationalist saw the classics as the basis of a liberal education. 'Nothing can compare with Latin' as a mental discipline, he said, and he did not believe other languages including English could be taught without Latin. As befitted a grammar school, 311 out of 331 boys did Latin in 1865 for 10 hours a week while those doing Greek added another six hours. As an educationalist, Lowe saw the need for his pupils to see Latin as the language of 'the home, the market place and the race course'. In 1866 he published Erasmus' *Colloquia* for use in conversation and declamation, and in 1868 *Porta Latina* with selections from Latin authors. As a realist he also admitted Latin was in the curriculum because it 'opened the way for advancement in life'.

As a Church school Hurst taught Divinity to all boys, but it is important to notice that even under Lowe Hurst was never totally Anglican. There were Nonconformists' sons in the school including a Quaker boy, and among their 'foreigners' there were occasionally Roman Catholics. There were, he told the commissioners, two Jews: one was baptised and the other ran away. In the classroom Lowe was keen to see Divinity 'studied and learned as a science', as he told an educational conference in 1867.

All studied history beginning with the rulers of Britain in the lower third, and including Roman history, and specialisation in the Tudor period using Hume's *History of England*. Geography was similarly studied by all. Unusually in the Victorian period Lowe was determined that English, both spoken and written, should be taught to all boys. English, he said, was 'a definite subject of study' with four and a half hours a week on grammar and literature. He edited for school use George Herbert's *Poems* in 1867, and in 1868 published *The Young Englishman's First Poetry Book*. There were declamation and essay prizes on Port Latin Day when scenes from 18th-century dramatists like Goldsmith and Sheridan were acted, and public speaking prizes for each form because, as he put it, 'in a free country free speech is the bond of freedom'.

Handwriting lessons were given to 181 boys in 1865, and there was even a remedial class (with 18 pupils) for those unable to read in the lower third.

Modern languages were another particular concern of Lowe's as his pamphlet *A Plea for the Study of Modern Languages* (1869) shows. 'Do we not', he said, 'show a blameable apathy about Continental nations and the tongues they speak?' All studied French from Arnold's *Grammar*, and a few studied German and Spanish. Although the commissioners criticised the accents used, Lowe was well ahead in his teaching of modern languages. In 1865 he appointed the first foreign assistant, Doktor Rüge, and in 1866 he was succeeded by Senor Herbert Martinucci who remained for 10 years. Foreign boys like Werner Stauffen or Alexandre des Essarts were asked to help with conversation. Lowe himself translated d'Azeglio's *Ettore Fieramosca* in the *Hurst Johnian*, and much later in life published a translation of Dante's *Divina Comedia*.

Arithmetic was studied by all, and mathematics by 174 boys in 1865. The double first in classics and mathematics was the Blue Riband of scholarship, and Hurst was to produce many excellent mathematicians. The department was effectively started by John Gorham, carried on for two years by 'Seppy' Phillpotts, and then by David Edwardes. 'The Euclid', said William Barrett, 'is the lesson I dislike most and so do all the fellows.' However, he and the others received six books of Euclid, mathematics up to calculus level, algebra, trigonometry and conic sections. In addition 59 boys studied book keeping and accounting, and 24 surveying, showing that these subjects were taught well beyond the bounds of the special school.

The surprises in Lowe's Victorian curriculum continue, for close behind these seven main subjects came two more with only slightly fewer boys doing them. Frederick Earp taught art from 1851 to 1856, and Baring-Gould thereafter for a time. From 1861 to 1866 the head of the Brighton School of Art was employed part-time, and twenty or more boys received certificates of merit in some years. 290 boys were doing art or drawing in 1865. Edwin Martin and John Dayson were the main music masters in Lowe's years, and there were at least five other music masters during these years including Baring-Gould, R. Gould, E. Tapsfield, T. Petherick, and J. Jackman. William Gates, bandmaster of the Brighton Town Band, assisted with orchestral music for plays. 293 boys studied singing using Hullah's method. There was even mention of a band or orchestra from time to time, but this was almost certainly not a boys' one.

Unfortunately one remark of Lowe's to the commissioners about science has been misinterpreted. He said, 'I do not attach value to it as an instrument of mental training'—meaning vis-à-vis Latin. In fact, Hurst was one of the first grammar schools to take science seriously. Expenditure varying from £10 to £14 a year on the laboratory started in the accounts in 1855 and in 1858 A. Goalen was the first appointed qualified science master. Among future science masters were George Pope, who also taught geography, from 1861 to 1865 and after him G.E. Dodson, the first master with a London University degree to be appointed. In 1865 chemistry and some limited physics including dynamics were studied by 26 boys for 2½ hours a week. In April 1870 Lowe's headmaster's book shows him re-organising science teaching so that all in the sixth not doing Greek (only 16 were so doing) should learn some 'natural science', as he put it. By then there were 32 boys doing chemistry, and 15 physics. Chemistry (1866), and physics (1875) prizes appeared on Port Latin Day. John Gorham encouraged the study of meteorology, and both he and Baring-Gould the study of Sussex flora, fauna and geology. There were a good many articles on scientific subjects in the *Hurst Johnian*, particularly ones relevant to agriculture.

As a result of science teaching taking place at all, Hurst produced many doctors—Martin Williams counted seventy or more taking up medical careers from 1852 when no less than seven did so in one year. Hurst built a reputation at London, Edinburgh, Glasgow and Liverpool medical schools, and produced a number of surgeons and medical writers of distinction including William Hayward, a physician at Adelaide Hospital and founder of the Australian B.M.A., Henry Powell, Fellow of the Royal Society of Medicine and expert on seasickness, Harold Hendley, an expert on typhus and Director General of the Indian Medical Service, and John Nixon, Emeritus Professor of Medicine at Bristol University and an expert on nutrition. The first *Lancet* war correspondent sent to the Sudan and South Africa was an Old Johnian, Charles Cunningham. Nor should Arthur Bulleid be forgotten, one of the greatest archaeologists, who discovered Glastonbury Lake Village in 1892.

Lowe was a great believer in exams which were held twice a year with good conduct prizes for forms turning into work prizes. There were 21 first-class and 37 second-class ones awarded in 1869. But when questioned by the commissioners Lowe firmly stated he had no intention of becoming a 'local centre' for external exams. With the help of Mark Pattison, an annual written and viva voce exam by two or three Oxbridge dons was begun in 1857. The dons came into residence and were paid £20 in fees for their pains. William Barrett commented on them in April 1869: 'their dinner was a grand one every night ... they all dined in full dress except the doctor. They had napkins, wine etc, and it did seem so beastly to me ... to be eating that dry bread and lukewarm milk and water whilst those masters were gorging.' The reports were read out on Port Latin Day, and published in the *Hurst Johnian*, acting as a good spur to the 'manly spirit of work' no doubt in masters and boys alike.

Port Latin Day in May was the great event in Hurst's secular calendar, even if it was named after 6 May in the Church calendar. This was the day on which St John the Evangelist was said to have suffered martyrdom by boiling oil at the Latin Gate of Rome. If not martyrdom then at least social exhaustion must have affected a good many on a day with so much crammed into it, sandwiched also between Old Johnian football and cricket matches. Between 1852 and 1855 Port Latin Day solidified into a set ceremony which lasted, with some reductions, until 1899. It was a grand day. A special train brought London guests. Mr. Gates's musicians arrived from Brighton. The *New Inn* handled the catering for up to three hundred guests. By 1860 the administration was costing £50 10s. 10d. and a charge for lunch was started. By 1869 there were 82 prizes awarded. Twenty-six of them were named prizes costing £42 9s. 6d. for embossed and leather-bound books that year. The ones already existing in 1853 were for Divinity, public speaking, mathematics, and English. Then came Latin prose and Latin translation, junior and senior French prizes, and in 1872 a German prize. The two Campion Essays (1858) were really the history prizes while the geography prize was given by Pennell on leaving in 1867. A natural science prize started in 1866, and there were music, choir (1859), freehand and technical drawing, public speaking and writing prizes.

1866 might be taken as typical of these Victorian occasions, beginning at 7.30 with a communion followed at 10.45 by service and sermon. The company entered upper school at 12 o'clock when the examiners' reports were read, university successes reported, the head reviewed the year, and the prizes were distributed. But that was only a beginning. That year choir and musicians provided four madrigals, and three part songs interspersed between the reading of prize essays, recitations, and dramatic scenes from plays. Walter Head was excused reading his essay due to his dormitory master's death, but four other essays were read. Then there were two Latin recitations, and six others in English, in prose and verse, including boys acting out an Erasmus *Colloquy* on 'boys asking for a holiday'. Lowe commented next year that some of these speakers should conquer their 'pardonable nervousness'. The play extracts were from *Julius Caesar*, *King Lear*, and *Henry IV*, *Part I*, and in other years both English and French play scenes were given, particularly from Sheridan and Molière. At 2.00 p.m. lunch was served followed by a surfeit of eight speeches interspersed with toasts in the hall. These events were followed by a corps or gym display in later times, and in Lowe's time by one of the two athletic sports that took place each year.

Port Latin in 1866, however, had one additional importance. Nathaniel Woodard was present to announce the award of the first Port Latin Exhibitions. They marked the completion of the ladder of advancement, and were in effect closed awards available to Hurst Johnians going to university. They were worth £16 13s. 4d. a year for three years and did not of course cover the full cost, estimates of which varied between a hundred and two hundred a year. To obtain them a stiff examination was taken, devised by Lowe earlier that year, in Divinity, classics, mathematics and English. Although the exam was weighted to classics, it is interesting that the first two winners, Thomas Chirol and Edward Forty, went on to obtain a first in mathematics and a second in natural science.

There were only four English universities at that time and those seeking positions in church or state had to obtain entry to Oxford and Cambridge. This was biased towards the rich, firstly, because the fees were large, and secondly, because there were many closed awards particularly for the older public schools. A royal commission investigated university finance in 1852-1854, but it took until 1879 to establish the system of exhibitions and scholarships which lasted just over a hundred years, providing many more open awards from re-organised college finances. For poorer students there were few opportunities of entry. Some colleges like Christ Church provided sizar or servitorships giving reduced fees for performing duties. There were halls with reduced fees. Woodard and Lowe had both been to Magdalen Hall and were familiar with the problem, and in the 1860s were particularly involved with St Edmund Hall where two former heads of Lancing were Principal and Vice-Principal.

According to a letter in the *Hurst Johnian* in September 1865 from William Boyd (OJ), the basic fees at St Edmund Hall were £73 7s. 4d. a year, and it was theoretically possible to survive on about £110 a year. However, in most colleges the basic fees had to be supplemented by others, and Boyd maintained that £200 a year was really needed. This point was confirmed by Samuel Brooke, a Lancing boy and later master at Hurst, who pointed out that scouts and bedwomen had to be paid extra for even basic services, and there were expensive 'wines' and other customs to be observed.

Providing for middle-class people at Oxbridge was a reformist cause of mid-Victorian England, and Mark Pattison, now Rector of Lincoln College, was at its forefront urging 800 places for those 'from national schools or commercial academies'. In 1867 at Wolverhampton Lowe made an important speech on the subject, published as *A Plea for Poor Scholars*. He disliked sizarships, or poor men's colleges, as it was necessary 'to reduce class jealousies'. He told the meeting, 'I have no small experience for nearly twenty years among poor men desiring the universities', and his solution was to lower fees by reforming endowments, providing more from the fees charged and making competitive awards or grants available. Lowe told Woodard that their schools could never compete with 'Rugby, Marlboro' and Eton in scholarships', and the commissioners that 'boys seldom go to university' from Hurst.

Once again a single remark has been misinterpreted, and at least two writers have said Hurst therefore failed to help the middle class break down this particular barrier. In fact, Hurst sent a very respectable number to university, agricultural and missionary colleges. Under Lowe at least forty boys went to Edinburgh, Glasgow, Durham, London, Dublin, and Lampeter. The figures for Oxford and Cambridge are as follows to 1879:

Years	Oxford (from 1852)	Cambridge (from 1864)	
Educated solely under Lowe	23	8	
Educated under Lowe and Awdry	19	7	
Educated solely under Awdry	4	10	
Total	**46**	**25**	**71**

Although many went to the poorer colleges All Souls', Balliol, and King's, Cambridge were among the successes. Hurst's 16 awards compares well with Lancing's 34 in the same period. The ladder upwards was a thin one, but it was there, and examination of the careers of Lowe's and Awdry's Hurst Johnians shows that a good many did indeed achieve the aim of putting middle-class men in professions.

Career details of only 689 out of the first 3,000 names in the register are available, and matters only improve slightly for the next 900 up to 1899. Figures given are therefore minimalist ones. During this time 127 Hurst Johnians entered the ministry. Eight of them reached the rank of cathedral canon or above. Eighty or so became schoolmasters, half of them teaching for a time in a Woodard school. Nine of them became headmasters. Including masters who served at Hurst, the Woodard Society benefited greatly from the school which provided six other Woodard headmasters, four bursars, and two second masters. Abroad Hurst provided head-masters for schools in New Zealand, Australia, South Africa, Hong Kong and Hawaii, and clergy of the ranks of archdeacon, canon and rural dean in New Zealand, South Africa, and Canada. Over seventy entered medicine, dentistry and agricultural science, and over eighty some sort of military service. Four reached the rank of major-general, and nine that of lieutenant-colonel. Both academically and socially Lowe's Hurst had established a reputation as a public school with a good Oxbridge record, and had started to fulfil Woodard's aims with a small but significant advance of its pupils into the professions and even the higher ranks of them.

THREE

GREAT DAYS
IN THE
DISTANCE ENCHANTED

The Life and Structure of a Victorian School

We are in anxiety again with one of the boys who is laid up with fever, typhus really, though we do not call it so, as it so alarms people ...

> Edward Lowe to Nathaniel Woodard,
> 11 March 1858
> Lancing Archives

At a second committee holden this day a report was laid before the members by Pole against Cooper max, and Sykes for insulting him on the football pitch by throwing sundry pellets of mud at him, and proceeding to violence ... After discussing the matter for some time the Committee came to the conclusion that Cooper and Sykes should be thrashed by the Captain of the Football, and that a public notice to this effect should be posted on the library door.

> Minutes of the Football Committee,
> 15 February 1867

Some mourn to hear the clang of arms along the cloister come,
The shrieking echo of the fife, the booming of the drum,
To see the classic quadrangle, meet haunt of stole and gown,
With long array of armed men, and horrid bayonet frown!
But God be praised as who thus raised a heart in English youth
To gird on armour for their land, and for their Church's truth.

> *The Hurst Johnian*, 43/121,
> August 1862

Walked over the fields to the College having sandwiches under the tall hedge by the white house with the long garden. Saw no boys until I turned the last corner—my heart beat with emotion as I neared the old, familiar places. I strode across the noisy yard with old prefect pride ... I went up to the Doctor's [Lowe's] room. He was dozing with Mrs Lowe over the fire—she left and we had a long talk together ...

> Journal of Edwin J. Fisher (Hurst 1861-1864),
> 1 April 1867

Those who lived near the new College set deep in rural Sussex had no doubt it was a religious institution. Latin hymns and plainsong chanting could be heard; religious processions with banners and surpliced choir could be seen moving along the cloisters day and night. There were two chapel services each day and a sung Eucharist every Sunday. Various days in the Church calendar were specially celebrated. These were the external signs that Woodard's foundation was fundamentally different from many public schools at that time, setting religion in the centre of its life, or, as Lowe put it on Port Latin Day 1854, they were training boys to look upon their lessons, sports and every aspect of school life as part of religious life.

The Hurst school year under Lowe developed a considerable number of ceremonies and services, some of which have survived to this day, adding variety to school life, giving the school an air of greater antiquity than it possessed, and reinforcing the centrality of religious observance in everyday life. On Rogation Day there was a cloister procession singing Psalm 104. From 1851, during Easter, Lowe would send a letter to Old Johnians with school news, and an appeal to attend communion frequently. On Easter Eve the cloister procession ended at midnight with the singing of *Jesus Christ is Risen Today* followed by a short service. On Ascension Day 'Danny' was climbed and a hymn sung. The last Sunday before Trinity was Stir Up Sunday from 1862 with emphasis on church missions. The first Sunday after All Saints' Day was Obit Sunday from 1868 when a list of Hurst Johnians, past and present, who had died during the year was fixed to the chapel door, and a service held based on the Communion of Saints. During the Octave of St Nicolas a procession carrying a boar's head sang another Latin hymn proceeding to festivities in the hall. St Etheldreda Sunday in October became the Old Johnians' day, starting with a banner procession into the chapel singing *Jerusalem, My Happy Home*.

Climbing 'Danny' was the one ceremony held in public outside the school, and was welcomed by the boys as a whole holiday as well as by the choir whose 12 seniors received half a crown (12½p) each, called Lowe's Dole. It began, as we saw, in 1850 and was first reported in some detail in 1858. Next year Lowe described how the boys 'displayed a courage worthy of the Alma charging up the slope', although it was the chase down afterwards for cakes and biscuits which was most exciting. May 1860 was a cold month with gales but nothing daunted 'the choir set out about six o'clock in great coats and plaids' accompanied by most of the boys. Wet through when they reached the top, it was decided to sing the hymn while processing round the fortifications. A letter about this particular day has survived from a boy in Red Shield who described how Lowe came in to the dormitory and advised them to sleep between blankets only to ward off any colds.

Christmas weather, too, could be harsh. In 1858 a severe frost 'knocked up the carriers' horses', and a farm wagon and horses had to be used to take luggage to the station. But Christmas was celebrated in true Dickensian fashion at Lowe's Hurst. A tree supplied by Borrer, Campion or Marshall was handsomely decorated and set up in Hall with presents provided by the local squirearchy for every member of the school. Lowe had seen the ceremony of carrying in the boar's head at The Queen's College, Oxford, and introduced it at Hurst, although its first use is not known. Certainly by 1860 when it was fully described for the first time the head was surrounded by tapers, and *Caput Apri Defero* was sung by the choir as they entered the Hall. Then there was a sing-song for the whole school with a mixture of carols like, *Hark the Herald* and *Good King Wenceslas*, and others popular then like *Mynheer Vandunck's Christmas*. The choir took their places at the high table with the junior chorister presiding like a boy bishop over proceedings. The choir had special food known as 'the stodge'. *Dulce Domum* was sung, and the 'boys gave vent to their feelings of holiday joy in cheering the masters or anyone else ...'.

The chaplain was the most important person in the school after the headmaster, appointed by Woodard and directly answerable to him. This led to difficulties in several Woodard schools, and it is interesting that while he was head Lowe complained several times to Woodard about chaplains going behind his back, whereas years later as Provost he took the opposite viewpoint in a dispute at Lancing. Woodard and Lowe acted as their own chaplains, hearing confession or taking communion at all the Sussex schools. John Knott, senior chaplain from 1850 to 1857, was given a non-residence dispensation and, although present at the opening of Hurst and on several other occasions (January 1854, June 1856), he had little to do with the school. Also present in 1853 was Edmund 'Mugs' Field, who took up residence as chaplain at Hurst in 1854 and became senior chaplain three years later. In 1863 he moved to Lancing as chaplain.

His successor was a distinguished Durham University scholar who had intended to take a curacy at Horbury Brig in Yorkshire—in fact, the one Baring-Gould obtained on leaving Hurst. Instead Joseph Fowler arrived as chaplain in 1864. After the wage dispute in 1869 Fowler left the next year, and a considerable search then took place to find a man of ability willing to accept a low salary. In the end this had to be raised to £100 a year, where it stayed until late in Coombes's day. Lowe's last chaplain was John Spencer Bartlett, another Durham man.

Although the crypt chapel was over-crowded and insanitary and the new chapel unfinished, every effort was successfully made to provide excellence in worship. There was a choir from Hurst's earliest days founded by Edwin Martin, choirmaster from 1851 to 1856, and brought to full power by John Dayson, officially appointed choir master and organist in June 1863. Singing was taught throughout the school, and every attempt made to secure distinguished musicians visiting Brighton, like Ouseley and Sterndale Bennett, to award music certificates. The external examiners sometimes examined music. The first part of *Messiah* was given as early as December 1858. The first Easter service in the new chapel had S.S. Wesley's service setting flanked by Mendelssohn's *Te Deum*, and the *Hallelujah* chorus. A number of sacred works were performed including Spohr's *Last Judgement* in 1872. In 1866 a separate choir fund appears in the accounts which provided for Lowe's Dole, and for an annual choir outing, usually to Lewes. As a result of the music teaching a number of Old Johnians became church musicians, including Arthur Morris at the Temple Church, Bristol, William Boyd, at Pembroke College, Oxford, and William Parry at St Bartholomew's, Dublin, although the most remarkable appointment was probably that of Horace Diamond, organist at Grace Church, Kansas City, said to have composed a hymn tune called 'Hurstpierpoint'.

Hurst was closely involved in supporting the Victorian missionary movement. Woodard had been drawn into it by Alexander Beresford Hope and Edward Coleridge, founders of St Augustine's Missionary College at Canterbury in 1848, to which many Hurst Johnians went. Lowe himself, through his wife's relations, also had a direct personal interest. One of her relatives was John Patteson, a Devon curate, who in 1855 became a missionary at the start of a career that would end in martyrdom in 1871. On the day after he left Hurst Lowe wrote to Woodard, 'I go to the Central Africa meeting at St James's [Hall]', and his wife was still writing to the magazine about missionary work 50 years later. In 1858 Oxford, Cambridge, Durham and Dublin formed the Universities Mission to Central Africa inspired by Livingstone's explorations, and in 1859 Woodard proposed the setting up of a missionary college at Ardingly where boys would lay aside 'considerations of birth and station' to train for the hard life of a mission priest or teacher or even to run a station.

On Port Latin Day 1859 the warden of St Augustine's, Henry Bailey, preached a missionary sermon, and the *Hurst Johnian* contained its first Missionary Paper—often reprints from missionary journals, or letters sent by Old Johnian missioners or colonial bishops who came to preach.

Francis Barchard was an official of the Diocesan Missionary Society. Woodard chaired its Henfield meetings and he and Lowe attended those at Lewes. The chapter accounts contain donations and the chapel offertory was frequently devoted to the missions. In 1862 came the first Stir Up Sunday sermon and the planting of an 'African' tree on West field. The preacher was a West Countryman and friend of Pennell, William Tozer, who came often to the College. Pennell became secretary of Hurst's Mission Fund, and decided to become a missionary himself. Bishop Tozer's sister, on returning from Africa in 1868, became superintendent of the sanatorium at Hurst for several years.

One immediate effect of this interest in missionary work was the early presence at Hurst of coloured boys: indeed they must have been among the very first to attend a public school in England. Two Old Johnians, Amos Knell and Thomas Fancourt, were involved in New Zealand missionary work, and in 1863 a baptised Maori chieftain's son, Wirimu Repa, was sent to Hurst. He was placed in Red Shield dormitory where he was looked after by Arthur Radford, member of the special school, and prefect of hall. Repa and Radford went to Osborne for an audience with Queen Victoria at which Repa was presented in Maori costume with trousers 'for modesty's sake'. Sadly he died on the return voyage to New Zealand.

When Tozer returned on leave in 1867 he brought with him five Yao boys freed from slavery. One of them, George Farajellah, was placed at Hurst, and this no doubt was the final event that persuaded Pennell to return with him and Tozer to Africa in 1868. Some years later a Zulu boy, Gregory Mpiwa Nycobo, was at Hurst where he was a cricketer. He went to St Augustine's Missionary College, and was ordained. He became a teacher at the mission school set up at the grim former battlefield of Isandhlwana in Zululand. Bertram Mitford, at Hurst during Lowe's last years, was a prolific and popular author of novels about the Empire, writing over forty-five books, many based on his own career in South Africa. In 1903 he published *Haviland's Chum*, a school story set in Lowe's Hurst. It must surely be unique among public school stories because Haviland's friend was Anthony Mpukuza, a 'lithe and well formed' Zulu, who joined in his poaching expeditions round the College.

Farajellah, Pennell and Tozer sailed for Africa in July 1868, and from October Pennell's letters were added to Tozer's in the *Hurst Johnian*. George Farajellah, and another Yao, John Swedi, were made subdeacons as the first move towards ordaining black Africans—a step not taken in that area until 1890. In March 1870 cholera struck their mission, and Farajellah died in agony with Pennell and six others trying to hold him down during his fever. Poor Pennell followed him to the grave two years later dying of a liver complaint, but he was not the only Hurst master to become a missionary. Among those that did were W.E. Fairbrass, who died comparatively young, W.G.A. Ransome, who went to Zanzibar, and C.O. Pickard Cambridge who went to Japan.

Being a missionary was hard and dangerous work not rewarded with a cure or cathedral post until late in life. It was work, Amos Knell said in a letter to the *Hurst Johnian*, well suited to 'the families of our artisans and labourers'. Although Lancing's rôle in spreading Anglicanism in Korea is well known—Seoul Cathedral is dedicated to St Mary and St Nicolas—it was Hurst's middle-class clientèle who provided a large number of missionaries over the years, and made another of Woodard's contributions to the growth of the Anglican Church.

If local press and public were suspicious of the religious atmosphere in their local school there were no doubts about the patriotic stance taken by Lowe along Palmerstonian lines, and his enthusiastic support for the Volunteer Movement and a school cadet force. 'I am,' he said, 'a Tory of the Younger Pitt's school'—as both Palmerston and Gladstone, his political heroes, had been. He wished Hurst to be seen 'rooted in patriotic attachment to old England', and such views of course endeared him to local gentry with military experience and Tory views. One obvious example of Lowe's attitude was the celebration of the Prince of Wales's birthday, a ceremony unique to Hurst, begun in 1852, and assuming grand proportions in the new building culminating in the scenes in 1863 when Prince Edward married Princess Alexandra of Denmark. There was an arch at the entrance, a service with the National Anthem sung in church, a most unusual event in those days, bonfire and fireworks, cakes that were 'masterpieces of the worthy confectioners' skill', and punch to drink. Lowe was quite carried away in praising the Princess until someone called out: 'oh, he's in love' to cheers and roars of laughter.

Hurst's opening years were spent against a background of continuous war in the Crimea, India, Persia, Burma and China and the bellicose years of Lord Palmerston. On Port Latin Day 1854 Lowe said they were 'most anxious as to the war that has just broken out', but told Old Johnians in his Easter letter to support the Military and Engineering School 'sending out soldiers and sailors to defend us from the Russians'. When Sebastopol fell there was a *Te Deum* in the chapel, and according to Charles Churton (OJ) 'they were turned out to the front to sing the National Anthem'. A similar *Te Deum* took place when the official end of the Indian Mutiny was proclaimed, and there was even a whole day holiday in 1860 for the taking of the Taku forts in China!

Ever since 1852 Henry Alford had been in charge of drilling for the boys, and in 1860 this was the only sporting activity Lowe ever made compulsory. It was announced in the *Hurst Johnian* the following year that 'every encouragement will be given to manly games, by reports of matches, feats of strength, and active exercise'. A drilling boys prize in 1858 was followed next year by a fencing prize. By the mid-1860s two posts and a bar were put up for gymnastic exercises in the quadrangle, and the 1865 commissioners commented that 'muscle was cultivated' as much as anywhere at Hurst. That year Lowe asked Woodard for a gymnasium, but all that was forthcoming was £20 for gym equipment. A vaulting horse, rings, bars, ropes and ladders were fitted up in the crypt after lessons, and Alford gave two gymnastic medals in 1868 when the first Port Latin Day gym display took place—Edward Harwood of the special school, captain of football, was winner of the first senior medal. A fund for a gym was started and when £260 had been collected a foundation stone was laid in December 1872.

When setting up a cadet corps was considered, Lowe stressed it would 'benefit the physique of the young levies', and Alford was to be the first corps drill instructor. But it was the patriotic motive that got Lowe involved in the Volunteer Movement in 1858-60. A Royal Commission on Naval Defence reported in 1860 and, to Gladstone's fury at the Exchequer, Palmerston insisted on spending £9½ million on naval fortification and the first English iron clad battleships in response to what was actually a non-existent French threat! He used the war scare atmosphere to revitalise the territorial forces (then known as the militia), but as no money was forthcoming this was done by means of a Circular to Lords Lieutenant in the counties, and they and their J.Ps were to be the commanding officers. The scheme was highly successful in recruiting 180,000 volunteers who were later (1871) embodied under the War Office as the reserves.

In mid-Sussex the meeting to discuss the volunteers took place at the *New Inn* on 13 December 1859, and on 28 March 1860 the 13th Sussex Volunteers came into existence with Colonels Campion and Moorsom among its officers. A great review was held at Brighton later that year. Some ten masters from Hurst joined the force including Baring-Gould, Ling, who was soon a sergeant, and Pratt, who later won all their shooting prizes. In the patriotic atmosphere the idea of starting a corps for the boys emerged, particularly in view of the training provided in the special school for those entering the military. On 18 June 1860 the corps came into existence, and Mrs. Campion presented them with a Union Jack and a corps colour. They were called No. 1 Cadet Company, 2nd Volunteer Battalion of the Royal Sussex Regiment, and were given the cap badge of the 35th Foot.

The College gave £30 a year throughout Lowe's period, and a small charge was added. The War Office provided 60 useless carbines complete with bayonets which were kept in racks in hall. The uniform first consisted of school cap, blue serge tunic with red facings, grey trousers and a tan belt. Gradually other items were added: a glengarry cap with scarlet band and streamers, a haversack with white strap, and boots and black gaiters. Full uniform appeared for the first time in March 1861. Hurst was one of six schools founding corps, but few others followed their example. By 1870 there were only 10 and, just before the Boer War, forty-two. Hurst's was the only one in Sussex until Eastbourne's started in 1896. Later, possession of a cadet force was one of the factors raising Hurst's status as a school able to take part in public school field days, camps, and Bisley shooting.

On 11 June 1860, led by Jackman, a corps band was set up and within a year had 12 fifes, two kettle drums, and one big drum. With Alford and Ling drilling them, the cadets began to provide 'guards' at school events, and on 11 October 1860 in torrential rain Colonel Moorsom carried out the first inspection. An amazing scene occurred in upper school after the guests had lunched in the fellows library. The band of the Royal Sussex Volunteers was playing in the cloisters, and the boys in upper school, confined there by the rain, were so gripped by the mazurkas and polkas that the corps took to the schoolroom floor 'soon thick with couples whose dancing was none the less spirited in the absence of fairer partners'.

By early 1861 over a hundred and forty boys were in the corps and it was fully organised. George Thomson became the first captain with two lieutenants, two ensigns, and 16 N.C.O.s. The boys who succeeded Thomson were O. Churchyard (January 1862), A. King (September 1863), R.M. Hill (February 1864), H.S. Cooper (July 1864) and, at some time before July 1865, A.S. Radford: thereafter the list disappears. From 1865 a sum of £10 appears in the accounts for a 'sergeant'. By then the Volunteer officers had lost interest, and so retired military personnel were employed—the names of Allen in 1867 and Waller in 1869 have survived, although the most prominent of them was Callaghan.

In March 1861 the corps marched to its first field day at Burgess Hill, and there is mention of other such occasions at Danny Park and on Ditchling Common. In September they attended the Volunteer Review at Stanmer Park, and there is mention, too, of attendance at Arundel Park. In 1862, 60 boys joined the Volunteers on the Old Steine in Brighton and marched with them to a spot on the Downs near the racecourse where the field day involved a mock battle with regular troops. Then they marched back behind the band to Brighton Station and returned to Hurst after a 14-hour day.

As the 1860s continued interest in the corps waned. In 1869 the *Hurst Johnian* carried a complaint about the band dying out. In 1870 the magazine contained a comment: 'we know the fellows will laugh at this letter but it is really essential that the corps should be properly drilled'. Callaghan did his best and introduced a section cup competition, so it is clear the corps in some form survived into Awdry's headship, but clearly the heady enthusiasm of the 1860s was not maintained.

While it did, the hall witnessed between 1861 and 1865 the annual ball of the Sussex Volunteers, and in scenes of 'great brilliancy and animation' county society set the seal of approval on the College, to Lowe's obvious delight from his reports in the magazine, in which he spoke of 'hearty and genial warmth and neighbourly good will and mutual respect' on these occasions. The dais was carpeted and provided with sofas for chaperons, and the band placed in front of them. The hall was decorated with evergreens and military trophies, and cadets who lived near were recalled to line the stairs and cloisters at intervals. Coffee and tea were served in the fellows library, and supper in upper school at midnight. Contrary to the image of Woodard as a rather austere figure, he, his wife and daughter Audrey were present with Edward and Harriet Lowe, and Alice Coleridge, and took part in the dancing. The associates common room was set aside as a smoking room and for card playing! Joined by the Campions, Blencowes, Dodsons and a 'large muster' of gentry the company enjoyed the balls so much that in 1861 it was 'not until six that the last votaries of the dance were exhausted' and carriages called for.

II

Although hours and terms were long and discipline harsh, Victorian Hurst in its early years was a much less regimented place than it was to become under Cooper later in the century. The boys were not under great compulsion in their spare time or on half holidays. The school had no gates or walls, and Lowe made much of the point that senior boys were not restricted to bounds apart from a two-hourly call over: 'it is left to the honour of the boys not to enter public houses'. School life for many of the boys themselves brought up in the country, or sharing the country pursuits of farmers and gentry, flowed easily in and out of the buildings into the surrounding countryside. William Barrett complained when he first arrived, 'these wet days are very miserable as we cannot go out of College', but later we find him writing, 'I have not seen one lamb yet although I have been over a great deal of country'.

Robert Hill (OJ) in his memoirs referred to eel trapping and how they would take them to be cooked by Eliza Davey, and Bertram Mitford (OJ) talked in his book of catching trout. He also mentioned birds nesting, talking of a 'really ripping afternoon' collecting them. One boy even swam pools to find coots' and moorhens' eggs. The eggs were formed into a collection in the fellows library and finds reported in the *Hurst Johnian*, and it was not until the 1890s that the practice was frowned on. Mitford described how, by putting a rope round two beds, boys got out of the dormitory at night to go owl hunting. In his own brief memoirs Lowe said he had forbidden poaching, but knew that it went on as close to the school as the South Woods.

Swimming took place a mile and a half away from the College at Pond Leigh. A swimming tragedy at Lancing in 1858 when three boys drowned persuaded Lowe to have the pond at the south-west corner of the property concreted in for £116 9s. 2d. in 1859, but this proved a failure because of the general drainage problems of the school, and boys returned to Pond Leigh. There in 1865 there was nearly another tragedy when Edwin Dean(e), a member of the special school, was trapped in weeds, and had it not been for the accidental presence of George Dodson a master who was 'not of the same party' he would have drowned. As it was, it was 'many minutes before Deane showed any sign of animation' and he was brought back to school on a farmer's cart.

Lowe now decided swimming should take place closer to school in the Ruckford Mill stream which was then larger than today as the mill itself was working. In the summer of 1866 swimming started there in a part with two islands although the sediment in an area of heavy clay soils caused problems. Lowe spent £20 to have an iron feeder pipe fitted, and Mr. Broad gave permission for the boys to dredge the stream. Edwin Fisher, seeing the new bathing place that summer, said 'very jolly it was', although boys still emerged caked in mud. Lowe introduced a rule that all, apart from prefects, must only swim with a master and two boys present, and a swimming certificate was introduced soon afterwards—only half the school had one by June 1873. Lowe's successor was more worried about the boys swimming naked and insisted they only leave the stream behind a protective fence erected on the bank. No attempt to repeat the swimming races of 1858 was made.

It may be true that Lowe told the commissioners he attached 'very great importance' to sport, but it was essentially as a means to fitness. That was why he insisted on compulsory drilling and had two athletic sports days a year, and he was not a supporter of the growing obsession with sport which was to dominate school life later in the century. In his day, Lowe said, 'sport and athletics had not absorbed the thought and study of all civilised man'. In the first place Hurst lacked facilities and Woodard had no intention of providing them, or as a Johnian poet put it: 'in their new quarters not a rood of land fit for their purposes was at their command'. The North field was used for football, athletics from 1862, and cricket from 1864, and no groundsman was employed. Apart from rolling, no pitch preparation took place except that done by the boys themselves. There were no changing facilities except a shed and, as hiring a horse brake for away matches was expensive, matches with other schools were few: under Lowe only with Ardingly, Lancing and Cranleigh at cricket, and Brighton at football.

There was confusion over the rôle of masters in sport. Lowe did say on one occasion that a master might be 'tutor, friend and perhaps play-fellow' with the boys, and the first masters versus boys match (in cricket) took place in 1872. Some masters were involved: John Gorham in cricket and Robert Wix in fives were rare examples. Most masters confined themselves to playing in teams, and not organising them. Although there were cricket umpires, for example, there was no football referee appointed until 1867. Lowe stressed far more frequently that boys should run their own sports, praising sports days arranged 'among themselves and with hardly a master on the ground'. This had risks. In 1865 a boy threw the hammer 'right in the midst of the crowd', but guide ropes did not appear for six more years!

Compulsion did not exist in the 1850s, and attempts to introduce it continued with considerable acrimony through the 1860s and were not fully achieved. In 1864 in March and September Cricket and Football Committees were set up, attended at first by Lowe, to introduce regulation into dress, fixture lists, colours, and team captains' rights, but in both games attempts to organise these things led to resistance. Games dress remained almost entirely a matter of personal preference during Lowe's time. In cricket a cap, red with white eagle, was introduced in 1864, but the players continued to wear coloured trousers held up by ornamental belts. In football rules, for example, forbidding iron-tipped boots gave an indication of what had been allowed. A football cap, red with a white tassel, was brought in, and by 1867 white jerseys with red hoops had appeared although the players refused to wear knickerbockers. Moreover, these changes were solely for first teams. Most boys played games in ordinary clothes, as a poem describing the steeplechase (cross-country over obstacles) shows very clearly:

> The coat is cast, the waistcoat gone,
> In trousers and in shirt alone,
> With streaming hair, unkept by cap
> Prepared for triumph or mishap.
> Well 'twas for him whose boots were strong
> With studded sole and toughest thong ...

There were three main sports in Lowe's Hurst. Although called football and played with a heavy round ball, the game seems to have been a variant of Big Side rugby of the kind described in *Tom Brown's Schooldays*. About a hundred boys were involved in melées on South

7 The First XI cricket team, *c*.1860. Note the windows of fellows library to their left, and the flowers of fellows garden to their right.

field. There were no referees, and breaches of rules were dealt with on the spot. The rules revealed the nature of the game. Players were only to be charged if they had the ball. No player was to hit or trip another. No fists were to be raised above the waist. No attempt was to be made to lift a player off his legs. In 1864 a Football XX was formed who 'shall be to football what the eleven was to cricket'. H.S. Cooper was the first captain of the game elected by the sixth as a whole. Four grades of matches were announced. Pitches were to be allocated by the captain. Referees in 1867 and corner flags in 1868 suggest that some kind of order was coming in, but it was very limited.

The bewildering variety in numbers of players and rules to be observed continued for the rest of the 1860s. Some advocated the Cambridge rules; others the Marlborough ones. Confusion reigned over whether rouges (tries) should even count in the score. They did in Lancing matches, but not in others, and in the first Old Johnian match in March 1866 rouges were not allowed. In two matches with Hove Football Club one match had fifteen a side playing, and the other, thirty! The football heroes of the period Jim Freeman, 'Gunner' Forty, Richard Osborne, and J.R. Forman were tough victors in games that could last for two hours into the dark, and were played in all weathers. An account of a prefects versus school match in which 'un-necessary and vicious hacking' prevailed, or the necessity of caning two boys for manhandling a prefect shows that the old ways died hard. Officially in September 1871 Rugby Union rules were introduced, but Lowe's successor was to bring this confused game to an end not long after taking up office.

Athletics developed at Oxford and Cambridge in the 1850s, and it seems Cheltenham College held the first athletics sports in 1853. Hurst held an experimental meeting in October 1857, and from 1858 there were two meetings a year in May and October. Individual challenges were made by boys to each other, and there were no dormitory or school contests. Courses varied. Tape measures were sloppily used. A cannon ball or stone of variable weight was used in putting the shot. The high jump was measured with a rope, or a cane. Races started with either a bell or a pistol. There were 'fun' events like three-legged races. Prizes were personal gifts donated by the local gentry who turned up to watch as did Woodard on occasion. A famous athlete like George Bulgin acquired among other prizes: pads, bats, a case of razors, ink stand, pencil case, boxing gloves and skates.

A letter from George Osborne (OJ) at Cambridge to the *Hurst Johnian* in 1865 was the beginning of improvements, and a year later the Amateur Athletic Association appeared. By the mid-1860s a regular programme of 20 events was in place including a hurdles race with eight hurdles, one, two, and three hundred yard races, throwing the cricket ball, putting the stone, throwing the hammer, pole vault, long and high jumps, and on the same day a steeplechase across neighbouring fields and streams. The presentation of sports trophies was among the first school duties performed by women, and among those who presented them were Audrey Woodard, Alice Coleridge, Harriet Lowe, Miss Tozer, and Miss Nickoll. In 1870 William Gleed became the first *Victor Ludorum*, and a medal for this was given next year although records of who held it were not kept until 1876. In 1872 a steeplechase cup was the first such cup to be awarded. The leading athletes of Lowe's time seem to have been Bulgin, Clapp, Gleed, Greenfield and Nicholas.

Cricket was the most organised and popular of the games played even though leaving much to be regulated in the future. The first two identifiable captains were T.W.H. Plaskett in 1856 and C.R. Whitbourn in 1857. A list was kept from 1858 when the first match was reported in the school magazine. In 1859 Charles Ellis was a part-time professional coach, and the first analysis of scores was made in the magazine. From 1861 detailed match reports appeared. 1858 also saw the first match with the Old Johnians who won easily. There was undoubtedly more interest generally in this game than in any other, perhaps because there was already a county side (from 1838), the gentry played, and there were many local cricket clubs where boys mixed with the local teams in pleasant social surroundings. The setting up of the Cricket Committee aroused 'an unusual degree of interest and excitement'. Rules about the various school sides and the captains' powers were established.

The captains had a hard task. Membership was voluntary, and the teams contained masters, associates, probationers and special school boys older than the captain. Advice on improving cricket first appeared in the 1862 magazine, but there was little technical practising. Things might improve, said a writer, 'if there were some regular Eleven practices'. The captain also had to look after the pitches. North field was described then as being rarely 'first class', and in 1871 the captain wrote to the *Hurst Johnian* asking for support in this task.

Matches were played with a great variety of local villages, the most frequent of course being Hurstpierpoint itself and elevens got together at Danny Park, Bolney and Ditchling, but matches also took place with Shoreham, Henfield, Wivelsfield and Cuckfield, and further afield at Horsham and East Grinstead. On one occasion at Horsham the Eleven beat a Sussex team including heroes like Charlwood and Fillery, and were chased off the pitch by indignant spectators. First and Second elevens played Ardingly and Lancing, and a regular fixture with Cranleigh.

Lack of good grounds or professional skills meant that much of the cricket was of the kind favoured by 'Burly' Crook, or 'Slogger' Stacey. Sustained innings were hard to come by with uneven pitches and poor batting technique, and the whole team were usually out for less than seventy runs. The first player regularly to score over thirty runs was J.P. Forman in the first season on the North field in 1864. W.C. Hand, Gorham's dormitory captain, scored 90 in a match the next year, described as the 'highest score ever'. At the end of the 1860s the first great batsmen appeared. J.R. Forman scored 401 runs in the 1868 season, and the first century

(104) in school cricket during a dormitory match next year. He was followed in a similar match by G.T. Clapp scoring 137 runs. Two brothers, A.J. and F.J. Greenfield, saw in the 1870s with more stylish cricket, taking 54 wickets and scoring 725 runs between them in two seasons, and it was F.J. Greenfield in a match against Bolney in 1871 who scored the first school match century of 218 while his brother took all 10 wickets.

III

Life indoors centred on a boy's dormitory. Hurst opened with two: Fleur de Lys and Red Cross on the west side of the buildings. Fleur's outstanding dormitory master in this period was Richard Pennell while Red Cross, starting with Lomax, then experienced a period of change under no less than six masters before settling down under Robert Wix from 1870 to 1877. On the east side on the first floor were the two doctors' dormitories which could only be reached along the corridor outside Lowe's rooms (the staircase was put in in 1892). Lowe received the capitation fees for these dormitories, but they had their own masters. Red Shield opened in 1856 and was run by Baring-Gould, and later by George Thomson. Blue Shield opened in 1858, and causes some confusion as its name changed to Red Star and Star at intervals. Its most noteworthy dormitory master was George Willes from 1867 to 1877. Present-day Chevron began life in 1859 beneath Red Shield in the south wing, and had a succession of dormitory masters until John Dayson moved from Fleur de Lys in 1873 for seven years. Crescent was the last house founded in 1861 on the ground floor of present-day Chevron. It began life under George Pope for four years, and was then under Frederick Bennett from 1865 to 1879 when he left to be the refounding headmaster of the Prebendal School, Chichester.

Although houses were eventually to take the names of these dormitories, there was, as yet, no concept of the house as an exclusive organisation to which loyalty was given even above that to the school. The dormitories were grouped together as North versus South, Doctor's versus School, or Oxford versus Cambridge. It seems likely that it was Baring-Gould who suggested the unusual heraldic names for them, but even these were not fully established until 1877. Dormitory masters with few exceptions were simply supervisors who came and went with such rapidity that it is doubtful if the existing lists are even correct.

Dormitory matches began in 1864. In the summer John Gorham arranged a match between the doctor's dormitories won by Blue Shield, and this was held for three years. In 1868 Phillpotts gave a cricket challenge cup, and a competition involving all six houses started. A combined Old Chevron and Crescent team won by one run over the two Shields. In October 1864 the first football match took place when Red Shield beat Red Cross. The Old Johnians at Oxford donated a challenge cup in 1865, won for the first time, in March 1866, by Blue Shield. The *Hurst Johnian* contained fairly frequent complaints that these matches were not taken seriously enough, and Thomson added his editorial voice to the complaints. Red Cross did not 'display the slightest pains' in one match and in another Crescent 'declined to exert themselves'.

The dormitories were a crowded and insanitary living space meant for three hundred and taking in nearer three hundred and fifty. Each had one fire with a chimney that often smoked, no ventilation apart from windows which could scarcely be opened in winter, one closet toilet, one basin, and one tap for washing. The beds were crammed together, made of wood, without storage space, and there were of course no carpets, curtains or pictures. The regulations issued from time to time are evidence of the conditions. In 1871 all under thirteen were to be inspected regularly for head lice 'under the eye of the matron', and boys were told to use separate combs. Bathing regulations at the same time required all under thirteen to take baths supervised by matron, and 'no boy was to get in until the water had been changed'. The older boys were to take baths in the order they were in for Latin in form. Two were to bath together, but the water was to be changed after every four.

A particularly ugly feature of this communal life was the opportunity for·sexual immorality or 'uncleanliness' as Lowe called it in his letters to Woodard. Dormitories with boys from eight to eighteen, largely unsupervised, was asking for trouble of several kinds. In Red Shield Lomax caught two boys in 1855 and while the younger one was locked in matron's room and dosed with rhubarb and magnesia, the older ran away, was caught, flogged and expelled. In 1869 Lowe wrote to Woodard, 'I feel quite disheartened' because four boys had been caught 'in that horrid sin' who had to be flogged and expelled. Bullying also prevailed. One of the 1855 offenders was described as 'a bully of little boys', and there can be no doubt absence of supervision—except when the dormitory master was in his bedroom from which a window looked into his dormitory—the wide age range, unofficial power wielded by older boys, close proximity, and long terms led in Hurst as elsewhere to what Honey has called 'the incidence of various forms of cruelty' inseparable from such conditions. When Frederick Farrar's *Eric or Little by Little* appeared he was accused of exaggeration, and replied, referring to King William's College, 'the things that did go on there were really far worse than I have described'. Boys were clearly unhappy. In 1856 runaway boys from Hurst were caught at Kingston-on-Thames and, refusing to be flogged, were expelled; but three more ran away next year.

Prefectorial organisation under Lowe varied widely. Sometimes there were restricted numbers; at others all the sixth were empowered. There were no house prefects, but from the school prefects each dormitory master appointed one dormitory prefect. The prefects had the right to cane and box on the ears, and they arrogated to themselves the places by the fire, the first baths, and the best meat in hall—sometimes leaving only juice, paper and string for the smallest boys on the table. The boys prided themselves on settling disputes by bare-fisted boxing although boxing with gloves was not a school sport until 1880. In spite of prize fighting being denounced on Port Latin Day in 1860, the practice continued. One day Lowe, seeing some boys the worse for wear, crossed North field and looking over the hedge saw 'three pairs stripped and hard at it'. Robert Hill said fights were then regulated by the prefects and took place before breakfast on South field.

Three times a day at eight, one, and six the boys went to hall for meals described by Lowe as 'plentiful and healthful' when they were neither, being of the meanest proportions and deficient in fresh dairy produce, fruit and vegetables. Heating and water problems in the kitchen or kitchens on a different level from hall did not help, but the main reason for poor food was deliberately practised economy. The food, said Joseph Fowler, was 'on distinctly frugal lines', and remained the most consistently criticised feature of school life until Howard's day. Breakfast and supper consisted for the vast majority of boys of bread and butter with occasional cheese, and a mixture of warmed milk and water. 'I know,' wrote Barrett, 'the mouldies and the milk get worse.' More senior boys could supplement these meals by paying for coffee, tea, and Couchman's beer, a barrel of which was kept near the crypt. Robert Hill described how he had pork pies sent from home, and how they cooked sausages in the probationers' studies, and ordered wine once a month.

But most boys were too poor to supplement the basic diet, and endured hardship. In 1857 parents removed two boys because of uncooked food, and in 1862 considerable trouble arose when a parent accused Lowe of starving boys by giving them rice when the prospectus claimed meat was served every day—Lowe hastened to announce an additional joint dinner with 'other comforts' to follow. They never did. In 1870 he found the servants had kept the meat which was supposed to be served to the smallest boys, and had to order in extra meat.

The diet actually served was as follows. There was a roast joint twice a week, boiled mutton or 'red elephant' twice a week, boiled beef, boiled rice, and meat pie made up of left-overs on the other three days. There were plum, treacle, and currant puddings on three days a week, and on Saturdays 'Freddy' pudding made up of left-overs. Bread and cheese was served on three days. The boys consumed this meagre fare on a metal plate with a knife and a two pronged fork, and a metal mug for the drink. It was hardly surprising they looked forward to occasional feast days and did all they could to get more food, although Lowe deprecated parents sending food. A shop by Hassocks Gate station supplied biscuits and sweets, and boys made their own toffee by the gas fires. A gypsy called Frenchie brought his barrow up the lane and, in spite of repeated attempts to get rid of him, he was still there in 1879. The Daveys served ginger beer, and were not averse to cooking poached fish and game for a consideration. Barrett wrote home, 'I shall buy some marmalade to eat with the mouldies', and in one term spent 10s. of his 30s. allowance on 'grub'. To take advantage of this demand the College opened a tuck shop which sold cakes and sweets in February 1872 to the north of the chapel in a shed manned by Mrs. Pierce from 1873 to 1899. In the first 20 years the profits amounted to £6,528, most of which went to improving sports facilities and the grounds.

Samuel Brooke wrote in his diary, 'I do not think I ever remember a half [term] without someone having died there', and Hurst certainly acquired a local reputation for being unhealthy in spite of the open country and the sport. It is important to realise that many of the conditions were the product of Victorian attitudes to children and medicine, and were neither better nor worse than elsewhere. Frederick Farrar's novels not to mention Charles Dickens's often had childhood death-bed scenes. These reflected high death rates and were true to life. Moberly of Winchester, for example, lost two of his sons of school age. It was considered best not to soften children's treatment but rather the opposite. Lack of bedclothes, fires, and warm clothing, cold or infrequent baths, and roughing it were part of growing up for boys. A piteous letter from Barrett described how his ordinary cold was far worse than at home. 'I cannot smell, breathe, taste or eat much', he wrote. He was put back in the dormitory where the coughing kept him awake and where 'no-one came and looked after you'. In another case this proved fatal when a small boy of 12 caught in 'a terrible blast of wind' died of pneumonia three days later.

Medical practice in general was seriously defective. Illnesses like bronchitis and influenza developed into pneumonia and this brought death. By no means all were immunised against diphtheria and small pox, and for other contagious diseases like measles and scarlet fever there were no drugs or injections, and complications were frequent. Illnesses like leukaemia, meningitis, consumption or anaemia were incurable and ill-diagnosed. Pain from brain tumours, stomach ulcers and appendicitis was endured until they were inoperable, and peritonitis set in with death. Lack of proper treatment of food, particularly milk and meat, and lack of clean water for cooking, drinking and washing clothes and people were fertile grounds for typhoid, while defective drains bred typhus lice. Such dangers lurked in all schools. When Ardingly opened in new buildings in 1870 Edwin Garcia, a Spanish servitor, died almost at once followed by seven more boys in two years. Lancing had its epidemic in 1886.

At Hurst there were undoubtedly additional factors that made matters worse. Three are particularly significant. The 1865 prospectus stated 'the School has its own medical officer on the spot' which was not true. For many years the matron, who was not a qualified nurse, handled day-to-day medical matters in the College, and only later does payment for a nurse appear in the accounts. As for doctors, the consultant was Dr. Ormerod of Brighton, but the local doctors were reluctant to call him in and they left much to be desired. George and Robert Weekes, later occupiers of the Mansion House, were the school's doctors. They were certainly expensive. For the first three years in the new buildings medical expenditure was £378 19s. 0d. and in the second three rose to £679 1s. 0d. But they were not particularly skilful, and quite often George sent down his less able partner, Robert. There were delays in coming at all, and in December 1862 Lowe complained that the doctors had refused to see two boys. Less than a year later Lowe complained that a boy with apparent blood poisoning was given a powerful purgative, and died soon afterwards from a 'dropsical effusion of the brain'. The Weekes were sacked as school doctors in December 1863 and replaced by Dr. Holman until 1881.

The second factor adding to Hurst's health problems was the lack of a sanatorium (infirmary), although one had been planned in the original buildings. In March 1859 Lowe told Woodard, 'I have been thinking ... about the infirmary scheme'. He urged that the surplus from the medical fee charged by the school should go into a fund for a building. Woodard rejected this. Lowe put forward several proposals for buying neighbouring properties all of which Woodard rejected. After grim events in 1862 Lowe told Woodard: 'had an infirmary existed how large an outlay of money and anxiety would have been saved.' Woodard compromised. Western House was rented for £80 a year, and Alice Coleridge put in charge at £10 a year with a servant and a nurse. This proved expensive because the distance required a cab—adding five pounds a year to costs—so in 1868 Lahore Cottage in the lane, renamed Port Latin Lodge, was rented for £70 a year, and a basket chair on wheels provided to take patients there. Miss Tozer, who was in charge until 1871, did at least have medical experience as a former missionary.

But it was the state of the buildings and the standard of living of the boys that were probably the most serious contributors to Hurst's fatal medical record. As we have seen, the boys lived in overcrowded and insanitary conditions with inadequate heating and under-nourishment from their food. Many came from poorish homes and were not strong anyway; nor did their parents have money to supplement their diet. Lowe began to complain about the inter-related issues of drains, water supply and sewage in February 1856 when he pointed out that bringing water to the toilets for flushing brought seepage in hot or wet weather in the heavy clay soil between sewage and water pipes. Next year he told Woodard he was in a 'fit of alarm' over the matter: Woodard issued his appeal for sanitary improvement funds, but it went unanswered. Not until February 1860, when a new drain northwards from the building was put in, did the *Hurst Johnian* unwisely announce, 'this long vexed question' was solved. In 1857 Lowe began to complain about water supply: there was not enough water for washing or even for drinking. Not until 1861-62 was an attempt to remedy this made with a new pump and tanks, deepening the existing well, and sinking a new one to the east at a cost of £150. This did not solve the problem and Lowe told the commissioners there would be 'an increase in bathing and washing facilities'—something which clearly did not happen. Lowe told Woodard in July 1871 that recent illness was 'distinctly traceable to well poisoning from an overflow' and in his last letter from the buildings in January 1873 told him 'the well is again poisoned and the drains are pouring into it at a serious rate'. The problem was inherited by his successor with even more grim consequences.

There were no deaths in the first three years in the buildings when there were few boys in them. The first death was of the holder of the local Hurstpierpoint Scholarship, Oliver Nye, in October 1856, and thereafter Samuel Brooke's remark seems justified. Curtis Coxwell died in 1857, William Coxwell and Charles Cocks in 1858, Charles Bryant and Walter Wadey in 1859. John Gifford died shortly after arriving in 1860 and too swiftly to notify his mother, who arrived the day after his death, and rushing into Lowe's study used 'most irrational and violent abuse' until Field was brought in to calm her and take her in a cab to the station.

In August 1862 came the first serious epidemic of scarlet fever starting with the death of William Griffith, a boy of 'frail figure' who died a week after arriving, immediately after writing his only letter home. A third of the boys were sent home, but many had to stay and in October, Cecil Turner, whose parents were in India, also died. The village Home of Rest took in the smaller boys and two cottages were rented for boys who could not go home, leading to complaints in the village about spreading the disease. Dr. Ormerod and a fever expert, Dr. Goodfellow of the Middlesex Hospital, were asked to make a report which was grossly complacent, saying the dormitories were 'excellent' from a health point of view and there was 'no affinity between the buildings and the disease'. Apart from the drainage changes all that was done was fumigation and whitewashing. The outbreak cost £165 10s. 7d. in medical bills, and led to the introduction of a medical charge of 16s. a year and a promise from Lowe of a sanatorium.

But the deaths continued. In 1863 Henry Andrewes was the first to die in Western House. Charles Kirby and William Pooley died. In March 1865 12-year-old Thomas Agnew died before relatives could reach him. According to the *Hurst Johnian* report, Lowe told him he must die and Agnew replied 'Heaven was Eternal Life' and busied himself giving away his few possessions to his schoolmates. Three days later masters and boys with his father and uncle stood by the grave in the village churchyard. Henry Wearing died in 1867, and in 1868 scarlet fever returned killing Harold Fisher, brother of the diarist so loyal to the school, and Octavius Washbourn, younger brother of one of the masters. In 1870 Vines Gibbs died a few weeks before his first confirmation, and in 1871 scarlet fever returned a third time. Francis Stone, Ernest Gates, and Robert Hickman all died that year, although it is unclear if it was from the epidemic, and in Lowe's last years came the deaths of the two servitors, James Dallison and Garibaldi Raishbrook.

It is something of a relief to turn to other aspects of school life in Victorian Hurst where Lowe proved to be an innovative headmaster. More than one account of the origins of the school magazine exists. Field maintained that the boys produced their own magazine called *The Knight Errant* and Edwin Martin produced a trial magazine during 1857. It is certainly true that Lowe took up the idea, writing to Woodard in March 1858 saying such a magazine would circulate to Old Johnians and present boys. In May 1858, priced fourpence, the *Hurst Johnian* appeared for the first time, only a month ahead of the *Tonbridgian*. It is the oldest magazine still in existence to have been in continuous publication, although other schools did produce magazines earlier. Lowe was editor until 1866, and there were 10 editions a year, later reduced to nine. Some memoirs also refer to another magazine produced by the boys called the *Grug*, but no details are known.

There are different ways of looking at the magazine. As a historical record its College Annals are invaluable and particularly so when dealing with domestic matters like health not usually referred to in school magazines. As a literary document it contains articles by some like Sabine Baring-Gould or John Kinchin Smith who were authors in their own right, and articles (unfortunately anonymous) by Lowe, Thomson and other masters. There is very little by the boys apart from reprinted prize essays and occasional poems or puzzles. Nevertheless it was soon having the desired effect. T.W.H. Plaskett, Hurst's first recorded captain of cricket, went into the army, and wrote from Vellore in India to say how he liked the cricket news in the magazine. 'The *Hurst Johnian*,' he said, 'carries me back to S. John's with the speed of an electric current.' Some eighteen Old Johnians took up careers in publishing and journalism.

School plays were produced at Westminster, Winchester and elsewhere, but Field maintained, more accurately this time, that it was Edwin Martin who in October 1854 suggested readings from Shakespeare on the hall dais with an armchair and a sofa for scenery, and some play extracts including *Richard III* were read. It is almost certain that the first few plays were read rather than acted: indeed apropos the *Merchant of Venice* in 1856 the *Sussex Advertiser* said, 'plays are read and criticised at the College'. Lowe sent for actors' marked copies from distinguished players like Edmund Kean. It may well have been Baring-Gould's presence that led to producing a play. In 1858 *Much Ado About Nothing* was put on as a full play. Lomax ran the box office, Baring-Gould did the scenery, Field the make up, and Jackman provided a small orchestra to play Arne's music. Some 180 seats were for guests of the school and these included Samuel Wilberforce, Bishop of Oxford, and pupils from Ardingly, Lancing and St Michael's.

Next year *Macbeth* was done for the first of four times under Lowe, the hall decorated with flags and coloured lanterns, and a table set out with coffee and tea. Nathaniel Woodard attended. For the first time a modern Prologue, usually spoken by the school captain (in this case George Thomson), was added making allusions to recent events. Baring-Gould later took a party of boys on the school's first theatre trip to see *Macbeth* at Drury Lane, and they stayed overnight in *Furnival's Inn*. In 1860 John Dayson took over as producer and continued until 1876. Costumes and a dresser were hired from Nathan in London, and James Pierce, the carpenter, took over making the sets. When Jackman left, William Gates and the Brighton Town Band took over the music providing what they thought suitable, such as Rossini's *William Tell* overture for the *Merchant of Venice*. On occasion their playing was so bad that Dayson had to conduct as well as rushing behind to do the special effects, but in 1866 at least the band did the play proud. *King John* was played to nine pieces, including four waltzes and two light overtures. Under Dayson the play moved from 'self-made dresses and rude scenery' to the 'well-appointed stage and brilliant lighting' of the 1871 production.

Apart from half a dozen years an annual Shakespeare play has been given ever since, and even in Hurst's early days about a dozen boys made careers later on the stage, something once again surprising for a Victorian public school. Among the leading boy actors under Lowe were G.W. Ling, G.O.L. Thomson, and H.S. Cooper, particularly in female leads. F.J. Greenfield had the distinction of being the first *Hamlet* in 1870, and returned to play the first *Henry V* in 1873.

From 1862 an Afterpiece was added to the Shakespeare night. It was usually a light farce like *A Regular Fix* that year, but even so prolonged the evening beyond 11 o'clock. One year, by trying to put on an abbreviated version of Sheridan's *She Stoops to Conquer*, they went too far and the clock passed midnight. By then members of the audience were surreptitiously withdrawing, according to the *Hurst Johnian*, because they were 'compelled to think of their horses standing out on a cold, frosty night'. Other Shakespeare scenes, English and French drama were acted on Port Latin Day.

Art, it will be recalled, was on the syllabus taught by part timers including Frederick Earp who taught locally—Borrer's children, for example—and Alexander White of the Brighton School of Art. Two drawing prizes were awarded and Lowe wanted the play profits used to endow an art scholarship. The Commissioners noticed that in art 'the more solid branches are preferred to the more showy'. Certainly, Hurst produced a good many competent and even well-known artists among its Old Johnians including Thomas Way, S.H. Fletcher, A.B. Hopkins, George Bulleid, C. Padday, E. Prynne, and B. Westmacott. Maurice Brockwell, who had been school captain, was an influential critic and writer on art, and cataloguing secretary of the National Gallery. George Wallis, in the special school in 1863, became art director of Nottingham Art Gallery as well as being a Royal College of Art medallist. The main Nottingham papers, incidentally, the *Guardian* and the *Evening Post*, were owned and edited by the three Formans, Arthur, Jesse, and James, at Hurst in Lowe's time.

Music in Lowe's Hurst was not confined to the sacred performed in chapel. Twice a year there were concerts which were mixtures of sing songs, light orchestral performances, and sketches or skits. In one Baring-Gould and Ling gave impressions while Maud Pratt sang to great amusement, *Come into the Garden, Maud*. Herr Bosco the conjuror was a great draw from time to time. On 17 October 1866 the first substantial orchestral concert gave a performance of Sterndale Bennett's *The May Queen*. Most concert pieces were solo piano or violin, and songs ranged from Mendelssohn and Schubert via Balfe, Benedict and Bishop to the music hall and items like *Good Morrow to my Lady Bright*. An old boy, Charles Murray Rumsey, was one of the many composers of such songs, his compositions including *The White Road* and *The Lord Mayor's Own*. By the end of the 1860s a concert would have as many as fourteen items, and would include original numbers like a stage adaptation of *The Pickwick Papers* performed by 24 masters and boys. Harsh though much of Lowe's Hurst might have been, it was both freer and more varied than the older public schools, and provided the basis for a wider choice of career in directions not usually associated with 19th-century schools.

IV

Nathaniel Woodard's appointment of Edward Lowe as headmaster of Hurst was probably the most important one he ever made. In the first place Lowe clearly succeeded in making a new kind of middle-class school into a well-regarded public school. Hurst experienced either satisfactory or very rapid growth for 20 years. Its debt was cleared in 1861, and its income rose sufficiently not only to cover its own expenditure but to make contributions to Woodard's other schools. From the early 1860s Hurst emerged in the Oxbridge stakes, and indeed sent more to Oxbridge in its first 25 years than Lancing. Hurst Johnians were found in all the major universities in England, Scotland and Ireland, and in the new training colleges for agriculture, priests, missionaries, and schoolmasters. Although we only have information about 689 careers of Lowe's pupils we know enough to accept Brian Heeney's view that the School succeeded in its central purpose of raising up the sons of middle- and even lower-class parents. Their careers embraced the clergy, grammar, public, and university education, medicine, law, accountancy, engineering, local and colonial administration, the armed services, and the colonial police forces, and contributed a good number to careers in architecture, drama, journalism, painting, music, and writing.

Lowe's authoritarian and even tough personality had been essential to win Hurst its enviable position. He had with Gilbert's and Woodard's help fought off the religious attack on the School's imagined Puseyism. Letters as wide apart as 1854 and 1871 to Woodard and the comments of the Commissioners show that Lowe often had to battle with parents who opposed his determination to introduce public school discipline with the birch and prefectorial power. With four different 'schools' in one building becoming more overcrowded the potential for trouble was great. There were contemporary examples—from Wilkinson at Marlborough to Mitchinson at King's, Canterbury—of what happened when discipline broke down. Lowe had some awkward moments, but he was always firmly in control.

But Lowe was not simply a disciplinarian. He established the Church of England credentials of the College. The chapel was built, the musical tradition of fine services started, and there was no doubt that Lowe saw his school as a religious college. Lowe's kindness to individuals, his support for servants and servitors just as much as for high flying scholars, his management of the Benefit Fund all reveal other, and probably deeper, aspects of his character than the outward image gave away. The Christian, kindly aspect of his character, of course, showed itself in his care for his invalid wife and help to his other relatives. His speeches revealed a sense of humour. His travels showed a breadth of experience. Within the school he was a traditionalist in some ways.

He accepted the primacy of Latin. He played the patriotic card and was most at home socially with the Tory local gentry. He did his best by introducing ceremonies to cast an aura of venerability over a new institution. Traditions made up by him, including the climbing of Danny, the Boar's Head Feast, and the Etheldreda Banner Procession, have remained ever since.

But Lowe was much more of an innovator than a traditionalist. The timetable was broad, some of the teaching methods imaginative, and he used every new competitive device including prizes, scholarships, a grand prize day, and internal and external exams to ensure that high standards were always being fought for even if not always achieved. He encouraged drama, art, singing and music. He backed the teaching of English and European languages. He allowed science to develop. He encouraged public speaking and started a magazine to encourage at least limited self-expression. Hurst was one of the first schools to have a choir, and a corps, and to produce an annual play and a magazine; and one of the earliest to have a gymnasium. He would have built a gymnasium and a sanatorium earlier and expanded the grounds for the purposes of games, if Woodard had allowed him. While he was a firm advocate of the 'manly' approach to life by boys it is clear he was deeply distressed by the poor living conditions and ugly medical record which Woodard's parsimonious and less sympathetic personality saddled him with, and for which he had to take the blame.

But it was not just Hurst's success for which Woodard had reason to be grateful to Lowe. Hurst was the fulcrum of the ladder of advancement, and it was Lowe who had to make it work. The only historian, Brian Heeney, who looked at this aspect of Woodard's plans, did so unwisely from the Lancing archives rather than those at Hurst, or even from the pages of the *Hurst Johnian*. Because none of the registers of Ardingly, Hurst, or Lancing give full details of those transferring between the schools in any degree of completeness and, as we have seen, the future careers of servitors, special school, and probationers are rarely given in the Hurst records, we do not have a complete picture. However, enough information does exist to show that Lowe made the scheme work. He accepted that the scholarship reducing fees at Lancing would tempt away some of his ablest boys. Between 1861 and 1902 at least seven won this scholarship, and only one failed to achieve professional distinction. On the other hand Hurst gained when Ardingly boys took advantage of the scholarship to Hurst, cutting fees to £15 5s. a year. The first to come in 1859 was George Follit, and between then and 1907 at least fifteen can be traced. They included such outstanding pupils as George Stallard, science and housemaster at Rugby School, James and Edward Orr, distinguished in Indian administration, and Walter Adams, metropolitan of Canada.

Heeney said he could find no examples of servitors taking advantage of their scholarship reducing fees at Ardingly to £10 10s. The first was awarded to Stephen Wells in 1859 who was later head boy at Ardingly. Thomas Warner (1862), Samuel Standege (1868), and Thomas Jackson (1874) are three others that can be traced. Moreover, these scholarships were only one of many ways in which fees were cut. Hurst had 18 scholarships reducing fees, and two for completely free education for day boys. Entrance fees to the special or the training school were cut if they were entered directly from the grammar school. Port Latin awards, payments to probationers, and the acquisition of degrees and ordination at a cheap rate all helped poorer boys in higher education. Far from Woodard's scheme strengthening and tightening class distinctions as Heeney claimed, it 'modified them by means of acknowledged merit' as Lowe said. It is perfectly clear from his evidence to the commissioners that he drew the attention of rich prospective parents to the prospectus because 'I do my best to keep off people that one thinks are taking advantage of us'.

Woodard was obviously delighted with Lowe's work even though there is hardly a word of praise or thanks in his letters to Lowe. With three schools established in Sussex, Woodard was now looking to the Midlands to replicate his scheme there, and Lowe with a brother at

Burton-on-Trent, and another at Abbot's Bromley, was ideally placed to be Woodard's right-hand man in a new Midlands Chapter. Lowe attended the inaugural meeting at Burton-on-Trent in 1867, and got to know Sir Percival Heywood, Woodard's principal financial backer in the Midlands, who visited Hurst and made small financial contributions to the school. Lowe was present at the foundation of Denstone next year. At last in December 1871 Woodard offered Lowe the provostship in tandem with headship of Hurst.

1869 had been the apogee of Lowe's Hurst in terms of numbers and revenue. In his last years, as his successor hastened to point out, numbers fell from 364 to 341, and revenue from £12,121 15s. 1d. to £10,139 17s. 6d. Lowe may have told Old Johnians, 'we go on evenly and satisfactorily' in his 1871 Easter letter, but he told Woodard, 'I have never known so few entrances and so few applications'. This fall may be partly explained by the pressures on Lowe which took him away from the school. He more or less ran the Southern Chapter while Woodard was ill, even organising the ceremony for the foundation of Lancing chapel, and he was clearly being drawn into Midlands affairs. In 1869 there were rumours of a bishopric and a year later he became a canon of Ely Cathedral. He was also active in educational affairs, speaking, for instance, at a conference at Wolverhampton. When Lowe wrote in rather depressive terms to Woodard in 1870 he remarked on 'indifference, worse than opposition, which has grown up in the last two or three years of slovenly and indeed neglected discipline'. He was most probably reflecting his own tiredness.

There was a good deal in these last years to depress him. In 1869 there was the clash over salaries led by the chaplain, Joseph Fowler, followed by his abrupt departure, so Lowe had to be chaplain himself for a term. The same year the bad perversion case distressed him. In 1871 scarlet fever returned. His friend and colleague's wife, Ann Edwards, died. His wife's relation Bishop Patteson was martyred at Santa Cruz in the Pacific. In 1872 his sister Eliza died, soon afterwards his niece Emily, aged only 23, and their school, Mayfield House, which Lowe had often visited, closed down. Lowe's constant requests for repairs to the domestic structure of the school, more land, and a sanatorium (last requested in April 1872) fell on deaf ears, particularly now Edmund Blackmore and William Woodard dealt with finance, coming between Lowe and Woodard in day-to-day matters. Lowe told Woodard in September 1872 of a 'growing feeling that my schoolmaster's days are numbered', and 'if you can relieve me at the year's end I shall be thankful'. Lowe's retirement was clearly brought about by the combination of his feeling that he had outlived his usefulness, and Woodard's determination to use him in the Midlands. So it was arranged. Lowe was to go at the end of 1872.

At the start of December a lavish Octave meeting at Hurst saw him give up his offices of vice-provost, librarian and examiner before a large audience including local clergy and gentry. His last sermon (unrecorded) was preached on 15 December. The Boar's Head festivities took place next day. The 18 December was the last day of term. The boys assembled in upper school, and Edward, Harriet, and Alice Coleridge came in to hear an address by H.C. Stevens, the school captain, to which Lowe replied, emphasising that Hurst was a public school, backing the prefect system, and encouraging them all to be loyal Old Hurst Johnians as he was about to become. He was given a silver grace cup and left amidst cheers. Lowe said little in his letters about retiring: indeed his of that day referred to a missionary meeting and Christmas arrangements. On 15 January 1873 Old Johnians and masters met at the *Freemasons Tavern* in Queen Street in the City where Lowe was given an ink stand, a desk, and a silver tea urn. After George Thomson and Robert Quick had spoken, Lowe replied briefly saying now he had a tea urn they must come to tea at Denstone. The same week Lowe left Hurst for the Midlands and William Awdry, the new headmaster, arrived.

Edward Lowe's Hurstpierpoint
1849-1872

Year	Grammar School	Special School	Servitors School	Day Boys	Probationary Associates	Highest Total of Boys Educated	A.S.N.C.	Assistant Masters inc. Fellows	Part-time Masters & Foreign Assistants	Total of Masters + Lowe + Chaplain	Exhibitioners	Scholars	Annual Income of College £	s.	d.	Highest Total of Academic Residents	Total Academic Roll of College
1849	9					9				1						10	10
1850	42					42		1		2		3				44	44
1851	103					103	1	3		5	1	3				108	108
1852	129					129	1	6		8	2	4	1,116	10	07	137	137
1853	135					135	3	6		10	2	6	1,464	12	00	145	145
1854	139		6		4	149	3	4		9	2	5	2,377	01	08	158	158
1855	126		6		3	135	2	6		10	1	9	2,659	13	05	145	145
1856	141	2	7		7	157	1	8		11	1	7	2,958	12	08	168	168
1857	172	7	8		8	195	1	6		9	1	7	3,286	12	06	204	204
1858	177	9	10		7	203	4	6		12	1	11	3,544	14	02	215	215
1859	202	5	10		10	227	2	6		10		13	4,068	19	03	237	237
1860	224	7	17	5	7	260	5	6		13		14	5,860	02	03	268	273
1861	256	10	15	6	10	297	4	6	1	13	1	14	7,091	18	04	303	310
1862	294	9	18	10	10	341	4	7	1	14	2	13	8,021	07	08	344	355
1863	299	16	17	6	8	346	3	6	1	12	2	15	9,138	09	02	351	358
1864	288	16	16	8	10	338	5	10	1	18		15	9,300	14	00	347	356
1865	299	12	15	8	10	344	5	8	1	16		17	10,380	05	08	351	359
1866	293	16	17	4	8	338	5	8	2	17		20	11,623	10	11	349	355
1867	294	15	14	3	7	333	8	8	1	19	3	20	10,816	11	07	348	352
1868	303	15	17	5	11	351	6	11	1	20	3	20	11,823	09	04	366	371
1869	309	13	19	9	14	364	4	9	2	17	4	21	12,121	15	01	370	381
1870	290	20	15	7	11	343	5	7	2	16	4	21	11,714	00	05	350	359
1871	277	13	16	6	12	324	4	8	1	15	3	22	10,470	19	02	332	339
1872	296	8	18	9	10	341	6	8	1	17	5	22	10,139	17	06	348	358

FOUR

THE VALLEY OF THE SHADOW
1873-1879

William Awdry and a Crisis of Confidence

Some cases of scarlatina having occurred in the School just at the close of the summer term ... There has been a general whitewashing and painting, during the holidays, and ... one of the wells has been emptied and thoroughly cleaned, and some alterations made in the ventilation of the drains ...

The Hurst Johnian, 185/186-187,
October 1876

The Headmaster came to the meeting and protested against the present football rules on account of the great risk, and said he could not allow them to be played any longer.

Playground Committee (P.G.C.) Minutes, p. 44,
25 July 1874

It may well be thought that I am not the right man for this post, or shall not be in view of altered ... circumstances ... . Under these circumstances I place my resignation in your hands to be used or not as you judge best.

Rev. Canon William Awdry to Nathaniel Woodard,
13 February 1878,
Lancing College Archives

If either Willes or Bennett should be appointed to the prebendal stall at Chichester, there would be the ground clear and ready for the change, but it would not be carried out, I think, without driving away some of the other masters of long standing— a good thing perhaps in the result, but to be achieved, if possible, in some other way than by making the place utterly unpalatable to them.

Rev. Canon William Awdry to Nathaniel Woodard,
3 February 1879,
Lancing College Archives

8 Rev. Canon William Awdry, Headmaster from 1873 to 1879.

Succeeding Lowe would have been difficult for anyone appointed as the next headmaster. There were already signs of decline that needed to be corrected, but it was also clear that the most difficult problems facing the College stemmed from the financial disciplines imposed by Woodard and Blackmore. Lowe had been a dynamic personality, and there were several Lowites in the common room, loyal to him since they had attended the school as pupils. The boys in the school were used to a firm hand. Unfortunately, Woodard made the wrong choice. Lowe's successor, William Awdry, had a personality painted in pale pastel shades instead of vivid oils. If Lowe had been a Churchillian figure dominating a generation, Awdry was to be an Anthony Eden whose short rule as successor ended in tears.

Woodard had drawn a good deal of his educational inspiration from Winchester College, and he had written to Awdry, then the lower master there, to ask for advice on a possible successor drawn from the Winchester common room. This was flying a little too high. Hurst had neither the social background nor high salary likely to attract a leading schoolmaster. Awdry wrote to Woodard several times saying, 'I have watched your work with the deepest interest', and that the headship of Hurst was in his view 'one of the highest positions open to a schoolmaster'. Woodard therefore took up his references, which came from the highest in the educational world, and he was appointed, taking up residence in January 1873.

William Awdry was one of five sons of Sir John Awdry. Born in 1842, he entered Winchester in 1855. He went to Balliol College, Oxford, where he obtained a First in Greats, and was a university rower. After a spell as a Fellow of The Queen's College he became Winchester Lower Master in 1868. That year he married Frances Moberly, sixth daughter of George Moberly, Bishop of Salisbury, and one of his sisters married George Ridding, headmaster of Winchester from 1866 to 1882. References from Moberly and Ridding talked of his 'philosophical power', and 'lofty views', but Woodard should have noticed a sentence saying Awdry 'has made a great advance in power of dealing effectively with a class'.

Awdry was clearly an academic most at home with the sixth form classics boys: the external examiners commented on the 'exceedingly satisfactory' teaching of the subject. But he had little idea how to handle what the examiners called 'rough material' at the other end of the ability range. Awdry continued to flog—in July 1875 Ross Gates, son of the Brighton bandmaster, was flogged for cutting lessons and lying—but he was not a strong disciplinarian. Boys noticed, that when referring to unpleasant matters like swearing, Awdry winced. As the 1870s advanced, with falling numbers reducing the better element in the school and the number of older boys, indiscipline grew. No less than three Old Johnians (F.C. Bayley, T.E. Lander and J.K. Smith) referred, for example, to a Boar's Head Feast in 1877 when the fourth form organised an unofficial procession, and some of the methylated spirits on the torches set alight paper below the floorboards, causing a fire. Awdry rushed in a dishevelled state to the scene to help put the fire out. When a call over was made in upper school, it was found that all but three of the prefects were absent from College having got out of a window to enjoy Christmas spirit in the village. They were dismissed. The eight fourth formers involved were birched next day, but by Awdry and Thomson alternately, rather than by the head alone. One boy maintained Awdry birched him gently as 'my illness had left me less robust than the other seven'. Thomson recorded next year that 'we have lost some who were not models to be imitated'. Inadequate prefects, bad behaviour among juniors, and expulsions are all indicators of poor discipline because effective discipline largely prevents all three occurring.

The Awdrys seem to have done their best to become involved in school life. Awdry played cricket in the school team with other masters, took five wickets in the Masters of the Three Schools match in 1874 and scored a century in 1877. He played fives. He was active in societies he set up like debating and natural history. His wife, Frances, was involved in dormitory matters and was given an entertainment allowance of £30 a year—she began the custom of tea parties for smaller boys, and was well liked by boys who had to reside in the holidays. She played the piano at the first concert given in the inner quad in July 1875. Their daughter frequently gave away the sports day prizes. Francis Awdry, a cousin, was educated at the College and one of his wife's relatives, Leonard Moberly, taught at Hurst for a short time. Senior boys like John Smith, who knew him well, respected him but socially Awdry did not succeed with several groups. He came into bitter conflict with the masters. The social contacts with the local gentry and clergy ceased—even the annual Christmas tree no longer arrived. In some ways Awdry was a shy academic who shrank from boisterous school life and clearly lost any real interest in the job when he found out what it really involved. He offered his resignation to Woodard as early as December 1878, and left a year later for another post he did not really want in which he suffered some kind of nervous breakdown.

At the very moment both school and neighbourhood needed reassurance about Hurst not least because of the last outbreak of fever in 1871, the College had a headmaster unable to give that assurance and, although there were many reasons for the sharp fall in the school's numbers and prestige in the 1870s, Awdry's appointment and Awdry's character are among the main ones. The figures chart the decline plainly enough during Awdry's seven years:

Year (June)	Day Boys	Grammar School	Probationers	Special School	Servitors	Total of Boys	Fee Income		
							£	s.	d.
1873	12	259	13	6	16	306	11,997	00	10
1874	10	241	11	4	15	281	12,963	14	01
1875	12	258	8	abolished	13	291	12,061	19	08
1876 (Oct)	8	217	7		14	246	10,861	04	04
1877 (Oct)	7	166	9		11	193	9,406	09	02
1878	4	179	6		13	179	8,519	04	09
1879	2	146	6		12	166	7,930	13	06

Awdry began by announcing in the school magazine in June an increase in fees, due to a rise in price of the 'chief articles of consumption', from 30 to 33 guineas a year, and a proportionate increase in his own capitation fees automatically followed. This had the effect of increasing income from a declining number of boys for Awdry's first three years, but as agricultural and industrial depression grew after 1876 and prices fell, this fee seemed unnecessarily high. In 1874 the special school was abolished by Woodard so it would not compete with the Modern Side starting at Lancing—even the small number of boys brought in £181 2s. 6d. in its last year—and its ending reduced the number of able and older boys. Revenue from the probationers fell from £203 3s. 6d. to £102 18s. 0d. under Awdry, and there were fewer of them to reduce the masters' salary bill. Servitor income fell from £118 6s. 8d. to £69 3s. 4d., as most were on the lower charge of £5 a year. The most serious decline was, of course, in grammar school numbers, fee income declining from £8,038 5s. 8d. to £5,275 0s. 0d., and within the fall in numbers from 259 to 146 the sharp decline in day boys clearly reflected local alarm about health and discipline in the school.

In December 1878 the Chapter finance committee chaired by Sanderson, the vice-provost, met for three and a half hours because, as Sanderson told Woodard, 'the state of things was serious enough to claim the attention of all your fellows'. Awdry himself admitted early the next year, 'there is no doubt that the financial aspect of things at Hurst is very serious indeed'. In spite of all Awdry's efforts, and they were not inconsiderable, the College was not paying its way: the deficit on current account had risen from £970 0s. 3d. to £1,907 2s. 8d. In 1879 Crescent dormitory closed.

In a long letter to Woodard in 1879 Awdry sounded quite aggrieved that he was being blamed for the financial position of the College and, although it is true that Awdry's own record is partly to blame, Woodard himself was to blame in more ways than one. His failure to meet Lowe's requests for domestic and medical improvements led to further outbreaks of illness under Awdry, and there was no change in Woodard's attitude. Even Awdry had to write directly to him in July 1875 to get the gutters repaired because, 'I cannot touch the funds without your sanction'. General repairs were so poor that Awdry himself found money to repair the upper school floor which now 'required almost weekly patching'. Pressure was kept up to reduce domestic expenditure. Servants' wages fell from £344 1s. 10d. to £278 7s. 6d. and Thomas Davey was the only one to secure an increase. In 1879 Awdry reported to Woodard, 'consumption of gas has been very much reduced by the close attention of the porter under the eye of the second master', and the new matron, Mrs. Crosslé's economies met with approval.

But while presiding over penny-pinching measures Woodard made no effort to end the corporate burden placed on Hurst, except for his own salary demand which was reduced. £375 went towards Lancing chapel under Awdry. In 1874 another gift, this time of £300, went to Ardingly. Edmund Blackmore's wages as bursar (£100 a year) remained unchanged, although Awdry managed to remove him from his living quarters in 1877 when Blackmore moved to Hayward's Heath. Similarly the chaplain's £100 a year remained unchanged although Awdry urged that he should also do some teaching in order to save money—a suggestion not acted upon. The abolition of the special school did not benefit Hurst. The consequences of stern economy, including lower masters' salaries and inadequate games facilities, added, as we shall see later, to internal unrest.

Awdry's Hurst also had to face competition and some of this came from the rest of Woodard's Society. Lowe had had a virtually clear field as regards competition. In 1870 Ardingly opened near Hayward's Heath in Hurst's catchment area with fees half as high. Three years later Lowe and Woodard launched the Midland Chapter which would set up similar schools, particularly Denstone, reducing Hurst's national catchment potential. After the acts of

1868 and 1869 the older public schools and the grammar schools were being reformed at the hands of the Charity Commissioners and, although this competition really got under way in the 1880s, there were already signs of it in Awdry's time. Steyning Grammar School, for example, re-opened its doors with 45 boys including boarders in 1875. There was a steady growth in Southern public schools including Brighton, Eastbourne, Cranleigh, and St John's, Leatherhead all in competition with Hurst.

Lowe's Hurst had grown against the background of mid-Victorian prosperity in agriculture and industry. Awdry's Hurst struggled on against a very different background. Awdry himself wrote to Woodard in 1879 about 'commercial depression and general distress'. Disraeli's government was to lose the election of 1880 primarily because higher taxation to meet foreign interventions and wars bore heavily on a population suffering from this depression. Prices of agricultural and industrial produce began to fall in 1876, and by 1882 the word 'unemployed' had entered the dictionary as industrial growth faltered before American and German competition. But it was agricultural depression that hit Hurst hardest. From 1875 to 1879 there were wet summers culminating in the worst harvest of the century in 1879 with blight, mildew and mould affecting the crops. Pastoral farming was hit by serious outbreaks of disease in 1877, 1879, and 1883, and both arable and pastoral farming were subjected to competition from overseas for the first time. A sizeable number of those sending sons to Hurst were obviously affected by these events and this, combined with their perception of troubles in the school, explains the rapid fall in numbers caused by lack of applicants and large numbers of early withdrawals.

The need for economy affected every aspect of Awdry's Hurst, but among its worst results was the poisoning of relations between the headmaster and many of the masters, although the reasons for the bad relations were more complex than a matter of money. We have already seen how in Lowe's last years there were salary demands and departures of skilled staff. Falling numbers of pupils meant reductions in masters, and this Awdry succeeded in achieving, numbers falling from 17 to 12, and he told Woodard in 1879 he had the same 'increase of strength and economy in the teaching power' as in Lowe's day. Awdry's problem was that, while he could easily make adjustments among junior masters, when it came to the leading Lowites this caused trouble: and it was in just this area of the common room that he wished to make changes. 'I think', he wrote, 'some new blood instead of some old seems very desirable and it could be had at a rather cheaper rate.' Because several of them were fellows and had long service records they were an increasing financial burden. Their salaries rose as follows:

Master	1873	Salary by 1879
Thomson	£ 125 + 25 for German	£ 196 13s. 06d. (with capitations)
Bennett	£ 83 06s. 8d.	£ 100 from 1874
Willes	£ 87 10s. 0d.	£ 100 from 1875
Dayson	£ 50 + 50 for other duties	£ 82 10s. 00d. (with no duties)
Pratt	£ 80 00s. 0d.	£ 100 from 1877

Awdry was specifically instructed to reduce staff numbers and costs, and had some success. When Henry Alford retired in 1878 his successor Mr. Moss was to draw his salary from cadet force subscriptions. Similarly after a modern languages master, William Kerry, left, there was only a German lektor, Herr Schütz and then Herr Neebe, who was to draw a salary from extra fees for German. The same applied to Prior, the music master, who was appointed in 1878 and drew his salary from tuition charges. Some new masters were offered even lower salaries than those paid under Lowe. However, in spite of such measures and the overall fall in numbers, the total salary bill fell only from £1,936 2s. 4d. in 1873 to £1,586 14s. 6d. in 1879 due to the long drawn out battle to reduce benefits and even remove Lowite masters. In one letter, when Awdry speculated on Willes or Bennett getting a vacant canonry at Chichester which would clear the ground for change, he said that driving them out would be 'a good thing in itself' although he did not want to make life 'utterly unpalatable to them'.

Oddly enough Awdry had, it seems, a fairly low opinion of George Thomson, the second master, saying in one letter to Woodard that he was 'the most unsatisfactory of all' the Lowites, and at the start of one term 'was more dead [than] alive that I have ever seen him'. This indicated Awdry's inability to read character, because Thomson already had a distinguished career behind him, and went on to be appointed headmaster of King's, Taunton by Woodard where he was the school's real founding headmaster for sixteen years! In fact, Awdry relied on Thomson in disciplinary matters and to deal with his salary introduced changes in the capitation system.

Lowe had received capitations on Red and Blue Shield dormitories. Awdry told Woodard that this brought him in, with the recent fee increase, '£275 more than by the original contract'. He reduced the capitation for the headmaster from £8 8s. per boy to £7 and used the money saved to repair the upper school floor. Awdry's salary which began at £626 a year therefore remained fairly constant and ended at £621 a year. Then in 1877 Blue Shield finally became Star and moved out of its dormitory. Red Shield was then called the second master's house, and Thomson was allowed to charge capitation fees two pounds below those of the headmaster.

To reduce the cost of the other Lowites it was necessary to reduce their financial perks and privileges, but for a group of resident bachelors, many of whom had known Hurst for their whole adult lives and had no real life outside the school, this was bound to lead to distress. Awdry was determined to reduce residence in College. He began by informing Old Johnians they might only stay two nights without paying. He told A.S.N.C.s they had no automatic right of residence. James Edmonds then wrote to Woodard in July 1875 asking if he could stay in College without charge 'as my sisters are partly, and I wholly dependent upon my salary'. Awdry had to give way. But it was the fellows like Bennett, Willes, and Wix that caused the real problem. Awdry said they should regard their salaries as 'board wages for the whole year'. He asked Woodard to approach them to give up their rights without financial compensation 'for the good of the School', but Woodard was unwilling to do this, so in the end Awdry had to resort gradually to cutting the standard of living of the Lowite masters. He reduced the bill for extra commons from £473 3s. 6d. to £196 0s. 7d., but at great cost in staff relations.

Awdry's opinion of the senior masters seems remarkably vindictive, and often plainly wrong. Apart from Mr. Bennett, he said on one occasion, 'there is not one of them whose removal would not in my opinion do more good than harm'. He pointed out that their ages would soon prevent them moving elsewhere and this would not benefit the school. He wrote of their 'schoolboy-like attachment' to Hurst, and their 'want of energy and enthusiasm'. Yet, when Robert Wix showed plenty of evidence of energy and enthusiasm, Awdry told Woodard he had stopped talking to him as all he got was 'anger and insult', and it would be 'greatly to the interest of the school' for him to leave. Pratt was described as 'very inefficient'. Awdry's judgement was seriously at fault about nearly all these men: Thomson, Wix, and Bennett became effective headmasters, and Willes chaplain of Westward Ho!

But the combined result of bad personal relations and financial difficulties was to disperse Lowe's common room. By the time Awdry left only four important members of it remained—

Dayson, Pratt, Edmonds, and Thomson. Under Awdry, Edwardes (1873), Arthy (1875), Wix (1877), Alford (1878), Bennett (1879), Willes (1879), and Bartlett (1879) left, and only one of his 22 appointments, Charles Banks, was of comparable stature. After Bartlett's departure an unpaid clergyman took chapel services for a term until Rev. Henry Bell was appointed to start in 1880. Apart from W.T. Kerry, a languages master, and A.J. Smith, who ran music well for four years, there were no particularly distinguished names among the new men. By the end of 1879 there were only four Oxbridge graduates on the staff, and it is clear that with the decline of common room calibre came a decline in results.

For a time Awdry was able to rely on Lowe's staff and pupils, but it is very clear that, once they left, the new intake was either of lower quality or badly taught by a less effective staff. The examiners' reports, although bland, did make criticisms of much of the work done in the lower forms. During Awdry's years Lancing overtook Hurst in the Oxbridge stakes and introduced the Oxford and Cambridge Local Exams in 1879, which Awdry refused to do at Hurst. In 1873-76 the number of Oxbridge entrants was 19; in 1877-80 it was six. In 1877 there were 13 Hurst Johnians at Oxford, and seven at Cambridge, including three scholars, but by 1880 these figures had fallen to eight and one respectively. Awdry was certainly no educationalist like Lowe and, when the latter published his revised account of the College in 1878, he was able to say no changes had been made in the curriculum or timetable since his time.

Shortage of money meant less building. The decline in numbers perhaps made some buildings less urgent, but it is hard to sympathise with Awdry's view that a sanatorium was unnecessary; indeed that Port Latin Lodge was an 'expensive luxury'. As early as June 1874 he was urging Woodard to sub-let the building as a rest home for city clergy. In spite of the 1876 epidemic, Awdry continued to urge its closure. In 1878 he complained that Ellen, the nurse, had been ill herself adding £16 to expenditure, and 'for all I know there might have been much waste besides'. In its last year of operations in 1879 Port Latin Lodge cost £130 18s. 3d., but with the closing of Crescent dormitory the ground floor of present Chevron became the sick bay for 10 years. Lowe had constantly urged, as well, building more dormitory space and with the opening of Awdry's house and the decline in numbers, this building problem at least was solved.

The only building in which Awdry displayed any genuine interest was the chapel, but the sole result of his interest was the installing of a fourth window in 1876—dedicated to the Glorious Dead—with an outstanding debt of £60. In April 1875 Awdry made much of a fund for a fine new organ the specifications for which were obtained from Sir John Stainer. As usual figures were of the vaguest—Awdry started with £700, and Woodard ended asking for £1,200. A first subscription list appeared showing the Southern Chapter had given £100, Henry Gibbs £50, Woodard and Lord Salisbury £25 each, and others smaller sums.

Woodard was oppressed quite often with the belief his life was ending, and he wanted to see Hurst chapel completed. He therefore pointed out that Carpenter's plans provided for an organ screen of stone at the western arch on which the new organ would be placed, and said he wished to finish this before the organ itself. As a result the fund collapsed and was abandoned in September 1877, the money eventually going to the windows of the chapel. The organ groaned and wheezed on until 1895.

Death cast its deep shadow over Awdry's Hurst at all levels of the College, and in 1876 scarlet fever returned for a fourth time. On Obit Sunday in 1875 an extension to the burial plot in the local churchyard 'stretching down the southern slope' was opened. Leonard Moberly, who came to teach in December 1873 died of rheumatic fever a month later. Emma Marchant, college servant since 1851, died in September 1876 and was buried 'beneath the old thorn tree' in the village churchyard with William Woodard representing the Provost. The Rev. Thomas Thomson, brother of the second master, came to teach in January 1874, but was forced to retire by ill health in 1876, and died at Ramsgate in May 1879.

The epidemic in 1876 affected only a small number of boys, but caused half the College to be dispersed. The problem Lowe alluded to in 1873 was the cause, and among measures taken, like whitewashing and ventilation improvements, the well was repaired yet again, and according to the *Hurst Johnian* 'the new water has been laid on and now meanders all over the College'. The epidemic cost £196 12s. 4d. in medical expenses. Two boys died during 1876: Thomas Clift who came in January and died in December, and Frederick Lloyd who came at the same time, but about whom no details are known. Edward Nichol, who also came in January 1876, died in January 1877, and is the only boy specifically said to have died at Port Latin Lodge. The school was most deeply affected by the death of the captain elect of the Cricket XI, Frank Sheerman, who died slowly during 1877 finally succumbing in a Brighton hospital in June. The *Hurst Johnian* printed a poem including these verses:

> Quiet and resolute, gentle and strong
> Friend of the weakest and foe to the wrong,
> Hope of our cricket field, pride of our stage,
> Ripe in the battle of life to engage ...
> Such was our brother. How changed is the scene,
> How have three weeks poured an ocean between.
> Helpless and suffering, silent he lies;
> Spirit half slumbering, half in the skies.

In Awdry's last four years there was, in fact, only one more boy death: that of Cyril Marsland, who died aged 15 in January 1879, but by then the damage to Hurst's reputation had been done as the stories no doubt spread through the village like wildfire.

II

In the chapel, too, Awdry managed to stir up opposition and engender bitterness. Apart from a reference to shortened and re-timed services on Sunday, there is no clear statement about what caused the trouble, although it seems that new choral arrangements introduced by A.J. Smith, music master from 1874 to 1878, were among other points at issue. Frederick Bennett, George Willes, and George Thomson were the most prominent opponents of the changes. A long letter from Bennett to Woodard objecting to the changes rehearses arguments that would surface many times in the future. He rejected the need to change the Sunday services, pointing out that similar reductions in parish church services had not increased congregations. There had been 'one change after another', and when he tried to keep up 'the customs and traditions of the place' he had received 'no encouragement'. If the changes 'are forced on me' he thought the result would be 'a termination to my work here'. Woodard forced him to withdraw his threat of resignation.

Thomson went further. As editor of the magazine he was able to comment on the services and in 1877 did so, saying, 'it is no secret that many would gladly hear other things ... than we have had of late years'. He complained that those with musical knowledge had been 'systematically ignored'. In his view 'it is no bad thing in a school to maintain traditional usages ... where the usages do no harm'. He was particularly annoyed, it seems, about the ending of the Easter midnight procession and service. However, it seems he came round to accept the changes because, when Smith was succeeded by H. Prior as choirmaster, he remarked in 1879 'the services were fairly well sung'.

Those who opposed Awdry fed Woodard with exaggerated stories of disrupted services and empty masters' seats, and Thomson had to write to Woodard to explain that John Dayson was not absent from services due to his opposition to the changes: on the contrary he has 'constantly hurried home from Hurst, where he has two or often three services, in order to be present at our Sunday afternoon chapel service and help in it'. As for the empty masters' seats, this was explained by the fact that six of the nine resident masters sat with the choir. It seems that Awdry got his way, but at a cost, and even in his last year the magazine contained criticism of proposals to replace choir surplices with cassocks and make the choir don mortar boards.

A more religious spirit prevailed when it came to Awdry's continued backing for the missionary movement. The *Hurst Johnian* contained so many articles on the subject it was criticised in other magazines for doing so. These included four articles by Edward Steere, a future successor of Tozer's as bishop, entitled *A Walk in Nyasa Country*, and five reports on the work of U.M.C.A. Other articles on missions ranged from a mission ship that sailed round the coasts of Newfoundland to remote fishing communities to events in Hawaii—then a British protectorate—where Hurst Johnians would later provide two headmasters for Iolani College. Awdry preached on missions on Port Latin Day 1875. The next year a missionary lecture on evangelising the Maoris was given in the inner quad, and in 1877 Sir Samuel Baker, the well-known explorer, spoke about Church missions in Africa urging the boys not to feel 'horror' at the thought of coloured clergymen.

Awdry's principal interest seems to have been in a new society he helped to found in July 1874. It was called the Port Latin Guild, and was affiliated to the Church Guilds Union. The guilds were secular organisations, and their main aims were to provide a forum for discussing current issues affecting the Church of England, to encourage members to be involved in Church voluntary work, and to ensure members attended church frequently. The Port Latin Guild was strongly backed by Woodard, Field and Lowe, and by Johnians like Herbert Low, secretary of Helmore's Gregorian Chant Society, and Frederick Dickinson, involved in East End mission work.

The first meeting took place on 23 February 1875 in St Paul's Chapter House, which was a frequent venue with members staying overnight at the nearby *Cathedral Hotel*. Membership rose from an initial 20 to over 70, and meetings were attended by sixth formers and probationers. Awdry spoke on several occasions: in 1877 on laymen in the Church, in 1878 on the Church in South Africa, for example, and Lowe, Field, and Woodard all made their contributions with Field's accounts of his trip to Palestine occupying many meetings. Woodard spoke in June 1877 on Church Education, and in June 1878 Lowe spoke, and Bishop Tozer preached the sermon at the Guild service. The *Hurst Johnian* reported that in the evening there was a programme of songs like the *Vicar of Bray*, and next morning after early communion a guild breakfast before they dispersed. Although the Guild made small contributions to chapel funds and the founding of an Old Johnian Club, it remains true that its activities were not directly part of school life, and it is reasonable to suggest that Awdry's absorption in its work was a distraction from his work as headmaster.

Although so far this chapter has been one of almost continuous criticism of Awdry's conduct and an account of sharp decline in many aspects of the College's life, there were positive gains from his time as head, some of which had a lasting influence on the history of the school. When he re-organised the capitations for himself and Thomson in 1877 Awdry took the opportunity, as he put it in a letter, to introduce 'the house system'. Although the word 'dormitory' was retained until the middle of Coombes's headship, the five dormitories left at the end of Awdry's headship were to be the five houses at Hurst until the mid-1950s. Blue Shield, finally named Star, was the headmaster's house run directly by the head and his wife until the late 1920s and without a separate housemaster. It had higher fees, but better facilities, and its prestige ensured it was always full, and therefore it secured a disproportionate number of sporting trophies over the years. Red Shield became the second master's house until that title was temporarily abolished in 1913. Chevron moved to its present position. Together with Red Cross and Fleur de Lys these made up the five dormitories, and the football matches in October 1877 were the first played under these names, with the addition of Crescent until its closure in 1879.

Awdry was responsible for founding two school societies, arguably the first of many, although there was a Sunday Social Society mentioned in Lowe's time. In 1874 the Natural History Society was founded with Awdry as the chairman. It was divided into four sections: entomology, zoology, botany and geology, and held meetings every three weeks. At these there were discussions of various scientific subjects often based on prepared papers some of which appeared in the *Hurst Johnian*. In February 1877 a Debating Society was formed, the first debate being on the exclusion of women from the learned professions. Both masters and boys took part including Awdry himself, and the Society gained immensely from 'a year of stirring events' in 1878-1879 with a Near Eastern crisis, and war in Afghanistan and Zululand. For the first time boys began to discuss imperial matters and the magazine, too, reflected this interest. There was an article by a Boer pupil, Jacob Swart, on 'Life in Natal', and two poems on the defeat of the British at Isandhlwana. It was the beginning of a shift in focus away from the Empire as a place of missionary endeavour to interest in imperial expansion and more secular occupations like engineering or the colonial police. A talk in Awdry's last term by Bishop Wilkinson of Zululand nicely captures the shift of emphasis. His main purpose was to talk about missions and the boys read aloud a hymn in Zulu, but the bishop then defended the Zulu War saying that although Zulus were possessed of 'mental, moral and physical qualities very far in advance of what we might expect from Africa' they were also capable of 'appalling cruelty'.

In dealing with Old Johnians Awdry had at first mainly succeeded in annoying them. At Port Latin and St Etheldreda ceremonies they had been accustomed to stay in College for some days. Awdry made it clear they had no 'right of residence', and restricted their stay to two days. He also laid down strict conditions saying they were not to enter dormitories, smoke in the buildings, or stay up after 11 o'clock. He also made considerable changes regarding Port Latin Day. The athletic sports on that day were abolished although he replaced them with a gymnastic display. Because of his changes with regard to football there was no Old Johnian match in the week prior to Port Latin, and the matches were not resumed until November 1881. He moved the cricket match in the week after Port Latin Day to a date near the Festival of St John the Baptist on 24 June.

But in 1877, no doubt, their annoyance was changed to pleasure on the setting up of the Hurst Johnian Club. Lowe had done a good deal to foster Old Johnian support for the school. He had started the old boys' football and cricket matches, and they had been welcomed for Port Latin Week and on St Etheldreda Sunday. He had written them an annual Easter letter and kept a register of their names. Woodard was determined, after the failure of the organ fund to take off in 1875-76, to create a Hurst Completion Fund, and to use Port Latin Day in 1877 to launch this new money raising effort. A network of 23 collecting secretaries was created and John Hooke (OJ) was made chairman of a London committee. Three subscription lists with small sums on them from this committee, the Port Latin Guild, and the Provost's Appeal exist. Port Latin Day was meant to be the grandest of occasions to launch this appeal to complete the chapel and indeed the rest of the buildings. A special train was laid on for the first time for many years, and there were 300 guests. The chapel service opened with Sullivan's *Te Deum*, and continued with a sermon by James Woodford, Bishop of Ely, a close colleague of Lowe's. Besides Bishop Woodford, Bishops Durnford of Chichester, Selwyn of Lichfield, and Mackarness of Argyll were present. Woodard's party included his daughter Audrey and his son William, and they were accompanied by the Lowes. The deans of Manchester and York were there, and members of the nobility including Lord Forbes and Lord Shrewsbury, the latter unfortunately dying the next day.

Splendid though the event was, it failed in its purpose. No other subscription lists exist, and no more was heard of completion until Lowe himself was Provost in the 1890s. But as part of this great effort the Old Johnians were circulated and Woodard suggested a club be set up in London which would hold an annual Old Johnian service in a city church. On 13 June 1877, with John Hooke as the first secretary and a committee of 12 old boys including G.W. Butler, F.J. Dickinson, C.R. Whitbourn, and G.O.L. Thomson, the Old Johnian Club was founded. On 23 June the first of the newly arranged cricket matches took place with the Old Johnians led by George Stallard winning by 17 runs. On 22 November at the *Guildhall Tavern* in Gresham Street about fifty sat down to dinner.

More by accident than design Awdry was also responsible for creating the first school committee which was to run games until 1970, and a programme of sports that remained basically unchanged until Bernard Tower became headmaster in 1924. The reason for the committee was financial. Even before Awdry arrived George Willes complained that over £500 had been spent by football and cricket committees without any accounts being presented. On 8 March 1873 the Playground Committee (P.G.C. hereafter) was established with Thomson as chairman and H.C. Stevens as secretary. The opening minutes make it clear it was to 'manage all monies' and its accounts were published in the school magazine for many years. The older football and cricket committees became sub-committees, and two further ones were added for fives and for the tuck shop—the profits of which were to be disbursed for sport. In the summer term there were athletics and occasionally swimming sub-committees. It was inevitable that these committees made up of captains and prefects came to make the rules covering every aspect of games, and to discuss all matters relating to them.

Awdry did not attend except on one famous occasion. During his first year he had watched the confusion of football rules with amazement. In one match between Lancing and Hurst the two sides played by different rules in spite of a referee. Although it was stressed again at the start of 1874 that Rugby Union rules applied, the violence continued and so did serious injuries. In September 1874 Awdry came to the P.G.C. and told them the school would play football according to Football Association rules. The first football match was played on 28 October, and was a draw with Ardingly. The first dormitory football cup was won by Chevron. Football lasted at Hurst until 1924, but its introduction, as indeed its abolition, was fraught with strong controversy. The Old Johnians declined to play such a soft game and there was no match with the school under Awdry. Old Johnians wrote silly letters to the magazine saying football was not right for the school because it was more dangerous than rugby, and too scientific to be mastered by Johnians, and more sensible ones saying it would end matches with other Woodard schools, although this did not prove to be the case as both Ardingly and Lancing accepted F.A. rules as well. Because football required a flat surface South field was abandoned and matches were transferred to North field to the fury of cricketers and athletes alike.

Apart from football the main sporting event of the Michaelmas Term was athletics sports day. Awdry insisted on one sports day only held in October, and a steeplechase was run at about the same time. The organisation continued unchanged, although in 1878 the tug-of-war was started, won by a team led by William Howard. Training remained perfunctory although in 1879 competitors were told that 'steady practice must have some effect. Let the coming generation look to it'. Only one contestant for the long jump actually reached the pit so there was some way to go! The list of *Victores Ludorum* remains fragmentary during Awdry's years apart from the names of J.A. Cooper (1876), Harry Howard (1878), and A.M. Seymour (1879). The account of the 1878 sports shows that the three Howard brothers, William, Harry and Charles, were the leading athletes.

In the Lent Term two new sports were introduced. In the summer of 1873 fives courts abutting on one side of the gymnasium were opened, and Robert Wix took charge. In September he presented cups for senior and junior house fives which became the most important sporting contest of the term until 1927. Wix was apparently a fiery tempered man who insisted on having his way with the sport. He created a fives VIII, replaced when he left with two fives pairs. He insisted on a blue cap with a white tassel which was the same as Lancing's. Again, when he left this was replaced with a red cap with white tassel. Wix spent a good deal of time at the P.G.C. attacking excessive cricket expenditure, and as we already know he did not get on with Awdry, leaving in 1877 to be headmaster elsewhere. The second innovation was the start of cross-country—or as it was at first—hare and hounds. This was modelled on Rugby School's Big and Little Side runs, and eventually became the Clayton Run which lasted until Tower's time. In Awdry's day the race was up College Lane to the Brighton Road, up Clayton Hill to the windmills, along the Downs to two miles beyond Plumpton, and t hen a return run across the country. An interesting account survives of the race in 1877 when the two hares, Charles Howard and Francis Awdry, ran out of paper for laying the trail just before Clayton Tunnel. They hid themselves in a hay stack where the hounds found them, and 'triumphantly brought [them] home'.

Swimming continued in the Summer Term, but the record of what happened is incomplete. About half the College managed to pass the swimming test. As for sports, these are mentioned only twice in 1876 and 1879 during Awdry's period. In 1876 there were races for over and under 15s including diving for coconuts, and in 1879 there was diving through a hoop in which Charles Howard excelled.

The opening of the gymnasium might have been expected to foreshadow the rapid growth of gymnastics, but both building and equipment were deficient. The mattresses and vaulting horses soon needed replacing, but in March 1879 the P.G.C. voted that there should be no extra money to help gymnastics which had to rely entirely on subscriptions for their equipment. Mr. Moss arrived in 1875, and in 1878 took over fully from Henry Alford after his 25 years' service. From 1876 the main gymnastics competition was held on Port Latin Day, and the first results to be published were in 1878. Although the building was improved by wall panelling installed by Pierce, it was already starting to reveal defects—the roof soon needed repairing—which continued until it was demolished over seventy years later.

The need for economy, in fact, affected all sports under Awdry, and battles over economies were a major theme of many P.G.C. minutes and, in spite of them and tuck shop profits, the P.G.C. recorded a debt of £32 in 1877. By 1879 the fives courts, gymnasium, and bathing place all needed attention. Typical of the measures adopted was one in the summer of 1876, when a late hay harvest meant that Mr. Broad the farmer at Ruckford delayed letting the water out of the stream. Instead of employing labourers to clear reeds and dredge mud, the boys were required to do it themselves.

But the two most costly major sports were football and cricket, and it was over their facilities that the fiercest battles raged. It was Wix who pointed out that the two cricket elevens used a horse brake or wagonette when they could well use trains and walk. This matter was not settled for three years when it was decided that horse drawn transport should only be hired if there was no railway available. The treatment of visitors was not good—only in 1877 was a second hut added on North field for them to change in. Cricket matches lasted long hours, and so in 1875 the P.G.C. agreed to provide a cricket lunch with bread and cheese and beer, only to be confronted by the footballers demanding a similar facility. Indeed in 1876 Brighton College refused to play football on account of the poor tea, and this forced the P.G.C.'s hand. Football teas started in September that year. The tent provided for teas was not of good quality, and in 1878 had to be sent to a sail-maker for repairs.

Cricket undoubtedly took the lion's share of expenditure. In 1877, for example, out of £242 9s. 0½d. spent on sport, £117 18s. 3½d. went to cricket, and it was inevitable that the majority of clashes occurred because the cricketers wanted good equipment, and a properly maintained North field. In 1874 cricket was short of balls, and later there was a shortage of presentation bats. In 1876 a request for screens was rejected by the P.G.C. as a 'needless expense'. Two years later a letter in the magazine complained about lack of rope to protect the pitches, and there was a shortage of seats for spectators. But it was the state of the field that caused most trouble. Moving football there, of course, added to the problems, and in 1875 the P.G.C. proposed that football and cricket should be played on different fields. The only concession they got was that West field should only be played on for dormitory football matches in the hope that it might recover for the season, but later this field was let to a local farmer to make money. The P.G.C. resolved in February 1878 that the 'North field is unsuitable for cricket and football games', and wrote to William Woodard, the custos. Matters remained unchanged. William Woodard did, however, agree to the removal of a tree impeding the field of play! So badly did the P.G.C. feel about the state of the field that three members resigned, and shortly afterwards George Willes resigned as chairman.

The problems surrounding seeding, mowing and rolling pitches required a groundsman. None was available, and these matters were largely in the hands of the captain to arrange. At first scythes were obtained and the boys did the work themselves. In October 1877 the P.G.C. resolved to use sheep on the grass and pay 9d. a day for a farmer's boy to look after them. A larger mower was bought but it needed horse power to pull it, and there was considerable debate on hiring either a donkey or a horse, resolved in favour of a horse. In 1878 a local farmer hired them one for 10s. a day and a 1s. a day for the boy to mind it. The mower then broke down. Rolling with the lethal large roller continued but, in spite of a special meeting at the start of term to arrange for this, letters appeared in the *Hurst Johnian* complaining that mowing and rolling were not being done properly.

Cricketers needed attention as well as their field. 'Cricket', said an article in the *Hurst Johnian* in 1874, 'wants teaching as well as Latin and Greek.' It was agreed to return to hiring a professional, but this only added to acrimony because it added to costs. One Stutterfield was appointed in 1875, but two years later the P.G.C. tried to cut his salary by removing journey money leaving him with 50s. a year, and used cricket balls. However, Awdry intervened to get his journey money put back. When the next coach, Joseph Burman, was appointed, he obtained wages of £2 10s. a week and £1 journey money.

There was one other issue which led to acrimony in the P.G.C., and showed Awdry's lack of control over events. It had been agreed in Lowe's time that the prefects appointed team captains who then selected their teams, and these rules were confirmed by the P.G.C. as late as April 1877. In football trouble arose when the appointed team captain, John Cooper, was criticised by the prefects who then insisted on his giving up the captaincy. Cooper wrote to

Awdry arguing that he was captain for life until he left, but Awdry disagreed, and Peter Burrell was elected in his place. In cricket the death of John Sheerman, who had been appointed, led to the vice-captain becoming captain *pro tem*. However, he was subjected to criticism from the prefects because William Howard was the outstanding cricketer of 1878. Awdry had to write to the magazine in July 1878 to ask for an end to open criticism. In the end changes in the rules were made. From December 1877 the Football XII and the Cricket XI were to be chosen by the captain, and in June 1878 it was agreed that existing team members would elect future captains. Arthur Shepherd and William Howard held office successfully.

Considering the large number of organisational and practical difficulties surrounding the two main games, it is hardly surprising that neither had a particularly good record under Awdry. For instance, the team captained by Cooper and then by Burrell played nine matches but won only two of them with Eastbourne College and Cuckfield Village. Although Arthur Shepherd boasted that in Awdry's last year the Football XII won half their games, the reality was that they lost to Brighton College and Lancing College, their only two school fixtures, managed a draw with Storrington Village, and won against Brighton Rangers and Brighton Engineers. Cricket was undoubtedly followed more closely and played more professionally than any of the other sports. From 1874 a full set of seasonal figures was given in the magazine, and from 1877 comments on individual players. Under Awdry there were only two years in which a fair number of matches were won: eight out of 14 in 1875, and seven out of 12 in 1876, but in his last years things were going badly. In 1878 they won only four out of 19 matches, and in 1879 only two out of eleven.

It is true that Awdry's seven years were not a complete disaster, and that he left behind him genuine contributions to the long-term history of the College: the P.G.C., a full games programme, a slimmed down Port Latin Day, the Hurst Johnian Club and sensibly placed Old Johnian cricket and football fixtures, five dormitories, the debating and natural history societies have all been discussed. It is also true that evidence from virtually every aspect of school life shows a spirit of acrimony and argument. This was prevalent in the common room, the chapel, and the P.G.C. and, although less marked in relation to Woodard himself, clearly the Provost believed he had failed to curb expenditure in line with falling numbers. Awdry disagreed with him, citing falling domestic expenditure, economies (clearly evident in sport, for instance), and reductions in staff costs. With the consequences of the inadequate buildings leading to illness, and further falls in numbers, and the general fall in numbers brought on particularly by agricultural depression it was only to be expected that Awdry would leave sooner rather than later.

He did so in December 1879, and the *Hurst Johnian* described 'great enthusiasm' among the present boys, and 'conspicuous sociability' among Old Johnians at the farewell ceremonies: he certainly continued to attend the Port Latin Guild, and visit the College. The College leaving gift was a silver epergne and two silver salvers, and a scroll signed by the whole school. Awdry had become a prebendary in 1877, and a residentiary canon in 1879 of Chichester Cathedral, and his next post was as Principal of Chichester Theological College which he told Woodard was a position he had 'little taste for'. He took parish work at Amport in 1886, and his career resumed in 1895 when he was the first suffragan bishop of Southampton for a year before going to Japan, first as Bishop of Osaka and then from 1897 to 1908 as Bishop of South Tokyo. His facility for upsetting people remained with him as the magazine reported he was accompanied everywhere in Tokyo with a bodyguard because of his critical remarks about Japanese religion. On returning for the Lambeth Conference in 1908 he was taken ill, retired to Winchester, and died there in 1910.

FIVE

RESTORER OF THE TEMPLE
1880-1891

Edward Cooper's Early Years

I would that you might see, even though it be only in some faint darksome manner, the real blessings of this, the goodly heritage, which is yours by being at Hurst; and therefore, as the knowledge of what others realise may be a beginning or a ground, I tell you today of what I, a Hurst boy, have learnt to know as a reality beyond doubt, a reality giving birth to conviction, and cherished with gratitude and love. For these are the feelings with which the name of Hurst must for ever be associated in the hearts of all who are her sons—conviction of her usefulness—gratitude for her guidance—love for her parental, fostering care.

> A chapel sermon by Rev. John K. Smith (OJ),
> Second Master 1884-1888, reprinted in full in
> *The Hurst Johnian*, 304/133-140, August 1888

At the end of this term we were sorry to lose N.B. Warde who went to Selwyn College, Cantab. He has been most useful to us on all matters connected with the success of the Dormitory as well as with the School; his most notable achievement being simultaneously Captain of School, and all the School teams. The last of his family, he has grandly sustained its reputation. At the end of term as a mark of their esteem the Dormitory presented him with a handsome Gladstone bag.

> Chevron Dormitory Book 1882-1924,
> Summer Term 1888

After Evensong the entire school, headed by all the masters, went down the road, past the Icehouse, to meet the Eleven. There they lined up and waited for the team, whose choruses could be heard afar off as they came up the road. When they got up pandemonium was let loose, and with cheers, yells, shrieks, hysteric sobs, and the bray of trombones, night was made hideous for the ten minutes occupied in getting back to College. Smith and Keeling were carried in shoulder high ...

> Account of the First XI returning on 12 June 1890 after victory
> over Lancing by 79 runs. B.F. Smith was the Captain, and
> H.W. Keeling took six wickets for 22 runs.
> *The Hurst Johnian*, 324/168-70, July 1890

Not surprisingly, as Woodard told Thomson, he looked for a new headmaster 'whose ability as a ruler would put a second failure out of the question'. But falling numbers, low salary, and poor reputation meant that the days of looking to Winchester or some similar school were over, and it took Woodard some time to find the right candidate. George Thomson was therefore acting headmaster for the first term of 1880, and then resumed his position as second master in April, leaving in July to be headmaster of King's College, Taunton. He was succeeded as second master in September by Charles Banks, who also took over Shield, the second master's dormitory. These appointments and dates have been incorrectly given in the past, but can be confirmed from the signatures in the P.G.C. minute book.

The new headmaster who arrived in April 1880 was Charles Edward Cooper. Like Lowe, he was a young man, aged only 28 when appointed, and also like Lowe he was to give 22 years to the school. Edward was born in 1852, and went to a small grammar school with a good academic record at Oakham in Rutland, and in 1869 he entered Emmanuel College, Cambridge where he obtained a degree in Classics in 1873. He obtained immediately a teaching post at King Edward's School in Birmingham which, after Prince Lee's headmastership, had a high academic reputation. The young master was soon on £220 a year. In 1874 he began work as a curate in Moseley, and a year later he was ordained at Worcester. Also in 1874 he met and married his wife, Louisa, and he was soon the father of four children: two sons, Harold and Wilfrid, and two daughters, Audrey and Margery. Sadly a third daughter, Hilda, born at Hurst in 1881, died two years later. A salary of £498 must have attracted a family man, and Woodard was rightly convinced of his High Churchmanship and disciplinary skills.

Edward concealed his comparative youth as headmaster beneath the large beard, mortarboard and voluminous silk gown seen in all photographs of him. There was never a hint under Cooper of any lack of discipline. Each day began with the boys assembled in upper school for calling over, and each day before lunch Cooper proceeded to the fellows library to cane those sent to him there. But 'Old Tick', as he was nicknamed, did not rule through fear alone. He and his family were actively involved in much school life. He attended school matches even if in cap and gown. He played cricket and fives. He and three other masters were members of the newly formed Pyecombe Golf Club where between them in 1896 they carried off all the trophies. With some assistance he produced 18 Shakespeare plays, and from 1884 took part in many termly Popular or 'Pop' concerts starting that year with a reading from Mark Twain given to 'roars of laughter'. Four years later he gave the first of many 'Hours with Dickens' when he imitated the characters, and it is no surprise that the most popular author in the school library as a result was Dickens. Edward Cooper gave his bound volumes of the *Spectator* to the library when he left, a small indication of his friendly and broad minded character which made him a man held in deep affection by the boys; not at all like the traditional image we have of the Victorian headmaster.

When Edward Cooper appointed Henry Woolsey second master in 1894, no school could have had two better, and more humane, leaders. Francis Rumsey (OJ) recalled a meeting with the 'dear old man' in his last years. Rumsey had a Kodak, and entered the headmaster's study to ask if he might photograph him. ' "How long do you want me to sit still?", said Cooper. "Two minutes", I said. And he did!' Few heads in the next century would have been so approachable. Both Cooper's sons attended the College, were good sportsmen, and one was school captain. Both went on to Keble College, Oxford. Louisa Cooper, described as a 'small, bird-like figure', was well liked particularly by boys who had to stay in the holidays and those

9 Rev. C. Edward Cooper, headmaster from 1880 to 1902, and the masters, *c.*1890. Seated from left to right, Rev. W. Back, Cooper, Rev. H.S. Milner, Rev. B.P. Bull. Standing, from left to right, H. Woolsey, G. Farrant, P.U. Henn, A.C. Moreton, W. Pratt, C. Marsh, C.H. Eckersley, W.H. Chappell.

she visited in the sanatorium. She often played the piano at concerts, and on one occasion husband, wife and eldest son played a trio. Louisa organised three bazaars to collect money for the sanatorium (infirmary, then). Funds for the mothers, and the sisters of the boys raised money for two more chapel windows.

Edward Cooper gave himself completely to the school, and by the time he retired at 50 his beard was grey, and his health partly undermined. The only activity he permitted himself outside the College was involvement in Woodard affairs. He was a fellow in 1881 and served as vice-provost twice. Lowe was often at the College and they became firm friends. Cooper was at Denstone Chapel dedication, and in 1889 and 1890 there were cricket matches between the two schools, even though this involved a journey with six changes of train. Lowe entertained the boys to tea in 1890. Cooper backed the Port Latin Guild now with over a hundred members. He was also Master of a Minor (Junior) Port Latin Guild for boys in the College, the highest membership of which was twenty-one. The Port Latin Guild lasted until 1888 when the *Hurst Johnian* said it was in 'suspended animation'.

The task he faced in the early 1880s would have left Cooper time for little else. The magazine might call for 'honest, hearty work and honest, hearty play', but the school was in poor shape. Numbers had fallen to 151, and income to £6,447 12s. 5d., the lowest it had been since 1860. There were only four Oxbridge masters in a small and poorly recruited common room where some salaries were as low as £20 a year. There were only 33 Old Johnians at the annual dinner. In September 1880 the P.G.C. minutes complained about the floor of the fives courts, and the north wall of the gym to which they had drawn attention 'several times before'. The organ in chapel was 'showing signs of dissolution'.

Behind the statistics lurked an atmosphere of apathy and bad will. In the chapel, services were 'not creditable to us' and singing produced 'intolerable discords'. The Debating Society had collapsed, and the *Hurst Johnian* urged a 'degree of reality and utility' be brought into corps affairs where even the officers' swords had disappeared. In football during 1880 there was a failure to play together and a lack of discipline, and in cricket next year 'members were heard growling about their positions in the field, or the place where they went in, and sometimes even refusing to go on bowling when desired to do so'. In tennis during 1882 the whole season was wrecked by a row involving defiance of the captain, a fight between members on the court, and sabotaging of equipment. It was all very well for the magazine to say, 'we must win more school matches this next season', but it also had to admit that there were plenty of boys 'mooning about the cloisters or crouching over the fire' when they should have been at games.

Cooper was not able to effect a rapid change in the situation because competition for the limited number of boys whose parents could afford secondary education was now developing, particularly in Sussex and Kent. Midhurst Grammar School re-opened in 1882 with 70 pupils. Rye Grammar School was re-organised in 1884. In 1889 Horsham Grammar School reformed, and soon had 130 boys including 24 boarders. Its fees were £4 a term, and there were 20 scholarships for poor boys. On the Sussex-Kent border The Skinners' Company, whose public school was Tonbridge, had been required by the Charity Commissioners to found two schools. This they did—a Middle Grammar School in Tunbridge Wells, and a Commercial School in Tonbridge—directly appealing to the kind of parents like the Wardes of Yalding who had sent five sons to Hurst. The fees at the two schools were £3 10s. and £2 10s. a term, and they both had scholarships to help with entry, and later with university fees. The school at Tonbridge negotiated a cheap season ticket with the South Eastern Railway. The new grammar schools provided almost exactly what Lowe's Hurst had provided almost exclusively, and they provided it more cheaply.

So recovery certainly came under Cooper, but only very slowly, as the figures show:

1880 151	1883 180	1886 180	1889 181
1881 163	1884 164	1887 187	1890 189
1882 172	1885 158	1888 189	1891 187

With a background in two academic grammar schools it was not surprising that Edward Cooper's first purpose was to restore confidence in the school's academic reputation. From the start a brisk and purposeful atmosphere was noticeable. 'We are sent into the world,' said Cooper in January 1881, 'to work; we are here to fit ourselves for good work in the world.'

Articles in the magazine criticised loafing around and cribbing work, and John Smith, when second master, urged boys to make the latter 'known to their masters' by reporting it. Boys were exhorted not to 'idle away time out of school', or to delay doing preparation 'in a singularly feeble and silly manner'. In the summer term of 1881 all forms started to take an annual promotional exam, and termly reports were introduced. The Oxford and Cambridge Local Exams had started in 1874, and we have seen that Awdry was against them at Hurst. Cooper was in favour, but Woodard insisted on continuing the old external Oxbridge annual three-day exam, and it was not until 1888 that S.E. Hickox and P.E. Turner became the first boys to obtain Higher Certificate (a kind of A Level). Then in 1890 Hurst began to take Oxford and Cambridge Local exams, and in the summer the old Crescent dormitory was cleared and desks placed there where the fourth form took the exam. Fourteen of them obtained passes.

All the limited indications we have are that Cooper succeeded and academic standards rose, with the possible exception of classics. Although the school clearly accepted the paramountcy of Latin in the curriculum—a debate in March 1889 saw the classics backed by fifteen votes to five—and Cooper was a classicist, Hurst could not compete with the high quality and almost exclusively classical curriculum of the great schools, except for a very small group of boys. The external examiners' reports are now supplemented by handwritten reports sent by the Board. In 1881 Latin was the subject they thought was 'poor', and in 1895 they were still commenting that 'the standard should certainly be higher'. Only Upper Sixth Greek New Testament was 'satisfactory'. Otherwise there were clearly improvements. Whereas in 1882 the report on lower school arithmetic remarked that the standard was lower than that for boys in a National (Church primary) School with over half those examined having great difficulties with even basic division and multiplication, a report in 1895 commented favourably on the same subject. By 1885 the examiners commented on the 'increased industry and intelligence of the lower portion of the boys', and by 1891 'the general character' of school work was 'very satisfactory'.

The improved academic atmosphere soon led to a recovery in the Oxbridge stakes. The probationers continued throughout Cooper's headship, and were increasingly interested in Oxbridge entry rather than taking the A.S.N.C. degree. Cooper succeeded in 1890 in having Lowe's entrance exam for probationers replaced by an appropriate pass in the Oxford and Cambridge Locals. Figures for 1882 and 1883 are not available, but in the other years from 1880 to 1891 Hurst sent 39 boys to Oxbridge, and there was a better balance between the two universities no doubt partly caused by Cooper's Cambridge background. Twenty-two went to Oxford, and 17 to Cambridge, although it is noticeable that High Church Keble College attracted a third of the Oxford entries after 1888. There were eight exhibitions or scholarships, and Hurst's name was known once more at the senior universities. In May 1885 eight Hurst Johnians were able to meet in William Buckland's (OJ) rooms at Gonville and Caius, and in 1889 he became the first member of the school to become fellow of a college (1889), later Professor of Civil Law, and eventually (1923) President of Gonville and Caius.

In one report the examiners commented on the text books, saying that in several subjects they were too difficult or were out of date, but Cooper could do little about this. Any academic improvement came about with no substantial increase in resources. The broad curriculum continued, and in 1888 the vast majority of boys—who stayed two or at the most three years —had a syllabus containing Latin, Divinity, French, German, English, history, arithmetic, algebra, Euclid (geometry), trigonometry, statics and hydrostatics (physics), chemistry, and physiology (biology). The only subject Cooper added to the curriculum was woodwork. A carpenter's shop was installed near the laboratory in Shield in Michaelmas Term 1882 under the control of P.A. Lemprière. Cooper justified this new subject saying, 'we shall not be satisfied till Hurst provides a much greater amount of technical instruction for the benefit of those who may desire in the colonies to earn an honest living by working with their hands ...'.

Throughout the 1880s upper and lower schools continued to be the site for most teaching, and the most noticeable improvement in facilities came in 1884 when £234 8s. 4d. was spent on new iron-bound, varnished desks because 'the old desks were so hacked with the initials of past and present Johnians' it was 'nearly impossible to write on them'. During the 1890s with the opening of a sanatorium it became possible to make three classrooms on the ground floor of Chevron, and other dormitory day rooms began to double up as classrooms as the concept of individual teaching rooms took over.

Shortage of money affected the second part of Cooper's programme for recovery—the improvement of the buildings and the grounds, and with falling prices for much of the 1880s and early 1890s there was no chance of increasing fees. Fees remained at £11 11s. term, and £15 15s. for the 50 Star boys, and it should be remembered that the proportion of those on reduced fees was higher when overall numbers were lower. These were £7 7s. for scholars, £10 for Sussex boys, and £3 3s. for day boys. Fee income was indeed reduced by the decision to end the servitors whose numbers in their last decade varied between seven and fourteen. In September 1890 Louis Coe, Alfred Cross and Alfred Absalom were the last to be admitted, and next year the accounts refer to them as 'servitors and pages'. They became the College servants, paid a pitiable wage, and survived until the Great War under the sole control of the butler. In 1898, 14 of them earned £42 11s. 3d. Fee income which was £6,447 in round figures in 1880 had only risen to £6,841 in 1884, and had actually fallen back to £6,297 in 1890. There is a gap in the accounts at this point but, even after some expansion in the 1890s and with rising prices, the fee income in 1898 was only £7,023.

Nevertheless the 1880s were a period of building development, even if two of the three main buildings were almost entirely built with money raised by appeals. In the chapel Louisa Cooper encouraged mothers of Hurst Johnians to contribute to a further stained glass window which was put in place in 1882 at a cost of £204 15s., but thereafter there was no more improvement, and funds for another window and the organ did not accumulate. Only £20 was spent on the increasingly moribund organ, and the only discernible improvement in chapel was a set of wall banners installed in 1887 to cover the brickwork. The reduction in numbers combined with the opening of an extension to Star dormitory in 1882, with a good size day room and improved washing facilities, undoubtedly ended the period of overcrowding. Dormitories set up their own improvement funds so that we find, for example, Chevron providing chairs, honours boards, and a hot shower from them. The winters of the early 1890s were nearly all severe, and the decade opened as usual with Hurst boys wearing greatcoats in class and 'breaking large plates of ice' from washing facilities. In 1893 hot pipes were extended throughout the College to the usual cries of horror at any improvements: a letter to the *Hurst Johnian* suggested that bath chairs to wheel out boys to football matches would soon be coming in. As Henry Woolsey pointed out later, the degree of domestic comfort in everyday life undoubtedly rose in Cooper's time. It is noticeable in this context that even food improved a little, when in 1883 the first resident steward was appointed at £40 a year to oversee the kitchens.

However, there was one domestic improvement above all others needed to restore Hurst's local reputation: a sanatorium, hopefully bringing with it an end to the death toll. Cooper's headship began in regrettable circumstances in this respect. He told parents on Port Latin Day in 1882 'we are free of epidemics' only to experience four deaths in 1883. Gerald Barron, 'a sunny fellow' in Star, died on 17 February and was buried in the local churchyard as usual.

Three days later a boy whose parents were in New Zealand, John Boyd, died with much suffering in his last hours. Three days more brought the death of the captain of school, Edward Bryant. An academic boy in the choir and editor of the magazine, he died while prayers were being said for him in chapel. Vested in cassock and surplice he was laid on a funeral bier so that boys could pay their last respects. Then the coffin was carried shoulder high by his fellow prefects to the hearse waiting at the gates while the choir sang *Brief Life is Here our Portion*. The lane to the village was lined by the boys. These three deaths were said to be due to bronchial pneumonia. The last a month later was said to be caused by galloping consumption when 16-year-old John Parsons died a fortnight after the disease took hold, watched in his last days by his mother and Cooper.

In fact, this was the last substantial number of deaths. A new school doctor, Dr. George Hawken, more sport, better food, and improved living conditions helped to improve the health record. But it remained true that using the ground floor of Chevron as the infirmary was unsatisfactory. Cooper seized the opportunity afforded by the deaths and in September 1883 an Infirmary Fund was set up which was largely run by Louisa Cooper. Woodard agreed that the former head's house in Carpenter's design, planned for the north-west corner of the property, should be the infirmary although William Woodard's estimate that it would cost only £700 was wide of the mark. Louisa Cooper sold photographs of the College and had a collection of extracts from the *Hurst Johnian* concerning the chapel published for sale, but perhaps her most noticeable fund-raising effort was to organise in 1884, 1887, and 1890 three fêtes, two outside and one in the hall. There was a series of stalls manned by the Misses Woodard, Campion, Borrer, and Cooper—the head's two daughters running the bran tub. The last fête in February 1890, opened by Lady Hampden, was a splendid affair with six stalls and various refreshments and stayed open until eight in the evening. Music by Sullivan, Handel and Haydn was played by the recently formed school orchestra. The fund rose slowly to £583 8s. 9d. in September 1887. Between then and September 1890 it rose to £1,047 6s. 9d., and among the largest contributors was the Prime Minister, Lord Salisbury, who sent £100. Building began in September 1888 and took two years, but even when it was complete Cooper said, 'expenses multiply and details increase the estimate of the sum required', and he had to appeal for a further £100 for the internal furnishings.

The building was opened on 25 September 1890 by Dr. W. Withers Moore, J.P., the local Medical Officer of Health, Dr. Fussell, and Dr. George Hawken. The *Sussex Daily News* carried a full report. Built by a local firm—Pearsey and Sons—the new sanatorium was described as 'light and cheery'. It had three wards: St Etheldreda on the ground floor, St Hilda and St Winifrid above, a nurse's room, and a small oratory for prayers where the choir sang *When Morning Gilds the Skies* at the opening. Withers Moore, who was consulting physician to the College, stressed the importance to health of isolation, and the proceedings ended with a vote of thanks proposed by Edmund Field. Furnishing went ahead. Mrs. John Otter paid for the door, and oak chairs and tables and a pine medicine chest were provided. The first resident school matron, Mrs. Martha Wanstall, described as a 'stiff backed, hard working lady' was appointed, and the first patient, C.S. Miller, admitted with tonsillitis. The new building undoubtedly created the best possible impression in the area, and featured prominently in the prospectus, including a photograph in that of 1899. It came none too soon because the bad winters of the 1890s culminating in the worst of the century in 1895 were to provide a new scourge for schools in the shape of a series of influenza epidemics, and Hurst passed through these relatively unscathed. Although they did not know it, the sanatorium was to be the last building of any importance on the site for over thirty-five years apart from completion work on the chapel.

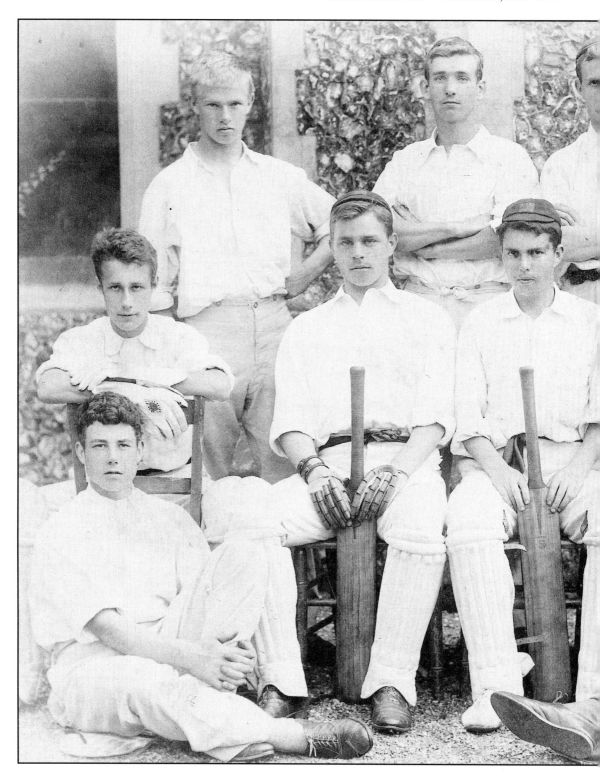

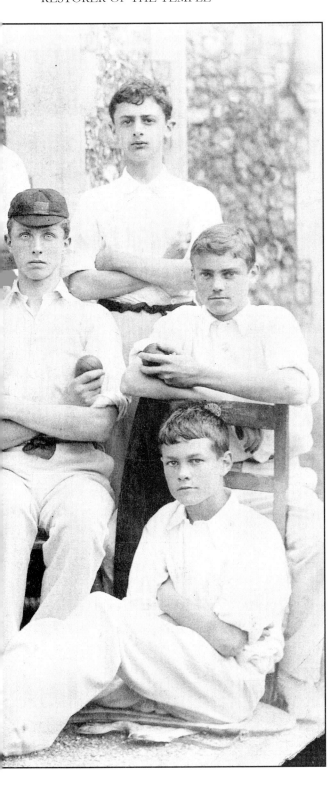

10 The First XI cricket team, 1891. In the middle row, second from left, is William P. Dean, who played football for Sussex, and was killed in the Boer War in 1901.

Good sports facilities benefited the boys and helped to raise school morale when teams won, and games could be enjoyed without the constant complaints of Awdry's day. Moreover, these facilities combined with attractive grounds to impress potential parents and visitors from other schools. During the 1880s virtually every aspect of the grounds and sports facilities received attention. The bathing place was properly cleared, although a tragic item occurs in the P.G.C. minutes for June 1883 when they voted a guinea to the widow of a labourer who died while hired to clean the pool. The fives courts were repaired. Tennis courts were provided on the grass in front of Star. A larger shed for the tuck shop was built and placed north of the chapel, facing the cricket field, and given a window so that Mrs. Pierce might view events. The ramshackle mess on the north-east corner including the Daveys' cottage, piggery, and stables was demolished. In 1883 a gymnasium sub-committee was added to the P.G.C. and annual subscriptions for the fives and gym building introduced. In the first year 52 took them out for both facilities, and 46 for the gym only, bringing in £59 for repairs. The walls of the gym were covered with panelling, and the floor with a coating of asphalt. In 1887 coke burning stoves were introduced for heating. A shed was provided for a new bicycle club although the P.G.C. minuted that it 'must not be attached in any way to the gymnasium' which remained a fragile building.

The North field's condition remained a problem, not least because every move had to be approved by William Woodard, the custos. In February 1884 the P.G.C. had to write to him to remove the branch of a tree 'over the path in the north field'. A water cart was purchased. The mower was repaired, and rolling became a punishment exercise rather than a duty imposed on captains to carry out. A poem expressed the feeling of those now involved:

> Rolling, rolling
> Pulling, pushing, running, rolling
> All the golden afternoon.
> Others at the nets are bowling,
> And the sight is not consoling
> When you're sent for extra rolling
> On a sultry day in June.

Although the field was re-turfed in 1884, complaints continued about the playing surface, and it was not until the field was closed for a year to re-seed it and rid it of plantain that it emerged as one of the best mid-Sussex grounds. Lastly, Cooper set himself to end the shabby changing conditions with two sheds on the field, and the utmost disorder in Fleur de Lys bath where visiting teams fought sponge battles. Early in 1888 proposals were put forward by John Smith for a pavilion for which £140 had been saved from tuck shop profits. Alfred Layman (OJ) and one of Hurst's first county players—for Kent—proposed that debentures at a guinea each with five per cent interest should be issued, and a loan also at five per cent made by the Old Johnian Club. Layman, Almeric Seymour and Charles Whitbourn formed a committee to carry out these proposals which was the first time the Old Johnians had formally helped the College financially. The boys themselves collected £21 18s. 11d. and, because the economy was picking up, from 1889 the debentures were taken up and the building was financed for about £260.

The pavilion was designed by Frank Edwards (OJ) and completed in the Summer Term of 1888. It was a wooden building with an oak shingled roof. On the ground floor was a changing room and an equipment store, and on the upper storey a scorer's box at the wrong end, and first team changing facilities with lockers. There was a balcony in front, and this rustic edifice survived until 1921. At first only the first and second teams were allowed to use the building, paying an annual fee of 10s., but it was later thrown open to any team members for a subscription of 2s. 6d. By 1891 lunches and teas were being provided in the pavilion by an outside caterer. Soon the pavilion had 'gay beds and borders', and was 'well covered with creeper' so that the North field at last assumed the dignity of a proper public school games field, clearly visible of course to the neighbourhood.

Economy continued to apply to masters' salaries. Here, too, Cooper had a major task on hand to rebuild a united and well qualified, or at least enthusiastic common room, and once again it was a long haul to eventual success. In spite of a steady rise in numbers the total in the common room was 10 in 1881 and the same 10 years later, and during that time the number with Oxbridge degrees had only risen slightly from four to six. Edward Cooper's own salary had risen well with the completion of Star, which gave him capitations from 50 boys, and it reached £738 16s. 8d. by 1892. Masters' salaries had shown no such increase, having risen in 10 years from £1,430 10s. 10d. to £1,772 4s. although the accounts show that their commons— food, heat, laundry, infirmary treatment and so forth—cost the College another £190 9s. 1d. Although some probationers came back to teach, like Chamberlain and Nixon, the overwhelming numbers of masters were now appointed in the ordinary way. Cooper made no less than 45 appointments, and of course the majority of these were birds of passage. What mattered was the creation of a solid core of able, involved, and reasonably long-serving masters, and in spite of early problems Cooper succeeded in this aim.

At first it was hard to stop the rot. The much maligned Thomson departed to be headmaster of King's College, Taunton, and John Dayson went with him as bursar. J.H. Walker, the mathematics master, was forced to retire from ill health and, returning soon afterwards to watch his dormitory Fleur de Lys playing, collapsed and died in July 1882. In 1883 the Rev. J.H. Edmonds left to be headmaster of East Devon County School, and next year Charles Banks left to be head of Arnold House School. It was unfortunate, too, that among his early appointments Cooper lost three men to the Church after short periods at the school. The Rev. J.H. Bebbington (1882-88), the Rev. H.T. Lewis (1884-88), and the Rev. R.S. Weallan (1885-88) went into the ministry at Pevensey, Horley, and St John's, Leeds respectively, and Bebbington later became a canon of Chichester in 1914. In 1888 Henry Bell, chaplain since 1880, also left and, although nothing is known of his work, he was a popular chaplain given a good send-off by the boys who presented him with a writing desk.

The departures enabled Cooper to mould a new staff. In his first years he was particularly fortunate to secure the services of John Smith (OJ), who returned in 1883 and next year became second master and dormitory master of Shield. Enthusiastic, loyal, and young he had considerable impact on the revival of school spirit, and when he left was given a clock, barometer, and thermometer by the boys. In 1882 Cooper had secured the services of Rev. Henry Smithson Milner, a Cambridge senior mathematics optime, and he succeeded Smith as second master in 1888, transferring from Chevron to Shield at the start of the new year. Responsible for the Oxbridge mathematics successes while he was at the school and for officering a refounded corps, he left in 1894.

1888 was clearly the year when the main staff changes took place, which dictated the mood of the school over the next decade when it experienced its greatest success under Cooper. The Rev. William Back became chaplain in 1889 but left in 1892 to be chaplain at Lancing, where he and Lowe as Provost did a good deal of harm to the authority of the headmaster there. Bertie Bull (OJ) was history master and Red Cross dormitory master from 1888 to 1891, leaving for a career as army chaplain and mission priest, and as a best-selling religious writer. Arthur Moreton (OJ), at Hurst from 1890 to 1898, who became chaplain in 1894 and left to become a naval chaplain, was similarly a young man full of the patriotic and gamesmanship spirit now increasingly coming into public schools. Bull's successor was

11   Rev. Henry Woolsey, 1862-1926.

W. Manning Sproston, who left in 1894 to be second master of Ardingly. In 1888 George Farrant became Hurst's most important music master since Dayson, and remained to 1896. He was to found the orchestra.

Three more crucial appointments followed in 1889. Percy Henn was dormitory master of Chevron and chaplain from 1891. He went in 1895 to be the founding headmaster of Worksop College, and later headmaster of Guildford Grammar School in Perth, Western Australia. Charles 'Monkey' Marsh arrived in 1889 and stayed 10 years. He was science master, and dormitory master of Chevron, and among his contributions were founding a bicycle club, and creating cross-country as a sport based on the Clayton run. He left to be headmaster of Beverley Grammar School. Most important of all Henry Woolsey, who had taught at the College for two years from 1884-86 and left to obtain a degree at Trinity College, Dublin, returned in 1888 as dormitory master of Fleur de Lys, and remained until 1903. In 1894 he became second master, and transferred to Shield dormitory. Although a harsh user of the cane, Woolsey was deeply popular because he was completely involved in boy life. He was the outstanding common room character of the 1890s. He was involved with the choir, orchestra, and many Pop concerts. He was a cadet force officer, and briefly commanded the force. He edited 232 issues of the *Hurst Johnian*, brought the magazine into profit, and made it a magazine for Old Johnians with a circulation of over four hundred. He was in charge of the tuck shop, and it made handsome profits. He was chairman of the P.G.C. and himself played football and cricket. He was a modern languages master it seems almost in his spare time, and he also found time to become the poet of 1890s Hurst writing dozens of school-day poems of the kind so popular with the rise of school community spirit.

It is clear from the eight promotions to higher posts (nine if Woolsey's later headship of Ellesmere is included) that Cooper found the right men and was able to retain them for only a limited time. In a way this was inevitable; Hurst being their first post, they were bound to move on if they had any ambition. It was almost certainly true that the low salaries meant that married men like Marsh could not afford to stay. However, in spite of the fairly frequent changes Cooper had managed to provide the College with enthusiastic, young masters, and this was important for two reasons. It helped dissolve away the apathy and malaise of Awdry's time. It was necessary at a time when the shape of school life was changing, becoming more confined to bounds, more organised and competitive, and masters willing to give up their working lives to the College were required. Cooper said in 1887, 'we fail at Hurst in these present days to offer a sufficiently varied form of recreation to those who pass so much of their school life within our walls'.

Dormitory life was becoming more important as a part of school life, and during the 1880s dormitories began to keep what became house books, recording their matches and miscellaneous information about themselves. The Chevron book shows how dormitory prefects, or captains as they were now known, like W.B. Warde in 1884 or N.B. Warde in 1888, were highly regarded for their efforts in connection with 'the success of the dormitory'. When the dormitory scored only four points in the athletics competition the comment was inserted: 'it is to be hoped that the Chevron will not appear in such a position again'. Clearly the sports which had been contested on an individual basis were being contested on a dormitory basis, and this was true of a range of sports. During a match between Chevron and Fleur de Lys in 1882 'many of the onlookers were attracted away to observe the transit of Venus', but by the end of the decade a different spirit prevailed. In 1890 a magazine article said they had 'no sympathy with the effeminate protests of maudlin writers' against compulsion in sport. In the summer term cricket was made compulsory on ordinary school days and, in the P.G.C., Clement Bigge, the leading sportsman of the time, proposed and carried a motion that day boys should be attached to dormitories 'as regards games'. The same year a master like Woolsey could write 'attendance and the shouting at this term's matches have not been what they should. Every fellow should attend every match'.

There were other indications of this change to integrated and supervised school activities. At the start of Cooper's headship a member of the First XI could boast of a birds' egg collection of 63 species. By 1890 birds nesting was denounced as being in the 'spirit of wanton cruelty'. In Cooper's early days boys were still roaming freely over the countryside. They would walk to Stanmer Park near Brighton, for instance, to attend a military review. A walk by a group to Cowfold was described in the magazine as they 'plunged headlong over ploughed fields, plantations and ditches' until reaching a stream into which one of them fell. 'After this', the article continued, 'nothing of any consequence happened with the exception of one or two trifling casualties such as falling into ditches and being pursued by cows.' Official trips now replaced these forays. When the Natural History Society was revived in 1889, organised expeditions became common: in May 1890, for instance, junior members began to try to complete Frances Awdry's collection of pressed flowers. There was an annual choir trip supervised by the chaplain and music master. In 1887 they swam at Brighton, picnicked in Arundel Park, rowed on the Arun, and had tea at the *Black Rabbit Inn*. Charles Marsh's bicycle club formed in 1889 went further afield but under masters' supervision.

Articles in the school magazine called for more activities from boxing to chess, and masters came forward willing to run them. One article wanted more carpentry and music, and a sketching club so that 'the very corridors and cloisters might be bright with frescos', and another in February 1890 ranged over a miscellany of topics of interest to 'the patriotic Hurst Johnian' including 'greater care of school buildings and property', making compulsory games 'a reality', attending societies, and doing well in exams.

In March 1887 the Debating Society came to life again, voting by 13 to six against Home Rule for Ireland, and started on a long flourishing period of existence defeating motions on conscription, strikes, prize fighting, and introducing rugby, in spite of an impassioned plea by Clement Bigge about the latter, and supporting muzzling of dangerous dogs, and the man of action in life. Cooper helped to extend the society into a Debating and Literary Society. In 1889 he started the practice of reading the annual choice for the Shakespeare play, and gave one of his 'Hours with Dickens'. It was something of a coup that year to secure the author's son, Charles Dickens, to come and read from his works. The first library catalogue was compiled in 1887 and holiday reading was encouraged. Bertie Bull introduced the idea that boys leaving should make donations to the library. The *Hurst Johnian* had been run by a committee until Henry Woolsey took over in 1889. Together with Percy Henn he raised money for the publication of *Hurst Echoes* the following year with extracts from old magazines, and he made the new magazine a journal for the new school patriotism or *esprit de corps*.

During this period the magazine ceased to be full of reprinted articles and masters' contributions, and became a journal of record. Old Johnians were urged to take it, and in 1886 the first *O.J. News* appeared. Two years later *valetes* began. Also in 1888 a feature 'Our Schools' started to give details of other Woodard schools and Hurst's contributions to them, noting proudly how both Denstone and Ellesmere had OJ headmasters. In 1884 the first suggestion for a College register was made. Woolsey's first poem in the magazine entitled *Reverie* appeared in March 1886 to be followed by scores of others, and by similar contributions by the boys. That affection for buildings and the school, and interest in aspects of school life like the College donkey or the peacocks called forth poems from master and boy was a very strong indicator of a changing ethos in which loyalty to the school was starting to become almost a religion, and certainly a deeply felt emotional experience. The early poems were not good, as some examples show:

> In summer when the leaves are green,
> When buds are blown and blossoms ripe,
> Here often have little birds been seen
> Taking their matutinal pipe

> Knock a hole into the stomach of a drum!
> Throw your hat about and yell until you're dumb!
> Let a loud defiant note
> Gurgle out from up your throat,
> For the holidays—the holidays have come!
> Go and shriek and laugh and sing and leap and dance,
> Go and kiss each other as they do in France!

> When the gay and beaming tennis player seizes with avidity
> His guinea Demon racket,
> When he smites the ball across the net with unction and rapidity,
> When the haughty batsman sees the ball, becoming rather jocular,
> And boasts how hard he'll whack it,
> But the swift and bounding globule hits him smartly in the ocular—
> Then it's summer!

Fortunately as the 1890s passed with the help of Kipling's, Longfellow's and Whitman's style, the quality of this verse was to improve.

With masters and boys involved in a range of activities it was sometimes difficult to tell them apart, and late Victorian and even more so Edwardian school life was much more relaxed than concentration on the evidence of posed photographs might suggest. There was still no school uniform, and off-duty masters, probationers and sixth formers mixed very much as equals, sharing the same interests and view of the College. In 1882 Cooper restored the Popular Concerts held in Lowe's time near Shrove Tuesday, and William Pratt obliged with *Hark to the Rolling Drum*, and *Allegiance We Swear*. In 1883 a second concert on St Etheldreda Day enabled old and present boys to mix together, and it is clear that there were other such occasions during the school year, because the magazine remarked that 'musical evenings given in the upper

12   The hall stage in November 1880 (prepared for *Henry V*).

school two or three times a term seem to be greatly appreciated'. In 1890 Woolsey, Henn and Farrant combined to produce a sketch with music and words entitled *Rookery Revels*, which was given frequently and in which boys and masters acted. They also did so in the afterpieces that followed the annual play like *Slasher and Crasher* in 1892, or the *Area Belle* in 1889. Together they found delight in entertainment, like that provided by a conjuror, Alfred Capper, who in April 1885 'discovered a boy thought of by Mr. Woolsey, a pin hidden in the Hall, and certain spots touched by [Arthur] Moreton'.

The new enthusiasm affected the established school activities as well. With Cooper as producer and Woolsey as box office manager the Shakespeare play entered on a long period of successful productions behind the oil lamp footlights in hall each November. The play was such a well known local event that many turned up even if they did not have tickets, and a policeman was hired for 10s. for crowd control. Even so Woolsey lamented that people got on stage in the intervals leaving cake and orange peel about. The school continued to rely on Nathan for costumes and even scenery, although this was not always wise. In 1891 Lowe and Bishop Durnford were present for *Macbeth*, the scenery of which contained a steam yacht, and the following year the wigs did not arrive for the female rôles. Even Woolsey made mistakes, issuing two sets of identical tickets one year! Technically the plays remained the same, although the addition of a trap door in 1889 helped with the problem of getting actors on and off a stage with no wing entrances. A battery operated electric star made an appearance. The main change came in the music once George Farrant arrived in 1888, and before long the after-piece had gone and there was overture, incidental music, and postlude. There was some confusion as to what music was appropriate. Farrant began with the *Merchant of Venice* played to tunes by Handel and Sullivan including *H.M.S. Pinafore*, and in 1890 the play featured Handel's *Largo*, Sullivan's *Lost Chord*, and a selection from *The Gondoliers*. Farrant then began to write his own music for the play; a tradition carried on until Horace Hawkins's day in the 1930s with variable results.

The early 1880s were not a good time for school music. The ablest music master, F.J. Karn, soon left, and his replacement for a time, B.N. Cogswell, came in on a daily basis. However, concerts were held from time to time. Sullivan's music first appears at an inner quad concert in 1883, and in 1887 the 'bold and manly music' of Charles Stanford was heard when *The Revenge* was performed, described then as a 'novel and difficult piece'. Directly he arrived in February 1888 Farrant got together with Milner and Woolsey to create a school orchestra. It gave tentative backing to the Christmas sing-song in December that year, and in 1889 its first major work, Sterndale Bennett's *The May Queen*. The play orchestra had 18 players including four masters, and this rose to 25 the following year. In October that year Farrant produced a Sullivan concert on St Etheldreda Day, and was presented with a silver mounted ivory baton for his services to music in his first two years.

In the chapel the poor quality organ made matters more difficult. The early 1880s continued the service settings of Garrett, Steggall, Monk, Ebdon and Hopkins although Stainer in E made an appearance. Anthems included Handel's *Worthy is the Lamb*, Wesley's *Blessed be God and the Father*, and Mozart's *Out of the Deep*, although the most frequently heard composer was Mendelssohn. The 1880s were to see the start of a great English musical renaissance which was to include church music and oratorio, and towards the end of the decade Stanford's *Te Deum* and *Magnificat* and *Nunc Dimittis* made their appearance alongside Mendelssohn and Sullivan.

II

Clearly by the end of the 1880s Cooper and his largely new common room of masters had overcome the main difficulties facing the school on Awdry's departure. Numbers were up and so were school spirits. In doing this he had been greatly helped by a new approach to school life which was developing during these years and reached fruition by the end of the century. Lowe's Hurst had thrived partly because it was a pioneering adventure, struggling against opposition, to find a position for itself in the public school world, but primarily because it was an Anglican community. There was no doubt that the driving force was Woodard's scheme. Now that scheme was slowly coming to an end: the special school went in 1874, and the servitors in 1891, and Hurst was emerging as a public school in its own right adopting the methods and educational philosophies of other public schools. The College was becoming part of what Honey calls 'the public school community', and its way of life part of what Gathorne-Hardy calls 'the monolith'—a basic set of values leading to various features of school life common to public schools. Loyalty to the school, the concept of what was called *esprit de corps* and 'school patriotism' was growing steadily in the 1880s. By the end of the next decade Hurst behaved and looked like a 'typical' public school in much of its life, and the process was completed under the next two heads, Coombes and Tower.

To some extent growth of loyalty to the buildings and the spirit of the school was inevitable with the passing years. Whereas *Hurst Johnian* Number 300 passed without comment, the 400th edition of the magazine produced a series of historical articles. In February and August 1888 the first reminiscence articles appeared by 'Old 'un' followed by others including some by Lowe himself. The foundation of the Hurst Johnian Club in 1877 began to bear fruit as it developed under two secretaries of this period—Herbert Low (1880-91) and Almeric Seymour (1891-98). In June 1881 Lowe made the first appeal in the magazine for boys to become members. Next year there were 132 members and a third of them attended the annual dinner. Lowe, Awdry and Cooper attended these dinners frequently, and Cooper began to give an annual report on the state of the school in his after dinner speech to Old Johnians. The presence of old boys at matches and services, and information about them in the magazine after 1886 aroused interest in past history and present achievements, enhanced as Lowe's generation began to occupy prominent positions in public life. Old Johnians sent sons now as well as brothers. Old Johnians taught in the College. In 1882 the first Old Johnian Football Club was formed with Almeric Seymour and Arthur Shepherd as captain and vice-captain, and although this collapsed in 1887 when the captain that year, Thomas Higley, was killed in a train accident, it was a presage of future developments when Old Johnians set up sports clubs and a Masons' Lodge.

Continuing interest in the College and loyalty towards it began to take on a practical dimension, it will be recalled, in 1888 when Alfred Layman had proposed and then administered with other old boys the scheme to raise money for the pavilion. In January 1889 an important discussion took place at the annual meeting. John Holford, a pupil in 1852, proposed that club funds should be available to help the College with individual projects. A number present opposed this, but it was carried with strong speeches by Cooper and Thomson in favour. The first fruits of this decision was a grant of £20 towards the infirmary, and over the years much valuable help was to be given.

The best way to understand what this new school patriotism meant for those at the College is to look at an editorial in the *Hurst Johnian* and a sermon, both by John Smith, at Hurst from 1873 to 1880, who was dormitory and second master. He went on later to write a novel about schoolboy life called *Out of the Depths, a Schoolboy's Story of St Wilfrid's* (1901), and to contribute to *Boys' Own Paper*. 'The school patriot', he said, 'is he who loves his school, who identifies himself with it, who is jealous of its good name', and 'longs to see it more highly esteemed and powerful.' His practical suggestions were first of all to take part in school societies and to work hard, but above all 'a school of healthy, active bodies will be a school of healthier, more active minds than those joined to weak and flabby frames'. He urged boys to shun groaners and moaners in school life, and support 'the sunny hearted, contented enthusiast who makes the best of everything'.

Although his sermon included a passage in which he said 'the spirit of Hurst' was to be found 'not in the school room, nor in the field, but here in this glorious chapel', the gist of the whole sermon was the wider theme of loyalty to the school's good name. If loyalty to the school was the highest patriotism, anyone against the school was 'guilty of a disloyalty as grave as any the human heart can be guilty of', and which was the product of a 'miserable and hateful spirit'. He went on: 'there is no meanness of mind worse or lower than his who will sneer at and disparage his own school'. There was, he said, 'no recommendation of a School' which was 'so forceful and effective on the recommendation given by a boy who does well at his school'. Boys should do well at school not for their own sakes, but for others, and for the good name of the school.

He then linked this emotional, even sentimental, view of school life to a boy's friends. On the last day, he said, 'there surges through us a mighty wave of love for what we are leaving behind, and we walk through cloister, schoolroom and chapel for one more last look'. In the future 'the sight of a Johnian friend whom we knew at Hurst awakes a thrill of pleasurable excitement'. It was a confused message. The school was described as a mother, father, fatherland, clan, and religious community. Loyalty to it was pitched in terms of religion, the *genius loci* of the buildings, and personal friendship, but nevertheless the emotional point of Smith's words was plain enough: 'Hurst is our country ... we have loved, we love, and will love her for ever'. For close on a hundred years such views, differently interpreted, vociferously opposed, even ridiculed by opponents, were central to the concept of Hurst as a public school.

There are many indications in the 1880s that such views were gaining ground not just in editorials and sermons but among ordinary Old Johnians, and in the teaching profession. Cooper, Woolsey, Milner, Bull, Moreton, Farrant, Henn and others expressed support for the new ideas, and in their deep commitment to school activities tried to reflect this loyalty in their professional lives. Public schools developed art forms to express these views. There were public school stories and Hurst had two by Bertram Mitford and John Smith. There were poems, and Henry Woolsey was Hurst's Henry Newbolt. There were school songs. At musical evenings the Winchester Ode or *Dulce Domum* began to decline in performance, while the Harrow School songs, written by Edward Bowen and set to music by John Farmer and Eaton Faning, were frequently sung. In 1889 Percy Henn wrote the words, and George Farrant the music, for a Hurst song. Entitled *Carmen Seculare* it was first sung on 30 July 1889, and was followed by others.

13   The College orchestra, 1889.

The magazine was a key vehicle for the new ideas under Smith and then Woolsey. A series of articles on 'Loafers' (May 1885), 'Cowards and Cads' (November 1885), 'Cribs and Cribbing' (November 1886), and 'Chums' (December 1892) reflected the new spirit and how it was to influence everyday life for boys and the image of the typical public school person. With so many boys taking up careers in the Empire or the Services where similar bonds and loyalties were required, and where Hurst seemed very far away, the emotional pull was strong, as letters to the *Hurst Johnian* began to show. Writing from the shores of Lake Winnipeg an old boy said, 'I would give anything for a game at Hurst, even in the worst mud'; or from the war front in the Boer War, ' I am lying on a mountain six thousand feet high. For height it beats Danny, but for nothing else ...'. As early as 1888 Smith was able to quote the following letter which summarises so well the beliefs involved:

> Before me as I write hang the pictures of the College, and the First Eleven in which I was taken. I seem never tired of looking at the photograph of the old buildings with the chapel in the background—a present from Mrs Cooper. Outside the rain is pouring, and a Kaffir hut is just visible shewing a contrast to the picture before me.

One part of school life particularly susceptible to the idea of school patriotism was sport. Cooper's first task had been to restore discipline to the sports field, and indications are that this was done in the early 1880s. Instead of disorderly scenes and lack of support, the authority of captains was restored and a more professional approach adopted to practising and playing most of the school's sports. The football captain in 1882, F. Knyvett, was said to be 'firm and good', and had kept 'games going regularly day after day'. There was now 'far more spirit and interest in the game'. Similarly, the cricket captain, J. Horstead, in 1883 'has had very little, if any difficulty in getting his orders attended to', and the boys played 'more for the team and less for themselves'.

Compulsion to play and proper practice sessions were both essential if teams were to shed their casual 1870s approach, and some advances were made in both spheres. There were calls for 'orderly practice' in gymnastics. 'Some sort of preparation for sports is absolutely necessary', said the magazine, and in one article urged athletes not to visit the tuck shop, avoiding at all cost Turkish delight and raspberry nogado, go for practice runs, and use skipping ropes. It was, said one article, a choice between 'dumb bells or obscurity'. In cricket a professional, Millard, was appointed in 1880 for up to seven weeks, but by the end of the decade Rogers was employed for the whole season and, as we have already mentioned, compulsion was first tried for cricket in 1890. Although Woolsey disliked it, saying it failed, it was rapidly extended to other games. In 1891 the last mixed probationers, masters and boys team played, and from then on teams consisted entirely of boys: Woolsey hoped masters would now lend a hand with coaching.

Professor J.A. Mangin in recent years has written the definitive study of public school athleticism. It had many strands: compulsion for house and school teams, and then for all boys at sport in all terms, practices, both house and school, the extension of the number of games played, games facilities, and fixture lists, compulsory watching of house and school games, the elaboration of customs and uniforms, colours and awards, medals and trophies at house and school level, the involvement of masters supervising, training, and umpiring, half holidays and club dinners to celebrate success, the assertation of the captain's authority, and the elevation of captains and leading games players to the level of 'bloods', or 'kings' and 'wangs' as they were known at Hurst. Above all it placed emphasis on the all-round character capable of leadership and skill at games, with physical and social graces, and perhaps with good academic results as well, able to command as a sixth former and later in many roles in the services or running the Empire. It took many years for this ethos to develop, and at Hurst it reached its peak in the 1930s under Tower, but there is every indication of its gaining ground from the 1880s.

Competing, said a magazine article, was not for individual prizes: 'from such we can only turn away in disgust'. The object was 'the honour of showing what a determined spirit in a well-regulated body can do towards the attainment of speed and muscular development'. Christian virtues of modesty and selfless regard were applied to sport or, as another article put it, 'let everyone practice assiduously but discreetly. Let everyone be moderate and self-controlled in all things. Let everyone do his best, and let no-one be discouraged.' The schoolboy heroes of Cooper's Hurst were increasingly the sportsmen like the Wardes, Stuarts, Michel, Bigge, and Russell. James Leary (Chevron 1886-1890) is a good exemplar of the ideal of the time. Captain of football, and a university player in hockey, water-polo and swimming, Leary was also a classicist, who won Greek and Divinity prizes, and went to Keble College, Oxford. From there he went to Wells Theological College. Ordained at Cape Town, he began work for the colonial church at Claremont in Cape Colony, and ended life as Archdeacon of Pondoland. Soon after his arrival in South Africa the *Johannesburg Times* ran an article entitled 'Muscular Christianity' describing Leary: 'he is still a young man, almost boyish to look at with his clean shaven face, impressive in its open-ness and frankness. He is modesty itself, well built, and every inch the athlete.' The article was reprinted in the school magazine as an example to others. The new enthusiasm for games began in 1880. Cooper asked William Dovers (OJ) who was in the Navy to return to revitalise gymnastics, and allied activities. Fencing with foils, cutlass drill, boxing, single stick work, bayonet and sabre drill, use of the quarter-staff, Indian clubs and dumbbell work were all included in the new course. 'Its object', said Cooper, 'will be to supply the place of other advantages attached to some larger public schools such as rowing.' Public Assaults at Arms would show off the skills. Two took place in 1880, and a third early in 1881 with Dovers taking part gallantly with an injured finger. Much praise was given to boys like Charles Rendell for his boxing, or Thomas West for his weight lifting. The *Hurst Johnian* said, 'it is with fellows who take no exercise that schoolmasters and doctors have most trouble'. Unfortunately lack of resources curbed the new activity, and many years later an Old Johnian letter explained that fencers had no jackets, and there was so little money they could not afford to replace a broken Indian club or supply boxing gloves.

Economy affected the gym master's salary as well. Mr. Moss who had succeeded Alford and remained into the 1890s was made part-time, and his salary reduced from £66 to £16, and it only grew by £3 in 10 years. On Port Latin Day the traditional display using horizontal bars, rings, horse, parallel bars, and ropes continued but, after the gymnasium subscription was started and repairs carried out, there was a sudden rise in popularity in 1887. E.L. Hunt and C.F.E. Bigge were Hurst's first competitors at the Public Schools Gymnastics Competition at Aldershot, then in its fourth year. Their train was late and they had to hire an expensive hansom cab from the station only to come next to last in the competition. However, the point had been made, and Milner urged 'older fellows' to come forward. At the Port Latin display in 1888 E.L. Hunt and E.V. White were the winners although Clement Brigge 'startled spectators by the sensation drop'. For the first time pyramids and shapes of boys were formed. Bigge and White improved to twelfth at Aldershot next year, although sadly there was a decline in the sport for some years thereafter.

For most of the 1880s running remained on a voluntary basis with hare and hounds covering much ground. Seniors ran to West Meston via Ditchling, or Cuckfield via Hayward's Heath: as one report put it, 'the hares took a very pleasant run of about thirteen miles' followed by 30 runners. The magazine commented on the Sussex villagers in places like Poynings who turned out to stare at the runners. It was Charles Marsh's arrival in 1889 that started organised cross-country, and that year a senior run of 18 miles was undertaken by

35 boys led by James Leary and Clement Bigge, although in subsequent years the course was usually more like 12 or 14 miles. A junior course of six or seven miles was started at this time although on one occasion when they ran through a farmyard the farmer took them all to Burgess Hill police station.

In 1881 the P.G.C. decided that Awdry's placing of the annual sports day in Michaelmas Term was a mistake and restored a sports day in the Lent Term in 1882, although not on Port Latin Day as before. There was still a degree of amateurism about, with three-legged and sack races, and the strange mix of prizes. On one occasion, when a team led by Armstrong won the tug-of-war, the prize was a bushel of apples which he shouldered and carried off to great applause. But in 1885 the first list of school athletics records was published and an annual effort began to improve them. In 1886 a dormitory cup for athletics was awarded and was won by Chevron who scored 34 out of 34 possible points. Each house managed to win this cup at least once in its first ten years. In 1891 it was decided to standardise some of the events—the steeplechase was fixed at one mile, one thousand, one hundred yards, and the hurdles at one hundred and twenty yards with ten hurdles to jump. The leading athlete of the 1880s was Clement Bigge who, when he became *Victor Ludorum* in 1889, won nine events, and scored 38 out of 38 possible points, which was an all-time record.

In football the list of fixtures with other schools was slowly expanding and now included Brighton College, Cranleigh, and St John's, Leatherhead, but the majority of matches remained with club sides from Burgess Hill, Seaford, Lewes, Brighton and Horsham. Hurst was a member of the Sussex Football Association from 1882 to 1891, withdrawing in a dispute over fixture dates. In most seasons the problem was Hurst's lack of size and strength compared with teams often older than themselves. A match against Horsham Town in March 1883 played in a northerly wind and driving snow 'against a heavy team' was lost three-one. Brighton Rangers 'as usual brought a team far heavier than ours', remarked the magazine on another occasion. Playing larger schools also had this drawback. Lancing was unbeaten against Hurst from 1875 to 1892, and won matches by spectacular totals like 16-0 in 1880 or 10-1 in 1889, the last match being described as 'an hour and a half's agony' for Hurst.

During Cooper's first decade there were only three teams which won more games than they lost. Under E.T. Seymour in 1885-1886, who was 'a heavy and vigorous half-back' who 'maintains excellent discipline', a team including H.D. Ozzard, J.P. Orr, and F. Michell won seven, drew one, and lost only one match. The 1889-90 team captained by Clement Bigge contained considerable talent such as W.P. Dean, C.F. Russell, H.W. Keeling, R.H. Newman, and James Leary, but had a very variable season, causing Cooper to write to Bigge to 'see to the sportsmanship and conduct of the team' which perhaps took its cue from the captain, who, while putting 'in some clinking good shots', was 'a trifle too rough' in tackling. The team won nine and lost six matches, including a victory over Burgess Hill 10-0 in 'snow, mud, wind and pelting rain'. In 1890-91 with R.H. Newman as captain, a team including William Dean, Thomas G. Le Mesurier, L.H. Nixon, A.C. Shippam, B.C. Rooke, and C.A. Waller won six out of its 10 matches.

Cricket clearly received more attention and encouragement than any other sport: better field maintenance, a new pavilion, a professional coach now full time, and compulsory practice have all been noticed. On 9 June 1882 Hurst played its first match with M.C.C. and Ground, a touring side, and managed a draw. J. Horstead in 1883, and even more so W.B. Warde in 1884, fully established the captain's authority on matters like bowling order and fielding positions, but it was not until the late 1880s that Hurst cricket first began to be impressive. This may in part have been due to the slow start of junior teams and coaching, because during the decade there are references to Under 14s, 13s, and even 12s playing long vanished local schools like the Ditchling prep school. The first junior fixture with Ardingly, for instance, took place in 1882, and after some years of disciplined experience and practice better senior teams appeared. By 1891 the Second XI was able to win four out of five matches.

The First XI's run of better seasons started in 1887 when they won half their 12 fixtures. The XIs of 1889 and 1890 captained by A.F. Nepean and B.F. Smith won eight out of 11, and six out of 13 matches, six boys being members of both teams. When this happened it took time to establish another team of sufficient age—1891 saw seven out of nine matches lost, and this was very much the pattern well into the next century: a small consistent group of players securing a short burst of success, and then a fallow period. The great matches of the 1889 and 1890 seasons were victory over Denstone on the occasion of the first visit from that school in 1889, and over Lancing by 79 runs in 1890, when in a fine display of the new school patriotism boys and masters turned out into the lane to receive the team back, and they were carried in shoulder high. In 1889 Nepean added to school centuries with one of 102. H.W. Keeling was the outstanding bowler, taking 8 for 8 in the Denstone match, and 6 for 22 in the Lancing one while Clement Bigge was excellent as a fielder (taking 12 catches in 1889), and as wicket keeper in 1890 with eight stumpings and five catches to his credit. With improved field conditions higher scores at last became possible, and in 1890 Bigge's 354 and B.F. Smith's 232 seasonal totals were impressive by the standards of the days. It was fitting perhaps that in so good a season umpires first appeared with white coats to add further to the traditional picture of North field—although whites for players had yet to come.

While there is no doubt that the growth of dormitory, team and school patriotism, a form of secular religious worship in a way, was the most important development of Cooper's years, Hurst's purpose and position as an Anglican foundation was still very much to the fore, although slowly beginning to decline. Of those leaving between 1886 and 1896 at least thirty were ordained, and 1899 seems to be the first year when none of the careers listed in the register was in any way involved with religion. Those educated under Lowe and Awdry were rising now in the career structure of the Church both at home and in the Empire, and some former Hurst Johnians were national names in various spheres of religious activity. Arthur Greaves, canon of Peterborough, archdeacon of Oakham and then Stowe, and precentor of Lincoln ended as suffragan bishop of Grantham, and Walter Adams, fellow of Durham University, and later Bishop of Cariboo became Metropolitan of Canada. Both these appointments were in the future, but there were already Hurst Johnians in many cathedral establishments.

George Daniell, chaplain of Alleyn's School, was diocesan secretary to Rochester, and canon and chancellor of Southwark Cathedral. Leigh Nixon, later chairman of the governors for many years, was canon and precentor of Westminster Abbey, and a priest in ordinary to George V. W.E. Drinkwater became prebend of Lichfield, George Osborne, canon of Sheffield, and Oliver Churchyard, chaplain of Bradfield and then Dulwich, and canon of Newcastle. Edward Cooper's son, Wilfrid, was chaplain to the bishop of Birmingham, and to the famous Bishop of Oxford, Charles Gore, becoming a canon of Christ Church, Oxford, and rural dean of Newbury. Abroad Amos Knell was rural dean, and Thomas Fancourt, archdeacon of Wellington Cathedral in New Zealand, Spencer Weigall, rural dean of Basutoland and then Grahamstown, and archdeacon of Bloemfontein, while he was succeeded as rural dean of Grahamstown by Walter White. James Leary became, as we saw, archdeacon of Pondoland. So there was no doubt that Woodard's plan for middle-class boys to rise to positions of influence in the Church had succeeded, and the careers of those concerned were detailed in the school magazine. Chichester and Ely Theological Colleges in particular were well-stocked with Hurst Johnians in the last quarter of the century.

At first sight it might be thought that enthusiasm for the missionary movement continued unabated as well. Certainly the *Hurst Johnian* continued its reprints of missionary magazine articles. During the 1880s there were articles on missions in Melanesia, Burma, India, orphans in Madras, famine relief in China, the building of schools and care for Indian orphans in Dakota and Minnesota, missions to Labrador and the Eskimos of Athabasca. In Canada, William Nicolls was priest at Moose Jaw and Medicine Hat, and George Ditcham at Fraser River. Nicolls wrote to the *Hurst Johnian* in 1888 saying his pictures of Hurst created great wonder among his parishioners who were mainly railway workers on the C.P.R. and Sioux Indians. He wanted £160 to build a church and the College subscribed £10 10s. Those serving the Church continued to die. Frederick Critchley, curate at St George's, Georgetown, British Guiana, died in 1883, and even years later the magazine would report Frank Gothard, vicar of St Peter's, Broken Hill, N.S.W. dying at 23 from years of overwork and typhoid, and Charles Zachary, aged 29, dying at Tinvelley in India the following year.

In Africa the clergy and missioners working for the U.M.C.A. were joined by the C.M.S. effort in East Africa. The missions were small. In 1893 there were 24 European and five black clergy in Central Africa, and 25 European and eight black clergy in East Africa, and about eight thousand Africans had been baptised. The Rev. W.H. Penny, who had been with Bishop Steere when he died in Africa, preached on Stir Up Sunday in 1883 urging boys to be missionaries, and those prominent in African work, including the Rev. L.H. Frere, Bishop Smythies, and Archdeacon Chauncey Maples, all visited Hurst. Among the most interesting visitors was the Rev. James Hannington, whose family owned the land to the south of the College, and who had ministered for a time in the small chapel of St George's in the village. He preached at Hurst in April 1884 before going next year to be the first Anglican Bishop in Uganda. Two letters from him were sent to the *Hurst Johnian* before he was martyred in July 1885.

But in fact interest in missions was changing and declining in the 1880s, and would die away greatly in the next decade. There was a swing towards teaching rather than preaching to the natives. Arthur Marsh was head of St Paul's, and second master of Queen's College in Hong Kong. J.F. Lane was head of Iolani College, Honolulu, and after he died young in 1899 was succeeded by another Old Johnian, Frank Fitz, the following year. Frederick Greenfield became head of Dundee School in Natal, and George Ditcham of the Indian Boys School at Lytton in British Columbia. The *Hurst Johnian* began to describe missionary work less in terms of conversions and saintly enterprise, and more in terms of civilising the heathen, and deeds of valour to help the Empire.

A good example of the changing attitude can be found in the magazine during 1887 describing a battle with Arab slave traders off Pemba when a ship with nine crew, commanded by Lieutenant Fegan, rescued 52 blacks in a struggle in which all the crew were injured. Medical aid took 11 days to reach them, and a young sailor whose thigh bone had been smashed survived the operation by only three days. The magazine comment was nicely balanced between Anglicanism and Imperialism: 'we do trust that there on that lonely island, far away from dear old England, the poor boy realised that God drew near him' after they fought 'true to the traditions of the British Navy'. Next year the Rev. L.H. Frere came to Stir Up Sunday, and 'kindly displayed in the Upper Schoolroom a most interesting collection of native implements and weapons among them being the slave yoke used to secure the gangs of slaves', and the collection raised £3 1s. 8d. for his mission work.

Although Woolsey as magazine editor put his weight behind such work, saying he hoped Stir Up Sunday would be followed by the 'accession of Hurst Johnians to the ranks of those who have furnished no small number of names to the roll of martyrs', in reality interest was declining. It was noted in 1886 that 'the part of the *Johnian* that is least read is the Mission Paper', and in 1891 a special article 'Why Do We Have It?' was put in to explain the papers. Two years later in March 1893 the last appeared, and it is significant that just under a year later in February 1894 Letter from Mashonaland had a very different tone describing blacks as 'awfully good servants', discussing Maxim guns, and the decision of the author to be a police-man in the Gold Coast. During the next few years Imperialism came to dominate the maga-zine's view of the world.

Hurst remained a staunchly Anglican school, and was drawn in to renewed national conflict over ceremonial and ritual in churches caused by the Public Worship Regulation Act of 1874. Passed by an unholy alliance of Archbishop Tait and Disraeli, this Act provided for prosecution of those who were said to have broken the laws defining what was and was not allowed in church: disputes raged over everything from cassocks to candles on altars, from eastwards facing, to statues of the Virgin Mary. Between 1877 and 1887 five clergy were imprisoned, and the one sent to prison for the longest was the Rev. Sydney Green, Vicar of Miles Platting in Manchester, who was in Lancaster Castle for 19 months. The bishop responsible was Fraser of Manchester whom Woodard disliked among other things for his lukewarm support for a Woodard school in Lancashire. Woodard was, of course, a canon of Manchester Cathedral, and battle was joined. Green's curate was Harry Cowgill (OJ), and Hurst gave him every support. He spoke to the Port Latin Guild, visited Hurst in 1887 and 1898, was among the first contributors to the infirmary fund, and later sent his son to the school. When Bishop Edward King of Lincoln was cited before Archbishop Benson's consistory court on ritual charges in 1889, a special eucharist was celebrated at Hurst, and there was another in 1891 during his trial.

For the first few years of Cooper's headship the Port Latin and Minor Port Latin Guilds remained the focus of religious activity and discussion. One of Cooper's earliest interests was in the Church of England Purity Society in which several headmasters like Butler of Harrow were involved. It was concerned with the 'besetting sin of our boys', and 'secret acts' of an immoral nature in schools. In 1884 H.M.C. had a secret discussion of the matter, tracts were published giving advice, and regional committees were set up. Cooper was one of nine Sussex headmasters at the inaugural meeting at Brighton in October 1886.

But the real interest of Port Latin proceedings until the Guild disappeared in 1888 was the way it illustrated a new development in High Church activity, in which as a Woodard school Hurst soon became deeply involved. The Oxford Movement had developed into the High Church party in the Church of England, and much of its work had been concerned with the government of the Church, its bishops and clergy, its synods and convocations, and with ceremonial, liturgy, ritual, buildings and the intellectual life of the Church. Hurst was still caught up in this side of the movement. All Saints', Margaret Street, built with Beresford-Hope's money, was an outstanding High church: its rector Beardmore Compton preached at Hurst, and M.B. Miller (OJ) was a clergyman there. The danger for the Church lay in losing contact with the everyday life of poor town parishes. Both by the evangelical wing with the start of the Salvation Army, and by the Roman Catholic wing with their new churches in slum parishes, the Anglicans were being squeezed. So in the same year that General Bramwell Booth published *In Darkest England And The Way Out*, parodying interest in African heathendom when English cities were pagan enough (1889), there met at Keble College under Charles Gore and Edward Talbot the Christian Social Union.

Its purpose was to rally Anglican clergy and laity to the cause of social reform. The parish was to become a little welfare state: family life, domestic violence, drink, crime, prostitutes, lack of healthy exercise, illiteracy, Sabbath observance, a vast range of causes were to be taken on board by clergy, and at the same time it was hoped to reclaim the poor for the Church's services. In Brighton the movement had started with the Rev. John Wakeford in 1883, and he was welcomed to the Port Latin Guild twice, and spoke on St Etheldreda Day in 1889. The Second XI played at St Wilfrid's Workingmen's Club in 1883 and lost by six wickets. His presence at Hurst showed that the College was going to be involved in the new mission movement, and the school in fact contributed a number of important clergy and laymen to it.

In 1884 two important articles appeared in the *Hurst Johnian*. One was from the Rev. Edward Hewett (OJ) in charge of the Margaret Street Mission in Glasgow where he found 'terrible indifference and even hostility to the Church', and served as mission priest from 1882 to 1895. A second article praised the work of Charles Lowder in the East End, and particularly the Deptford Lay Mission. There several OJs were working, including F.J. Dickinson, running a Sunday school for 500 children who lived 'in the most abject scenes of misery'. In 1889 Edwin Layman (OJ) took charge of this mission. The Rev. C.H. Turner (OJ) was similarly involved at All Saints Church near the East India Docks. In Bristol the Rev. C.E. Burkitt (OJ), and the Rev. B. Maturin (OJ) ran the All Souls Mission, and there were several other examples of such involvement.

Among those who listened to the Rev. John Wakeford was a secretary of the Minor Port Latin Guild, Bertie Paul Bull (1864-1942), a boy and, as we have seen, master at Hurst. In 1891 he joined the mission movement working in Brighton, and then moved to help the famous Robert Dolling Mission at St Agatha's in Portsmouth. His later work as army chaplain will be discussed in the next chapter. Here it is important to outline his prominence as a national figure in the mission movement. In 1904 his *The Missioner's Handbook* came out, and was a best-seller. He wrote over thirty books, and the titles of some of them show the nature of the work: *Gambling Among Men*, 1908, *Marriage and Divorce*, 1924, and *A Man's Guide to Courtship and Marriage*, 1932. His 46 small pamphlets on various aspects of religion, called *Manuals for the Million*, and his *Preacher's Notebook*, containing sermons and sayings for every Sunday and saint's day, were also best-sellers.

In his last years Woodard had no reason to doubt that his original purpose in founding Hurst was being fulfilled in many fields of church activity: the range of Hurst Johnian careers are clear evidence of the breadth of Victorian horizons rather than the contrary which is often stressed, and of the commitment at the cost of income and prestige of many educated at the College to hard, and ill-rewarded church work in missions at home and abroad. Nathaniel Woodard last visited Hurst in 1886: thereafter he was failing rapidly, too old to attend the dedication of Denstone Chapel or the laying of Worksop's foundation stone. In 1887 the jubilee of the first school at Shoreham was celebrated at Hurst with an open air *Te Deum* sung in the inner quad, and a special tea. Unwisely, as it turned out, Edward Cooper published a letter in the *Hurst Johnian* in February 1891 about Hurst's Jubilee, which (rather oddly) he thought would be 50 years after the laying of the foundation stone. The letter stressed that the aim should be to complete the chapel. He listed 12 items, and even then did not include the rest of the stained glass windows. The estimated cost would be £7,000, which was of course completely beyond the College's means in the short term. He mentioned that Lowe would come to speak on Port Latin Day, but this did not happen.

On 24 April 1891 Woodard died at Martyn Lodge, Henfield. Port Latin was replaced by a solemn eucharist, and on 30 April Woodard was buried in the unfinished Lancing chapel when 'the wind beat bleakly round the chapel buttresses' according to the *Hurst Johnian* report. After early communion the Hurst contingent arrived at Shoreham in time to help line the route taken by the bier on a black hearse escorted by Lancing prefects as it made its way to the chapel. As Lancing had not returned from the holidays it fell to Farrant's Hurst choir to supply the music throughout. The fellows, including Cooper, processed from the Library to the strains of *Now the Labourers Task is O'er*. The Hurst choir provided the burial service with anthems by Purcell and Croft, and Lowe read the lesson. Woodard was buried in the crypt of the chapel.

There was no doubt that Lowe would be the new Provost. A letter went from the school captain, the Prefect of Hall, and the Senior Scholar of Hurst congratulating him, and Lowe replied, noting that chapel completion was in the air: 'I shall feel it a duty', he replied, 'to co-operate as far as justice to other claims allows me.' On 15 October he was installed as Provost, and 20 October he visited Hurst. Lowe was to be Provost until 1898, to continue active in school affairs until 1905, and to pay his last visit in 1907. Both Cooper and his successor Coombes in the new century were to find the venerable Lowe more of an incumbrance than a help. Keen though he was to launch the Completion Fund and bring it to fruition for the Jubilee, it was his fixed intention that the chapel should take precedence over all other uses for the money raised. As a result the chapel was not completed until 1914, or even 1930, it might be argued, while no important building was erected to accommodate new educational ideas, nor help to cope with a decline in numbers which, after Cooper's successful years in the 1890s, again began to menace the College's existence at the start of the new century.

SIX

FOR GOD AND OUR SOLDIERS
1891-1902

Edward Cooper's Later Years and the Boer War

The third lecture was given in Hall on 14 March 1896 by Mr Peatling on the subject of the Transvaal ... he had an excellent lantern which made us long to possess one of our own, and he gave us excellent views and an entertaining lecture ... we vented our patriotism very lustily indeed, we screamed at the German Emperor ... we cheered Cecil Rhodes ... then with cheers for Dr. Jim [Jameson] we dispersed.

The Hurst Johnian, 380/120-21, April 1896

Percy Clements (OJ) was captured, and Harry Shepherd (OJ) was killed in January 1896 when the Jameson Raid was defeated by the Boers

> Dimly the light of day on distant Danny is dying,
> Sweetly through bee-laden limes the bells of Hurst are resounding,
> Homeward the cawing rook his way is peacefully winging,
> While in the golden west now the sun sets in glory ...
> I am at peace and glad, as I see these things from my window,
> Over the masses of rosy may and golden laburnum.
> Joy in the Hurst summer term, and the beauty lavished around me,
> Bid me continually say with gratitude, ay, and devotion,
> Manifold are Thy works, the earth is full of Thy riches.
> Henry Woolsey, 'A June Evening at Hurst'

The Hurst Johnian, 343/100-101, July 1892

A club run took place on May 18th ... and having expended half an hour on mending an eleventh hour puncture, a start was made for Turner's Hill. Owing to stoppages en route for the aforesaid tyre two hours were occupied in getting nearly to Turner's Hill. It was then deemed expedient to [make a] run for Balcombe and Cuckfield at once, in which latter town tea at the hostelry of *The Talbot* refreshed the bodies, and the merry wit of one of the party, the minds of the Club. Home via Pond Leigh in good time. Distance thirty miles. The ride was uneventful but with roads good, and weather glorious it was very beautiful.

Bicycle Club *The Hurst Johnian*, 432/215-216, June 1901

Evening preparation was postponed till Monday, and in its stead a Patriotic Pop took place. The items were all received with the greatest enthusiasm, and vigorous agitation of many flags. 'Rule Britannia' by the headmaster had a tremendous reception.

The day the relief of Mafeking was announced *The Hurst Johnian*, 422/217, June 1900

The title of this chapter is that of a book written by Rev. Bertie Paul Bull (OJ) in 1904 about his experiences as chaplain to the 4th Cavalry Brigade during the Boer War.

The most important and interesting part of school life in Edward Cooper's last decade, the 1890s and the Boer War years, was the intensification of school 'patriotism' as it came to influence every aspect of College life. 'Every community', said Alec Waugh in *Public School Life*, 'must have a religion', and worship of dormitory, teams and games 'bloods', and the College's reputation overshadowed and eventually replaced Woodard's vision of Hurst as a middle grammar school at the nexus of a ladder of advancement, and even to a degree the centrality of Anglicanism in College life as far as many of the boys were concerned. While lip service had to be paid to Woodard's ideals, certainly as long as Lowe was Provost, the reality was that Hurst wished to be seen as typical of the public school community at large. The first substantial prospectus issued in 1899 described Hurst as 'a public school of the Woodard Foundation', but it is interesting to see that in the *Victoria County History of Sussex* published in 1907 it was stressed that 'all ideas of class [are] swept away', and that Hurst was 'a public school like all the rest'.

These years were the defining years for the extended use of the term 'public school' to cover not just the former great schools, but a large number of the 450 boys' secondary schools in England in the 1890s of which only seven were run by local authorities. The rest were endowed, proprietary, or private schools, and there was much dispute about which were and were not entitled to be called public schools. The Headmasters' Conference list in 1902 contained 104 schools, and Hurst was not among them. In 1906 H.M.C. was to draw up rules for membership including numbers in schools, numbers at university, and composition of governing bodies, and by none of these was Hurst justifiably called a public school. Whereas Lancing was one of the top 77 schools obtaining Oxbridge awards, Hurst had very few pupils there by the early 1900s. Although Hurst had started taking the Higher Certificate under Cooper it stopped doing so for six years under Coombes.

But there was no doubt that Hurst had been, even since Lowe's time, regarded as a public school. From 1898 to 1902 there appeared the *Public School Magazine* in which Hurst featured several times, and later in 1909 the College received an invitation to join the newly formed Public Schools Club. In 1977 John Honey's investigation of the problem of defining public schools was published, and interestingly showed that about one hundred and sixty schools were regarded as public schools by other schools; what counted was acceptance as part of the public school community. He divided the schools into groups by 'interaction', and by this he meant how far they were involved in public school events, or had activities regarded as essential to being a public school in the eyes of others, and remarked: 'the position achieved by Lancing, and, even more significantly by Hurstpierpoint, is noteworthy' because Woodard had seen them as catering for boys beyond the pale of the older public schools.

Honey found that if a school participated in certain events, played certain games, and was involved in certain activities it became a public school by common consent. In academic terms he referred to taking the Oxford and Cambridge local exams, which Hurst did from 1890, the Higher Certificate, in which Hurst's involvement was patchy, and basing entry on the Common Entrance Exam devised by H.M.C. in 1902 which Hurst adopted. The presence of Hurst Johnians at Oxbridge, and Sandhurst, and later at Dartmouth, played its part, but the main reason for Hurst's acceptance as a public school lay in the fields of corps and games activities. When the cadet corps was reformed Cooper wrote, 'it would be to the advantage of the school for the corps to join other public school corps in their annual field day, and to shoot for the public school challenge cup'.

As we shall see in more detail later, Hurst attended the Public Schools Corps Camp at Aldershot in 1892, and the Public Schools Field Day intermittently from 1898. The Ashburton

Shield had started at Bisley in 1861. Hurst established a Shooting Eight in 1896, and attended Bisley for the first time in 1897. Hurst attended the Public Schools Gymnastic Competition at Aldershot in 1889-90, and again after 1898, and also the Public Schools Athletics Championships held from 1898 to 1901. Fencing was taught, although Hurst did not attend the Public Schools Fencing Championships. From 1882 Hurst's First XI had played an MCC/Ground team each year, and her football XI played other public schools like Lancing. So it was parity of esteem that made Hurst a public school, and this remained true until the 1920s when Hurst became a H.M.C. school, and it explains why a later head like Tower was so desperate that Hurst should win at Bisley, take part in public school squash at the Queen's Club, and in public school cross-country and swimming events.

Hurst's integration into the public school community and its adoption of virtually every aspect of life in a 'typical' public school was certainly Cooper's, and even more so Coombes' and Tower's wish, and it was the way forward not only in educational-theoretical terms, but in guaranteeing new clients and a rise in numbers. Unfortunately, Cooper's years showed that the transition from High Church, middle-class Woodard school to a public school like all the rest was not going to be easy. As late as 1898 Cooper identified the old 'Puseyite' criticism as still playing a part in deterring parents. What he could not say was that Edward Lowe, Provost from 1891 to 1898, was the main cause of a fresh decline in school numbers which set in during 1897, and threatened to extinguish the College altogether in the early 1900s. It was no coincidence that Lancing similarly suffered a serious fall in numbers in the 1890s, and although Cooper's age and lack of grip, and defects in the Lancing head, were a little to blame, the main reason was that Lowe was unwilling to accept the change to the kind of public school Hurst needed to become. Speaking to the Old Johnians in 1900 he said: 'let them not forget that they were one of a Corporation'.

Competition from the restored and new endowed grammar schools continued, and in 1902 an Education Act began the state system of secondary education, many of the grammar schools taking advantage of partial integration with the local education authorities in return for funding so that, for example, Chatham House, a private school, became a state grammar school in 1909 serving the Thanet area. The competition stressed academic matters, and provision of public school facilities and training whether it was boxing and swimming or prefects and Oxbridge entry. Lowe was faithful to the Anglican and middle-class appeal of 50 years before, and for this reason although outwardly Cooper's Hurst was a happy, thriving school it was also losing numbers, and unable to provide facilities because Lowe insisted that the Completion Fund and the Jubilee Appeal should both go to completing the chapel. As we shall see, this was not only a financial task beyond a school with less than 160 boys, but drained away money from essential building. No building of any importance to the academic progress of the College was built under Cooper or Coombes. Cooper built a Hurst which had the devotion and pride of its Old Johnians and pupils, but one which had a divided purpose: to carry on as a specifically Woodard school in educational terms, or be a typical public school of its time.

'I am sure', said Cooper in November 1895, 'that love for the School is as strong now as it has ever been', and there is plenty of evidence that the mood captured by John Smith in his 1888 sermon was strengthening in Cooper's last years, and indeed remained powerful for a hundred years or so. It produced absurdities like two editions of the magazine full of poems about the sad death of the College donkey, and it produced a sense of companionship and loyalty which was to the school's advantage. Two examples will illustrate it. Henry Keeling, who had entered in 1885, and left to be, among other things, a county cricket player for Kent, died aged only 25 in 1898. Hurst Johnians were concerned enough not only to have a

14   The Cadet Force in 1901. The
Commander, the Hon. Lieutenant Henry
Woolsey, is seated in the centre of the
picture. On the far right, same row, is
Sergeant Copp.

Notice the black boy in the back row.
He was Christopher Ordahl Fayé, a Zulu
at the College from 1901 to 1904 who later
became a Lutheran minister at Eshowe.

memorial brass erected in chapel, but to subscribe £43 2s. for a memorial fountain with six
cups erected by the pavilion in 1900. Edward Shears had come to Hurst in 1892 'weak and
ailing', but had forced himself to be a top sportsman and became school captain. He was 'a
model among captains of school', and was always present at early eucharists as well as being
an outstanding runner, and winner of the Fives Cup in 1900. He had, as we shall see, disciplinary problems, but won through in the end. He left to train for the ministry, but died early
the next year in 1901. There was a genuine outpouring of grief in the magazine for 'Boo' Shears
and £15 was raised for a local memorial. To be a Hurst Johnian was now to be the member
of a closely-knit community. By 1900, 240 Old Johnians took the magazine, and 100 put down
for the Dinner that year, even if illness and the war cut the number to ninety-one.

It was no bad thing if school life was seen with more than a practical eye, and if the poetry
which flooded the magazine for thirty years or more was not of the highest quality of verse
it did pay tribute to qualities of loyalty and respect for the traditions of a particular school:

> But how can I sing tonight, boys,
> With a heart so full of woe;
> For look, when the morning light, boys,
> Dawns on us, I must go,
> Go from the place that has known me,
> All thro' the days of youth,
> Go from the friends that own me,
> Fellow and friend in truth.

II

As the 1890s advanced so did an increasingly bombastic and strident nationalism as Britain
became the world's greatest power, and created the Empire covering a quarter of the land
surface of the globe on which the sun never set. Imperialism and militarism were in the air in
politics, and in public schools, and the politics of both boys and masters began to take on a
conservative tone which eventually became second nature for most people in the College until
the 'revolution' period of the 1960s and 1970s. In 1895 the Debating Society discussed a
motion of no confidence in the last of Gladstone's Liberal governments, and carried it by 12
to nine votes. There was a 'mock' election the mood of which was summarised by a poster
on the Upper Third classroom door, 'No Liberals allowed in the rooms or quadrangles'. In
March 1899 the Debating Society voted by 12 to four that the Liberal Party 'has ceased to be
of importance'. It was perhaps a little unfortunate that Hurst's first member of Parliament in
1900 was J.G. Shipman, elected in the radical town of Northampton (seat of Bradlaugh and
Labouchère) although he was a Liberal Imperialist backing the Boer War then in progress.

Gladstone, according to the *Hurst Johnian*, incurred much odium because in 1893 he had
refused to declare a public holiday for George, Duke of York's marriage to Mary of Teck. Both
College and village took a holiday, though, on 6 July and the magazine described the boys
visiting the Chinese gardens at Burgess Hill. The school declared a half holiday for the birth
of their son—the future Edward VIII—the following year. When the Diamond Jubilee was
celebrated in June 1897 Arthur Moreton, the chaplain, was driven to write most abominable
verse in the magazine like:

> Look on her, as she rides in regal fashion,
> Centre and idol of this mighty throng.
> Victoria, hear the cries of loyal passion
> From the great people thou hast ruled so long!

Wilfrid Cooper, the school captain, sent a loyal address to the Queen. Cooper himself used a favourite Anglican text from the days of the Stuarts, 'Fear God, and honour the King' for his sermon before the public holiday. In the evening a torchlight procession made its way to Wolstonbury Hill where a beacon was lit. Fifty-five boys went to attend a review of 4,000 cadets in Windsor Great Park, and saw her drive past in an open carriage under her parasol, and watch them through a lorgnette as they marched past. When Victoria died the magazine appeared with a black border, and on the day of her funeral—2 February 1901— a requiem service was held in a chapel heavily decorated in black crepe. The choir entered singing *When our heads are bowed with woe*, and Cooper himself sang the responses. At midday the school returned to chapel where Cooper read the lesson, and Chopin's *Funeral March* was played.

On 20 February 1901 the Debating Society voted England has reached the zenith of her power. In the library *Boys' Own Paper* was taken, and it was noted with pride that John Smith (OJ) had an article in it. Books given by boys leaving show that everyday reading was now far removed from religious works. G.A. Henty was by far the most popular author. When Cosmo Blount left in 1897 his library gifts were *In Savage Africa* and *Sturdy and Strong*. Even Louisa Cooper donated *Fix Bayonets*, and *With Buller in Natal* although a copy of the latter had already been placed there by the Copemans. J.G. Poole donated five Hentys. Kipling's poetry first appeared in the magazine in 1893, and many of his poems were set to music and enthusiastically sung at Pop concerts. Sullivan set *The Absent Minded Beggar* to music which received two performances in its first week in December 1899. C. Murray Rumsey (OJ) scored a popular hit with *The Lord Mayor's Own*, commemorating the City Imperial Volunteers going to South Africa.

A patriotic prologue was added to *Twelfth Night* in 1899, and *Henry V* deliberately chosen in 1900 to suit the 'military temper of the times'. Cooper frequently read speeches from the play. The termly Pop concerts contained increasing numbers of patriotic songs. That held to celebrate the Coopers' silver wedding in 1899 included J.P. Freemantle, a sporting blood, and future school captain, singing *Soldiers of the Queen*, and H.M. Parham who had just arrived as a master 'evoked great enthusiasm' with *When Britain Really Ruled* to which an anti-Boer verse was added. Moreton's verse grew steadily worse:

> Warriors in red as ye are, well proven in many a fight;
> To whom is entrusted the power of the Empire, and placed in your hands,
> Stern is your tale, silent watch, swift marches by night;
> Fierce charge, and dark ambuscade, and fightings in many lands,
> Ye to the ends of the earth have carried the flag, and fought;
> That never the Flag might be lost in the fray, nor droop in defeat ...
> Ye who have built up the Empire with toil and with pain,
> And with your bones a foundation have laid for it sure;
> Failing, and falling at times, but only to conquer again;
> Giving your lives for a Purpose that shall endure!

There can be no doubt from studying Hurst's history under Cooper, during the Boer War, and indeed in Edwardian times when the mood remained imperialist, that the middle classes were as influenced as anyone else by imperialism, contrary to the views of some historians.

About the link between public school training, of the kind provided by Hurst and other schools, and the Empire there is no doubt. Every historian like Mack, Bamford, Honey and Mangin has stressed how the school, as regiment, with its colours and flag, ordered and regulated, with its emphasis on fitness, sport, and worship of athletic heroes; and on loyalty to the house, team and school; rather than on individual rights; its toughness of régime, and emphasis on conformity, produced the necessary human material to make an empire work. 'The life of a planter', said one OJ in the magazine, 'is a very ordinary one; it is based on routine like school life.' Of the total of 4,000 boys who entered the College to 1899 one eighth, and this is likely to be an underestimate for lack of information, emigrated. Some went to North and South America, but the majority went to Canada, Australia, New Zealand, South Africa, India, and Ceylon. Then from the 1880s the tropical colonies began to attract more. About a quarter of those between 1882 and 1908 went there, mainly to South East Asia and West Africa. The Rhodesias were added to South Africa as a popular destination. Instead of missionary deeds it was the work of engineers, ranchers, planters, miners, police-men, soldiers, and politicians in the Empire that dominated OJ News and filled the pages of the school magazine. If they were not all as versatile as Cyril Burkitt (Hurst 1891-93) who was a lawyer's clerk, painter, tinsmith, blacksmith, fruit farmer, cowboy, store keeper in Texas, sugar planter, engineer, goldminer, navvy, drover, sheep shearer, member of Royal Australian Artillery in the Boer War, university student, dentist, and manager of a coconut plantation on the Solomon Islands, there was no doubt Hurst was turning out 'manly, well-adjusted, honourable boys' capable of taking positions of authority, or those requiring hard work, self-reliance, willpower, and physical strength.

Because of Hurst's social composition few of its members were likely to reach the higher échelons of the political and diplomatic services then monopolised by wealthy men from the leading 30 public schools, but in the colonies things were different. George Johnson, in Newfoundland, Francis Wilmot in Western Australia, and Robert Wilson in Queensland were among Hurst M.P.s. Martin Burrell, M.P. for Cariboo, held four ministerial posts in Canadian government from 1912 to 1920, and Lewis Byron, a Natal M.P., was a member of the Natal government. In Natal, as well, James Stuart was Assistant-Secretary for Native Affairs while in neighbouring Rhodesia his brother, Charles, was a Native Commissioner. In India, Sir James Orr and his brother Edward became members respectively of the Bombay and Madras legislative councils. James Orr was well described in the *Hurst Johnian* in his earlier Indian days when he 'worked up the football' as typical of the imperial type required: 'the natives bow down and worship him when he appears in the Hurst shirt, and to keep himself in training he plays polo, and takes 20 mile drives in his horse trap'. Sir Lancelot Hare was on the Governor-General's council and became Lieutenant-Governor of East Bengal.

Most Hurst Johnians found themselves in more mundane imperial rôles like the great athlete, Clement Bigge, who was a Ceylon tea planter and then a Canadian rancher. In Ceylon, W.S. Coombe noted five old boys in his immediate neighbourhood while a more lonely C.D. Martyn urged more of them to come out to Borneo. From time to time the *Hurst Johnian* published letters encouraging emigration—Warde wrote one as early as April 1887. There was one on ranch life in British Columbia in 1896, and C. Vernon May said that with a capital of £700 and proper training he had started fruit growing in British Columbia which was now 'his rôle in the expansion of His Majesty's realm'. The Immigration League of Australia sent material to the magazine. M.P. Hughes wrote that with a capital of £500 he had bought a half share in a pineapple and banana farm near Brisbane. Among others in Canada were Wallace Goldring, fruit farming in Ontario, and George Goodall, ranching in Alberta and, in Australia, Hansard Yockney, a sheep farmer, and Sydney Hodge, a sugar planter. Others went to America like Ambrose and Herbert Warde from Yalding in Kent who went to Florida for fruit farming. In South Africa Lancelot Tonkin was an ostrich farmer while others had more conventional holdings like Hurst Farm near Bulawayo run by David Williams, or Edward Sawyer, a forestry expert in Rhodesia.

Although Old Johnians were involved in law, banking, and business abroad, far more of them, perhaps because of their mathematical and scientific teaching at the school, were involved in mining, surveying, engineering, and public works. Their lives were as risky as those in the armed services. Francis Darby, after trying rubber planting in Perak, became a tin mine manager only to be drowned in a dam burst. Arthur Le Mesurier, former captain of cricket, died of yellow fever working as an engineer in Mexico at the age of twenty-three. Eustace Bird, working in Egypt as an engineer, died of typhoid aged only twenty-six. Cyril Michel, a mining engineer, was killed by a rock outcrop while travelling in a skip in Rhodesia. Again, the magazine contained letters urging boys to take up engineering as a career. Stanley Turrill, a mining engineer, wrote to explain how boys might enter the Royal School of Mines. Bernard Creasey became Director of Public Works in Ceylon, and Herbert Groves, after becoming Chief Engineer for the Burmese railways, ended as Governor of Mysore in India.

National patriotism, school patriotism, and the new emphasis on the athletic and physical side of life all came together in a school institution which had flourished in Lowe's day, and survived Awdry's time, although it is unclear if it has a continuous history under Cooper in the 1880s. Sergeant Callaghan who had presented a section competition cup had left, and in 1884 complaint was made that the cup was gathering dust in the library: the reply given was 'the numbers of the corps were too small' for competition. Trouble on the North-West frontier of India at Pendjeh in 1885 led to demands for the corps to be revitalised. At first Cooper said it would be too expensive, but in October 1886 it was announced that the corps 'disbanded some years ago' would be reconstituted. After War Office permission was granted the corps was attached to the Second Volunteer Battalion of the Royal Sussex Regiment, and reformed in September 1887.

Milner, the second master, was placed in command because he trained with K Company of the Volunteer regiment in the village, and this enabled the corps to use the range at Wellcombe Bottom. Sergeant Duffy of the Dublin Fusiliers, the first school sergeant to be appointed, was, however, not particularly successful. In 1894 Milner was succeeded by Marsh for five years, and then by H. Rowe, the new music master, who was also a local Volunteer, and in 1900-1901 went to serve in South Africa where he was decorated and reached the rank of captain. The same year Sergeant-Major Morgan, formerly of the Grenadier Guards, became the sergeant, and was greatly respected. When he left in 1899 to be succeeded by Sergeant Copp of the Royal Sussex Regiment. Morgan paraded in his full Guards uniform, and was presented with a silver watch. Woolsey took over command while Rowe was away although he had left the corps in 1894, and Rowe resumed command when he returned from South Africa.

The corps grew rapidly, and was by far the most popular school activity. It began with a dozen members, and by the time it was inspected in 1888 had 30 members. When H.J. Stafford was Colour-Sergeant in 1894 the corps became popular with the sixth form—Stafford himself later served in South Africa—and the Jameson Raid brought in six new members at once the following year. The corps was 45 strong in 1896, 59 strong in 1899, and 72 strong by 1902. Two of the old kettledrums were found and the band restored, and by 1899 it had six buglers, three side drums, and a bass drum. Sounding Retreat at night in the front quad began in 1897, and continued until Ronald Howard abruptly terminated the practice in 1945! Hurst and Eastbourne were the only Sussex public schools with corps until the Boer War, when Lancing and Brighton started them in 1900 with Hurst proudly giving advice on how to do so.

A basic uniform as before of glengarry cap, blue trousers, and scarlet tunic was issued, and to this were gradually added during the 1890s kit bags, belts and slings, and in 1893 a helmet like that worn in the army. Under the impact of the Boer War the helmet was replaced briefly by first a slouch hat, and then the Brodrick cap which lasted until the Great War. Weapons of any use were harder to come by. The rifles which arrived in time for the first inspection on 12 December 1887 were condemned Snider carbines to be replaced at first with Martini-Henrys which only fired blanks. It was not until 1897 that the corps was fully equipped with working rifles, and by 1902 these were standardised as Martini-Henry carbines.

The War Office did not provide any training courses for officers so there was close operation with the local Volunteers K Company. There was joint training with them at Sayers Common followed by beer, bread and cheese in the village hall. A typical evening route march in 1898 started at 6 p.m. passing 'a numerous throng of wondering civilians' in Burgess Hill on the way to Ditchling Common, and back to beer, bread and cheese at the *Burgess Hill Inn* before returning from their 12-mile march at 11.30 p.m. It is also interesting to notice that whereas beer was removed from the school menu in 1891 by Cooper, Milner invited the corps to a supper in Shield with beer, pies and sausages, and next year the corps attended chapel in uniform first as the corps supper became a new school tradition. When Woolsey injured his ankle training he was carried in by two members of the corps to the 1900 supper.

Corps training was relevant to the kind of small colonial war which any members joining the army would then have experienced, and every effort was made to ensure that training was modern and realistic. In 1888 they attended the Volunteer field day at Sheffield Park, and inspection in camp at Arundel Park which were both fixtures for many years. In 1896 Marsh provided a new cup for a section competition in manual firing, the section in attack, tent pegging, and other exercises. There was a corps band bugle competition. In 1900 examinations for N.C.O.s were started. A signalling section using semaphore flags began in 1894, and soon afterwards an ambulance section, who came to the rescue of P.A. Stuart when he collapsed in the 1895 steeplechase. A cyclists' section started in 1901. Sadly modernisation meant that in 1903 the red coat had to give way to khaki uniform.

Shooting began with borrowed K company rifles at Wellcombe Bottom, and the first class firing at targets was recorded on 6 October 1888. In 1894 Stanley Chapman was the first boy to qualify as a marksman while at camp at Aldershot, and as he was followed by others it became possible in 1896 to form a Shooting VIII. H.S. Claye (OJ), a captain in the Cheshire Volunteers, gave a cup for the highest individual marksman's score. On 19 May 1896 the first shooting match took place with Weymouth College, resulting in no score because the two teams used different methods of scoring! Shooting matches took place by means of exchanging results cards, and this enabled Hurst to shoot with a variety of schools including Cheltenham, Rossall, and Sherborne. On 14 July 1897 Hurst went to Bisley for the first time, and not surprisingly came last in the Ashburton although by 1900 they had worked up five places from the bottom. With suitable warnings about safety Cooper permitted a Morris Tube range on the North field, but it was not until Edwardian times that a full size range appeared.

As the shooting showed, the corps enabled Hurst to hold its own with more prominent schools, and Cooper had made no secret of his belief that the corps would benefit Hurst in this way. Much was made when the *Sporting and Dramatic News* in March 1900, for example, carried a picture of the Hurst corps at a Public School Field Day at Aldershot, and every effort was made to attend the annual camps and the less frequent field days held at Aldershot. Haileybury had started the camps in 1889, and in 1892 Hurst attended for the first time. That year there were only 14 schools and 590 cadets. By 1906 there were 35 schools and 2,500 cadets. Apart from 1900, when prevented by measles, Hurst attended every year. The basic pattern from 5.30 a.m. reveille, when they rose from their straw palliasses in their tents, to the evening entertainments, consisted of the usual military chores and training with mock battles and night operations, and a ceremonial or church parade. Although dampened occasionally by the rain as in 1895, the communal life with canteen-brewed tea, illicit smoking on Cove Common in early twilight, camp-fire sing-songs, and talks by lantern light in tents was greatly enjoyed. Sometimes, too, there were treats. In 1899 the Royal Sussex Regiment served them a special breakfast at tables set under the trees.

Not only was the routine and training to prove useful to many in the Boer War, but camp provided more. The boys watched real military manoeuvres with troops advancing in line, or regiments of cavalry galloping and charging. The troops were reviewed by military heroes like General Sir Redvers Buller. They were given talks on military campaigns—in 1894 on the Matabele Campaign, and in 1896 on Rorke's Drift. Other subjects were raised—temperance in 1894, for example, and Bertie Bull was the garrison church preacher in 1899. There were military bands to watch, and gymnastic displays including boxing, fencing, and tugs-of-war by regular troops, all good propaganda for the military life. Less successful were attempts at Aldershot field days. Hurst went in 1898, getting up at 5.45 a.m. on a bitterly cold March morning to catch the Aldershot train. They had no greatcoats or proper food, and snow fell. The mock battle was chaotic, and they shivered long in unheated railway carriages before returning at 7.50 p.m.

The growth of empire, and the almost constant little wars this involved, aroused interest in military careers, and the cadet force brought military matters into the very heart of school life. At Port Latin Day in 1886 Cooper was the first head to refer to military careers, and during the decade from then to 1896 about eighty of the listed careers of Hurst Johnians were in the armed services. In 1883 W.G.A. Bond was the first successful Sandhurst entrant for many years, followed by H.D. Ozzard (1886), M.F. Harding (1888) and others. The magazine began to take an interest in military careers, and carry reports on Victoria's little wars where those like Martin Copeman were 'slaying ferocious savages', in his case with the King's 4th African Rifles on the Sudan border. Clement Bigge's brother, Herbert Bigge, served in the Manipur Campaign in 1891, and in the early 1890s at least, events in India attracted more attention than those in Africa. In 1897 Bindon Blood's Malakand Expedition contained Major Herbert Wharry (OJ) on his staff, and John Henry (OJ) among the troops. Henry described the battlefield at Chakdam Fort, in a letter to the magazine, where 'the vultures and crows were too gorged to fly'. He omitted to mention five of the dead were English, and 2,000 of them Indians. Henry later commanded the First Welsh Brigade of the Royal Artillery in the First World War. The *Hurst Johnian* did, however, have to report the death of Captain Henry Ozzard in India in 1896.

Hurst's distinguished military men included Major-General William Hill, who served on the North-West frontier and was Inspector General of the Indian Volunteers, Major-General John Steevens who became Inspector and then Director-General of Ordnance and Supplies for the army in 1917, Major-General Charles Westmoreland who became commander of the Karachi Brigade in 1907, and Richard Davies, a major-general who commanded the 3rd New Zealand Contingent in the Boer War and the Sixth Infantry Brigade in the First World War. Among Hurst soldiers who reached the rank of lieutenant-colonel were John Henry, Samuel Thomson, Herbert Lawson, Robert Platt, Maynard Harding, Herbert Wharry, Samuel Bradley, Harry Stafford, and Travers Clarke. At the end of the 1890s interest switched to Southern Africa, and as we shall see towards the end of this chapter reached fever pitch during the Boer War when, in the magazine's words, 'the martial spirit that pervades this isle of Albion the blessed, is passing over the School'.

III

In Cooper's last years there can be no doubt that many school activities including academic work began to take second place in the minds of the majority of the boys, and not a few masters, too, to athletic and sporting achievement. Although neither Cooper nor Lowe would have agreed with Alec Waugh's view that 'the position of a school is decided by its performance on the field', it is clear that only a minority of boys left with any kind of academic qualification, and that those held in highest esteem were the 'bloods' whose *valetes* are simply a record of sporting achievement. The combination of school patriotism, admiration for the corps and military careers, respect for the manly virtues, and the need in prestige terms to compete in sporting and corps matters with other public schools focused attention on sport at Hurst as elsewhere in ways that would have deeply shocked Woodard. What would he have thought of a Harrow housemaster like Edward Bowen who said 'there lives more soul in honest play, believe me, than in half the hymn books', and at his house suppers had a toast to 'The Muscles' or sportsmen? It was no coincidence that Harrow songs, many with words by Bowen, were among the most popular items at Hurst Pop concerts, and never more so than when they were sung by the sporting heroes of the day as they were at the end of the summer term in 1900 with D.N. Milestone rendering *Giants*, and F.G. Freemantle *Forty Years On*.

In 1894 an attempt was made to start a similar body of songs for the school with *Play Up, Hurst*, but this did not succeed. One verse from the song, however, captures the mood of the times very well:

> Let's give them a cheer who have done so well
> And fought for the honour of Hurst,
> And then three more for the School we adore
> With a rousing chorus first.
> Play Up, Hurst!
> Play up, 'till the game is o'er!,
> Play 'till you can play no more,
> Play Up, Hurst, Play Up!

Sport was a matter now to be taken with the utmost seriousness, and to be organised down to the last detail. The Playground Committee came into its own with endless discussion of dress, colours, competition rules, conduct, membership of teams, and other aspects of sport. In 1897 the chairman had to use his casting vote four times such was the deadlock on the matters discussed. The composition of junior dormitory teams was first considered in 1893. Junior teams were to consist of those who were under 15 on the first day of the Michaelmas Term in 1897, and only in 1900 was it finally agreed that junior and senior dormitory matches should be played by means of the same competitive draw and rules for procedure. Cooper had to intervene twice in 1897 to curb the enthusiasm of the P.G.C. In April he insisted they reduced the First Eleven fixture list from 18 to 14 matches because the team was depriving 'boys not in the elevens of their fair share of school cricket'. In June he refused to allow daily drill to come under P.G.C. control: 'drill and gymnastics' he said will stay 'under my direct control for the moment'.

The P.G.C. was anxious to 'abandon all practices that are unsportsmanlike', and to impose a code of conduct. Rough charging was banned in football in 1894. In 1897 after a letter by 'Anti-Vulgarity' to the magazine about cat-calling at cricket matches a lengthy code of good cricketing behaviour was proposed. Boys were told to clap opponents' successes as much as their own, not to comment on poor fielding, dropped catches, or poor wicket keeping by the opponents, and not to go 'wild with enthusiasm' for their own side. Calling at individuals and shouting advice to the umpires was frowned on, and spectators were told 'don't ballyrag on the banks'. A determined effort was made to sort out rules. When Hurst met Lancing for cross country in 1896, for instance, it was necessary to decide the size of teams, and length of the course because Hurst wanted eight to run, and six to count on the Clayton 12-mile run, and Lancing wanted 15 to run and 10 to count on a course of five miles. Privileges were extended to sportsmen. All those with school colours were permitted free use of the pavilion, and exempted from any cricket duties whereas everyone else, including prefects, was to pay or do the duties. Rules of all sorts appeared—balls were not to be used on the path 'south of North field between the third opening and the little gate'. Prefectorial power increased to enforce these new conventions and rules.

And nowhere were there more rules than those concerning dress and kit. The sportsman was clad in a panoply of clothes off the field worthy of etiquette in a Hapsburg court, and kit on the field was minutely regulated, although photographs show that it took many years for the rules to be fully enforced. Athletics kit was standardised in 1894 with white jersey, black, blue or white knee length shorts, and a coloured arm band to identify a boy's dormitory. Cross-country kit was standardised two years later with black shorts, and a white vest with scarlet elbow bands. In 1896 Cooper asked for a fashion parade before the P.G.C. with a boy wearing various proposed blazers for cricket. That year caps, boater ribbons, and blazers for the First and Second XIs were fixed. The Firsts were to have a white cap with scarlet eagle, a scarlet boater ribbon with two white bands, and a white blazer with scarlet piping, eagle and buttons. Not surprisingly an Old Johnian wrote to ask: 'are you women at Hurst now that you must be changing your costumes and your customs?'

First XI football players were to wear black shorts, a white jersey, and red socks with a white stripe. From 1900 they were permitted to wear a red scarf, but they were forbidden to play with either belts or scarves on. First XI cricketers had emerged all in white by 1899 when the prospectus detailed their kit even down to white boots. Some latitude was allowed in the wearing of white slouch hats instead of caps, but in 1897 belts and handkerchiefs (cravats) were forbidden. Ties are not yet mentioned: the first sports tie seems to be for the Shooting VIII in 1902.

It was now made very plain that sport was an essential part of the school programme. From May 1892 the College agreed to provide a photographer for annual team photographs, and the first picture of a team appeared in the magazine two years later. Masters were now in charge of games. Charles Marsh was made Overseer of the Paperchases in 1895, and Edward Eckersley put in charge of swimming. In 1897 Sergeant Hiatt, formerly of the King's Own Scottish Borderers, was appointed to run boxing and the gymnastics. He was a noted gymnast, who won a silver medal at Paris in 1900, and 'the pocket Hercules', as he was known, was well liked. Compulsory runs started when he arrived and 'those who could not run are required to walk'. A compulsory gym test started in 1900. Hiatt was succeeded in turn by Sergeant Howell in 1905, and Sergeant-Instructor H.L.A. Dearing, but when he left in 1911 no further gym sergeants were appointed. Lastly, in 1901 Harry L. Johnson, who succeeded Woolsey as second master two years later, was appointed as the first master in charge of games. The school prospectus now stated: 'all boys go regularly by forms to the gymnasium for physical training', and 'regular exercise' is provided for 'all boys in the school according to size and age'.

While school numbers fell in Cooper's last years from 202 in 1897 to 132 in 1902, as we shall see later, the number of sports offered increased, and so did the number of teams, so there could be no doubt that sport was occupying more and more energy and time: among all the reasons for decline put forward, excessive concentration on sport was never mentioned although it will be suggested it did have an impact on academic results. By the end of Cooper's headship Hurst played the following sports: football, cricket, fives, gymnastics, athletics, steeple chase, hare and hounds, cross-country, boxing, fencing, swimming and shooting. Sporting heroes could well be involved in nearly all of them at both dormitory and school level, and in cadet force field days, marches, and training. No changes occurred in this programme until Tower became head in 1924, and he increased the number of sports by developing tennis, and adding hockey and squash!

Apart from the chapel the only buildings to receive any substantial attention in Cooper's last years were the gymnasium and swimming facilities. The same year as Sergeant Hiatt arrived the gymnasium was fully refurbished with a wooden floor, wall panels, gas lighting, a clock, and new equipment. All boys were required to do basic gymnastics, and for those new boys incapable of this a remedial class was set up. The basic exercises were those used then in the services, and survived at Hurst until the 1950s. About thirty boys took up gymnastics as a sport with a course involving 12 exercises on the ropes, bars, rings, and box. Dumbbells and Indian clubs were in use, and from December 1897 elaborate displays with the boys forming pyramids and other shapes were given. In 1898 a Gymnasium IV was selected by competition, and a new cap (scarlet with a white tassel) provided for them.

The same year an inter-dormitory gym competition started with the Shield Pair being the first winners. The Gaydon Cup for this was presented by the parents of A.G. Gaydon. During the year the Hurst IV went into training for Aldershot, and managed to win bronze medals in an Amateur Athletic Association gym meeting, but the first appearance at Aldershot in 1899 was disappointing. They came thirtieth, next to last—who were Lancing! During 1897 boxing was restarted and in June 1898 the P.G.C. agreed the rules for an inter-house boxing competition for which a Mr. J.L. Thomas presented medals for the various weights. An 18ft. ring was erected on North field near the pavilion, and the first competition was won by Edward Shears.

Swimming in the Ruckford stream was clearly unsuitable now for the era of organised sport. In December 1899 William Knowles, a distinguished Old Johnian county cricket player for Kent—he scored two centuries for them next year—proposed financing a pool in the same way as the pavilion. Debentures of a pound in value would be issued at four per cent interest, and a swimming pool fund set up in the school. Tuck shop profits would also go to the new pool. Permission was given in March, and work began in September 1900, fortunately coinciding with the introduction of mains drainage and water by the Rural District Council. The pool was opened in June 1901 although it was of the most primitive—unheated, with no changing or diving facilities. However, it was an improvement on a muddy stream, and was accompanied by detailed rules for swimming, including the wearing of trunks for the first time and the banning of Sunday swimming now they were close to the buildings. The total cost was £492 5s. 8d.

In 1894 the P.G.C. passed cross-country rules, and the Clayton Run was defined as an eight-mile course crossing the railway line a third of a mile north of Hassocks Gate Station, going south of the windmills past the chalkpit to Warren Farm, across the road near Hassocks Farm, and back down College Lane. Among other runs were those to Henfield, Ditchling, West Meston, and Poynings. An account of the Clayton Run in 1901 says that the hares took 66 minutes, and the winning runner, W. Whitmore-Searle, 61 minutes to complete the course. Thirty boys ran and 21 finished. In other races the number of finishers was considerably less— one to Albourne the same year started with 109 and ended with sixty-eight. Charles Marsh clearly brought the era of amateurism to an end, and other masters like Bassano, Rowe, and Eckersley also ran with the boys. In 1893 the first Old Johnian match took place in torrents of rain with a victory for the old boys. In 1894 junior teams and an inter-dormitory run started.

15   A group of boys outside the tuck shop, 1897. It was then situated north of the chapel.

16   The swimming pool as it was from 1901 to 1949. Note Herbert B.I. Pocock (with the pipe!) in the top left-hand corner.

This was on a 10-mile course to Albourne, Wolstonbury and the village, won the first time by Fleur de Lys. In 1896 the first inter-school fixture was held with Lancing who won then, and next year, when the full Clayton was run.

Amateurism vanished, too, from athletics in this period, although there were a few survivals like the race for College servants, and sack, and egg and spoon races, and as late as 1892 the 100-yard race turned out to be a 90-yard one due to mismeasuring. Sports Day in 1894, organised by Marsh and described as 'successful and well managed', seems to have been the first in which accurate records were taken for all events, and divided into junior and senior ones. That year three records were broken, and three inaccurate ones replaced by precise ones. In 1895 Gregory Nycobo was Hurst's first black athlete in the high jump and hurdles, and took part in his dormitory's, Star's, winning tug-of-war. By the end of those sports all but four of the original records standing in 1893 had been broken, and in 1900 Douglas Milestone broke the famous James Bulgin's 'throwing the cricket ball' record. By 1897 the sports were a well attended local event and were run with starters, time-keepers, handicappers, marksmen, stewards, judges, and referees. Among the leading athletes were Harold and Douglas Milestone, David Williams, later a Rhodesian farmer, *Victor Ludorum* in 1898 and 1899, and Ronald Turner, a future Cambridge football Blue, *Victor Ludorum* in 1902 and 1903. Douglas Milestone, *Victor* in 1900, won five events, and came second in three more.

Hurst was not lacking in fine players of football and cricket. By 1914 the school had produced 19 football, and 10 cricket county players, several Blues, and national team players, but the results of the First XIs in football and cricket were probably the most disappointing feature of school life in these years. The magazine was hard put to it year after year, having praised the potential of teams, to explain the poor results. The grounds were well prepared. Team captains had full authority. There was plenty of practice, and mass support from the rest of the school. Yet the overall figures show how badly the two main teams fared. Between 1891 and 1902 the Football XI won 73, drew 27, and lost 82 matches, and the Cricket XI won 37, drew 17, tied one, and lost 87 matches. Football did record three good seasons—1893-94 with 11 wins and three draws, 1897-98 with 10 wins and four draws, and 1899-1900 with eight wins and two draws, but in cricket the highest number of wins in a season was six in 1894, and in 1900 the total of victories was reduced to one.

The reasons for this situation were reasonably clear, and indeed they persisted for many years. Hurst was a small school with a small sixth form, and could not raise teams to compete with larger schools with older boys. This was made worse because the fixture lists contained a majority of club fixtures, and therefore of older and now better trained players. In 1897 the boys found the Royal Sussex Regiment 'of one size and hard as nails', and next year had a 'most unpleasant match' with them in which there was rough play and intimidation of the referee. Cricket did have outside coaches, but not every year, or even for the whole season, and G.H. Price who coached in 1900 commented on the lack of basic skills so that, for instance, 14 catches were missed that season. Neither game had any masters at this time who were themselves skilled players to supervise them. The matter of playing club sides was endlessly debated—in May 1899 for example—but cost of transport prevented lengthy journeys, and as far as football was concerned the situation became worse as other schools like Eastbourne College switched to rugby. Woolsey also argued in the magazine that there were too many fixtures, when four matches in a week brought the comment this was 'rather too much of a good thing'. But clearly the main problems were not in the hands of games players to solve, and so teams contained talented players without back up, or occasionally built up strength when boys were in them for two or even three years, but otherwise had to face many a disappointment. The bloods of the late 1890s, Harold and

Douglas Milestone, William and George Smith, and G.P. Freemantle were admired and featured at every Pop concert to thunderous applause, and did their best, but it was not until the time of Dingwall's headship in the 1940s that Hurst's major sports records became outstanding.

School life still had its rough edges. Francis Rumsey's memoirs referred to his tearful early weeks when he had days of 'constant fear' and 'days of misery'. He spoke of 'bullying' senior men, and Cooper made it plain that bullying was a caning offence. When Rumsey himself was sent to be caned by Woolsey: 'I nearly fainted. Woolsey's caning was notorious'. He described a typical fight held behind the gym in the presence of the school captain when Hubert Williams of Star, 'a proper bruiser', fought Philip Hargreaves, who had had him banned from the corps supper. Williams beat him up badly, and he was removed to the sanatorium. Rumsey complained too about the 'sweaty mutton' and salted beef or 'red elephant' as it was known, and 'woe betide the fellow who got the dregs—a sediment of scraps of paper in which the meat had been wrapped'. The Rumseys sent six boys to Red Cross, and C. Murray Rumsey was then engaged in giving annual concerts for the chapel fund, and little attention was paid to Francis's letters home when he returned from school 'looking so well'.

Most of the evidence suggests that school life was more comfortable and better organised, and that relations between masters and boys in everyday life were often close and friendly. Pride in the school led to the gradual appearance of school uniform although pictures of Cooper's and Coombe's Hurst show that full uniform did not come until after 1914. The school cap was introduced on 5 September 1890—black with white piping and a red eagle for seniors, black with red piping and a white eagle for juniors—although it was not compulsory wear. Boaters came in, and in 1895 a scarlet ribbon for Hurst ones was introduced. Several letters to the magazine asked for a blazer, and in the summer of 1901 a blue blazer with a white pocket eagle was introduced. Ties were not yet part of the uniform.

Cooper was now sufficiently popular and in control to relax the severe discipline of the past. When he left he said he believed 'the relations of masters and boys have been for the most part friendly ...'. He had little time, he said, 'for the master whose one aim when school hours were over, was to ... put the greatest possible distance between himself and the College'. He set the example, as we know, by his involvement in concerts, playing games, producing the play, and giving readings. In 1894 at an orchestral concert Cooper played the flute, Louisa, his wife, the piano, and his son, Wilfrid, the school captain, the violin. At the concert on the night the relief of Mafeking was announced Cooper sang *Rule Britannia* which had 'a tremendous reception', and in the last concert of his career he read from *David Copperfield*. His family, too, were very much part of school life. Audrey, his daughter, was given an etching and a volume of poetry by the boys on her 18th birthday by a school captain 'struggling with emotion', and she rewarded her swains with the song *When Love is Kind*. Next year, 1899, was the Cooper's silver wedding, and this was seen very much as a school occasion for which a half holiday was given. The Coopers received silver candlesticks from the masters, a silver bowl from Star, and a silver flower vase from the school. At the evening concert the Head read from *Pickwick*.

Throughout the 1890s Cooper was concerned to reduce the severity of punishment. After finding that prefects were taking a good run before using their canes he stopped prefects beating in September 1890. Instead a Cuts Book was used in which the offence, and the recommended number of cuts was entered, Cooper himself doing the caning. In September 1892 probationers when teaching were forbidden to cane, and in September 1894 the cane was restricted to dormitory masters. This led, inevitably, to the use of other punishments, but Cooper was not happy with them either. In a surviving fragment of his Headmaster's Book

17 The Bicycle Club in the early 1890s before they acquired safety bicycles.

he is seen taking constant action against over-zealous punishment. In 1894 he restricted the practice of 'standing out' in hall or the corridors to 15 minutes, and forbade holding arms outstretched. In 1896 he criticised over-long impositions that interfered with work, and in 1898 he told masters to punish less and reward more. He started a system of 'sending up for good' to him, saying exceptional work could earn a boy a half holiday. Due perhaps to old age as well, Cooper in his last years shrank from the need to cane. Rumsey described him with 'his left hand to his temple, and a worried look upon his face' as he gave three cuts 'very quickly and very lightly'.

Toward the end of the 1890s this lenient approach led to some kind of trouble involving the prefects and possibly the bloods, although no precise details survive. Edward Shears was School Captain and Prefect of Hall from 1898 to 1900 and, although an athlete through sheer persistence, he was clearly a religious and academic boy determined to carry out his job at whatever cost. His tragic early death in 1901, already noted, did not prevent Woolsey in the magazine commenting 'loveable he was not to everybody' and as a result 'he had much opposition to face'. Wilfrid Cooper had been captain from 1896 to 1898, and therefore none of the outstanding games players, the Milestones and Smiths, had occupied the top position. The bitterness created alarmed Cooper. He appointed F.G. Freemantle for the summer term of 1900 and then, highly unusually for a public school and uniquely in Hurst's case, appointed no school captain or prefect of hall: even the new prefects in 1900 were referred to as 'sub-

prefects' in the magazine and, when it came to public occasions, Cooper relied on Herbert Wadman, a probationer.

Certainly there is evidence that in Cooper's last four terms discipline was affected by this dispute. Boys did not perform their duties on the cricket field where dandelions and stones were to be found, and the First XI performance was among the worst ever seen, with pathetic fielding. In cross-country there were complaints that corners were cut in the inter-dormitory race, and paper ran out on one occasion with the hare and hounds. The corps was criticised for slovenly turn out, and the gym test was failed by many boys. The gymnastic display on Prize Day showed that several contestants 'were obviously not in very good training'. It is significant that among the new head's first acts were a restoration of prefects' power and appointment of a school captain. He also added detention for work—previously called Imposition School— to punishment drill for misdemeanours.

Woolsey, who had come in 1884, thought the quality of life had improved greatly under Cooper. The influenza scourge of the 1890s, particularly bad in 1895, the coldest winter of the century, measles in 1900, and mumps in 1901 were coped with well in the new sanatorium. There was only one death to record when the inappropriately named John Fitness, who came in September 1896 and was already 'ailing', died in November 1897. Hot pipes were extended to dormitories and classrooms with hot water, and, as we have seen, the gymnasium too acquired some heating. The school was connected to the local drains and sewers in 1900 and new toilets called 'courts' with enamel basins were built, a development mentioned not only in the magazine but also at the Old Johnian dinner next year, bringing to an end another long-term problem. In the dormitories a strip of carpet was placed down the middle, and rugs allowed by beds. Pictures appeared on the walls and honours boards were put up. Similarly in dormitories like Star which had a day room there were books and newspapers, a display cabinet for trophies, and more honours boards. In 1896 the walls of upper school received boards recording Oxbridge awards. In hall cutlery and crockery were provided, and in the dormitories metal replaced wooden bedsteads. In 1897 a school telephone was installed, and a line to the sanatorium was soon added.

There was another change in school life that Woolsey noticed. As yet it was not dramatic, but it was in reality the end of an isolated existence deep in the countryside. Woolsey sarcastically referred to the village as Pierpointville, as 'ruthless jerry builders' began to put up villas on the Wickham estate when it was sold, and to the 'semi-detached pride of Burgess Hill'. In November 1896 the boys stood at the *King's Head* at Sayers Common to watch the motor cars drive past to Brighton. Woolsey denounced 'parlous noise' and 'intolerable odour of petroleum', and seemed quite pleased when there was a crash at Newtimber throwing some passengers over a hedge. The magazine commented that before long boys would be ordering their end of term motors or going home by balloon! Ten years later the magazine noted the appearance of a 'fiendish' motor cycle. In 1894 an Edison phonograph with an immense horn was demonstrated and a recording made of Cooper's voice. In 1906 the College acquired its first gramophone, and it was used at a pop concert. Before long there were to be letters criticising the noise of Alexander's Rag Time Band echoing round the College. A new epidiascope appeared at long last in 1905 for showing slides. Young Rumsey's camera and Cooper's telephone were signs that life was becoming more mechanised and less isolated.

If Woolsey was put out by these changes there was one change of which he heartily approved: the bicycle. Indeed, it was to be one of the paradoxes of Edwardian times that appreciation of the countryside began the process of destroying its beauty and peace as bicycles, cars, and motor bicycles began to disturb dust that had lain undisturbed since the end of the coaching age. Charles Marsh founded the Bicycle Club in February 1890, and it was run in turn by Woolsey (1899), Haines (1903), and Scott (1909), coming to an end during the Great War. In 1893 they still found it 'necessary to appeal for members'; but thereafter it became the most popular school society with a membership of up to forty boys, and several masters, because it enabled them to leave the College for the beauty of the surrounding countryside, and to enjoy various social activities as well as the physical challenge of long runs. Once the Rover bicycle and the pneumatic Dunlop tyre were combined in the safety bicycle, long runs were possible, and on one to Sheffield Park in 1896 it was noted all members now used the safety bicycle.

There was little other traffic on the roads, although two members were unseated by a fast trap on a corner at Cobb's Mill, and two others had 'a difference with a cart'. The road surfaces were dusty, gritty, uneven, and loose stoned. A 34-mile ride to Horsham in 1898 to look at the start of the Christ's Hospital buildings had its pleasures, including elderberry wine at Lower Beeding and tea at the *Talbot*, Cuckfield, but the minute book recorded: 'punctures, two, saddle, broken, one, weather, warm, dust, considerable'. A similar trip in 1901 produced other problems including someone hiding their machines, an awful tea at the *Black Horse*, and 'punctures and spills were frequent on the way home. One rider came such a cropper he had to return by train via Brighton'. Lack of signposts also led to problems. On a trip to Steyning they arrived on the wrong side of the river, and had to cross by a dangerous bridge, and on a ride to Balcombe 'members encountered other members going in opposite directions'. Nevertheless amply clad in cap or boater, Norfolk jacket, knickerbockers, high socks and strong boots the boys enjoyed a variety of delights. There were trips to Lancing or Sheffield Park to watch cricket. When visiting Chanctonbury it was usual to climb to the top for a picnic. In May 1896 they did this and visited the church. Visits to Steyning ended with tea at the *White Horse*, a visit to Bramber Castle, and a swim in the Adur. Similarly there was an opportunity to swim at Shoreham, and at Slaugham lakes there was rowing and a pleasure garden with a tea house. Visits to Cowfold were followed by tea at the *White Hart* in Henfield. For 6d. members had boiled eggs, bread and butter, cake and strawberry squash.

If school work plays a small part in this chapter it is because it played a small part in many people's lives at the College in this period. At every level academic standards fell. Although between 1892 and 1902 43 boys went to Oxford and Cambridge and there were 18 Old Johnians in residence in 1895 (compared with 45 from Lancing in 1894), the number fell to five by 1902. In Cooper's last three years only two boys, C.H. Giles and E.H. Cox, are mentioned as going to Oxbridge. Hurst was to drop out of the Higher Certificate lists from 1903 to 1909 as the quality of sixth-form teaching fell. For remove boys taking the Oxford and Cambridge Locals there was little chance of success. The extremely easy preliminary test was only passed by 16 boys in 1896, and this fell to 12 in years like 1898 and 1900. Those passing the exam were 12 in 1896, and 14 in 1900. It was hardly surprising that when Cooper confronted the problem of falling numbers in several meetings with the masters in February 1898 the academic programme was among the topics discussed.

The fundamental reason for the situation was that the major public schools and the reformed grammar schools took the cream of academic boys, and, although we have no means of measuring it, clearly Hurst's intake was unlikely to provide a base for substantial exam success. Nor was taking exams high on the list of boys', parents', and even masters' priorities. The school was seen as providing a practical training for the life most of its pupils would lead, a substantial number of them as farmers in Britain or the colonies; others increasingly in the armed services or the colonial police forces. The athlete, the holder of prefectship, captaincies, and cadet force ranks, the good 'all-rounder' was the beau ideal, and this substantial shift away from Lowe's and Awdry's priorities was bound to have its effect.

This is seen most clearly in the composition of the common room. Cooper was neither an academic nor an inspirational teacher. While Cooper had been able to attract good quality masters in the 1880s he was unable to keep them: Bull, Milner, Henn, Sproston, Farrant, Back, and Moreton all left during the 1890s. Only Woolsey in Shield and Marsh in Chevron provided any dormitory master continuity. Fleur had four, and Red Cross five dormitory masters during the decade, and in the classroom there was even less continuity with virtually all masters appointed in Cooper's last years staying less than four years. The only exceptions to this were E. Eckersley (1892-99) and P. Bone (1894-98). Cooper's most successful appointment was that of Harry Johnson in 1896, who stayed until 1905 becoming dormitory master of Red Cross and Shield, games master, second master, an effective history master who edited the first register, active in many school activities, and later a long serving official of the Old Johnians. Cooper appointed two men who would serve the College for long years—H.M. Parham in 1898 and P.W. Scott in 1901, both promoted dormitory masters within a year, but their work lay in the future. The majority of common room members were young men who were birds of passage: two of them were attracted away to the new Christ's Hospital with better facilities and salaries. The others threw themselves enthusiastically into the corps, sport, and social life of the College, but clearly less so into the work of the classroom.

Very little was done to improve matters. As a result of his 1898 meetings Cooper increased time in school—it was to be five hours on half holidays, for example—but the number of 'halves' granted rose in the heady days of the Boer War. In 1900 the external examiner was the distinguished head of University College School, H.W. Eve. Cooper read and discussed his report with the masters before the start of the Michaelmas Term, but the only practical change seems to have been the start of morning break.

Hurst's second decline in Cooper's last years carried on through the 1903 Jubilee into Coombes' early ones, and is clear enough:

1892.....186	1894 186	1896........211	1898 189	1900......162	1902.....132
1893.....188	1895 191	1897........202	1899 166	1901......145	1903.....128

When Cooper discussed the decline with the masters in February 1898 he emphasised domestic reasons for it. He said that new Protestant agitation over education led by Rev. John Kensit and the Rev. Hugh Price Hughes was reviving the old anti-Puseyite cry against Hurst. He spoke of poor bath and toilet facilities, and the continued circulation of the bad health stories. He referred to harsh punishments, bullying and an ineffective timetable. There may have been some truth in these points. Clearly, too, Cooper's own weakening hold, lack of backing by a highly qualified, stable staff, and the slackness resulting from the prefects' dispute all made matters worse.

But the real reasons for decline lay outside his control. The first was more effective competition from other schools in a limited market. The second was Lowe's rule as Provost, and his continuing power in College affairs up to and even beyond the Jubilee. Other Woodard schools nearer to peoples' homes, more public schools, more grammar schools, and from 1902 state grammar schools provided the competition. The re-organised endowments provided hundreds of scholarships nationwide, and in 1907 the start of the direct grant enabled famous grammar schools to cut their fees still further. Not for nothing did Edwardes, head of Denstone at this time, write to Lowe about the Education Bill of 1902 to say 'we must try our best that the Education Bill does not produce anything to eclipse' their sort of school. To meet this competition Cooper did take some action. In 1899 the first school prospectus with pictures was produced, describing the domestic arrangements as 'thoroughly up to date' and the well-organised sports programme. In January 1900 Hurst participated in the English Educational Exhibition at the Imperial Institute where it had a stall displaying photographs of the boys and the buildings, the prospectus, a report card, and a coloured diagram of the timetable.

That Lowe would become Provost in 1891 and take a close interest in Hurst was more or less inevitable. His was an active provostship. He published the constitution of the Society or Corporation as it was now being called. Bloxham was added to the Southern Chapter in 1896. The Western Chapter was founded in 1897. He visited Hurst within five days of being installed as Provost, and thereafter rarely missed a Port Latin Day or other great function to which he was able to attract distinguished guests like Alwyne Compton, Bishop of Ely, or Dr. Lock, Warden of Keble College. He moved to Martyn Lodge at Henfield, and the Bicycle Club visited him there and had tea with him at the *White Hart*.

What was less satisfactory, although, perhaps in view of his age and closeness to Woodard, also more or less inevitable, was his failure to see that the exclusive Anglican and middle-class basis of the Woodard schools had to change. We have seen that there was now substantial competition, and competition, moreover, that benefited from Hurst's previous associations with High Churchism and Woodard's ladder of advancement. Some of the past had gone, but in 1902 Hurst still had scholars in gowns, probationers, Port Latin exhibitions, external examiners, scholarships to it from Ardingly, and away from it to Lancing. It was self-evident from parallel events at Lancing that retaining the old system was damaging: while Lowe was Provost two headmasters gave up the task of modernisation, and numbers sank to 89 by the end of the century. Even in the Church things were changing. When Bishop Durnford died in 1896 his successor was Ernest Wilberforce. He became Visitor and was at Hurst's Jubilee, but, as Cooper told Lowe, the bishop 'has not betrayed the slightest interest in the completion of the chapel'.

18 The ceremony at the start of the second stage of the chapel construction, 20 October 1892. Front left, Rev. Canon E.C. Lowe, fourth from left, Rt. Rev. Richard Durnford, Bishop of Chichester.

Lowe simply refused to change, and he was backed by William Woodard and Edmund Blackmore who remained in place throughout the period. It was only when the Hon. Arthur Lyttelton, Bishop of Southampton (1898) succeeded Lowe as Provost than any kind of change occurred, and sadly he died in 1903. But in 1901 he had provided each school with its first governing body. It was significant that it was called a committee, and only later the council, and that its members were not called governors. For many years the School Committee had no real power. It was composed at first of the Provost, bursar, custos, headmaster, and four well-known people connected with the College: William Campion, Major Maberley, R. Griffith Boscawen, and William Knowles (OJ). It had no impact on events because, as we shall see in the next chapter, Lowe continued to dictate matters including the Jubilee, even though he had no official right to do so. Perhaps there was some significance that numbers began to rise in the year Lowe last visited the College—1907!

Unwisely Cooper had already committed himself to completing the chapel for the Jubilee which should have been held in 1899, was planned for 1901, and lastly postponed to 1903 in a vain attempt to raise the money for this purpose. On 20 October 1891 Lowe said in Hall that 'the completion of the chapel' was to be achieved 'at an early date', and Cooper never dissented from this viewpoint as far as we know—indeed his sermon at Port Latin Day in 1893 endorsed it. On Richard Carpenter's death in 1893 *The Builder* published his original design for the building, and it was this and nothing less that Lowe determined upon. Through the 1890s Cooper continued to improve the chapel. The last stained glass window went in for £220 in 1893. The organ gave its last gasp at Advent Sunday in 1894, and was replaced the following year by a centrally placed instrument costing £500. Louisa Cooper collected the money (£97 3s. 6d.) for a pulpit put in place in 1896. But to complete the chapel, including all the stained glass, panelling, and building would have been a daunting task for a school of 300, and was impossible for one which had only 113 boys in 1905.

Lowe wrote to Archbishop Benson in November 1891 saying 'the needs of the people are still the same' as they were in Woodard's day, and asking him to support the raising of £50,000 to complete the buildings of the Southern Chapter schools as a whole—£5,000 was to go to Hurst for its chapel. Benson was not High Church, and he did not contribute. Perhaps Lowe should have been warned by this. Instead on 23 February 1892 an old-style Woodard meeting was held at Brighton Pavilion to launch the appeal with Bishop Durnford in the chair. A committee of six churchmen and six Woodard officials was set up, and Cooper made secretary. The first subscription list that month contained £30 from Gladstone, and £100 from Salisbury, and other substantial contributions, but the accounts printed in the *Hurst Johnian* show that the Fund petered out having raised less than £6,000, and most of this money went to Lancing chapel, Bloxham, and Ardingly. It was to be the last national Woodard appeal.

However, in September 1892 work began on completing Hurst chapel, and it was to go on intermittently for 13 years when it was by no means finished, start up again and stop in 1914, and not finally cease until 1930. So it was to be a continuing *leit motiv* in school building and finance for three headmasters. On 20 October 1892 the foundation stone of the western end was laid by Lowe, in the presence of Bishop Durnford, at a grand ceremony. The sermon was preached by George Ridding, the former great headmaster of Winchester, now Bishop of Southwell. The money raised at this early stage all went into foundations and gas pipes, the cost of which exceeded the £628 in hand by nearly £150, causing delay until this money was raised.

1894 marked the next stage. Internal panelling had begun and Lowe's Completion Fund gave the first £1,000 towards this: the rest was eventually paid for by Lowe himself in his will

19 The chaplain's study when the Rev. F.C. Haines was chaplain between 1900 and 1909.

and not finished until 1926. Sabine Baring-Gould returned to preach and wrote a short story in the magazine. It was announced that the next stage was to build the giant piers and arches to support the future tower. Clearly Lowe was doing what Woodard had done with Lancing chapel—sketch in the groundwork to prevent a smaller building emerging. As he could not have anticipated the need one day for a chapel seating 500 it would have been far more sensible to cut costs. He must have seen from the paltry £50 raised that Port Latin Day and £16 4s. 3d. from a concert of Edward German's music, that raising thousands was more or less impossible. The foundation and structural work cost £1,225, and of course contributors saw nothing of artistic interest as yet. In 1896 Lowe brought over Benjamin Ingelow, the architect until his death in 1911, and explained how William Woodard would supply labour from the College maintenance staff when not needed at Lancing.

In May 1898 the work on the west end began, followed by the south transept. A bazaar with the usual stalls was held in July to raise money. It was a pleasant enough day: strawberries and cream, the orchestra played negro spirituals, and it raised £130. The walls were 24 ft. from the ground now, and Woolsey's month-by-month account of how they grew is boring enough. The length of time involved made it increasingly difficult to raise money. C. Murray Rumsey held three London concerts—and a mere £12 14s. 4d. was forthcoming. There was a windfall £100 in the will of a boy killed in the Boer War, but from 1896 to 1900 only £1,632 1s. 6d. was subscribed, and during 1901 the sum collected fell to £30. The total money spent on the chapel from 1892 to 1901 was £3,172 17s. 5d.

It may be argued that if this had not been done Hurst would never have had a fine chapel, let alone one capable of meeting every need of the College in expansive years ahead. At the time the effects were nearly all bad. The endless collecting of money for 10 years meant that, when it was decided the Jubilee Fund should be for the same purpose, this had the effect of lowering this considerably. Building under Cooper was of two kinds. Subscriptions, Old Johnian debentures, and tuck shop profits between them provided an infirmary, a pavilion, a refurbished gymnasium, and a pool. The school itself provided panels for the dining hall, a new staircase in the south-west corner of the building, hot pipes, toilets, and new classrooms. It was a small programme indeed. The school needed a good library, classrooms, books, equipment, good salaries for qualified masters, and better living conditions. Just on £2,000 was provided by voluntary effort for the buildings mentioned above, and there was no difficulty in raising the swimming pool money. Had the College chosen to spend its money on secular buildings and improve its facilities, the fall in numbers would obviously have been far less, and the income for further improvement correspondingly more. Cooper left this problem to his successor.

He was also fortunate that in his last years, when numbers fell, discipline declined, and academic standards were poor, attention was focused on the Boer War. The school was gripped with imperialist sentiment, and the magazine full of the war: publishing over fifty letters from Old Johnians at the front, for example. Woolsey remarked that with the country at war 'we naturally find ourselves affected by the enthusiasm. Maps are to be seen posted up on all coigns of vantage ...', and boys were more interested in the war than the football results, according to him. As we have seen, patriotism found its way into the choice of play, and the prologue at its start, and into termly pop concerts where everyone from Cooper to the young Parham was to be found singing jingoistic songs. The corps rapidly increased its membership, and while Woolsey temporarily commanded it in 1900-1901 he used the magazine to criticise 'craven civilians' who had not joined.

Among the most dramatic examples of Boer War patriotism at Hurst was the treatment of Henry Rowe, the music master, who was a Volunteer in the First Royal Sussex Regiment, and was called up in March 1900. Although it was pouring with rain the day he left the corps marched with him to Hassocks Station. 'At Stone Pound [now the traffic lights at the Brighton Road] the horse was taken from his cab, and members of the corps dragged him in triumph to the station.' As the train drew in the corps burst into the National Anthem on the station, and the train moved out 'amidst the wildest enthusiasm'. Rowe did well in South Africa. He rose in rank from corporal to captain, was mentioned in despatches and decorated, and later received the freedom of Chichester. When he returned in June 1901 the corps were at the station to meet the 6.26 p.m. Led by the band playing *Georgia*, they marched back escorting Rowe and a villager, Private Spratley, to the village before marching down the lane to the College entrance where 'the Headmaster in cap and gown standing in front of a triumphal arch welcomed Mr. Rowe'. Rowe resumed command of the corps and school music, and his account of his war experiences was added to others heard by the boys, including a talk by the Rev. Bertie Bull, now chaplain to the 4th Cavalry Brigade, in April 1901.

The whole College, however, was involved in a day of imperialist fervour when on 17 May 1900 a small township called Mafeking was relieved after a siege lasting 216 days. 'Breakfast ended in chaos', and Cooper announced a whole-day holiday. 'Excited crowds produced Union Jacks from unsuspected places, and marched everywhere singing and shouting.' The corps paraded at 9.15, salutes and cheers were given for Queen Victoria and Colonel Robert Baden-Powell. Led by the band the whole school, including masters, then marched to the village. The fountain on the green was dispensing lemonade instead of water to the boys' delight, and they marched on 'through the village resplendent with flags, and thronged with people cheering and waving things at us'. They marched back past Latchetts to the front quad where the National Anthem was sung. That evening at the pop concert the school captain sang *Hearts of Oak*, Parham, *Soldiers of the Queen*, and Johnson *There's a Land*, all to tumultuous receptions.

Reporting in the national papers, and in the school magazine was equally jingoist. Even the *Church Times* carried stories, including Bertie Bull's, and one about James Leary, now chaplain with the 21st Brigade, who rescued wounded men under fire at a place called Bryce's Store. 'It was ripping', wrote F.N. Turner from Bloemfontein, 'to march into the town as part of an invading army, and you should have seen how we stuck out our chests and swaggered.' However, the reality of war at last broke in, and Woolsey wrote, 'we have at length to record the inevitable casualties in Old Johnian ranks'. About seventy Old Johnians served in the Boer War, the majority in yeomanry companies or various colonial contingents. No attempt was made to compile records either of casualties or decorations, and even when it came to recording deaths a mistake was made on the war memorial. Never before had an empire campaign taken more than one Johnian life. The Boer War took six. One was a civilian, Frederick Greenfield, sometime captain of Cambridge University cricket, and at the time of the war a headmaster at Dundee in Natal, who was captured and beaten up by the Boers dying in October 1900. Two well-known footballers died. Francis Welsby, who had badgered the authorities to let him go out in spite of an injured knee, died aged 20 of enteric in 1900, and William Dean was killed in 1901. He left £100 for the chapel in his will. Cosmo Blount, who wrote several war letters to the magazine, died aged 21 of enteric in February 1901. Edwin Waller was killed accidentally in camp in June 1900 and Roger Hammond was killed at Barnard's Kop in December 1901. £6 10s. was subscribed for a small brass memorial later replaced by the names carved in the memorial chapel.

In 1901 Cooper was approaching his 50th birthday, and young Rumsey described him as a 'dear old man'. His beard was nearly grey, and it is clear he was ageing rapidly from the days when he played golf at Pyecombe or sat on the parish council. He told Old Johnians he 'felt unequal to the endless strain, and void of the vigour required'. Louisa, seen by Rumsey as very much an elderly Victorian lady in black, was ill in the winter of 1901-1902. After 22 years the time to move had clearly come and, although no one blamed him for the decline in the College's fortunes, the task of restoring them needed to go to a younger man. At the end of the Lent Term in 1902 the boys assembled in upper school, and Herbert Wadman, the sole probationer, took the place of the school captain. The Coopers received silver entrée dishes from the boys who also gave a silver photographic frame to Louisa. The masters gave him a Turkey carpet, and Star, a silver salver. The school servants gave him a plated silver reading lamp. In June the Old Johnian farewell meeting presented him with a cheque for 200 guineas.

From 1903 to 1911 Cooper was vicar of St Andrew's, Portslade, and their Church Lads Brigade came to play cricket at Hurst. He was vice-provost, but in 1906 had a major operation and his health declined further. He moved to a country parish at St Thomas à Becket, Brightling, and died there in August 1912. Although he left in July 1903, Woolsey's departure should be dealt with at the same time as Cooper's because they had worked together from 1889, and the school that entered Edwardian times was very much a joint creation by two like-minded men. Woolsey was given books by Shield, a desk and chairs by the boys, a silver inkstand by the servants, and £83 by the Old Johnians. He still had an active career ahead of him, and was a less than successful headmaster of Ellesmere College from 1907 to 1910 before becoming a parish priest at Holy Trinity, Gosport, where he died in 1926. His writing and poetry in the school magazine will always encapsulate the era of the 1890s and the Boer War, one in which, in spite of difficulties, lack of development, and falling numbers, Cooper and he had made school patriotism central to school life, as his poem *The Last Time* so well illustrates:

> When the merry sun of morning
> Laughing gilded all the tree tops,
> And the Johnians loudly shouting,
> Clambered on the omnibuses,
> Eager for their homes and holidays,
> There I saw him, but not shouting,
> Noted him, but not rejoicing,
> Gazing hard as eyes can gaze that
> Look through tears that ever blind them.
> Saw him raise his hand, and wave it
> Till the White Gates lay behind him,
> Closed by gloomy fate, while onward
> From the certain to the unseen
> From the has been to the will be
> Rushed he, broken with his sorrow
> To the country of the future.

SEVEN

EDWARDIAN CONTRASTS
1902-1914

The First Jubilee and Arthur Coombes's Early Years

> I have to place one startling fact [before you] which I should not shirk in any case, but which I want to impress upon you here especially, because I believe that with you to a certain extent lies the remedy. The fact is this: in 1903 I entered fifty-one new boys; in 1904 I entered twenty-seven ...
>
> Arthur Coombes speaking to Old Johnians at their December 1904 Dinner
> *The Hurst Johnian* 468/31, January 1905
>
> The sun is shining gloriously and the only cool places are the swimming bath and the bank. It is too early to bathe so I commandeer a deck chair, and sit under the shade of the oaks that fringe the North Field. There is an exciting game proceeding on the Second Club ground where the impertinent striplings of the Under Fifteen have challenged the bearded veterans of the Second Club. I can't see who is batting, and I am much too lazy to find out. First Eleven heroes are lolling here and there giving patronising advice or fatuous criticism. Small boys eat 'bouncers' and talk volubly on things about which they know nothing. Cyclists career up and down the path and run into one another with painful, but assiduous regularity. Far away an occasional ping of a rifle bullet, and the glimpse of a recumbent figure in a red and white chair, tell me that the Shooting Eight, amid protracted intervals of repose, are practising.
>
> North Field in the summer of 1905
> *The Hurst Johnian*, 473/235, July 1905

Arthur Coombes, at 39, was the oldest man to be appointed headmaster of Hurst so far. His early years were in the Edwardian Age, later seen after the horrors of the First World War as a golden era, and Coombes also bore the burdens of the war years, while increasingly ill himself with arthritis, until he retired aged 60 in 1923. Outwardly Coombes's early years coincided with two national and one Hurst event that made for celebration: behind the scenes Hurst faced its worst ever crisis in numbers. 1902 was a Coronation year, and the year when peace came in South Africa. The news reached the school on 1 June and next day cheers were given and volleys fired for the King, Roberts, Kitchener and the Old Johnians in the war, and, as on previous occasions, a half holiday was granted, and the boys marched to the village and fired a volley on the green, watched by crowds of children from the neighbouring primary school. The afternoon was spent in the pool, and the evening in a school decked with Chinese lanterns. That day the cycling club made a familiar run to Turner's Hill through villages decorated for peace (or victory) and stopped for tea at the *Talbot* in Cuckfield where the boys were joined by Arthur Coombes and his wife, Isabel. On 8 June there was a thanksgiving service in chapel, and Coombes wrote to Lowe: 'my bike has been out of order of late, so we have not yet been able to return Mrs. Lowe's call, but hope to do so shortly. We have the Provost [Lyttelton] here, and are rejoicing at peace.'

The atmosphere of frenetic patriotism that had characterised a good deal of school life since the end of 1899 really came to an end on Prize Day, 26 June, which started with the choir processing into chapel singing Baring-Gould's *Onward Christian Soldiers*, and ended with a *Te Deum* on the altar steps. Prizes were distributed in the sunny inner quad, followed by a gymnastic display, and orchestral concert. This was brought to an end as the choir started *Lords of the Waves We Are*, and a torrential downpour occurred. Moreover, the *Hurst Johnian* pointed out that next year, 1903, they would be celebrating their own jubilee: it would be, said Woolsey, 'the second greatest year of our existence'.

20   Jubilee Day, 25 June 1903. In the centre of the picture is Rev. Canon Arthur H. Coombes, headmaster from 1902 to 1923. Seated in front of him, from left to right: Mrs. Henrietta Lowe, Mrs. Isabel Coombes and Mrs. Louisa Cooper.

This was far too sanguine an appraisal. 1899 should have been the year of jubilee. Cooper had announced it would be 1901. In fact, it turned out to be the last possible date of 1903 and, although the magazine explained this away by referring to the war, Victoria's death, and the coronation, the real reasons were purely domestic. In five years to 1903 school numbers fell by a third to 128, and the fall was to continue to 1906. In 1905 the smallest number ever in the school's history, 113, was to be reached. This had seriously affected collecting money for chapel completion and, as we saw, in 1901 just £30 was collected. Cooper told Lowe, 'the future of the chapel completion scheme is a source of grave anxiety to us'. When Coombes arrived there was £300 in hand and debts to both the architect and builder had to be settled while the work had come to a standstill. Clearly Coombes's main job was to address the numbers and financial problems, but unfortunately he was unable to do so as he would have wished. Instead for 18 months he had to acquiesce to policies that were wrong, and it was only after he was established as head, and had the backing of a new Provost, that he was able to stem the tide of disaster, by which time he had himself been threatened with dismissal if things did not improve.

Arthur Henry Coombes was born in Oxford in August 1862. He attended Magdalen College School, probably from 1874 to 1881, entering the sixth form in 1879. He was in the First XI cricket, and First XV rugby, and played the latter for Oxford. He obtained several prizes, and entered Magdalen College with a demyship. He obtained a first in Mods, and a second in mathematics. In 1886 he went as a master to Dover College and three years later left on marrying Isabel Parker. They had one daughter, Sibyl. The Coombes went to New South Wales and he taught at the King's School, Paramatta (a suburb of Sydney). He was ordained in 1896. In 1900 he returned to England and became senior mathematics master at Clifton College, from where he came to Hurst. Athletic and well turned out, and with a charming and handsome wife, Coombes struck boys like Rumsey as sweeping away the 'old régime', although he was able to do little at first.

He continued the tradition of Awdry and Cooper as a games playing headmaster. He played cricket and fives, and was an active member of the Bicycle Club. Soon after his visit to Cuckfield he cycled with Woolsey and the boys to Chanctonbury, climbed the hill, descended to explore Steyning church, and had tea in the *White Horse*. In his personal life he was a keen piano player and stamp collector. In school he took part in pop concerts—he sang in *Ruddigore* in May 1908, for example. He taught geography and the examiners thought this the best taught subject in the school. William Carter, an orphan, who had to stay in the holidays from 1910 to 1918, described Coombes as an 'humane and cultivated person', and his wife as a delightfully kind woman and a good cook. In school legend Coombes has always been seen, as he was at the end of his career, a broken man in many ways, but in his early years he was the bright young man appointed to produce change. He was a strong Anglican, but clearly saw chapel more as part of the system than the fulcrum of every activity and thought. He was regarded as a clear, plain preacher although on one occasion, due to the presence of Rev. Leigh Nixon as precentor, he preached at Westminster Abbey in March 1913.

The combination of a new head and an impending Jubilee, with its financial possibilities, might have seemed the ideal moment for a change in policy. Instead the Jubilee was celebrated as an old-fashioned Woodard occasion and the appeal money went to the chapel: both serious mistakes even though unfortunately probably unavoidable. As a new head Coombes had to tread warily and found Lowe, although now only a fellow and with no official authority, Cooper, who had retired and should have known better than to interfere, Haines, the chaplain, and a largely indifferent Lyttelton as Provost, united on a course of action. 1903 saw the Northern Province or Division created, but this actually marked the high water mark of Woodard expansion—the Eastern one did not come until 1968, and all the signs at Hurst and Lancing were that change was needed in the direction of ending the middle-school cachet attaching to Hurst and giving the two heads more autonomy to modernise buildings and curriculums. It was all very well for the magazine to say of Lowe, 'he can never come too often'. He was present a good deal too much, and even when the Jubilee was reported Lowe was praised, more should have been done (it was said) to involve Cooper, and Coombes's speech was not reported. The school remained 'A Church of England Public School' in the new prospectus.

As soon as possible after Coombes arrived Haines told Lowe he would cycle over to Martyn Lodge to discuss chapel completion. He was clearly put out—perhaps Coombes had suggested other priorities for spending. 'The headmaster,' said Haines, 'does not want to take a very active part in the matter as I fancy he wishes to devote his energies to other departments.' Soon afterwards Cooper wrote to Lowe, 'I know not how he stands towards the completion of the ante-chapel'. All three men determined that the chapel should be completed to the original design (except for the west end organ on a screen), and ignored, for instance, the bishop's lack of interest and the evidence of the dwindling subscriptions for the chapel as compared with the swift provision of money for a pool. So Cooper urged Lowe to continue running the Completion Fund because 'nothing could be better'. 'It would be well,' he told Lowe, 'to get from the Provost a statement that you represent the Chapter in your efforts to build the ante-chapel.' Lyttelton gave him backing although this was quite unfair—the chapel fund had nothing to do with Lowe's Provost's Completion Fund of 1892. Cooper told Lowe he would back him 'but I must keep well in the background'. A Jubilee Committee was set up in May 1902 to organise the day, but in October another committee was set up to run the Jubilee Fund and it was announced that this money would go towards the chapel.

Confusion surrounded just how much money was to be raised. The appeal was for £2,200, but the school magazine said it was for £1,700 and that £3,400 would be needed to complete the work. The fund was a failure, and this is hardly surprising since money had been poured into the chapel since 1892 with very little to show for it except an incomplete shell of a west end. By Jubilee Day the amount raised was £765 9s. 9d. and the fund reached £985 11s. 9d. by October. This was the contrast behind the celebrations in June 1903, which were actually organised by a third committee set up in March that year to replace the May 1902 one and consisting of Lowe, Campion, Haines, Woolsey, Maberley, and Coombes for the first time. On Wednesday 24 June there was the first day of a two-day cricket match. The Present including Herbert Wadman and Randolph Rogers played the Past including A.P. Nepean, H.R. Dotteridge, and the Rev. T.G. Le Mesurier. After Evensong an audience in full evening dress attended a concert in hall conducted by the new music master, A.A. Engelhardt. Among the soloists were C. Murray Rumsey, and Coombes himself, followed by a 'mob of the Lower School' in the choruses to *Drake's Drum*. Edward German's and Coleridge Taylor's music was played.

Next day opened with early Communion attended by the bishops present, Cooper, Lowe, and the Provost, but not by Coombes. A procession led by 70 Old Johnians was formed and moved into chapel to the strains of *Jerusalem, My Happy Home*. The school was so small it was accommodated on the lower flight of the altar steps while the chapel filled with representatives of other Woodard schools, each under their banners. Coombes entered early with the other Woodard heads leaving the places of honour at the end to Lowe and Cooper. The service was *Stainer in A*, and the sermon was preached by Cosmo Lang, then suffragan bishop of Stepney (1901-1909). The presence of only one other bishop, Randall of Reading, who was also a suffragan, was not an impressive episcopal representation. The offertory raised only £76, and the service ended rather surprisingly with a *Te Deum* specially composed for the day by Engelhardt. The Old Johnian Club paid for the lunch in their second donation to the College, and 400 people crammed into hall to hear G.J. Goschen, M.P. for West Grinstead, a former Tory Chancellor, and First Lord of the Admiralty, Wilberforce of Chichester, Southwell, the Provost, Lang, Coombes, and lastly Lowe. While the cricket continued to a school victory tea was served on Chevron lawn presided over by Isabel Coombes, but the pictures show how thin the guests were on the ground, and they had all gone by six o'clock.

For all Woolsey's efforts in the magazine the lack of great names, the size of the offertory, and lack of local press comment all indicate that it was not a complete success—in 1949 the atmosphere could hardly have been more different when the buildings were crowded with notabilities. Work on the chapel came to a halt, but Lowe was determined to press ahead and a year later, in the summer of 1904, it resumed once again using in part money collected for two stained glass windows. Lowe paid for the west doors, and George Hames (OJ) for the south doors, in memory of his wife, and at long last in September 1905 the brick wall in the west arch, there since 1865, was removed, and in October Cooper preached at the dedication of the ante-chapel in defensive terms, stressing that people had given the money voluntarily to 'endorse the views of the Founder', and that religion should take place in buildings reflecting the 'greatness, dignity and beauty of God'. Bernard Tower—who gave £10,000 to Lancing chapel when it was given to the school—was there and praised the building, but Lowe was unable to attend through illness. All Coombes could muster at the lunch was 'a few remarks'. Perhaps he heaved a sigh of relief that building really did seem to have come to an end. The offertory raised £64 towards settling an outstanding debt of £280.

It took until 1908 to clear this debt, and it was only done in the end by holding a fête in June, opened by Viscountess Halifax in glorious weather with music provided by the Royal Marines Artillery Band and the Southwark Glee Singers. £150 was taken. According to the speeches in 1905 £4,700 had been raised since 1892, and Lowe would have taken comfort that this was near the £5,000 he had originally proposed. Unfortunately the building was far from complete and barren inside at the west end, and under Coombes the total raised had only been £1,528 including the whole of the Jubilee money. This money was needed elsewhere and at least part of the money should have been spent on other facilities.

Lowe's illness was the beginning of the end for him. He visited the school until 1907 and thereafter was too infirm to do more than lean out of the window to talk to boys visiting him at Martyn Lodge. Lyttelton died young and there was a new Provost possibly just in time to start the necessary resuscitation of Hurst and Lancing. Henry Southwell (1861-1937) was, after Woodard, the most important of the early provosts. Educated at Charterhouse and Magdalen College, Oxford, he was vicar of Bodmin when he became Provost of the Western Chapter in 1902 and almost immediately Provost of the whole Society. He served as an army chaplain in the Boer War, and in the First World War was chaplain-general for a time, before ill health led him to resign in 1916. He took his D.D., and in 1920 became suffragan bishop of Lewes. However, he remained vice-provost and in 1926 resumed the Provostship until his death in 1937. In May 1903 he had chaired a meeting at Caxton Hall of all the schools' representatives and made it plain that they needed to change.

Years later Coombes admitted that in 1904 Southwell told him that if numbers did not improve he would have to go, although within two years of this the Provost was praising Coombes in public for his success. Success did not come, however, until the nadir had been reached in 1905 when numbers fell to 113, and Red Cross closed with its few boys transferred to Chevron. A rise of one in total numbers next year was followed from 1907 by a steady recovery sustained until 1913. By 1910 Red Cross dormitory was re-opened, and Coombes said there were 'marked signs of improvement' in nearly every department of school life. Sadly there was still one more fall in numbers in store for him—not for nothing was his nickname 'Bulldog'—but at least the crucial issue of actual survival was behind him, as the figures show.

Year	Numbers	Total gross fee income		
		£	s.	d.
1904	114	6,059	13	10
1905	113	5,762	01	03
1906	114	5,746	16	08
1907	122	5,964	19	05
1908	130	6,599	11	03
1909	161	7,073	08	07
1910	161	7,503	07	00
1911	171	8,173	16	03
1912	176	8,177	01	00
1913	183	7,838	19	03
1914	174	7,958	00	10

Fees were not increased. Variations in income resulted from number of boys admitted on various kinds of reduced fees.

The first necessity was to bring to an end Woodard's ladder of advancement and other features which bound the College too closely to the Woodard organisation. Coombes himself did not often refer in his surviving speeches to Woodardry and the departure from the scene of Pratt (1908), Blackmore (1909), and Lowe (1912) made it less necessary. It is significant of the trouble caused by too close control that William Woodard as custos survived until 1918 and was the source of future trouble for Coombes. In the magazine the missionary movement disappeared almost completely. So did detailed reporting of chapel services—there was a complaint about this in 1913—and Woodard occasions, so that the dedication of Lancing chapel in 1911 received only a few lines whereas ten years before there would have been detailed attention.

Practical steps were taken. In 1902 E.F. Morison was the last Hurst scholar to go to Lancing and in 1908 B.F.F. Krall, the last Ardingly scholar to come to Hurst, left. Port Latin Day had gone: now the Port Latin exhibitions disappeared. Charles Martyn, who went to teach at Ardingly before entering St Edmund Hall, was the last probationer, and he left in 1908, incidentally providing accommodation for masters which was adequate for many years in the former rookeries. The term 'rooker' was transferred to the room occupied by the dormitory prefects. The long Winchester gown for scholars was replaced by a short one only worn on limited occasions and then abolished. Coombes was determined that scholarships reducing fees should be seen as academic achievements not charitable concessions. From 1902 he embraced the Common Entrance exam for most entrants, and in 1911 a scholarship exam for anyone seeking reduced fees was introduced; the concessions, for instance to Sussex boys or Hurstpierpoint and Cuckfield scholars, merged into the general provision of scholarship places. There is mention too, although not in any detail, of an Old Johnian scholarship, possibly first held by Leighton Flindt (1908-14), son of an Old Johnian.

Coombes tackled head on local criticisms of poor health and living conditions in a new prospectus which presented what must be admitted was an extremely rosy picture of the College. It was on an 'extremely healthy site' and was equipped with 'a perfect system of drainage', and an 'excellent water supply'. A doctor attended daily, and there was a resident qualified sister (matron). The prospectus said, 'the greatest care is taken with the boys' food' and 'the diet is carefully considered and unlimited in quantity'. In remarkably modern terms it went on: 'the keenest attention is paid to the health and comfort of the boys by the dormitory masters, the headmaster's wife, and the matrons in charge, and the domestic supervision is thorough and minute.' Clearly this last paragraph was aimed at allaying fears of bullying. Speaking to Old Johnians in 1904, Coombes had sharply criticised this (although cloaking his remarks by saying he referred to a much earlier era), commenting: 'I have become painfully aware during the last twelve months of the existence of Old Johnians who look back on their time at Hurst as a bad dream.'

Memoirs from Francis Rumsey at the start of Coombes's headship to those of J.P.F. Saffell at the end show that conditions did not improve in line with these claims. However, there were improvements. When he took over no-one was in control of the domestic staff although the pages came under the control of the butler, Mahon, described by Rumsey as 'of gross appearance with a fat, red and objectionably shiny face, and a small quantity of greasy hair on the top of his head'. In 1904 Coombes appointed David Llewelyn Evans, who had been at King's College, Taunton, as steward, which meant that he was responsible for the domestic affairs of the College. He was a friendly and well-liked man who did some teaching and coached football. He was paid £60 as a master and £40 as steward, and did all he could within the scrooge-like grasp of Blackmore to improve matters until he left for a similar post at Worksop in 1911.

The health of the College did improve and, when scarlet fever returned in 1907, 1910, and 1912, there were no deaths and the only casualty was the Shakespeare play. The kitchens were rebuilt, and by 1913 it was claimed that masters and boys ate food cooked in the same ovens. The drains were overhauled. Roofs were repaired and windows releaded. The heating system was overhauled.

Efficiency was to be found in the handling of discipline. Coombes ended Cooper's daily calling over and caning, but 'he wielded the cane well' in the privacy of his study. In May 1902 B.T. Verver was appointed school captain and Coombes did all he could to restore prefectorial authority. Dormitory captains were permitted to cane, and other prefects used a variety of instruments including slippers and Indian clubs, according to the memoirs of a Star member who was caned for not shouting loudly enough at a dormitory match. Punishment drill was handed over to the prefects and was to consist of manual labour. Their other power was to exact fines for such matters as walking on the grass, running in cloisters, or wearing slippers round the school. For work Coombes changed imposition school to detention in 1902 for use by masters only. There was never any hint throughout Coombes's time that general discipline was not excellent, even if some of the masters appointed left much to be desired in this department.

Academic efficiency was central to Coombes's revival of College fortunes. Prize Day 1909 was the first time when percentage pass rates were mentioned, Coombes taking pride in success in public exams and condemning boys who were 'loafing through the middle forms'. Coombes introduced 'a uniform course of instruction' in the lower forms, aimed to take boys through the Preliminary and actual Oxford Local exams in the fourth and fifth forms. Results were published in the magazine from 1904, and in the first year 15 boys passed in between three and seven subjects. The sixth form took Higher Certificate in one year and in 1909, with the success of E.W. Gilbert and G. Perkins, Hurst resumed its place as a Higher Certificate school. Sufficiently high pass-marks in this exam exempted boys from London Matriculation and thus enabled them to enter university. Precise figures for Oxbridge entry do not exist for Coombes's early years, but by 1910 numbers were increasing again following a good intake of six boys in 1908. Between 1910 and 1914, 16 boys entered, four going to Cambridge, but it was significant that they went to the poorer colleges and that half of them went to Keble College, Oxford. Hurst was no longer in the Denstone or Lancing league—schools with over 25 boys there, and its results were comparable with Ellesmere or Worksop.

The changes Coombes made in the teaching programme were very limited. The timetable was altered three times in his first three years to get it right. Prep was increased first of all in the summer terms, and eventually throughout the year it lasted from 6.45 to 9.00 p.m. The sixth form was organised into classics, languages, and science divisions. Coombes tried to raise the academic content of the school programme as a whole. In 1904 he started a general knowledge test, the first papers of which produced the usual howlers: flying buttress was a butler's wife, Balfour was a music hall performer (actually he was Prime Minister), *Vanity Fair* was by John Bunyan, and F.R.C.O. meant Fellow of the Royal Cocoa Organisation. Next year with the arrival of a new epidiascope a programme of lectures started, and from 1911 this was compulsory in the Michaelmas Term.

There was plenty of variety: in the first few years subjects included the Bayeux Tapestry, Spain, Stars, Ants, Palestine, British Birds, Architecture, Stamp Collecting, Exploration, Cameras, and Sicily, Land of the Mafia. Some of the lectures were clearly useful. One by a companion of Shackleton and Scott was followed by a debate on the usefulness of Antarctic exploration. Others seem to have been more like pure entertainment. Mr. Bellingham's talk on 'Caravan and Camera' produced the comment, 'We liked best Mr. Bellingham bathing, Mr. Bellingham unshaven, and the farmer's daughter', whilst A. Radclyffe Dugmore's 'Stalking Big Game with a Camera' was particularly enjoyed for 'Mr. Dugmore's realistic impression of the growls of an angry lioness'.

Both libraries received attention. The boys' received new bookcases, and a catalogue was compiled by Haines, the chaplain, who was made the first library master. Everything was done to encourage donations, which came from many sources including Lowe and Alice Coleridge. Among the boys' serious minded ones like Rumsey donated lives of Church, Liddon and Wilberforce while the offerings of W.H. Colquhoun, including Wallace's *The Four Just Men* and E.W. Hornung's *Raffles*, were more typical! Isabel Coombes compiled albums of all the existing school photographs. Coombes said the fellows library would now become the museum and for 10 years the magazine was full of donations. By 1914 this room contained a valuable religious library in Baring-Gould's bookcases, portraits of Keble, Newman and other Oxford Movement churchmen, Sussex flora and fauna, including a large stuffed bird collection, coins from Greece and Rome, weapons from various parts of the Empire, a stamp collection of 'considerable dimension' and many other items. Its complete disappearance during Dingwall's headship is one of the unsolved mysteries of Hurst history.

The success of academic recovery depended on recruiting a better and more permanent staff, and Coombes took on 34 masters before 1914. Although many of them were birds of passage as usual, there was a reasonably solid core of masters during the Edwardian period. Salaries remained low, usually starting at £60 a year, and could still fall as well as rise—A.C. Axe, the music master's fell from £110 to £95 a year. Dormitory masters were now receiving a better salary. Percy Scott's salary rose from £94 in 1904 to £161 a year by 1914, and H.M. Parham was on £160 the same year. The total masters' salary bill was £2,539 2s. 0d. in 1914. An important change was that in 1913 for a time the title of second master was abolished when H.M. Parham succeeded as senior master and stayed with Fleur de Lys. Shield ceased to be the second master's dormitory with special capitations.

Hurst common room's 'Big Three' of the first half of the century were all at work as young men in Coombes's school. H.M. Parham was involved with Fleur de Lys and singing. Percy Scott was dormitory master of Chevron, where he stayed until 1950, and took over the corps in 1903. He ran the Bicycle Club for a time and the tuck shop. In 1908 they were joined by H.B.I. Pocock who would teach science to 1954. He was active in fives and tennis, and on the masters' bowling green, and in 1910 took over the reopened Red Cross. H.L. Johnson, the second master, was a popular live wire among the masters: P.G.C. treasurer, cadet force officer, editor of the magazine, and producer of four plays. His marriage at Holy Trinity Church was followed by his departure in 1905. His successor as second master was the Rev. F.H. George, dormitory master of Shield, editor of the magazine, play producer and, like Johnson, popular. When he left in 1913 to be headmaster of King's College, Taunton, he was presented with a desk and chair. P.P. Mallam (1903-1908) was involved in the cadet force, the gymnasium, swimming, athletics, and as stage manager while R.J. Wood (1903-1913), a portly biologist with discipline problems, ran the tuck shop, chess, the Natural History Society, debates, and produced two plays. Sadly he died in College, aged only 48, after a major operation in November 1913.

21 The masters in 1912. Seated H.B.I. Pocock, P.W. Scott, Rev. J.R. Fowler, Rev. A.H. Coombes, Rev. F.H. George, H.M. Parham and R.J. Wood.

22 The First XI football team, 1902-1903. Seated (from the left) are W. Whitmore-Searle, who died aged 21 in India in 1906; H.A. Wadman, probationer; O.C. McMahon, probationer; Ronald Turner, who played football for Cambridge, Sussex and England, and was killed at Gallipoli in August 1915 and V. Randolph Rogers, master and chaplain, 1919-25.

While there was still great fluidity—six music masters before A.C. Axe, five play producers, and four *Hurst Johnian* editors, for example, Coombes was clearly building a staff willing to take part intensely in school life. In 1913 the first 'masters versus boys' football match took place, and Coombes remarked that this was 'great testimony to the keenness and eternal youth of the staff'. By then he had three young masters in place, each making a fine contribution. A.C. Axe had revived music and composed church music for use in the chapel. T.A. Straughan took over editing the magazine and R. Willis ran cricket for two seasons. Sadly, all three were to leave, and entered the army in the First World War only to meet an early death.

Among the enthusiastically involved masters was Rev. F.C. Haines, chaplain from 1900 to 1909, whose 'parties have earned him undying fame', and who was 'delighted to surround himself with boys and books'. He began work on the College register, which H.L. Johnson carried on after leaving so that the book was published in 1914. He was in charge of the library and ran the bicycle and photographic clubs. He left to be rector of Blackford in Somerset where he died in 1926. His two successors soon left for overseas work in India and Mauritius, and Coombes himself had to be chaplain for a term before the Rev. H.S. Barber was appointed in September 1913, an enthusiastic sportsman as well as cleric.

Coombes's success in improving buildings, as might be expected, was considerably less, little enough money was coming in, and the chapel took away any chance of another appeal. Only one addition was made to the main buildings when in 1910 a woodwork shop was opened near Fleur de Lys, a building which was to have an interesting history as an engine room, tuck box store, music room, and history department. It enabled the former woodwork room in Shield to be converted into a second laboratory for physics next to the existing chemistry one. Although upper school still continued to be used for some lessons, Coombes between 1904 and 1911 created five classrooms in the existing building, each one associated with a dormitory and serving the additional purpose of a day room. Prep was moved to day rooms and dormitory libraries started. Some dormitories like Chevron began to provide cabinets for cups and to move their honours boards into the new rooms.

In the grounds Coombes was able to achieve a good deal. West field was purchased, and made fit for games in 1912. Frederick Rooke (OJ) died in 1909 aged only 30, and left £342 to the College. This was invested, and together with £600 from the Chapter used to buy the first land to the east owned by the school, when Rooke's field of seven acres was bought in 1914. It is now divided into Highfields, the sanatorium, and Martlet gardens. Ground improvements were helped by an increase in the chapter grant in 1904 from £75 to £100, tuck shop profits, and above all by the setting up of an Improvement Fund by the Old Johnians. Created in 1906, this was run in turn by B.T. Verver, F.K. Rooke, and R.C. Petherbridge until it came to an end in 1912. During those six years about £300 was given, the largest sum being £189 3s. 9d. for renovating the fives courts, and other sums went to the tuck shop, range, and improvement of West field. Money for the first school register was provided, and also for cricket nets and screens. Sadly, as we shall see, this useful fund ended when the chapel once more began its demands on peoples' pockets. It enabled Coombes to use other money on improvements. In 1906 a miniature range was put on the far side of North field and in 1908 a full-scale range in the south-west corner of the grounds. A new tuck shop hut was built.

23 The cast of *King John*, 1907. Second row from the front, fifth from the left, is R.C. Petherbridge dressed as Faulconbridge, then A.S. Grant as King John.

II

In his distinguished study of public schools Jonathan Gathorne-Hardy gave the title 'The Final Picture' to his Edwardian chapter. These were the years when public school histories, memoirs, and novels became a major literary genre and did much to fix in peoples' mind the 'typical image' of public school life then, and unfortunately long afterwards, when it had little relationship to reality. In 1906 Hurst library acquired Lionel Portman's *Hugh Rendal*, and an even more notorious school novel, Horace Vachell's *The Hill*. Hurst's own two novels about its school life, John Smith's *Out of The Depths, a Schoolboy's Story of St Wilfrid's*, and Bertram Mitford's *Haviland's Chum*, came out in 1901 and 1903 respectively. In the new day rooms *The Gem* (1906) and *The Magnet* (1908) had started Billy Bunter's long career at Greyfriars, and it would be true to say that the majority of non-serious reading by boys in the 1900s was of imperialist, military, naval, and public school stories, if they were middle class or above.

Both Cooper and Coombes did their best to ensure that Hurst was accepted as part of the public-school community and was 'like all the rest'. The school did not have every typical feature—few did—lacking a school song, for instance, but in other ways it was stepping into line. It adopted a language peculiar to public schools both in general—the word 'chaps' replaced 'fellows' in the magazine at this time—and to itself with words like 'courts' for toilets, 'rooker' for dormitory prefects' room, or 'flooders' for a dip in a lane north of the College. Blazers and boaters, caps and lengthy scarves, and the panoply of games' dress with special caps, scarves, badges, colours, and later ties, had completely conquered individuality in dress. Athleticism, *esprit de corps*, and playing the game were the core of a code of conduct as rigorous as any religious observance, with social excommunication awaiting those who did not conform. Prefectorial power was established and a host of rules for prefects to enforce. Hurst, as we have seen, played the right sports, attended the right public-school events, and through its corps mixed with the right and more famous schools. The substantial collection of Edwardian pictures in the archives shows a school apparently full of confident, happy, healthy boys and masters. The substantial number of poems in the magazine reflects affection and loyalty to the College. So perhaps it would be true to say that Edwardian Hurst was the high peak in the evolution of the public-school system—before it the system was growing; after it, some might say, the system was either declining, or changing into something unrecognisable to Coombes and his generation—a process he himself was to criticise as it started soon after the First World War.

Edwardian Hurst was part of another more general golden age, the existence of which some historians have disputed, maintaining that this was wishful thinking, looking back across the trenches of 1914-18, which would make practically anything that went before look idyllic. It depends of course from which angle you look at the period: J.B. Priestley maintained in *The Edwardians* that there was never a golden age, but W. Macqueen-Pope, on the contrary, said there was one for the middle classes during The Golden Sovereign Age. He particularly drew attention to 'that quiet, peaceful, spacious England of the golden days' in part of which Hurst was set; 'this sweet, Sussex land', as Cooper called it in his last sermon. If one narrows the definition of the Edwardian Golden Age a little, it can hardly be doubted that there was indeed one when the countryside of Brooke's poetry or Sassoon's Kent was really as idyllic as that for a minority.

For boys at Hurst, Coombes's years were the last when it was really a school set deep in unspoilt countryside, appreciated and visited by boys and masters alike, although even then the magazine was critical of semi-detached houses in Burgess Hill (1905) and bungalows appearing at Shoreham (1906). When Cooper left to be vicar of Portslade, it was 'a pretty inland village on a hill'. This is the description in E.V. Lucas's *Highways and Byways of Sussex* (1904), where Angmering is described as 'a typical dusty Sussex village with white houses and thatched roofs' and Rottingdean as a village 'hardly ever likely to creep across the surrounding hills'. 'Nothing,' said Woolsey, 'is more delightful than a run through our lovely country', and part at least of happy remembrance and loyalty was to the setting as well as the school itself; the magazine in its descriptions, particularly of the Bicycle Club's travels but also in prose pieces most probably by Woolsey and Johnson, certainly reflects a golden age for public-school boys living in the country.

So the riders set off to explore 'the glamorous Downs, and the green goodness of the Weald' where 'sunlight breathes through the pale leafed woods and the air is sweet with the scent of Spring'. Along lanes they went where the hedges 'are full of naive faced daisies, buttercups, glistening gold, and dandelions, like ragged medals'. All round the riders was 'an indiscreet profusion of colour, trees everywhere, and orchards, low sloping roofs, moss grown, the colour of gold, ragged farm yards, and here and there a church spire rising over all'. Villages they passed through were 'a glimmer of dull red', and as evening drew on 'the Downs will soon be rippling towards a glorious sunset of liquid gold'. After chapel the boys would often go to masters' studies for music or talk, their windows opened to the lime trees and fellows garden to the west of the College, or the musk of honeysuckle on the walls to the east of the building. There they would listen to the piano, 'the light on distant Danny dying, the bells of Hurst resounding sweetly ..., and the sun setting in glory in the golden west'.

Passing through these idyllic surroundings the bicycles had their problems. Punctures prevented them reaching chapel in time in 1904 and were 'two a penny' next year. In 1907 one boy had to be towed back from Bolney when his chain broke, and there was a plague of flies, but by and large the magazine and minute book record many pleasures, including visits to watch building at Christ's Hospital and Lancing, and to Cowfold Monastery, Bramber Castle, and several churches. They could swim at Shoreham or in the new municipal baths at Lewes, or enjoy boating on the lake at Slaugham. They could ramble on the Downs or Ashdown Forest. There was tea at cafés like those at Slaugham or Lewes, or inns at Steyning, Cuckfield and Henfield. At the last village they were entertained by Lowe in the *White Hart* in July 1904, and continued to make visits until May 1908 when Harriet entertained them in the Martyn Lodge garden, and Lowe spoke to them through a window.

By contrast to this pleasant picture some of the masters at least believed they were actually menaced by change. We have seen Woolsey upset by building from Shoreham to Turner's Hill over the years. Haines said they lived in 'an age of hurry' and in June 1908 the first accident involving a motor vehicle took place at Cooksbridge when two boys were struck from their machines by a motor taxi cab, and had to go back on the train with Scott. Cars, motor bicycles, cameras, phonographs, and telephones were all indications that the world was changing, and in a debate in November 1913 the boys voted 12-6 that 'savagery' was preferable to 'civilisation'. What they meant by this emerged in the debate. Norman Bannister said man was content to live the simple life unlike the 'civilised man who had his motor car'. Aeroplanes, another speaker said, were 'suicidal, besides being a nuisance and eyesore'.

The Debating Society was revived by R.J. Wood in January 1912, and its discussions show that the boys were overwhelmingly conservative in attitude to life and politics: perhaps that was why a new master like T.A. Straughan criticised 'lack of originality' in school life. The boys voted against striking miners, Home Rule for Ireland, Socialism, tariff reform, and votes for women, and supported compulsory military service, the cane, and the waging of war if necessary. But their debates also reveal that outside influences were making themselves felt, particularly in the sixth form. In February and November 1913 there was much criticism of the 'masher' or 'the nut' with bright ties, yellow socks, brilliantined hair, and a vocabulary including 'rotten show', 'priceless', and 'the giddy limit'. This paralleled the magazine's criticism of the 'devastating course' of the first jazz music. There were complaints of a lack of respect for the prefects, and a lack of self-reliance. The boys voted that they were not suffering from 'degeneracy' in such matters, and on another occasion proved it by voting in favour of cold baths, long walks, and camping, although they drew the line at the reintroduction of duelling.

This contrast between change and tradition can be seen, too, in the musical life of the College, particularly after A.C. Axe arrived in September 1907, and later when T.A. Straughan and R. Willis brought in the latest songs from outside. Patriotic music certainly continued to flourish throughout the period. Kipling's poems like *Troopin'* and even the *Just So Stories* were set to music. Edward German's light operettas replaced those of Sullivan, and the most popular was *The Yeomen of England* in which Coombes himself sang. Elgar's music was frequently played including his *Imperial March* and cantata *The Banner of St George*, while Axe set *Land of Hope and Glory* to a piano arrangement. For a time Boer War songs like *Goodbye Dolly Grey* and *Tommy Atkins* were popular.

The traditional chorus songs and ballads, too, remained popular like *John Peel*, *Tom Bowling*, and *Widdicombe Fair*, but it was noticeable that music hall and dance music was making an appearance. Among contemporary songs sung were *Two Lovely Black Eyes*, *By the Light of the Silvery Moon*, and two extremely popular songs with the astonishing titles of *Tooralli*, and *Yippi Addy I Aye*. Parham's rendering of the *Belle of Bethnal Green* was considered a little risqué by the magazine editor on one occasion. Both the school songs, and the Harrow songs popular in the 1890s died out, and black minstrels and jazz music were considered the latest thing.

It is noticeable that there was a decline in serious music. The choir is rarely mentioned in the magazine, and there were no great choral works performed. Axe added to school music his settings of services and play music, but most classical music performances were by soloists or small ensembles, and most of the leading players were masters rather than boys including Parham, Axe, and Straughan.

In one aspect of school life there was no change from Cooper's day. The boys remained strongly imperialist in sentiment, and the cadet corps flourished to give some expression to such sentiments by training boys for possible military service in the Empire. Empire Day was first celebrated at Hurst on 24 May 1905 with a corps volley, cheers for the King, and a setting by Fielden, the music master, of Kipling's *Recessional* sung in chapel. The day continued to be celebrated at Hurst until the early 1930s, although it never caught on with the general public. Coronation Day in 1911 was quite different, of course, and the corps marched to the village green to fire its volley. There was a *Te Deum* in chapel, and a cricket match with Billingshurst stopped by rain after tea when Billingshurst were 136 for 3! Although the rain dampened the firework display that evening, the school went ahead with a torchlight procession up Danny, and they 'slithered and slid and struggled to the top through the wind and the rain' with torches still burning, and there sang the National Anthem.

Lieutenant H. Knox spoke about the Navy League at the school in 1906, but an attempt to make Trafalgar Day a school occasion did not succeed. *The Hurst Johnian* had plenty of material on the Empire and three examples will illustrate this. The Rev. Bertie Bull who had talked on the Boer War now published *For God and Our Soldiers*, the aim being to show how Christian English soldiers were at war listening to their padres round camp fires and attending services: it was, said the magazine, 'a vivid and trenchant reply to all those who try to blacken the character of our soldiers'. When Bull preached at Hurst he made strong appeals for moral behaviour based on examples from the lives of Lord Roberts and General Redvers Buller. Harry Mckenzie Rew (OJ) had served in South Africa where he was decorated several times. His brother was a master at Worksop, who died young in 1909, and the same year Rew went there as secretary. In 1908 he published *Records of the Rough Riders* which the magazine described as a 'remarkably complete account of the war compiled from diaries kept at the time'. Lastly, James Stuart, the distinguished member of the Natal government, whose career has already been discussed, published in 1913 *The Zulu Rebellion of 1906* which was given an eight-page review in the magazine. Unusually for its time the book made an effort to see matters from the Zulu point of view as well as pointing out that, in a year of drought, locusts, and rinderpest, the Natal government imposed a poll tax starting the rebellion.

Percy Scott, later Captain Scott, took over the corps in 1903, and the ground floor of Chevron became the armoury. Numbers rose from 72 in 1903 to a hundred in 1913. The corps now paraded in khaki and the Brodrick cap which they continued to wear until the First World War when it was replaced by an officer-style cap. The most important event in corps history was the result of the Liberal government's decision to modernise every aspect of British forces once the failures of the Boer War had been studied. In 1909 the corps became the Officers Training

24 The Boar's Head entering hall in December 1913. Note the condition of the hall as it was until Tower's headship, P.W. Scott, bottom right, and the two pages wearing the servitors' aprons.

Corps (O.T.C.), seen less as a broad training ground for military service than as a means to providing a ready pool for rapidly expanding the officer cadre. 'Our soldiering', said the magazine, 'is more serious than it was', and under Scott there would have been little time for amusement. He was so laconic that corps reports virtually disappear from the magazine by 1914. However, its first inspection as an O.T.C. in June 1909 indicates that they performed well.

The annual visit to Aldershot for the public schools camp remained the highlight of the year. In 1906 it was so hot shirt-sleeve order was allowed even for the parade after which Lord Roberts rode down the lines. The first O.T.C. camp in 1909 was attended by three thousand boys. There were two field days and a night operation, and they were inspected by General Smith-Dorien. They were able to see a complete division parade in Long Valley with 18,000 men, 600 officers, 6,800 horses, and 100 guns. In 1907 the Lee-Enfield rifle replaced the old carbines, and with two ranges Hurst was able to improve its shooting, and Coombes stressed that 'every boy should learn to use a rifle'. Local night operations had their inevitably funny side. On one occasion the Hurst Corps was in battle with the local Territorials on Danny, but an attempted flank march fell foul of barbed wire, a stream and an ash pit: 'one man fell into a stream and was with difficulty extricated: one man encouraged a master to advance with 'get on you fool'. The band challenged and chased another officer who tripped over his great coat. In 1907 a joint field-day was held with Cranleigh and Reading Grammar School, and in 1913 the local press reported in some detail a field-day on Ditchling Common when an invading army represented by Lancing College attacked Hurst on the defensive. Post cards of corps activity were popular, and one showing them marching through the village in dappled sunlight in the summer of 1914 was soon to achieve poignancy when a real and terrible war engulfed the public-school corps that autumn.

The athletic god continued to be worshipped in Edwardian Hurst. At St Etheldreda Day in 1913 the archdeacon of London preached a sermon based on the odd text of St John 'the famous athlete', because he ran the half mile to Jesus's tomb faster than St Peter! He went on to talk about running to win, but being modest in victory and gracious in defeat. Doctrine was scarcely mentioned, but the theme was sufficiently interesting for it to be the only sermon commented on at any length in the magazine. The only time Kipling was unpopular with the boys was when he denounced the 'flannelled fool and muddied oaf' for playing a part in the disasters of the Boer War. In a heated debate he was criticised, one speaker asking: 'who is this Kipling? He is not even a knight!'

Enthusiasm was not everything, however, and the fundamental problems making it hard for Hurst to win consistently at major sports remained, with the exception of playing fields of which there were at last enough. Between 1902 and 1914 there were four seasons of cricket which might be described as good—1904, 1906, 1907 and 1914—and only 1907 was outstanding when they won 10 out of 15 matches. Captained by J.E. de W. Denning, their most effective bowler, and with R.C. Petherbridge as their main scorer the team showed their paces in their most difficult matches, particularly that with Lancing. Petherbridge scored 96, and R.B. Neill 138, so Hurst declared at 266 for two. Lancing went in to bat at 4.15 p.m., and with a minute left the last Lancing batsman was caught by Neill off a ball by Bird, and they were all out for 159. The usual scene on North field was less enthralling. In both 1905 and 1910 only one match was won, and overall of 174 games played only 66 were victories. The magazine commented in 1913 that the matches were 'quite devoid of interest because in them we know we must be hopelessly beaten'.

Sadly, the record in football, due to the large number of early leavers, was even worse. Only in 1904 and 1907 did the First XI win more than they lost. In 1907 with six players who had been in the team three years they played superbly and won 11 out of 12 matches. The Lancing match won 12-1 at Lancing was a good example of that season's play, when Petherbridge scored four of the goals in a match played in heavy rain and a tearing gale. 1909 was the worst year with 10 defeats. Of 136 matches played at Edwardian Hurst only 52 were victories. The football XI of 1914, soon to be put to the test on other fields, was described as displaying 'want of skill, energy, and enthusiasm'.

This record in the two major sports must have been galling to Old Johnians because Hurst had established a good reputation as a sporting school among county and old boy sides. By 1914, 19 had played football for their county, and in the 1900s Hursts provided two players— Harold Milestone and Ronald Turner—for internationals with France and Bohemia. Ten had played cricket for their county. Hurst Johnians had played for 13 counties in different sports, and 11 had played for Oxford or Cambridge at cricket, football, athletics, cross country, hockey, water polo and swimming. In the past Hurst had provided, in George Osborne, an early rugby international. Three had played cricket for Sussex, and 12 had represented the county in football. In June 1913 the Old Johnian Football Club was refounded, and in their first season (1913-1914) captained by G.W. O'Neill Butler they won the Arthur Dunn Cup in March 1914.

By now there were 10 trophies available for competition. There were dormitory cups for football, cricket, fives, athletics, gymnastics, boxing and swimming. There was a cadet force section cup. In 1905 a *Victor Ludorum* Cup was presented, and the first junior dormitory cup— for football—started to be followed by others. Not all these sports were enthusiastically followed, although fives, athletics and gymnastics remained well supported. Although Robert Kup, father of F.C. Kup, presented a cup the first competition for it suffered from faulty timing. The magazine commented that 'few people at Hurst take their swimming seriously'. House swimming was reorganised, and in July 1913 the first match with another school—Ardingly—took place with Kup as the best swimmer also helping Chevron to win the dormitory cup that year.

Although running was maintained throughout the period there were frequent complaints about inadequate supervision. One year the hare and hounds had to abandon a fixture when the paper blew away! Runners were accused of cutting corners, eating on the course, and, of course, walking, and some runs were described as 'farcical'. Although a captain of running appears in 1907 the post was not consistently filled. Once Mallam left, boxing too declined, until the P.G.C. intervened in 1912 and the dormitory competition was organised to take place daily for a fortnight on North field. But the standards were low. Bouts between heavyweights (in those days boys over nine stone) were 'tame and disappointing', and many fights were 'little more than the usual whirl of gloves and arms'.

By the late 1900s just as everything was improving at last it seemed that Coombes might be able to benefit from a financial windfall, even if it was one brought about by the deaths of the three previous heads within a short space of time. In 1910 Awdry died, but the memorial fund for him raised only £24. This was not because people lacked generosity in giving for chapel memorials—those to William Pratt, George Thomson, and R. J. Wood attracted a good response. Clearly it was because Awdry was distant, even remote, history. Then on 30 March 1912 Edward Lowe died, and was buried at Ely. Harriet left Martyn Lodge for Medina Villas, Hove, and it was soon apparent that Lowe's will gave most generously to the College, starting with money to endow permanently the Dole which was paid into the chapel account. In July a meeting took place to consider a suitable memorial: a stained glass window, scholarships, a portrait, and completion of the chapel were considered. On 17 August 1912 Edward Cooper died. On 28 September a Memorial Committee was set up under R.A. Bennett (OJ) and

H.L. Johnson to consider the joint commemoration of the three heads. This was a unique situation in which a considerable amount of money could be raised.

Speaking to the Old Johnians in 1911 Arthur Coombes had made it plain where his wishes lay. He pointed out then that the chapel fund contained £10 1s. 3d. and that £7,000 was needed to complete Carpenter's original design, going on later in the speech to talk about the need for new school buildings. There are no records apart from financial ones for Coombes's years, and we do not know what he asked for in 1912. We do know the committee decided on three portraits—installed in Hall in 1914—and on completing the north transept of the chapel. This ended the Old Johnian Improvements Fund, and it prevented again any of the money raised being used for pressing educational needs.

The fund was launched in October 1912 and by March 1914 had collected £644 17s. 8d. Building started again in August 1913 and the work finished in May 1914. By finished, one means that the south and north transepts and the ante-chapel were now complete, the windows filled with the cheapest glass, and the building completely bare. The cost was £1,034 leaving a debt of about £380 which William Woodard refused to finance in any way. The committee ended its work in June 1915, and the debt was slowly whittled away until the last £40 was stumped up at the Old Johnian Dinner in 1921.

1914 was in many ways a good year. Numbers were slightly down, but revenue slightly up. Academic results were starting to show the effectiveness of Arthur Coombes's emphasis on work. There were five Higher Certificates and two exemptions from London Matriculation. There were eight Old Johnians in residence at Oxbridge where E.A.T. Dutton was 'punting on the Cher although usually without the pole'. It was a summer of 'perfect weather', and the magazine noticed that boaters were out early, and that boys took forked sticks with them to trap adders when they climbed Wolstonbury Hill. The First XI had its best season for some time, winning half of its matches, due in part to R. Willis's coaching. D.R. Baylis, the captain, was ill and Richard Crux was acting captain of a team including M.A. and E.L. Pitcher as bowlers, and R. Lintott as best batsman. Match followed match 'on a baked wicket and under a scorching sun' and, in a spectacular victory over Whitgift, Richard Crux took six wickets for nine runs, and Richard Lintott scored eighty-seven.

So term drew pleasantly to a close. Carts and cabs arrived to take luggage and boys to the station, and the magazine wished 'goodbye to all those who are leaving—and to all a happy holiday'. Among 30 leavers were Frank Carter, the school captain, prefects like Richard Lintott and Norman Cartledge, and some familiar Hurst names like Lock, Norman and Pitcher. The same day as term ended the corps went off to camp at Mytchett Farm, Aldershot, and it was there that the First World War came upon them as the hot summer dissolved in thundery rain. On 2 August they found all the officers, orderlies, cooks, and even horses had gone and they had to fend for themselves. On Tuesday 4 August 1914 war was declared, and the Hurst corps marched to Aldershot Station singing this year's most popular tune, *It's a Long Way to Tipperary*, soon to be sung in other dusty lanes and other circumstances.

EIGHT

VALIANT HEARTS
1914-1923

The First World War and Arthur Coombes's Later Years

The very sight of the waking beauty of the Spring brings other thoughts than those of pleasure ... Even as we gaze on the dim, blue goodness of the Weald, a vision rises of the ruined homes and blackened fields of Flanders less than a hundred miles away.

Arthur Coombes writing in *The Hurst Johnian* 564/133, May 1915

O valiant hearts, who to your glory came
Through dust of conflict, and through battle flame:
Tranquil you lie, your knightly virtue proved,
Your memory hallowed in the land you loved.

The first verse of a hymn, words by J.S. Arkwright (1872-1954), sung on Armistice Sunday 1919, and Remembrance Sunday since

... since August, I have had to tell fifty-nine people that the School is full until 1920. When we say full, we mean this: that, after sacrificing every guest-chamber in the College and Headmaster's House we can provide 218 beds, giving to each the cubic space required by the sanitary authorities ... An opportunity occurred in the early months of the year of acquiring sleeping accommodation in the largest and best house in the neighbourhood [Hurst Wickham]. This term there are twenty-two boys there, and these with twelve day boys, make up a total of 255.

Arthur Coombes speaking on St Etheldreda Day, October 1918
The Hurst Johnian, 594/284 November 1918

Reaction to the outbreak of the First World War varied from school to school. At Wellington College all games were cancelled and each afternoon was spent in corps training, but in most it seems to have been business as usual. At neighbouring Brighton College, for example, 'the war barely disrupted school routine'. Fifty-eight per cent of casualties on the Western front were caused by artillery fire, and the *Hurst Johnian* commented in 1916 that this bombardment could be heard in Sussex. Unlike the very different picture of life totally altered by the impact of the Second World War, this was as near as the direct impact of war came to the College, although blackout was purchased for possible use. The only war work

153

involving the boys was labour on the vegetables grown on the West field to help meet the food shortage: yield from these rose from £213 1s. 7d. in 1914 to £411 11s. 7d. in 1918. In the last year of the war 50 boys went to Chew Magna and East Harptree in Somerset to do farm work, and spent a month cultivating swedes and bringing in the harvest. A picture shows Pocock and Parham in the fields, the latter in a billycock hat raising aloft a sheaf of corn.

Unfortunately for Coombes the war had a switch-back effect on intake, first producing a fall, then a spectacular rise, and then a further fall. The immediate fall from 174 in 1914 to 159 in 1916 was caused mainly by early leavers, including those keen to get into the war like Charles Gepp, member of the First XI, and runner up as *Victor Ludorum*, who left in December 1915. He entered the London Scottish under age and was killed on 1 July 1916 on that most terrible of days in British military history, the first day of the Somme. Then came a rise: in 1917 to 174 and in 1919 to a spectacular 255. Numbers remained high until 1922. Other public schools experienced a similar rise for which various explanations are given including bombing in the London area, the absence of fathers from home, and the cheapness of catering at school when rationing at last imposed restrictions at home. From September 1918 to July 1919, Hurst Wickham, a neighbouring large house, was rented to accommodate the sudden rush of boys, and the rooms formerly set aside for the Provost to lodge in were taken over as well: for a brief moment Coombes had the unusual job of turning away applicants. But the boom was short lived. By the end of 1919, 107 boys had left during the year, and by 1923 numbers at 195 were returning to normal.

NUMBERS 1915-1923

Year	Total in School	Entry
1915	163	51
1916	159	65
1917	174	87
1918	217	82
1919	255	50
1920	231	64
1921	220	47
1922	209	38
1923	195	51

Numbers from 1915 to 1937 are taken from the Woodard Calendars.

As usual the Chapter were slow to respond to increasing demand, and fees were not raised until 1919 when they increased from £53 11s. to £64 10s. a year for the entrants on full fees. Nevertheless Coombes was for a time in the pleasing position of receiving increased revenues. Although the accounts are not entirely clear for this period, the increase in fee income was as follows: 1916—£8,781 1s. 1d.; 1917—£10,587 17s. 8d.; 1918 to July—£8,430 7s. 4d.; 1918 to December and 1919—£19,001 12s. 9d.

However, virtually none of this money found its way into development. It was eaten up by war-time and post-war boom inflation as Coombes explained on St Etheldreda Day in 1923. Rather unfairly he singled out as an example of this trend the rise in masters' salaries brought about by the setting up of the Burnham Committee (in effect a wages council for teachers) in 1919. Masters' salaries had indeed risen during the war years from £2,305 8s. 2d.

to £3,514 7s. 4d. while numbers remained constant, but this was only part of the inflationary problem. Although male domestic staff had left and the overall domestic labour force was cut, their wages bill had risen during the same period from £524 8s. 11d. to £674 17s. 7d. Incidentally, Coombes' own salary rose during these years from £895 18s. 2d. to £1,270 13s. 10d.

The accounts have plenty of examples to show how school life was affected by this six-year period of inflation. The cost of prizes rose from £20 to £60. Producing the *Hurst Johnian* cost £93 18s. 7d. in 1913 and £204 5s. 5d. by 1918. The last play before the war cost £74 1s. 8d. to produce, and the first one after it £115 17s. 2d.—the play committee was soon over £50 in debt. The P.G.C. minuted in 1915 that 'the strictest economy will have to be observed this year' but, in spite of cuts, as we shall see, expenditure rose from £252 0s. 11d. to £316 18s. 4d. Most serious of all, of course, was the rise in domestic expenditure with the increase in food and fuel costs. Between 1915 and 1917 the domestic account rose from £3,133 10s. 2d. to £4,241 10s. 8d. and increased numbers coincided with increased inflation. The cost of coal in the Michaelmas Term alone rose from £68 7s. 10d. to £169 7s. 3d.

Response to this situation was at two levels. First of all, there were small, almost cosmetic, economies. After donating the 'stodge' to Belgian refugees in 1914 the Boar's Head Feast ceased during the war. Climbing Danny on Ascension Day continued, but the tuck distributed came to an end in 1917. The Shakespeare play was suspended. The fixture list was cut. The number of servants was reduced, and there were mutterings that masters were having to do their own washing up and boys to stoke the boilers. The gas supply was turned off for part of the day. The responsibility for keeping the wheels turning in these difficult times fell on the school steward. Evans had been succeeded in 1911 by R.C. Reid. He fell ill with pleurisy and Edward Balshaw, a language master since 1908, took over in 1915. He was a jovial man, interested in art and cricket, and according to the magazine 'kept Hurst decently fed even in the leanest days of rationing'. By the end of 1919 he was ill and he died in February 1920 aged only fifty-four.

The second line of response was stern economy. Provost Southwell was away as an army chaplain and the Chapter was in the hands of William Woodard, who maintained his grip until his death in 1918, as his refusal to help with the north transept debt and his haggling over payment for the war memorial roll of honour indicate. G.E. Baker was the Chapter bursar for a time and was succeeded by P.C. Bates. He also died comparatively young in October 1921 and G.E. Baker returned until 1925. Although there are no Committee records for this period there can be no doubt that the most rigorous policies were adopted with one exception. As the post-war boom ended land prices fell spectacularly and, in 1919, 22 acres (East field and Ruckford) lying to the east of the College were bought. This was a valuable acquisition, protecting the College from future building development and ensuring it was centrally placed on its sports fields, although for the time being the Chapter leased it to neighbouring farmers because there was no money for development.

In 1919 architect's scale drawings of the buildings were made and in 1921 Harry Adnitt's series of six sketches of these buildings were produced. Both show that the Victorian buildings remained unchanged, and the worst result of the war years was that many of the gains in building improvements made by Coombes prior to 1914 were lost, and conditions degenerated as a result of deliberate economies and then inflation. 'We have,' said Coombes in 1922, 'to carry out a thorough overhaul of all our buildings': but this was not done. Whatever Coombes may have meant when he told the Provost next year, 'I am handing back to you a school in a thoroughly good working order', he clearly could not have been referring to the buildings and indeed he had referred publicly to the fact that 'all our buildings are from fifty to sixty years old'. The infirmary had started to collapse and was sustained by buttresses to the outer walls, with steel rods bolting together the upper floors. By 1922 the gymnasium could no longer be used, being held together by four new buttresses against the north wall sunk in seven feet of concrete and iron rods in the west and east walls. A contemporary refers to the cold, gas-lit buildings, the clouds of dust rising as they played football in the crypt, and the green sludge that gathered on the swimming pool.

By the time Coombes left, the common room, like the buildings, stood in need of renewal. There was always a brisk turn over of masters, but the war accelerated the process, and because there were no reserved occupations some of the youngest, involved in corps and sport, particularly felt they should join up. Nineteen former and present members of the common room were involved in some sort of war service, including two forces' chaplains and service in the censor's department. Of 14 masters present in 1914 only five were left at the war's end, and of the 28 war-time appointments only one was of any lasting value. Four masters died who are commemorated by the pavilion clock given by the P.G.C. after the war. R. Willis and T.A. Straughan had actually left in July but they both joined up at once. Willis was in the Honourable Artillery Company, and then the 9th Lancashire Regiment and was killed occupying a crater at Vimy in May 1917. 'Shall we not,' said the *Hurst Johnian*, in the extraordinary language of those nationalist times, 'envy him his glorious death, sudden and painless, in the glow of a great achievement?' Straughan was in the Northumberland Regiment and was seriously wounded at Suvla Bay in July 1915. He told Coombes he would like to return, but soon after visiting the College he died of blood poisoning in February 1918.

A.C. Axe, the talented music master, left in May 1915 and, after being turned down for a commission, entered the Yorkshire Regiment as a private. He was killed on 1 July 1916, and the memorial money collected on his behalf was used to publish his religious music with the help of Canon Leigh Nixon (OJ) and Dr. Walter Alcock at Westminster Abbey. H.V. Lee was a master at Hurst from September 1912 to March 1915, when he left to join the Suffolk Regiment. After a spell in Egypt he went to the Salonika Front and from there sent a few letters to the magazine. In November 1916 he was shot during a dawn attack on Bulgarian positions. Three masters—C.B. Williams, W.S. Bell, and N.E. Robinson—were invalided out of the forces. Robinson had only been in the school a term before he volunteered. He returned in 1918 and took over the editorship of the magazine among other duties. After two years he had to leave and he died from his wounds in 1922—one of many not listed in totals of war dead.

The five masters who stayed during the war were Edward Balshaw (1908-1920) who, as we saw, was also steward, G.H. Gregory (1903-1924) the last writing master, Percy Scott who was running Chevron and the corps, H.B.I. Pocock teaching science, and running Red Cross from 1910 to 1921 when he was married, and H.M. Parham, running Fleur de Lys, who in 1923 was the first member of staff to complete 25 continuous years' service receiving a silver tea service and silver cigarette box. Three clergymen helped to sustain the life of the school in the war years. The Rev. H.S. Barber had just been appointed in 1913, and for four years he helped run football, cricket, fives and cross-country before going to be chaplain of Glenalmond. His successor was the Rev. K.G. Packard, who left in 1921 to be chaplain of Bradford College: 'we shall not soon forget his telescope, and his socialism, his wild animals and his bowling', remarked the magazine. From May 1915 to July 1921 the Rev. P.R.B. Brown, described as 'our best scholar', was at the College as Shield dormitory master with 'accomplishments many and various'. Old Johnians were called on to fill gaps including R.F. Crux, R.A. Cumming, J.M. Rolleston, and later L.E. Cartridge who stayed for a short time, but two old boy appointments proved highly successful.

Claud Gurney, who had been an Open Scholar at St John's, Oxford in modern languages, returned to Hurst as Shield housemaster in September 1920. From then until 1924 he produced four plays and edited the magazine, introducing tentative literary criticism, and, although he disliked swimming himself, he restored it as a major sport. He lifted French teaching 'out of the dust of drudgery to the height of a mild adventure'. But within a year of the new head's arrival he had left; some years later meeting John Muriel (OJ) it emerged that he left because Tower was 'essentially a little man'. After a distinguished career as a West End producer he was killed in a car accident in 1946. Vincent Randolph Rogers (1885-1925), who had left Hurst in 1904, was a noted cricket and football player, who had entered the church as vicar of Warminster. He married Margaret O'Hagan in 1909. He became an army chaplain, but resigned this post to take up active service in September 1917 in the Royal Artillery. He returned to Hurst in January 1919, and that year revived the Shakespeare play with *Twelfth Night*. Affable and easy going, handsome and with a beautiful wife, whose sister, Kathleen, was married to Douglas Smith, another Old Johnian, Rogers was immediately popular. He organised the first Old Johnian cricket week, and in 1921 Coombes promoted him to be chaplain. A third successful appointment of a master who was to be deeply involved in school life was made in September 1923 when Coombes appointed Francis Wright, whose main work lay ahead in Tower's time.

The one war-time appointment of lasting value took place in September 1915 when Horace A. Hawkins took over music. He remained until July 1938, and during that time he was destined to establish Hurst's reputation as a school of musical distinction and to begin a long line of music awards to Oxbridge. Other appointments could only be described as unfortunate, and it was no surprise that Tower was to make a clean sweep of some of them, even if he foolishly offended Gurney at the same time. The Rev. O. Darrell Brown was at Hurst from September 1920 to September 1925. He was a well-intentioned cleric who contributed to the sports day and swimming prizes as much as £30 a year. But he was also an eccentric given to rushing round stuffing a clenched handkerchief in his mouth. His room was raided two or three times a term. His classroom was bedlam with ink pellets flying everywhere and crude drawings of himself on the board. On hall duty he usually presided over a riot with butter pats flying, and boys would snip pieces off his gown as he passed. Once a term he was let loose in the chapel pulpit and gave sermons popular with the non-religious element in the school, in which he behaved like an Old Testament prophet gesticulating and roaring. On one famous occasion while preaching on Bunyan's *Pilgrim's Progress* he was so worked up that his gestures and great weight edged the pulpit to the top of the altar steps, and it was only saved from toppling over when some boys rushed forward to hold it up!

If Darrell Brown was eccentric, Sidney Mavor was bizarre. One of the most interesting Old Johnians was Reginald Turner—subject of a biography by Stanley Weintraub in 1965— who was part of the artistic circle in the 1890s West End. He was author of a dozen books including *Castles in Kensington* in 1904 and *Dorothy Raeburn* in 1905, and was a close friend of Oscar Wilde's; indeed he was one of those who helped him when he came out of prison. Among the charges brought against Wilde were two involving one Sidney Mavor. Lord Alfred Douglas told him to deny the charges: 'remember you are a gentleman and a public school boy', and this was one of two counts on which Wilde was found not guilty. It is therefore highly likely that it was Turner who recommended Mavor to Hurst, where he arrived as a master in January 1917 and remained until July 1925. 'Sammy' Mavor was respected for his culture, according to John Muriel, and not ragged, although his behaviour might have led to it, as his rooms were hung with dark curtains kept drawn during the day and he spent hours kneeling at a *prié dieu* surrounded by flowers and incense.

Lack of records and register alike from 1914 make it difficult to quantify results, but the overall position remains clear enough: only a small percentage of the College were successful in any of the several exams then taken, which included Higher Certificate and from 1921 School Certificate; as Coombes himself put it in 1923, 'the intellect of the School was confined to quite a small number of boys, and they were looked upon with a certain amount of suspicion, as possessing more than their fair share of brains'. Indeed the new School Certificate exam led to the 'greatest difficulty' and a reorganisation of the lower forms. No records of university entry were kept, but at the end of the First World War deferred entry and new entries meant that between 1918 and 1924 there were at least twenty-one Hurst Johnians at Oxbridge, although all but six of them were at Oxford. Of those 15, five were at Keble and five at St John's.

In the same speech in 1923 Coombes was equally scathing about the life of the school. If Woodard returned, he said, he would find 'originality, enthusiasm, and devotion looked on as rather dangerous eccentricities', and there is little evidence in the magazine of the thriving school life of Edwardian times: even the photographs show dour and solemn-faced boys replacing the cheery looks of earlier years. The war inevitably made the corps a major school activity and under Captain Percy Scott, without a sergeant to help him, numbers rose to 180 by 1918. Scott retired as commander in July 1919 and was given a clock, later presenting the corps himself with a platoon challenge shield, but during his years of command scarcely a word appeared in the magazine, and it was only when Captain H.B.I. Pocock took over that limited reports briefly appear, before silence descends again on their activities.

The only area of school life where there was plenty of vitality was in music and the play, where Hawkins, Rogers and Gurney combined to provide a varied programme. The three men produced between 1919 and 1924 *Twelfth Night*, *The Merchant of Venice*, *A Midsummer Night's Dream*, *Macbeth*, *Hamlet*, and *Much Ado About Nothing*, which was an ambitious line up of plays compared with previous years. Photographs show they were experimenting with lighting and scenery, and Hawkins wrote special music for each play, some of which, like that for *A Midsummer Night's Dream* and *Macbeth*, was published. Also published a year after it was written in 1921 was a *Hurst March*.

But in his early years Hawkins's two main achievements were to establish a carol service and to restore an orchestra. On Sunday 19 December 1915 six carols were sung after Even-song, and next year he was able to be more ambitious. On the Feast of St Nicolas the hymn of St Nicolas was sung in plainsong, not heard for many years. On 16 December there was a programme of Christmas music in chapel with five early carols and organ music by Hawkins 'played as splendidly as ever'. Following Evensong on the next night there were seven more carols. In December 1919 the Boar's Head procession was restored, but it was decided that the sing-song in hall would not be restored. Instead they would have the carols in chapel because 'they had won a place in our hearts from which they could not be evicted'. A week later the first full carol service took place.

Re-establishing classical music in the College was not easy. In June 1916 the choir was used to present *Trial by Jury* on a makeshift stage, and Coombes commented he was 'frankly astonished by its success'. Hawkins gave talks on European music, and works by Franck, Sibelius, and Widor began to appear in chapel services. On the night of 11 April 1916 in a darkened chapel (there was no gas) the first of Hawkins's concerts was given, with W.J. Lines singing the solo with the aid of a torch, and music by Frank and Widor. Over the next few years French composers like these and others such as Fauré and Saint-Saëns were a regular, and in those days unusual, part of the concert repertoire at Hurst. At first only the brass parts were played by boys, but by 1922 an orchestra of 19 players performed at the Shakespeare play. There was some opposition to the repertoire chosen by Hawkins: the magazine remarked on a concert in 1920 that it was 'the breaking of ice, which were better left unbroken', referring to music by Grieg and Sibelius. But as the programme of music expanded with pieces of Schubert, Tchaikovsky, and Wagner, Hawkins's efforts came to be appreciated, and by 1923 his concert was 'an eagerly awaited event at the end of the dullest term in the year'.

With reduced facilities, lack of competent masters, and smaller fixture lists, sport, like societies, does not receive detailed treatment in the magazine as in years past. Perhaps something of the spirit summed up in a Wellington College magazine affected other schools: 'we have come to understand that in the presence of the real thing, games are after all only games, useful though they may be'. Early leavers made the traditional problem of a lack of older players worse. By 1916 the *victor ludorum*, the runner up, and the winner of the Clayton Run were all under fifteen, and the First XI cricket team in 1917 had no less than 18 players during the season. Football's task continued to be made more difficult as other schools switched to rugby—Brighton did so in 1918—and by the early 1920s there were only three matches with other schools in the fixture list. Coombes suggested a switch to rugby but did not pursue the matter as there was such an outcry, particularly from Old Johnians whose club side under M.A. Pitcher was doing so well.

In cricket there were a number of fine players in the war years like W.H.B. Wolstencroft, D.H.O. Woodhams, and L.E. Cartridge, but they could not save the First XI from a succession of poor seasons: in 1917 only two boys, Woodhams and Cartridge, scored half the team's runs, although this did include a century of 120 by Cartridge in the Ardingly match. In 1918 for the first time in College history all First XI matches were lost. Every effort was made to keep a full fixture list, and this led to a series of matches with older teams like those from the 16th Royal Fusiliers, 3rd Battalion of the Sussex Regiment, and the Royal Army Medical Corps.

As some compensation for poor showing in the main sports there was a revival in two sports—swimming and cross-country. From 1916 there were 'fun sports' at the pool in the summer term including races in corps kit, evening dress, and night shirts, three-a-side tug-of-war, blind-folded water polo, and bobbing for apples. This rekindled interest and, with the help of Mr. Kellingly of the Brighton Club, a returned Sergeant Couch, and the arrival of Claud Gurney, proper training began and new strokes like the crawl were introduced. A group of boys including L.T. Good, H.L. Good, E.J. Stratford, R.E. Stratford, L.B. Yaldwyn, H.H. Wells, and A.W. Gibbs led successful teams for some years, and several went on to swim for their universities. In 1918 L.T. Good became the first captain of swimming and colours were to be awarded.

On 20 June 1918 the first match with another school since 1913 took place and by 1922 a fixture list of eight matches was established, Hurst winning four of them that year. In 1921 Hurst went for the first time to the Bath Club public schools' events and on their third visit in 1923 came second equal with St Paul's. In 1922 water polo fixtures began in which Hurst won two and drew two that year. The swimming test for all boys was restored, and in order to pass boys had to swim 400 yards, swim 75 yards fully dressed, and 50 yards in 50 seconds, carry out two rescues, and dive from three boards. House swimming revived and in 1921 there were swimming sports with nine events.

In 1919 G.L. Hankey was only seven seconds behind the winner of the steeplechase although three years younger; the first indication of his excellence, which, as he later became school captain, focused attention on this sport. He won the steeplechase in 1920. The Clayton Run started up again although on a reduced course of six and a half miles, and Hankey won it in 1921, and again in 1922 when his time of 40.13 minutes established a record that lasted until 1930. He won the steeplechase and was *Victor Ludorum* in both 1921 and 1922, and so in April 1922 the P.G.C. agreed there should be a captain of running and colours awarded. The same year school fixtures last heard of in Victorian times started again with a victory over the South London Harriers, although they were soon to be frequent winners of the Clayton Run. Hankey's successor as captain was another school captain, F. du B. Wilson, winner of the Clayton and *Victor Ludorum* in 1923. By then there were over sixty steeplechase runners and over ninety doing the Clayton Run, showing the sport to be well-established once more.

While Coombes was editing the magazine during the war he encouraged a series of articles on the history of the College, and in particular managed to reconstruct, with inaccuracies, lists of dormitory masters. In January 1916 Coombes began the replacement of the word 'dormitory' by 'house', and as usual change ran into opposition: Chevron did not adopt the new title in its house book until 1918. In May 1917 boards listing house masters were placed in the upper cloisters, and during the year the *Hurst Johnian* contains references to house leagues, house colours, and every house match was reported at length for the first time for many years. From January 1919 house captains, prefects and monitors were listed in the magazine, and the same year house colours were finalised: Fleur de Lys, light blue and gold, Star, dark and light blue, Chevron, black and gold, Red Cross, red and black, Shield, light blue, and day boys, green. Star house banner was completed in 1917, so all five could carry them in processions. The five house day rooms were painted in their respective colours.

At first there was some doubt about house loyalty—a letter to the magazine pointed out that at one junior house match only one supporter turned out, but the writer need not have worried. Early the following year a robust letter from Parham showed that house spirit was well alight. Fleur had been accused in a report of behaving in an unsportsmanlike way in a football match with Shield which they lost 14-9. Reading such a letter, said Parham, was 'horrible'. 'I feel very bitter about it', he went on because the accusation would be read about widely. The editor refused to withdraw the criticism, but the letters themselves show that house loyalty was an accepted part of school life. Another feature of public-school life had been introduced, and in the annual house photographs taken from 1916 onwards it is noticeable, too, that uniform had been fully introduced, all the boys now having dark or tweed suits, and shirts with stiff collars.

II

Some years after the end of the war Pocock compiled a war record, and this heavy volume containing the combatants and the dead is the most sombre book in the archives. The book contained 895 names of which about six hundred and fifty saw war service. Of these 108 were killed, and 117 'invalided out', some to die later, others to spend the rest of their lives suffering. Eighty-two of the deaths were in the army, and 38 of them in 1916. Apart from Major-General R. Hutton Davies, who commanded the 6th Brigade in Haig's 1st Corps, few Johnians reached commands of any eminence although Lieutenant-General Sir Edward Clarke and Major General Sir John Steevens were staff officers. Hurst supplied the lieutenants and the captains. One hundred and one Johnians were mentioned in despatches. Thirty-seven received British, and 26 foreign decorations for services in war time, and 90 received military decorations including 62 Military Crosses, one with two bars, and three with one bar, three Distinguished Service Crosses, one with two bars, and three Distinguished Flying Crosses. One other interesting characteristic of the war record was that a sixth of the Old Johnians serving were in Imperial units from every part of the Empire, and in command of Labour Corps of Fijians, Indians or South African Blacks.

25 The armoury which occupied the ground floor of the present Chevron house.

26 A mathematics lesson in upper school in the Summer Term of 1912.

27 Frederick N. Bosher who was at the College from 1907 to 1911 and afterwards a farmer. He was killed by shell fire near Armentières on 3 April 1915; one of the 108 First World War Hurst dead.

Few Hurst Johnians were found at sea: only one of the deaths is recorded there, and those not in the army served in the Royal Naval Air Service, the Royal Flying Corps and, from 1918, the Royal Air Force, which attracted over sixty boys including several who transferred from the army. Thirteen, that is about one in six, were killed including H.G. Reeves and T. Le Mesurier, described by Coombes as 'our two most distinguished flyers', while others like E.H. Dimmock and T.G. Edwards were invalided out. John Norton obtained his Military Cross for a reconnaissance at 300 feet, and his bar for driving off two attacking planes while observing, and later his D.F.C. for putting two anti-aircraft guns out of action while flying with a wounded foot. Thomas Le Mesurier took part in 14 bombing raids, his plane painted in the Hurst colours, and received his D.S.C. for actions including low-level bombing of Ostend docks.

War dead are usually young: it is all too easy to forget that remembrance services are attended more often than not by older people, but the majority of casualties were under thirty years old. If one looks at the programme for *Julius Caesar* in 1913 name after name—Lintott, Carter, Lascelles, Adamson, Gepp, Lys, and Gault among them—was soon to be numbered among the war dead. Perhaps Richard Lintott's life might be cited as an example. Richard was one of three brothers from Horsham who were in Chevron. He had been a corps sergeant. He had been a keen debater voting with the majority that modern youth was not degenerate in that 1913 debate. In the play he 'had all the attributes of the young Octavius'. He was a member of the First XI Football and Cricket, and in the summer of 1914 he was a prefect, and the best batsman in the team, scoring 87 in his last school match and 75 not out in his last house match. In the autumn he joined the London Rifle Brigade. He was commissioned on 3 April, and killed on 3 May 1915 at Ypres.

Six school captains who had held office since 1902 died in the First World War:

Name	At Hurst	Date of Death	Place Killed
R. Turner	1898-1904	15.08.15	Gallipoli
H. Corbett	1901-1910	23.07.16	Ovilliers
R.M. Lascelles	1908-1913	15.09.17	Oppy Wood
F.L. Carter	1910-1914	22.04.17	In the air
T.F. Adamson	1908-1914	01.07.16	Somme
W.H.B. Wolstencroft	1911-1916	12.04.18	Loçon

Turner had been an outstanding athlete, twice *Victor Ludorum*, captain of football and cricket, a Cambridge Blue, before becoming a preparatory school master at Rottingdean. He was killed attacking a Turkish trench. Corbett had been in the two elevens and a fives player, and had taken a degree in history at Oxford. A lieutenant in the Gloucestershire Regiment, he was wounded at Ypres, invalided home, returned to the front in June 1916, and was killed a month later in an attack on a machine-gun post. Lascelles had been captain of football, and was training to be a civil servant when he joined the Artists Rifles. He was killed by a bullet in the head while scouting. Carter served with the East Surreys, transferred to the Royal Flying Corps, and was killed on an observation flight. Adamson had reached the Second XI in football, and intended to serve in the Indian Police. Instead he obtained a commission and became a lieutenant in the Devonshire Regiment and was killed, like Mr. Axe and Gepp on the first day of the Somme battle. William Wolstencroft was school captain from September 1915 to July 1916, and although not a talented young man had great qualities of perseverance. Although low in the Sandhurst entry he passed out eleventh in his year, and became a second lieutenant in the Royal Scots Fusiliers. He was popular with his fellow officers and known as 'The Boy', and on his first tour of duty at the front was killed while helping a wounded man.

The war tested in grim earnest the principles which had influenced so many boys under Cooper and Coombes, their imperialism and nationalism, and concepts of duty, discipline and toughness acquired through corps, games, leadership positions, and the general rough and tumble of school life. 'When a man joins the army', said a letter to the *Hurst Johnian*, 'one of the first lessons he learns from his fellows is the spirit of comradeship, *esprit de corps*' which 'plays a prominent part in public school education.' To those brought up in the peace and security of Edwardian times the war, in Stephen King-Hall's words, was 'more horrible, more heroic, more gigantic, more nearly universal, more costly, more destructive' than any previous war in history. It was the worst war in British history. Of the British and Imperial forces, 3,260,581 were killed or wounded, and of those 702,410 were British dead. Although it is true, as historians like John Terraine have argued, that the casualties need to be related to the vast size of the armed forces, with Haig commanding over fifty divisions on the Western front alone; and that taking population figures as a whole there was no 'lost generation', the impact on public schools was perhaps more intense than the general figures indicate.

Dr. J.M. Winter's work has confirmed that 70 per cent of casualties were under thirty, and this figure rises to over eighty per cent for the public school dead. Moreover, the proportion of junior officer ranks killed was higher than that of senior officers or privates, and it was in this section of the forces, as we have seen, that a high proportion of Hurst's and other schools' boys were serving. Similarly the casualty rate for those joining the flying services of one in six killed was higher than for the army and navy, and again these services were heavily weighted towards public-school men. As year by year the magazine detailed the deaths and wounds as well as the heroism and medals, there was clearly a sense of shock and of there being a lost generation. This led to an increase in loyalty towards the school by those who lived through the war, and to determination to provide a whole series of memorials to those that had died.

The Old Johnians became more numerous and active. In April 1919 a new constitution for the Old Johnian Club was drawn up providing a council and an executive committee. Club colours were fixed, and F.C. Bayley's (OJ) shop in the Strand reported increased purchase of Old Johnian blazers, boaters, and ties. Numbers at the annual dinner reached 109 in 1923, and several of the guest speakers were military Old Johnians like Major-General Sir John Steevens and Major Cuthbert Keeson. The dinner was transferred from the Holborn Restaurant to more spacious premises at the *Hotel Victoria*, and such was the wish to meet more frequently that a

28   Chevron dormitory in the 1920s. Note the window at the end to the master's bedroom which was closed up in 1932.

City Dining Club was formed in 1923 which met at the Comedy Restaurant in Panton Street. The Old Johnian Football Club continued to flourish, and in July 1920 M.A. Pitcher and Randolph Rogers organised the first Old Johnian cricket week. The same year there was the first swimming match with old boys, and a year later the first athletics match, and under Tower there was a continued increase in the sporting activities of the Old Johnians. In September 1922 the Club began to circularise boys to join. The Club helped the College with settling the chapel debt and of course with the financing of several of the war memorials.

In October 1915 there was a Chapter meeting to discuss war memorials in the Woodard schools and Temple Lushington Moore was made architect so there should not be a proliferation of unsuitable memorials. Hurst was fortunate to have in the recently completed north transept an ideal memorial chapel, and in January 1917 the Hurst Committee decided this would be the case and launched a memorial appeal. By then the furnishing of this chapel had begun. The altar and piscina were given in memory of R.J. Wood, the recently dead biology master, and by the parents of Norman Bannister who died soon after leaving, and in memory of his wife by Henry Smith, of Ruckford House. The altar had been dedicated at a ceremony in October 1916. Henry Smith also provided the altar candlesticks, and the O.T.C. the altar cross. The panel behind the altar was in memory of Francis Lys, the credence table, of Cecil Gault, the stalls, of Dennis Gambell, and the screen, of William Wolstencroft.

At their meeting the Chapter had agreed to fund the memorial panels with names to be erected in each school. Hurst was allotted £140, but the actual cost was £271 15s. 8d., and as the Chapter refused any more money the Old Johnians stepped in to cover this debt. The panel with

108 names was installed in August 1920. In January 1920 the Old Johnians met to consider what should be done with the memorial fund which by then amounted to £1,147 16s. 6d., and because the chapel and panels were in being it was possible to devote this money to other purposes. It was agreed to endow a scholarship for the son of a dead Hurst Johnian who had served in the war, and the bulk of the money was to go to a new pavilion and improvement of the South field shooting range. John Hunt (OJ) designed the building which was the only one erected in the first quarter of the century, and it was opened in July 1921 with a short service held by Provost Edwin Lance, followed by a cricket match. The building was incomplete—the boys dug the drains next year—and in debt; so the fund remained open until July 1923 when it had raised £2,379 16s. 1d. Even then a debt remained which Tower had to pay off.

The other visible memorials to the war were two trophies. Richard Lintott's parents gave the Lintott Cup in the shape of a 17th-century porringer awarded for house shooting, and John Sidley's parents gave a two-handled cup with a winged figure holding a wreath for the house gymnastic competition. In upper school a portrait of Major-General R. Hutton Davies, Hurst's only brigade commander, was placed. Since 1909, Amos Davey, Tom Davey's son, had been carpenter. In 1921 he was put in charge of a works team so that Hurst would not need to employ outside contractors for carpentry and other work. He continued panelling hall and upper school and the house day rooms. Each room had a wooden frieze containing pictures of the war dead which remained in place until the 1970s.

29   The War Memorial Chapel, designed by Temple Lushington Moore, and dedicated on 23 July 1921.

Besides memorials, services to commemorate both the end of war and the war dead were a feature of life in Coombes's last years, starting with a *Te Deum* and a half holiday on 11 November 1918. On 29 June 1919, the day after the signing of the Versailles Treaty, there were three services, and on 6 July the official peace service took place with Hawkins's setting of the Communion Service, and Stanford's *Te Deum*. 19 July was a public holiday and after cricket in the morning the boys went to the village green for tea and buns or to a fair at Hassocks. In the evening a procession formed, led by the prefects (in a donkey cart), wearing fancy dress and made its way with torches to the top of Danny, where there were fireworks, and the last boys were not back in College until one in the morning.

It had been decided to keep 11 November as Armistice Day when a two-minute silence took place nationwide, and it was inevitable that the Sunday nearest to this soon had a special church service and, once memorials were erected, special ceremonies like wreath-laying and the playing of the Last Post. Hurst already had Obit Sunday, and therefore under Coombes the main remembrance service took place on this day, the first falling on 2 November 1919, when Hawkins's *Requiem*, dedicated to the memory of A.C. Axe, and his *Ave Verum*, dedicated to the memory of William Wolstenholme, were played during three services held that day, at one of which Coombes preached on the themes of death, grief and pain, including the remark, 'I like to think of them [the dead] as those who have passed the strictest of examinations and are now safely within the fold'. On 11 November there was a brief service and a wreath-laying before the two-minute silence, and from 1922 an Old Johnian wreath was laid as well. Obit Sunday, however, remained the most important service until Tower's time.

III

The shadow of war and its remembrance hung over Arthur Coombes's last years. Numbers and revenue were falling once more, and the buildings lacked new facilities and proper maintenance. The common room had several unsatisfactory staff, and with the growth of house feeling the prefects were arrogating power to themselves: contemporaries write of 'roustering' in Red Cross, where a house captain claimed he could kick a boy up onto a bed, and the use of brushes, clubs and slippers to beat boys. Memoirs by members of Red Cross, Star, and Fleur de Lys for these years paint similar pictures. Domestic and wartime conditions led to considerable illness in the College. In Michaelmas Term 1917 and Lent Term 1918 there was a danger of diphtheria and £400 was spent on medical swabbing of throats. Alexander Bean (OJ) was called in to examine the drains—he had been Bournemouth's civil engineer—and the drains were relaid over a period of three years. In Summer Term 1918 came the European influenza epidemic. Dr. F.H. Kelly (1917-1939) called in three assistants. Only half the school could take exams, and there was a sharp rise in medical expenditure. On 16 July D.W. Castle died at home of pleural complications. In Lent Term 1919, influenza returned at a time of bad weather, so cold that boys went to chapel clutching hot water bottles and wearing overcoats. In March A.J. Soward died in the infirmary and term finished with a mumps outbreak.

John Muriel, in his semi-autobiographical *When All the World Was Young*, gives an excellent account of life under Canon Wheat (Coombes) and Mr. Spire (Tower). Although there were in theory four meals a day, three of them were really only bread and butter and tea supplied by the College. The butter tasted rancid, and the tea was of a peculiar bluish tint. In winter porridge was added to breakfast but it went first to the senior boys 'with results that can be foreseen'. Lunch-time meat was of poor quality, and two old boys maintain it was maggoty on occasion. The puddings were so solid one of them was known as 'rock of ages'! Boys were forced to supplement this diet themselves, and at the foot of hall stairs at supper time was 'an unruly rabble clutching variously tins of sardines and salmon, apricots and peaches, lumps of cheese, radishes in season and other delicacies'. From their pocket money boys were given up to four pence a day for 'extras' including bacon, egg or sausage for breakfast.

Muriel pointed out that the head created a very unfavourable impression on parents. In 1917 Coombes first alluded to arthritis which attacked him eventually in both legs. He came into school unbathed and unshaven on cold mornings, and walked with a stick which he laid about him with when annoyed. He was unable to concentrate for long in lessons, and in geography sent boys to start digging the garden he had started on Rooke's field. His eyes were bloodshot and his face strained with pain. He was the first head to have a car, having bought a Swift, but it is clear that his thought processes were now far from mobile. His favourite remarks were, 'I never move till I must', and 'it seems to me the line of least resistance'. Although it is true he recommended a prep school, and changing to rugby, his remarks in general were a strong defence of traditional pre-war methods of running public schools which he felt were under attack.

He frankly admitted on one occasion: 'anyhow we do produce men, even if we fail to evolve scholars or scientists', and on another that 'the main interests of the boys ... were simply athletic'. Jonathan Gathorne-Hardy's chapter on the post-First World War public schools is entitled 'The Monolith Starts to Crumble'. It was early days yet for this, although A.S. Neill (an Old Tonbridgian) founded Summerhill in 1924, and other progressive schools like Dartington Hall and Bedales were appearing. In 1917 a novel by Alec Waugh, who had been at Sherborne, called *The Loom of Youth* was savagely denounced by Coombes who said the author had taken a broom to sweep up all the dirt he could find about public schools. Alec Waugh's *Public School Life* (1922) contained many criticisms of athleticism, the bloods, and a system that 'stands in drastic need of repair'. Waugh said that in many schools:

> It is some time since the drains were attended to; electric light is more serviceable than gas, the tapestries are a little moth eaten, the books in the library are dusty. The house wants to be spring-cleaned.

Coombes on the contrary denounced interference in education by those speaking with 'profound ignorance'. Lloyd George's government was bringing in a package of education measures: the Education Act of 1918, teachers' superannuation, and the Burnham Committee on Salaries, the University Grants Committee, and 200 state scholarships to grammar schools. Coombes remarked: 'monumental is the waste of paper and human energy' involved in government interference. He was equally scathing about proposals for smoothing 'the rough road' of school life so that 'a boy never knows when he is at work and when at play'. It was necessary, he argued, for education to rub off 'the corners' and for boys to play games and even hear sermons they found dull, for education which failed 'to develop character would be no sort of training for life'. On St Etheldreda Day in 1921 he spoke for some time in this vein, stressing that boys should not be minutely supervised; all the new proposals tying up boys so they 'had not room to breathe'.

Coombes was partly right to emphasise that the training at Hurst met a need. Indeed the war added the Middle East to the British Empire, and the R.A.F. to the fighting services, and the *Hurst Johnian* survey of careers made it clear that many boys still needed the kind of training Coombes believed in, and would continue to need it until empire and armed forces melted away. Those like G. Bayzard 'in the thick of the Moplah Rebellion', L.E. Davies 'making good in Kenya', C. Gault 'in action against the ever lively Waziris', W.B. Thomas, 'who has been taking part in a punitive expedition in Kurdistan', B.T.S. Leete 'with the RAF 5th Squadron at Mosul', or M.G.B. Copeman 'commanding the 2nd Armoured Car Company at Heliopolis' benefited from the kind of school Coombes was defending.

On the other hand Victorian England was really passing away now. In 1918 William Woodard and Harriet Lowe died, followed in November 1919 by Henry Holford, the last Mansion House boy to survive. Colonel William Campion died in 1923, Sabine Baring-Gould in 1924, and Henry Woolsey in 1926. After a long period in which warfare and patriotism had been well to the fore in national life there was bound to be a reaction: the 1920s were to develop into a very different decade particularly among middle-class people whose Victorian values were to be questioned by Bloomsbury writers, and later by the literature critical of the First World War. Coombes had outstayed his usefulness, and Muriel admirably describes how Tower's reputation 'reached us from the School of which he had been head', and 'spread gloom and despondency among the elderly members of the staff' because he was rumoured to be 'a man of action'.

Arthur Coombes left in December 1923 and Provost Southwell came back to make the farewell speech thanking him for his fearless and dogged determination. The masters gave him an armchair and a dining table, the boys, a sideboard, a wardrobe, and the *Times Atlas*, Star gave him a set of carvers, and the Old Johnians, silver coffee and tea services, and the cost of his hall portrait. Coombes became a canon and subdean of Chichester Cathedral, was as active as possible in parish life, and completed a thesis on St John for his D.D. degree. On 11 February 1926 he collapsed while at a choir supper and died the next day. A distinguished congregation at his funeral was led by Bishop Winfrid Burrows. Tower was unwell and did not attend, but the pall bearers included Parham, Scott, Johnson, and Keeson, and the congregation, M.D. Rhoden, the school captain, and many masters and Old Johnians. Present also was the Coombes' daughter, Sibyl, who in September 1916 had married Dudley Baylis (Hurst 1911-1914), a captain in the R.A.F. Isabel Coombes lived at Haywards Heath, and then at Holland Park, and in July 1934 was killed in a car accident at Shillingford in Oxfordshire when Sibyl was seriously injured. 'I am sure', Coombes had said in his farewell speech, 'that what little has been done here could not have been done without her.'

NINE

SPREADING CANVAS AND TAKING IN SAIL
1924-1937

The Rise and Fall of Bernard Tower

The Headmaster then read his report, and laid stress on the great need of the buildings generally receiving the attention of the Chapter ... The Bursar informed the Committee [Council] that the Chapter had no funds at its disposal.

Committee [Council] Minutes, 28 May 1926

... so we in Mr Spire's [Tower's] Greek set saw less and less of Mr Spire, whose days were spent with architects and surveyors; with builders and plumbers and masons; with butchers and bakers and greengrocers for the improvement of the food; with a hundred and one other concerns that, unseen, claimed his attention until long after I had left, the then Duke of Kent came to declare the Tower open ...

Simon Dewes, *When All the World Was Young*,
Hutchinson, 1961, p. 53

The Secretaries of the Fund [for Improvement] presented their report which showed there was no more money available for further improvements.

Committee Minutes, 21 October 1930

For architectural beauty of appearance the main buildings of Hurst will stand comparison with any school in the country. I think we may claim that the forty or fifty thousand pounds spent upon them during the past ten years has played no small part in establishing our position in this respect.

Bernard Tower speaking on Prize Day, 1935
The Hurst Johnian, 746/318, November 1935

The Headmaster expressed the conviction that the present fees with the compulsory charges were too high, and gave figures in support of this . . . The probable receipts and expenditure for the term showed an overdraft of £1,500 could be required at the end of the term ... The Secretary's report showed that the amount of the Loan outstanding was £12,000.

Committee Minutes, 19 February 1937

John St Clair Muriel was a member of Fleur de Lys House from 1923 to 1927 and, after he left, under his two pseudonyms, Simon Dewes and John Lindsey, he was author of over fifty books including biographies, fiction, and autobiographical works. *When All the World Was Young*, published in 1961, was dedicated 'with affection' to H.B. T[ower] just three years before his death and was an account of life at Hurst during Muriel's time at the school. Although a fictionalised account, it is remarkably accurate in many respects. It deals with Tower's unpopular personal image and his reforms, and contains a good many critical passages although the personal account of his five years was one of 'ever deepening happiness'.

By contrast, another writer about Tower's Hurst, far from finding deepening happiness, clearly found the experience of life during the same years a bitter one. Bernard Tower's wife, Stella (1891-1983) was an authoress under the pseudonym, Faith Wolseley, and in 1936 published a detective novel with the title *Which Way Came Death*. From the historian's viewpoint the book is important because it shows her dislike for the school her husband and she found on arrival, and her unhappiness at the reaction to her husband's reforms. While John Muriel, for instance, paints a picture of H. Parham, his housemaster, as a reactionary whose favourite phrase under Tower was 'Canon Coombes would never have allowed it', Stella described him as an arrogant and vindictive man with a face like 'a ram caught in a thicket' when it came to the character in the book clearly based on Parham.

30   Rev. H. Bernard Tower, headmaster from 1924 to 1937, in the hall of the headmaster's house (now the library). With him is his wife, Stella (1891-1983), and their children Penelope (1916-1975), and William (1918-1940).

'I sometimes think', she wrote, 'that masters who stay a long time in one school had jobs which atrophy every decent impulse and quality in the human make-up'. The headmaster's wife in the book felt surrounded by eyes 'either green with jealousy, or black with suspicion'. The school in the book, in Stella's words, 'lacked most of the attributes of a public school' and had a complacent self-satisfaction that 'turned obvious failures and disabilities into unique school features'. Her main character was so unhappy at the backbiting and intrigue directed against her husband that she frequently retired to her garden to escape them. Stella's own garden at Hurst, planted with over a thousand bulbs at a cost of £100 in 1928, was just one of the many points of criticism levelled at the Towers at the time.

We are much better informed about Tower's years than those of either of his two predecessors. The typewriter came into use in school administration and School Committee (Council) Minutes are now available. It has been possible to use Old Johnian memoirs, among the most valuable of which are those by Frank Whitbourn (Hurst 1923-1929). Tower, he says, 'won grudging respect, but not any affection', and it is clear that few old boys were even willing to concede the respect. We have Muriel's and Stella Tower's partly fictionalised accounts. What emerges is that Tower's headship was an unhappy one certainly for him personally. During the first six years, while he was increasing numbers, reforming, raising the College's status, and carrying out the first sustained building programme in the College's history, he was subject to strong criticism both of the reforms and of his attitudes and mannerisms. In Muriel's words, 'his greatness was always thwarted by the forces he stirred up against himself'. His last seven years, due to economic circumstances quite outside his control and reluctance on the governors' part to take actions he recommended quickly enough, were years of decline leading to the third financial crisis in the College's development. He left a school with substantial debts, small numbers, and a poor academic record, and of course bore the brunt of criticism for these events as well. A prosperous voyage for the school ended in near shipwreck.

Son of a clergyman, Bernard Tower was born in 1882, and educated at Marlborough from 1893 to 1901 although there is no mention of him in the magazine. He was a Classical Exhibitioner at St Catharine's College, Cambridge, and trained to be a priest at Ely Theological College. He was ordained in 1905 and was for a time curate at Berwick-on-Tweed and then at Benwell. In 1912 he became a master at The King's School, Canterbury, and a minor canon of the cathedral. Two years later he left to be domestic chaplain to Henry Hodgson, Bishop of St Albans (1914-1921). In 1915 he married Stella, the bishop's daughter. They were to have two children: Penelope (1916-1975) and William, born in 1918 and killed at Dunkirk. In 1916 Tower returned to The King's School where he was head of the junior school and then second master. After three years he became headmaster of Churcher's College, Petersfield, from where he came to Hurst.

The real reason for his unpopularity was his reforms and, once many had made up their minds to oppose them as far as they dared, nothing Tower did could please them. It must also be admitted that Tower himself was partly to blame by giving hostages to fortune. After Coombes's solid and traditional approach, Tower seemed lightweight and idiosyncratic. His panama hats and his yellow cigarette holder were easy to parody. He did not get on well with boys. Two years after arriving he handed direct responsibility for the headmaster's house to F.B. 'Sticky' Lisle, who remained in charge until 1935, when he left to be head of Kingsbridge School and was succeeded by Robin Gregory. Muriel points out that Tower neglected his Greek set for administrative matters. His sermons were prosaic and didactic, and on public occasions he unwisely made jokes that parodied his own reputation for being rather full of himself and his successes. On Prize Day 1928, for example, he said, 'Hurst is certainly becoming known for what it is really meant to be—a really well organised—I organise it—and progressive school for boys'. On another occasion, referring to reform, he said, 'I do not promise Minty chairs for the dear boys, nor ice cream soda fountains', and when Scott succeeded Parham as second master he described this as 'one more proof of the headmaster's wisdom'.

Public occasions were something Tower liked. They were an opportunity for raising the school's status by securing distinguished speakers whose presence would be reported in the local press. For a time he tried to make Empire Day into such an occasion, and secured some well-known military figures like General Sir Reginald Buckland (Chief Engineer to the 4th Army) in 1928, and General Sir Herbert Lawrence (Haig's Chief of Staff) in 1931. That year he was even more delighted to secure the presence of Lord Freeman Willingdon, who had recently been Governor-General of Canada and was about to be Viceroy of India. 'No, we do not object to viceroys', said the magazine. Tower started next year a Viceroy of India's Prize first won by D.S. Allen, but both the prize and Empire Day faded away during his last years, and in 1937 they had to make do with a corps parade and a lecture on Joseph Chamberlain.

Prize Day and St Etheldreda Day falling at the same time until Dingwall's headship, this was clearly the main public occasion of the year. Muriel devoted a whole chapter to these impressive occasions. For some years Tower succeeded in attracting well-known educational and religious figures of the day, including the deans of Chichester, Exeter, and St Paul's, and the bishops of Chichester and London among clergy, and four leading headmasters—Alington of Eton, Norwood of Harrow, Turner of Marlborough, and Williams of Winchester. Tower's speeches are given in the magazine and today seem unctuous to the visitors and overfull of snobbish attempts to equate Hurst with the most important public schools. In 1928, typically, he told the story that local bus conductors thought Lancing was a girls' school or a theological college; its fame paled before that of Hurst. This was nonsense. Perhaps delivered to an audience thick with clerical collars, cloche hats, and old school ties the speeches sounded better. Here too Tower was unable to keep up the momentum, and in his last three years the speakers were of considerably less fame: the Mayor of Brighton; John Greig, former bishop of Guildford; and Arthur Greaves (OJ), in turn suffragan bishop of Grantham (1935-1937) and Grimsby (1937-1958).

Nor is all publicity good publicity. Tower's name-dropping and snobbishness was not appreciated. Frank Whitbourn said 'we had no wish to see our photographs in the *Tatler* or the *Bystander*' where Tower was determined to put them. The county image was enhanced by photographs of the Brighton Foot Beagles (February 1927) and the South Downs Hunt (October 1929) in the outer quad, and there were several articles on the College like those in the *Monthly Pictorial* (December 1926) and *The Graphic* (October 1931). Tower appeared in one of the articles wearing his mortar board even in the play green-room, and every effort was made to give the impression that Hurst was no different from the great schools even down to using the special public school language then favoured in them. Bloods were called 'wangs', and the captain of school and captain of rugby, J.W.H. Watts, was shown in another article 'leading his strapping henchmen to the playing fields for pragger'. There is no evidence that Tower's search for publicity and prestige at this superficial level increased numbers, and it did not endear him to boys who, as Muriel rightly pointed out, 'were connected in a subordinate way with trade ... there were just a few sons of parsons and solicitors and doctors'.

So there was little Tower did that was not subject to personal criticism. When he appointed Lisle to run Star, Tower gave up capitations in favour of a lump sum of £250. By 1930 his salary was £1,800, and he only lost £150 as numbers fell in the 1930s. But his life-style was the subject of frequent criticism. He, and presumably Stella, were determined to improve the head's living accommodation, and no less than three different sets of plans costing £250 16s. 10d.

in architect's fees were drawn up. Since the improvements would be accompanied by improvements to Star House the Chapter argued these fees should be paid out of the Improvement Fund: Tower said the Chapter should pay them. Eventually a special meeting in December 1927 ruled that improvements to the existing house would go ahead, and the garden on the opposite side of the road would also receive funds. All kinds of difficulties arose and the improvements took three terms, for which Tower got a grant of £150 to cover living out expenses. £450 was agreed on for internal furnishing, but there were rows over blinds, cupboards, and even a coal shed, and Tower obtained a further £92 17s. 11d. for a gas range and a garden shed. Star was extended to the north and the entrance porch added to the front. Nor did people fail to notice that the architect employed was Walter Tower, a relative, and the surveyor, W.A.T. Carter, from Petersfield.

II

Tower told an early Committee [Council] meeting, 'Hurst itself was in need of so much', and his first six years were years of reform in nearly every aspect of school life. Speaking on Prize Day 1925 Sir John Sankey turned to Tower and said, 'the mantle of Elijah has fallen upon Elisha', referring to the fact that it was a Tower who had restored Lancing's fortunes, and now it was Bernard Tower who was restoring Hurst's. He certainly saw himself as an innovator, remarking on another Prize Day that 'nothing is a sadder mutilation of great possibilities than to watch a living society hardening into a dead tradition'. Muriel believed Tower 'made too many sweeping changes too quickly', but Tower did not think so. It was only lack of finance that prevented him from continuing: at the height of his achievements in 1930 he outlined further grandiose plans, and at a later Prize Day said, 'I do not pretend that I should not like to see faster moving change'.

As a clergyman Tower naturally was interested in the chapel and the religious aspect of school life, but after a reference on his first Prize Day to the 'Church of England Chapter as by statutes appointed' there are hardly any more references to Woodardry. The Oxford Movement which had lain at the heart of Woodard's work celebrated its centenary in 1933. Tower invited the Professor of Education at the University College of Southampton to speak about the Movement. There was an essay prize, won jointly by E.A.C. Balshaw and R.H. Marchant, and a special eucharist. Victorian traditions like Obit Sunday and Stir Up Sunday ceased to be commemorated by the end of the 1920s and, apart from a momentary flurry of excitement when the chaplain, Rev. L.E. Cartridge (OJ), left to be a Melanesian missionary in 1927, no more mention is made of the missionary movement. Frank Whitbourn pointed out that there was no Divinity time-tabled for the majority of boys and, although Hurst continued to send young men into the Church—10 were in theological colleges in 1935—it is clear Tower wished to play down the Woodard element in Hurst's reputation.

Instead he played up the 'typical public school' image which Coombes had moved some way towards. In 1924 Hurst obtained H.M.C. membership. The same year Tower had an inspection by the Ministry of Education, so that the school could be recognised as efficient, and another inspection took place in 1930. It is interesting to notice that the Ministry of Education gave recognised public schools the right to nominate a boy to Sandhurst and later to Dartmouth. This naturally pleased Tower who proudly announced the first successful nomination. This was of George Allison, captain of Star and the First XI, who was sadly killed in a car accident in 1937. On 28 October 1927 Hurst was 'brought into line with

31   The Southern Railway locomotive, *Hurstpierpoint*, which entered service in 1933 and was scrapped in 1961.

other public schools' when Masons Lodge Number 4937 was established, five years after Lancing had established theirs, due to the work of the Rev. John Hooke and others. There was discussion in the Committee for some years about acquiring a coat of arms, the Chapter bursar querying the cost, but in 1931 one was registered with the College of Arms. Soon after arriving Tower had managed to get the words 'Alight here for Hurstpierpoint College' added to the station name boards, and was naturally delighted enough to grant a half holiday in October 1933 when Hurst was one of the named locomotives in the Southern Railways' Schools Class of 4-4-0 engines.

Hurst was certainly a solidly Conservative society by the 1930s, and in a mock election in November 1935 J.W. Millar won for the Tories with a majority of seventy-four. Debates nearly always returned solid conservative, even reactionary, majorities. Tower's Hurst experienced none of the problems of the greater public schools he so admired. During the 1930s the mood that Coombes had been so offended by in the 1920s spread to a substantial section of informed opinion. These were the days when at Marlborough the Oxford vote that they would not fight for King and Country was carried in the Debating Society, and at Wellington Esmond Romilly edited *Out of Bounds* in one copy of which he attacked 'the semi-compulsory nature of the O.T.C.', 'the hypocritical bluff about character building', and the 'absurd restrictions and petty rules and regulations' unsuited to boys over fourteen. The *Hurst Johnian* remarked, 'our attention has been drawn to the fact that some school magazines publish socialistic articles' and commented this was 'the lowest depths of degradation' a magazine could sink to. The corps commander did feel it necessary in March 1931 to have an article in the magazine on the value of the corps and there was a two-hour debate on the issue the same month.

But while Tower had no disciplinary problems, the conservative nature of the school posed a difficulty to many of his reforms which were aimed at civilising, liberalising, and widening horizons, and were therefore seen as radical or soft. It is to Tower's credit that he persisted in his reforms throughout his time as head. Tower sought to make chapel worship more relevant to an age in which the churches were increasingly involved in social issues like unemployment. He extended the range of chapel preachers to include outside speakers. He insisted that half the year's collection money should go to worthy causes like the London School for the Blind or Russian Church Aid. The R.S.P.C.A. gave their first lecture at the school in December 1932 and the school was among the first to collect for the R.N.L.I. In the winter sixth-form lecture topics like working class housing in November 1935 and Brighton's unemployed in February 1936 made an appearance.

Three good causes in particular were supported by Tower, and it is not without significance that all three disappeared from the school programme when he left. Talbot House (referred to as Toc H) was a chain of Recreation Centres for all ranks who had served in the First World War, and in May 1927 their founder the Rev. Philip 'Tubby' Clayton spoke to the College. In January 1931 a group of boys visited the slums of Southwark and boys' clubs there, and were the guests of Talbot House at Denmark Hill. From 1924 Hurst hosted at least six Sussex Boys Summer Camps. The aim was for boys from public schools to mix with working-class boys whose country holiday would be paid for by employers. Francis Wright was in charge and the camps were near Ringmer. The boys played games, visited beauty spots, and enjoyed camp life. In 1929 the camp was greatly improved by a 'ripping party of fellows from Christ's Hospital', and Tower even turned up, joined in the sing-song, and was given rare cheers.

In November 1935, in co-operation with the National Council for Social Service, Tower took 16 boys on a Priestleyesque tour of Northern England to Durham, South Shields and the Cumbrian coal field to see the appalling conditions. The N.C.S.S. was involved in various schemes of a limited nature to help the poor, including training boys as butlers and chauffeurs and girls as house maids and, in fact, some girls from Tyneside were employed at Hurst. In the magazine Tower wrote,

> they shall learn up there that the public school boys in the South who know, do care, and that our patriotism is not merely a readiness to shoulder arms, but also to shoulder such burdens as we can help to bear.

In February 1936 Contact was set up to provide holidays for poor boys. A fund was started, and £50 raised to entertain 20 South Shields boys for two days at Hurst. The visit took place on 4-5 July and was run by the chaplain, the Rev. K.B. Batchelor. An article by one of the boys spoke of their 'ceaseless wonder and interest' at their experience, and Tower made much of this social experiment on his last Prize Day.

Another aspect of widening horizons and sympathies was foreign travel. In the summer of 1926 the first overseas visit took place. This was organised by H.P. Hughes, a language master from 1924 to 1930, who took 17 boys for three weeks' French study at Calais with tutors from the University of Lille. The trip cost six guineas! In December 1929 Hughes was also responsible for the first ski visit to Switzerland. Horace Hawkins used his friendship with leading figures in French music to provide the basis for no less than three choir trips to Paris in 1931, 1934 and 1936. On the first trip they visited a large number of churches and gave two performances in the concert room of Cardinal Mazarin's palace and at St Eustache Church, while Hawkins played the organ at the Sacré Coeur. In 1934 their performances included one in Nôtre Dame, and besides visiting many churches their relaxations included the Tour Eiffel and a Russian restaurant. On their last trip they met Vallombrosa and Dupré and paid a visit to Widor when they sang his *Ave Maria* with its dedication to Hawkins.

In his last year Tower entered boys unsuccessfully for the E.S.P.U. scholarships for the first time, and in his last term the first visit by a group of overseas boys took place at Hurst. The members of the School Council paid a proportion of the expenses involved, and 16 Canadians came for three weeks sponsored by the National Education Council of Canada. They introduced the Hurst boys to baseball and to ice hockey at the Brighton ice rink.

The most important of Tower's reforms was his attempt to develop and modernise the buildings, and his first six years were undoubtedly dominated by this first co-ordinated building programme in the School's history and the necessary fund raising. These funds were not provided in the main from current income, but by a policy of borrowing and some lucky windfalls in the form of donations to the College. Fees were certainly raised during Tower's early years from £105 to £126 and eventually in 1928 to £135 a year, but numbers remained consistent during the 1920s boom, and gross fee income rose only slightly from about £14,000 to about £17,000. The figures for intake in Tower's early years were as follows:

Year	Total in College	Total entry
1924	186	53
1925	187	50
1926	186	49
1927	197	48
1928	184	47
1929	187	42
1930	174	42

These figures show that the financial basis of the College remained extremely precarious, but Tower argued, and rightly, that they would not attract more boys unless they brought the buildings up to date, and by various means at least £40,000 pounds were found for development in just under six years.

In February 1926 a works committee was formed to consider the needs of the school as regards its buildings, and in October the same year the Hurst Improvement Fund Number 1 was established with the aim of raising £15,000 by means of a loan at six per cent interest. This loan coincided with the Baldwin boom years and was successfully taken up. The rest of the money was made up in a variety of ways. Lowe's will provided money spent on the interior of the chapel until 1926. Five hundred National Savings Certificates purchased by Coombes in February 1923 were sold and so was £100 of War Loan. Legacies from Randolph Rogers, Canon Coombes, Henry Woolsey, and George Oliver (OJ), combined with memorial appeals, raised more money. Above all one Old Johnian, Captain R.F. Norman and his step-daughter, Miss Williams-Bulkeley, between them gave nearly £5,000.

It is very clear that this was an extremely risky way of financing development, which depended for its success on rising numbers and continuing national prosperity. The Council of those days was not at its best dealing with financial matters as is shown by their handling of the College rates. In 1925 Chamberlain's Act established a new rating system; the College's assessment rose from £612 to £888 a year, and eventually reached £910 by the end of Tower's headship. The next headmaster found this was £200 more than the College should have been paying. However, for the time being all went well as new buildings rose, and on Prize Day 1930 Tower was still talking of raising another £20,000 to complete the building programme with a school hall and classroom block.

In 1926 three army huts made their appearance on West field to provide 10 classrooms, two laboratories, and a small lecture room. This enabled Tower to provide four music practice rooms for Hawkins in the main building, and studies for house prefects. With the money from the Randolph Rogers legacy and appeal the Randolph was opened in 1928 at a cost of £600 to provide a dignified, centrally placed room, which was soon panelled and equipped with bookcases by donors. With the Woolsey fund and legacy combined with that of George Oliver, an Old Johnian doctor who died young, it was possible to open the two vestries in 1928. In the same year the confusion of small rooms surrounding the kitchens and used by domestic staff were swept away and a Matrons Block was built northwards from the main buildings. The same year the last butler, Bennett, retired with a pension of 10s. a week, and domestic arrangements were centralised with the rest of the administration in Scott's hands who now became a bursar in all but name. The new wing enabled Tower for the first time to employ a matron for each house. Similarly the unsightly north end of Star was removed and the house was extended at a cost of £11,000.

The school hall received particular attention as it was the area of the College seen most by visitors. The windows in the north wall were unbricked and glazed and the panelling completed. At the east end a platform and proscenium arch were built out over the cloister, enlarging the hall's capacity and improving play facilities, while at the west end the Coombes legacy and memorial fund contributed towards the creation of a gallery opened in 1930, sweeping away the servitors' quarters.

32 Horace A. Hawkins was the music master from 1915-1938. In this photograph he is with the choir and C.M. Widor outside St Sulpice in Paris, 1931.

In her book, Stella Tower referred to the 'over-powering smell of gas' in the school and one of Tower's first tasks was to bring in electricity. During 1926 and 1927 the Alpha Electricity Company installed electricity at a cost of £2,486 2s. 2d., the system being run by a petrol-driven engine installed in the Coombes carpentry shop. In fact, the supply was not good, and in Tower's last year at a further cost of £356 16s. the College was joined to the National Grid by the Central Sussex Generating Company. A new woodwork room was built adjacent to the old one.

Something was done to improve living conditions in the College. At a cost of £583 dormer windows were inserted in the dormitory roofs to help with the long-standing ventilation problem. Two years later in 1928 the provision of cold and hot water to the dormitories was improved at a cost of £1,814. In 1932 the window between the housemaster's bedroom and the dormitory was bricked up, now that the house prefect system was fully established. But Tower did not get his way when he proposed iron fire-escapes, the governors minuting that it was 'un-necessary to take any action'. To help with diet Tower had the menu reorganised after consulting food experts, and there were limited improvements to the kitchen ranges. His last building was in fact a new tuck shop, opened in 1934 near the sanatorium after an arrangement had been made with a caterer and an outfitter to supply food and the school uniform from the new building.

Tower was concerned about provision for school health and told the Council early on that it was inadequate. He began with the opening of a surgery at the main cloister end of Chevron, and he had substantial plans for an improved sanatorium costing perhaps £4,000. The Council would not accept these and placed a ceiling of £2,600 on any new building. As a result the existing sanatorium had two unsightly wings added to it which Tower hastened to have flinted by Ridley, the school workman, responsible for several areas of flinting at this time, and then covered with creeper. However, the enlarged sanatorium fulfilled its purpose because, whereas in Tower's early years an epidemic, according to Muriel, led to a great upheaval with two dormitories being taken over temporarily including even the housemasters' bedrooms and the taking on of extra nurses from a Brighton agency, one in 1931 was coped with when about sixty boys were admitted to the sanatorium, and Tower was able to report to the governors that he was pleased with the general health of the College.

So within the space of a few years seven either new or greatly modernised buildings had been achieved and, simultaneously, an improvement in facilities within them. All this time the chapel was also being improved, but entirely (apart from roof repairs) from money which did not come from the Improvement Fund. When Tower arrived the provisions of Lowe's will for the furnishing of the chapel interior were well under way, in the less than capable hands of F.C. Eden, and causing not a little resentment. The east end was completed with panelling, sedilae, and a substantial stone altar. A Portland stone floor was put in, and the panelling throughout the building stained to a uniform colour. Panelling beneath the organ was given as a memorial to W.D.C. Cuthbert-Keeson. The screen and stalls at the west end were inserted together with the memorial to Henrietta Lowe. After electricity came in, the organ was rebuilt over a long period between 1928 and 1934. Lastly, Tower encouraged individual gifts to the chapel: an altar cross came from the Lowe bequest and candlesticks from Randolph Rogers' family. Pocock was asked to prepare a chapel donation book in which each gift was recorded and the Tower years are prolific in gifts.

The problem of completion remained to be tackled. At first Tower supported the idea of completing the tower to the original Carpenter design and in 1925 a Jubilee Fund was launched to complete the chapel by the 65th year of its existence. Like previous funds it failed, and after several years had reached only £1,196 7s. 6d. It was at this point in 1929 that Captain R.F. Norman stepped in with his offer of £3,500, but it was clear that even with this generous sum the original tower could not be built. It was decided to use a design by Walter Tower, clearly based on Rye church, and to join the hall and chapel by a cloister to be known as the Norman cloister over which the hall extension could go ahead. Norman and Gates estimate of £4,247 was accepted and the work was completed within 24 weeks. The Old Johnians provided the clock and John Paice (OJ) the bell, and at the time it was intended to insert a peal of bells and use the tower room for campanology.

With the hall refurbished and the chapel completed Tower was determined on a great ceremonial for Saturday 18 October 1930, although he was to be disappointed by refusals from Lord Sankey, the Lord Lieutenant, and Cosmo Lang, now Archbishop of Canterbury, who had been at the 1903 ceremony. However, Tower was able to gather a considerable number of distinguished clerics. George Bell (1885-1958) the previous year had just taken over as Bishop of Chichester, and would hold the see until his death. He came in his capacity as Visitor. Hugh Hordern, suffragan bishop of Lewes from 1929 to 1946, came, and a clutch of three colonial bishops. From Westminster Abbey came Dr. Foxley Norris, the dean, and Canon Leigh H. Nixon (OJ), the precentor. Southwell, the Provost, and Lance, the previous provost, were there together with Sir John Otter, Woodard's son-in-law, and a cousin of Edward Lowe's.

33 A Hurst banner procession approaching the chapel in 1930 carrying the College and five house banners.

34   H.R.H. Prince George speaking after the chapel completion ceremony, 18 October 1930.

Royalty seemed to have looked favourably on Sussex schools at this time: St Michael's had recently been visited by Queen Mary, and Lancing by Henry, Duke of Gloucester. Hurst secured George, Duke of Kent, who interestingly enough was back in Sussex a week later at Brighton College! After lunch and presentations Prince George entered the chapel where a brief dedication service took place, and the Prince rather oddly declared the tower open before proceeding to his seat to a fanfare of trumpets. The service was admirably done by Hawkins who could not resist an arrangement of his own for the anthem. Bell preached on counting the cost of a building from Luke XIV, 28, and the service ended with Hawkins at the organ and the corps band. Prince George then went to the hall where he made a speech praising Hurst for some of its recent triumphs at Ranelagh and Bisley. Tower was no doubt a little nearer to heaven on this day and his speech is more than ever full of baroque phrases. The clergy present probably did not appreciate his praise of Bell's sermon as a 'seismic disturbance' which would 'shake the county of Sussex from that sedentary self-satisfaction which was the Church's worst foe'.

Tower also expressed his pleasure that the collection of over £50 had cleared a small remaining debt on the building. At the Council meeting prior to the ceremony 'it was decided that plans for a block of new classrooms should be obtained', and in his speech Tower mentioned this and said he hoped the Prince would return to open them. Yet only three days after the great occasion the Council minutes recorded that there was no money left for further improvements. Although no-one could have known it the days of build and spend were about to be abruptly terminated by economic depression and a further fall in numbers.

III

Sport predominated in school life under Tower to an increasing degree: after all, as we shall see, there were few academic results to cheer. By the 1930s the magazine was almost exclusivel y a sports report—the whole edition of July 1933, which, apart from one item, was devoted to sport, was not untypical. The school played 12 sports and tried to turn out teams at all levels while numbers continued to fall—by 1936 house rugby had to be played with 12 a side. In 1927 the purchase of a £400 Morris 17-seater helped to expand fixture lists particularly for minor sports. It was inevitable that with a declining sixth form the best sportsmen would be heavily committed. Looking at the *valetes* for 1933 and 1937, for example, one finds in the first year a boy who was member of six first teams, was captain of five, and obtained colours for five, while in the latter year another boy was in eight first teams, captained three, and obtained colours in six. Nor should it be forgotten that house matches also took place in nearly all sports. Tower is not on record as ever having deplored this situation: indeed the 15 trophies existing when he became head had grown to 23 when he left, if shooting awards are included. The Sidley Cup was transferred from gymnastics to hockey, the Standley and Varney cups were given for tennis, the Norman and Williams-Bulkeley for squash, the Rust for boxing, the Laurence for junior hockey, and two kicking cups—the Richmond and Tower—for rugby.

Tower's influence was felt on the games programme in two main ways. The first was that he changed the programme which had been fundamentally the same since Awdry's time. Coombes had already proposed switching to rugby, and Tower announced his intention to do this as soon as possible, encountering strong opposition particularly from Old Johnians whose football team did well in the Arthur Dunn Cup. There was trouble at the Old Johnian dinner in 1925 and the report of the event was delayed: when it came out it in- cluded the remark, 'no-one who was present appears to be able to remember clearly the details of the speeches'. Tower simply pointed out that most schools had switched and a fixture list was not possible without the change.

During the Michaelmas Term of 1924 articles in the magazine, lectures, and training began under Mr. Reginald Loverock, an enthusiastic new history master, who was also an Oxford Blue and a former member of Harlequins. He was appropriately accommo- dated in the room previously occupied by Sidney Mavor's devotions. The last Football XI was captained by W.G. Michels and had a good season, winning nine of its 12 matches including the last official one played on 6 December 1924. The first rugby match played was an Under 14 one lost to Cottesmore by

35 Climbing Danny—Wolstonbury Hill. Danny House is at the bottom, and the College is in the distance.

20 points to six on 25 October 1924. Rugby began in the Michaelmas Term of 1925, and the First XV captained by H.K.A. Denyer played—and won—their first match against Storrington by 16 points to three on 24 October. Junior house matches started in the Lent Term of 1926, and senior ones a year later. The first effective team was that captained by J.E. Stevens in 1927, which won five of its seven matches including the first one with the Old Johnians on 9 November. An Old Johnian Rugby Club was founded in 1929 playing at New Barnet, and did well for a time—in 1934 they won 11 of their 17 games. The school team found themselves playing much bigger sides and the only XV worth recalling from Tower's later years was that of 1935, captained by S.H. Dowse, which won six of its nine matches. In Tower's last year all nine fixtures were lost.

The Lent Term had always been the awkward one as far as a sports programme was concerned, and the virtual closure of the gymnasium and the end of the house competition added to the problem at the end of the 1920s. Hockey was introduced in the Lent Term of 1929. The First XI was captained by W.A. Michels, and played their first fixture on 16 February when they were defeated nine goals to none by Chichester School. The same month house matches started. By the mid-1930s hockey had established itself, and W.I.M. Nightingale was the first Hurst player for Sussex in 1935. Captained by G.A.B. Docker, the First XI that year won four and drew one of its eight fixtures. The other change Tower made in the Lent Term was not popular because during the mid-1920s fives underwent a short revival, due to William Carter forming an Old Johnian team and the chaplain, the Rev. L.E. Cartridge (OJ), being an enthusiast; the 1927 team captained by M.H. Rhoden won seven of its nine matches. But Tower saw that squash was the up-and-coming game—the Squash Rackets Association was founded in 1928—and after Norman and Williams-Bulkeley had provided the courts, fives died a natural death: no captain is recorded after 1935, and no house fixtures after 1936. Squash, as we see in more detail later, was popular and the outstanding team under Tower was that of 1936 captained by A.H.J. Muirhead which won four of its six matches.

Hurst cricket remained weak due to a lack of lower teams—in 1934 there was no Under 15 and only two Second XI games, for reasons already outlined in Cooper's and Coombes's day. Throughout Tower's years until his last two, only two teams could be regarded as good and only two others managed any significant number of wins. The best First XI was that of 1927 captained by M.H. Rhoden with seven victories and two draws. Next year under W.A. Michels they managed five wins and a draw, and in 1930 and 1934 there were five victories. If anything the fixture list deteriorated. The game with Lancing ceased, and by the mid-1930s the Victorian position had re-asserted itself with 12 out of 14 fixtures against non-school sides. Matches with Ardingly and Whitgift were the only regular school fixtures so that, of the five victories in 1930, for instance, only one was against another school. In 1936 and 1937 it did seem as if at last a nucleus of cricketers was emerging, with Mr. Robert Bury in charge and boys like S.H. Dowse, J.N. Lock, A.H.J. Muirhead, and K.L. Millar. In 1936 the First XI beat Ardingly and Whitgift and even the Second XI won four of its six matches. In 1937 the First XI managed four victories, but the overall figures tell the story. Out of 108 First XI matches played from 1930 to 1937 only 28 were victories.

The second way Tower's influence was felt in sport was in his determination that Hurst teams should compete in all the public-school competitions. By raising the standard of what are unfairly called 'minor' sports at Hurst, Tower was also able to provide Prize Day with plenty of sports victories. The progress of squash was one obvious example of these two points. S.W.R. Howell captained the first squash team which played—and lost by 15 to nil—their first game on 18 February 1930 with the Sussex County Sports Club. The first match with the Old Johnians occurred on 12 November 1931. By 1933 Hurst had produced the first of many winning squash teams when under G.H. Freeman's captaincy they won six out of seven fixtures. That year the College joined the County Squash Association and matches took place in the most congenial surroundings at R.A.F. Tangmere, Lewes, Hove, Arundel, Worthing, and with the officers at Preston Barracks. In 1934 G.H. Freeman and C.H. Simmons entered the Public Schools Rackets at Queen's Club and managed to reach the third round. The same year Hurst had six players in the R.A.C. Drysdale Cup matches and, although there were some black spots—half the fixtures were scrapped in 1937—squash had clearly been a great success not least because it was actively played by four masters—Robert Bury, Kenneth Mason, Robin Gregory and Arthur Hodgson.

Swimming continued to be successful in the mid-1920s with C.W. Yates, G.H. Young, R.E.S. Stafford, J.G. and A. Murdoch among the leading swimmers. Red Cross was the leading sports house at this time due in part to Lyndon Evelyn in the house from 1923 to 1927 who came from the West Indies, to which he returned as a doctor. He helped the house to win the last four gymnastic cups competed for, the house shooting for three years, and the house swimming for two years. Evelyn, incidentally, was also in the First XV, the best bowler in the 1927 First XI, and was an athlete performing well in the high and long jumps. By the 1930s, although Hurst continued to attend the Bath Club, her position was usually fourth or fifth in a field of 14 or so schools. There was a brief return to former glory in 1932 when the swimmers were unbeaten—G.H. Freeman and C.F. Freeman being among the most outstanding—and the year was noteworthy also for the first Under-15 fixtures swum against St John's Leatherhead and Christ's Hospital.

Cross-country like swimming was strong in the early and mid-1920s and then declined, before recovering in the early 1930s with a group of runners including D.M. Baylis, W.I.M. Nightingale, J.P. Watt, A. Etheridge, and G.H. Freeman. In 1930 Hurst entered the Public School Cross-Country race for the Ranelagh Cup. They won it on their first attempt and again in 1932, securing good positions in 1931 and 1933. In 1930 also the Hurst team managed to defeat their main rivals, South London Harriers, on the Clayton Run now officially stated to be 6 miles and 462 yards. Nightingale achieved the course record of 38.39 minutes. In 1932 a shorter training course was introduced and matches were often run on this course. The cross country success was not maintained and, like squash and swimming, showed weakness in the last Tower years. By 1935 the school was eighth in the Ranelagh Cup.

Apart from a short period in the mid-1930s shooting, however, was consistently successful and Hurst established a good reputation nationally in this sport: these were the years that produced G.E. Twine, later winner twice of the Queen's Prize at Bisley. Hurst's success was due primarily to the school doctor, F.H. Kelly, who from 1919 to 1932 was a prolific prize winner at Bisley including the King's Prize in 1926. He and his wife presented two Kelly Cups, and in 1925 the Ingall Cup was presented in memory of B.B. Ingall who died in Malaya six years after leaving. Captain Francis Wright, the cadet force commander, and Sergeant-Major H. Gladman, who helped to train teams, also played a part in the successful record. Hurst returned to Bisley in 1924 and could only manage 60th in the Ashburton but by 1927, when G.E. Twine was captain, they had reached 21st, and in 1928 Twine's team came second to Clifton College by only four points.

As a result the quality of the fixture list improved with matches against Clifton, Dulwich, and St Paul's and in 1929, captained by G.A. Brett, the team won half its fixtures against such schools. In 1927 Hurst entered the Country Life Competition for the first time and came fourth in the contest for the Cusack-Smith trophy. They won it next year. In 1930 Hurst won the Oakley Cup at the Sussex Public Schools meeting. After a lull, success continued in 1935 with J.V. Burnside as captain. P.P. Beecroft won the Spencer-Mellish Cup at Bisley. In 1936

J.W. Millar won the Sutton Vase at the Sussex Public Schools meeting, and the next year he and P.T. Harrington were in the Sussex Public Schools Eight.

As far as everyday life in school went Tower believed he had made it more attractive and Muriel would certainly have agreed. On Prize Day 1931 Tower said he had to report 'progress and promise'. There has been, he said, 'happiness and health among the boys, satisfaction and subscription from the parents'. It is true a number of older societies were revitalised—Debates in 1931 with a junior society two years later—and that a range of new societies existed from time to time during these years. These included angling, cinematograph, model railway, aeroplane, wireless, naturalist and drawing clubs. A news exam was added to the General Knowledge competition when it was re-organised in 1929. And to supplement lectures the College acquired its first cinema projector in 1929. The silent films shown first were *Raffles*, a Charlie Chaplin, and a Wild West one. The last silent film was *Felix the Cat* in October 1933 and the same month the first talking pictures arrived with a newsreel and a film about African exploration.

Going by the *Hurst Johnian* reports of school activities, however, it would appear that only three involved substantial numbers of boys: the cadet force, the Shakespeare play and, above all, music. Captain Pocock's years in command of the cadets are barely mentioned in the magazine before he retired in 1925 to be succeeded by Captain Francis Wright. When he left in 1933 his successor was Captain G.B. Morgan who married and left to join the R.A.F. in 1935, his successor in command being Captain Kenneth Mason. Throughout the period Sergeant Couch continued as sergeant-major, celebrating 25 years in the post in 1936.

Few corps activities are reported in the magazine, and perhaps this reflected lack of interest in things military, particularly in the late 1920s and early 1930s. Wright was careful to present the corps in terms of specialist skills like the band, shooting and signalling rather than as a preparation for army life. Each year there were the two ceremonial parades on inspection and Empire days, field days, the platoon competition, and the annual camp at Mytchett or Tidworth. Under Morgan 1935 was a particularly active year. The corps returned to the Aldershot Public Schools Field Day, although it is noticeable that only seven schools attended, and the first non-Aldershot camp was held at Strensall near York. At this camp a lecture on aerial co-ordination was a small indicator of a new challenge to interest in army matters—flying. The first Hurst boys entered Cranwell, and in 1936 the R.A.F. Volunteer Reserve was formed with 13 training schools and five flight schools, and by the late 1930s it was the air force rather than the army that commanded most interest among those thinking of a service career.

In Tower's early years there was quite a succession of play producers. Randolph Rogers produced that of 1924 and Claud Gurney that of 1925. Although he left he returned to produce the play of 1926. That year C.W. Thomas began his many years as stage manager. In 1927 the play was produced by Francis Wright and Reginald Loverock, and from 1928 to 1932 Wright and F.B. Lisle were the producers. Stella Tower did the make up; matrons, the costumes; and Parham handled the box office. According to Muriel, Parham, who was an English master, fulfilled an important rôle in encouraging the play. First, he talent-spotted boys and Muriel says, if it had not been for him, 'I should never have got into the play at all'. He also devoted lessons to reading the plays in his 'frightful adenoidal squawk', using his voluminous gown as costume, and this performance the boys found rivetting.

1926 was the first time *Romeo and Juliet* was given with L.W.A.T. Drake as Romeo and Ronald Neame as Juliet—who was later to be a distinguished film producer particularly of Dickens' films like *Oliver Twist* and *Nicholas Nickleby*. The 1928 play was *The Merchant of Venice*, which ran into casting difficulties and in which R.C. Heiser played Gratiano a few weeks before he died, aged 16, early in 1929. The first play produced with the benefit of the new hall stage was *Richard III* in 1930. Next year lighting and special effects were greatly improved for *Hamlet* with K.R. Prebble in the title rôle, and the orchestra for the first time consisted entirely of boy musicians. 1932's *Twelfth Night* was dominated by R.P.K. Harrison's Feste, an accomplished actor in his third play, while the female leads for four years were taken by J.N. Perkins.

Robert Bury produced his first play, *Henry IV Part II*, in 1933 and he and Thomas worked together on the plays until 1939. Basil Roper Cooke was Henry IV although his speaking was inhibited due to an accident to his throat on the first night. He was Theseus in *A Midsummer Night's Dream* in 1934 when Hawkins's music was performed again. This production received praise for every aspect of the play and it was clear that Bury's attention to detail and to diction was having an effect. Some amusement was caused by giving the part of Hippolyta to J.T. Griffiths, 'a somewhat muscular female' even for an Amazon queen! Next year he had the more congenial rôle of Macbeth and R.S. Meade was Lady Macbeth. That year the last Prologue was given and two performances instead of one. The last play under Tower was *The Tempest* with N.V. Hall as Ariel and J.G. Richards as Caliban.

By the time Tower arrived, 'Hawkey' was established as a distinguished music master and a well-known school character. He was a short man with a crew cut, thick pebble spectacles, and a shambling walk, with his head down and his arms waving rather like a penguin. Stella Tower described him less pleasantly as 'a monkey at the organ'. In Muriel's day he taught French and geography and his classes were the scene of friendly disorder. Muriel says he was respected for his musical skills and there was 'a real love for him and his odd and endearing ways'. In 1924 he had built and moved into the Tudor House by North field and there tragedy struck in 1927 when his wife died giving birth to their daughter. She was baptised in June as Ann Winifred Le Conte with Christian Widor and Siegfried Wagner's wife as her god-parents. Hawkins was a respected figure in the world of music known for his organ playing (he went on to be organist of Chichester Cathedral for 20 years) and his enthusiasm for early English music and French classical music, which he pushed to the point of obsession in his concert and recital repertoires. Widor and Potiron dedicated pieces to him.

His work was prodigious. He wrote music for the Shakespeare plays. He wrote religious music and set all parts of the service. He provided alternative arrangements for well-known music and, although this composition, like that of Farrant and Axe before him, was not distinguished, it helped to raise the prestige of music in school life and to stimulate interest. He wrote a *Hurst March*, and a *Grace* for the Boar's Head Feast. He gave organ recitals, conducted choir and orchestra, and trained the corps band. Music teaching expanded and he coached the first two of many successful Hurst music scholars who went to King's College, Cambridge— R. W. Carrington in 1933 and P.A. Stevens in 1936. Through Canon Nixon (OJ) Hurst was able to attract some young choristers from Westminster Abbey. Hawkins was an F.R.C.O. and an F.R.S.A. and Tower characteristically could not help noticing on one occasion that in Westerby's *Complete Organ Recitalist* there were three photographs of organs—Hurst's and 'the other two being of Eton and Harrow'.

Certainly for a small public school in the inter-war period, Hawkins' music programme was unusually weighted towards music which would have been heavy going for many listeners: at times he seems to have deliberately avoided 'pop' classics. In July 1928 a stir was caused in chapel when 'bold' and 'severe' music by Potiron was used during communion. Certainly concerts including Widor, Dubois, and Arcadelt (1927), Gebauer's *Fourth Symphony* (1933), or Widor, Vierne, Wilhelj, and Vallombrosa (1936) would not have been heard in other Sussex schools at that time. Later this became a criticism of Hawkins, but for most of Tower's time he managed to strike a balance between his own interests and those of ordinary boys. A concert in July 1927, for instance, with 18 items included the Sussex composer, Frank Bridge, Schubert, Schumann, Mozart and Vaughan Williams. The concert in 1933 had Ireland, Grieg, and Quilter, and that in 1935 Gershwin, Schubert and Sullivan. Even his organ recital on 21 March 1937 commemorating Widor's death a few days earlier included two pieces by him and also Bach and Handel.

Under Tower Hawkins continued to be a musical innovator, adding to his carol service and orchestra started in Coombes's day. In June 1926 the choir gave its first outside recital for many years at St Martin's, Brighton, where they returned on two subsequent occasions. On 6 March 1927 wireless listeners heard 'London calling. We are now going over to the school chapel of Hurstpierpoint College'. This was for the first radio broadcast with pieces by Widor, Bach, some hymns, and some of Hawkins's own work. On 2 April 1927 the first orchestral concert when all the players were boys was given including works by Schumann and Sullivan. In February 1928 the choir took part in a plainsong concert at St Thomas's, Hove, and was entertained by Ambrose Gorham (OJ) at the *Queen's Hotel*. On 3 April 1935 the first house music competition took place for the Hawkins Cup, given in memory of his wife. Chevron won in 1935 and 1936 with P.A. Stevens as their star assisted by K.L. Millar, R.E.S. Chapman, H.E. Franks, and J.W. Millar in a programme including music by Sullivan, Wagner, Bach and Schubert. On 30 March 1937 a joint concert with girls from St Michael's and Burgess Hill School for Girls took place in the hall with a piece specially composed for the occasion by Vallombrosa, and music by Arne, Bridge, Howell, Widor, and others, the performance ending with the *Hurst March*.

IV

There is little that can be said about Hurst's academic record in Tower's time. The only bright spot was the continuing presence at Oxbridge of a reasonable number of boys. According to the calendars the number of Hurst Johnians in residence in each of Tower's years was 11, 13, 14, 10, 12, 10, 11, 11, 12, 8, 11, 9 and 9 which was a good record considering the smallness of the sixth form. In 1928, 1930 and 1935 there were five entrants. Entrance to Sandhurst and Cranwell was also satisfactory—there were four in 1936, for example. And there were even some awards: two music ones already mentioned, one classics (E.A.L. Balshaw), and two historians (H.S. Deighton and K.L. Millar).

For the majority of the College exams seem to have played a small part in life and, because other local schools like Brighton College were improving academically in the mid-1930s, Hurst had clearly fallen a rung or two down the academic ladder. Between 1932 and 1937 there were about 258 leavers. Of these seven obtained Higher Certificates and 98, School Certificates. 69 obtained exemption from London Matriculation and, when it is borne in mind that the same boys achieved some of these passes, the overall position is bad and there is no other word for it: Tower admitted at Prize Day in 1936 that only 11 per cent managed exam passes. No task apart from financial recovery was more important than academic recovery if Hurst was to survive.

Tower, it will be recalled, inherited a staff that needed the academic pruning hook, and he quickly dispensed with Darrell Brown, Mavor, and one Cumming who was found to have falsified his references. Sadly, he also lost Gurney and two other masters who died. On 6 November 1925 the chaplain, Randolph Rogers, died aged only forty. On 8 November Coombes returned to preach at what proved to be the last Obit Sunday service. Rogers's body was placed on a catafalque in the chapel with a guard of honour of boys and masters overnight, and next day the burial service was conducted by the Rev. F.C. Haines—the first part in the chapel, and the second at the graveside in the village churchyard where the boys holding wreaths lined the paths. The last death in the College treated in this Victorian manner was actually that of a boy, Kenneth Suffield, who died in the sanatorium during the holidays in August 1934. He too was laid out in his coffin in the Memorial Chapel, and on 13 August he was the last boy buried in the village churchyard. F.N. White, a science master appointed early in 1926, died aged only 24 in January 1928.

Tower was faced with a *fait accompli* when it came to the common room. Three men— Parham, housemaster of Fleur de Lys and second master, Scott, housemaster of Chevron and secretary-bursar, and Pocock, housemaster of Red Cross until his marriage, corps commander and science master—were the first long-serving masters in the century. Clearly Stella Tower saw them as reactionaries determined to resist any sort of change. This is certainly true of Parham (1898-1931) who was never a popular figure: indeed his nickname was 'Turpy' from the Latin *turpis*. The small, rotund figure, encased in voluminous gown and giving forth orders in his squeaky voice, much given to favourites and often spiteful in enforcing petty rules, clearly aroused Muriel's wrath. Parham had two operations in the 1920s, but was allowed to carry on as Fleur housemaster while the equally diminutive C.W. 'Hundred Weight' Thomas (1920-1945) did all the work! There was no public ceremony when Parham retired, although he obtained a pension of £300 a year from the General Purposes Woodard Fund and a gift of fish knives and forks from Old Johnians.

Percy 'Weasel' Scott (1901-1950), described by Stella as 'colourless and with a hatchet face', was an uninspiring master, the epitome of the backwoodsman bachelor—a type of public school master then to be found in most schools. His whole life was the school, and there can be no doubt that his firmness in discipline and his rigour as bursar was invaluable to the College. He reached his 25 years in 1927 and was given a cheque and a silver cigarette box. Scott gave the impression that his life's work was a life sentence and once going in to the chapel confided in a colleague: 'you know, I never really liked people'.

Herbert 'Bip' Pocock (1908-1954) was an altogether more humane man. But his life was saddened by domestic tragedy. Pocock gave up the corps in 1925 to concentrate more on his home life when his daughter was born, but only four years later his wife died. It was unfair of Stella Tower to describe him passing round the buildings with a 'look of dum dog endurance' because in spite of the loss he was an active squash player in the 1930s, and ran cricket in the war years. He received a silver cruet for his 25 years in 1935.

These three men were not the only long-serving members of the common room: indeed an element of stability was at last entering into the staff with others staying for long periods and a good group of medium-term stayers developed. Hawkins remained throughout Tower's headship. C.W. Thomas who had done Parham's donkey-work was housemaster of Fleur for three years, was stage manager, and ran hockey for some years. In 1928 Tower appointed Arthur Hodgson, his brother-in-law, as a geography master. He was housemaster of Shield for 20 years, and in 1935 was the first careers master. He left in 1950. The medium-term stayers among the masters who made substantial contributions to school life under Tower were H.P. Hughes (1924-1930), modern languages master who started foreign trips and rugby coaching; Reginald Loverock (1925-1928), who established rugby, edited the magazine for three years, and taught history; Francis Wright (1923-1933), housemaster of Red Cross, who produced plays, edited the magazine, founded the aeroplane club, organised the summer boys' camps, officered the corps, and helped develop shooting; F.B. Lisle (1926-1935), who did Tower's donkey-work in Star, and was play producer, and G.B. Morgan (1927-1935), housemaster of Red Cross and corps commander.

A common room of 12 reached 15 in 1929 but fell back again to 12 in 1937, although Tower was actually able to increase the number of Oxbridge graduates from six to eight during that time. In May 1934 the first modern salary scale for masters was announced, to come into operation in September. The starting salary was to be £200 a year and this would rise over 26 years to a maximum of £560. Masters were expected to live in, receiving free board and lodging, but provision was made for three to live out and receive an extra £80. Housemasters were to be paid £50 a year, and the principle of allowances began with one of £30 a year for running the corps followed by £50 a year for running the Junior House. Sadly, however, before these scales could come into force a five per cent cut in salaries was ordered in October 1934.

This was just one result of a deep economic crisis affecting the College, more serious than either of those under Awdry or Coombes because, although its origins lay in financial decisions taken in the 1920s and were compounded by muddle in the 1930s, there was also a national economic crisis of such serious proportions that one like it was not to be seen again until the 1990s when, incidentally, it had equally serious effects. The seriousness of matters did not enter the public domain. Tower told Old Johnians in 1934 that Hurst 'was weathering the storm of financial depression, and was showing signs of prosperity', and on Prize Day 1935 he said entry was 'keeping up well'. The figures are, however, plain enough:

Year	Total in School	Total entry	Junior School
1931	171	42	(included in
1932	157	37	Total in School)
1933	136	50	4
1934	142	46	12
1935	139	46	24
1936	147	50	25
1937	137	48	24

So too were the comments in the Council minutes which by 1934 referred to the 'rather alarming state of the financial position', and two years later to the 'unsatisfactory state of the school's finances'.

The 1930s were a grave time for many small public schools as the depression affected middle-class incomes, with falling returns on investments and declining salaries. A more academic school like Brighton College saw its numbers fall from 501 in 1930 to 241 in 1937, and a report in 1937 said 'the present financial position threatens the existence of the College'. Ardingly College was in a worse position—its numbers fell to 84 in 1937, and even a well-known school like Lancing dropped to 160, and the master of Wellington College was concerned to keep fees as low as £140 a year. Some schools like Margate and Weymouth Colleges closed their doors.

In 1930 Tower had been confident that Improvement Fund Number 1 would be repaid and wished to start an Improvement Fund Number 2, which would have completed the building programme, who knows with what beneficial results? But the fall in fee income meant there was no money for development and no money to repay the loan. Fortunately those who had taken out money were prepared to wait, but this meant that in 1937 there was still a debt of £11,950 to be cleared. This inhibited banks from extending limitless credit and made the

Chapter wary of starting to bail out Hurst from the General Purpose Fund. The Chapter gave £350 over three years to cope with emergency demands for maintenance. By 1937 expenditure exceeded fee income by £1,309 7s. 11d. and an overdraft of £1,500 had to be obtained.

Looking back, particularly after Walter Dingwall had saved the situation, there does seem to be some ineptitude by Chapter and Council alike in responding to the situation. The Chapter bursar, Henry Pelham, was another Edmund Blackmore: economy was his only answer and in February 1937 Tower was required to clear every item of expenditure with the Chapter. The Council, as we have already mentioned, mishandled the rates payable by the College and in 1933 they were congratulating themselves on finding money in a fund they did not know they had! In 1933 Ambrose Gorham (OJ) died at Telscombe. He had always enjoyed entertaining the boys after cricket and was a wealthy man, having won the 1902 Grand National. He left £1,000 for the chapel without specifying conditions and, instead of investing this money, half of it was spent on the organ, and the rest disappeared piecemeal over the years rather than being used for a new north window, for which a design was commissioned (it is in the archives) and which had to be turned down in May 1936.

Tower believed part of the problem was high fees and as early as June 1931 raised the matter. In February and October 1932 he advocated reduction, but not until February 1933 did the Council set up a committee to consider reductions and they rejected the idea in June of the same year. In October Council changed its mind and agreed to reduce basic fees from £135 to £105 a year, and this change was to operate from September 1934. However, within two years they had to some extent nullified their policy because they introduced charges for science, games, laundry and the doctor while making the smallest gesture of a £2 reduction in corps charges, so that by 1937 fees were back to £110 5s. Moreover, Star boys were to pay £5 more, although Tower did not directly supervise the House.

Tower's second idea for coping with the crisis was to start a junior house. He wished anyway to end the entry of boys under 13 to the main school. So in April 1933 four boys started the Junior House with the young Kenneth Mason in charge. Robert Bury took over in September 1934 and the Junior House was successful: it numbered 24 by 1937, but it did not really help the problem. Its fees were lower and some of the boys at least would have entered the main school at the higher fee. There was not a hundred per cent feed through into the senior school. Roger Moulton has shown that the total of boys in the school given in the calendar includes the Junior House intake, so to an extent all it did was rearrange boys: the total in the College rose by one between 1933 and 1937.

Small though the entry was, if it had been retained, matters would not have reached the state of crisis they did. Tower at one point advocated cutting sixth-form fees if parents agreed to keep their sons at the College for at least four years, but the economic crisis and the lack of academic success meant that the annual leave was as large as the annual intake, and by 1937 there were only 76 boys over 13 in the College. When Arthur Hodgson became careers master in 1935 he invited a spokesman from Selfridges to talk about trainee managers. An Old Johnian commented in the magazine, 'every other O.J. we meet these days is a policeman ... this is awful', and among the names he mentioned was one of the outstanding athletes of the 1930s. Job insecurity was clearly persuading boys that leaving to get a job was more sensible than staying on. But without a sixth form there could not be academic and sporting triumphs, and without that publicity numbers would not rise. This was to be one of Walter Dingwall's most difficult problems.

Hurst survived, but only just. By Tower's last year cancelled fixtures, house rugby with 12 a side, and the obvious absence of boys in the school created what Dingwall called in his first

Council meeting 'a general lethargic air'. Although Tower was only 55 years old he clearly had had enough, and there can be little doubt that Stella, too, was eager to leave. Tower left in July 1937 and it is interesting that he is the only headmaster for whom no farewell ceremony is recorded in the magazine although the Old Johnians gave him a desk and chair. The Towers' departures was typical in some ways of their self-centred lives. Stella took the kitchen range so that Dingwall had to buy a new Esse Stove (£80) and he did not receive the cost of this until he left. Bernard sold the green house and tool shed to Dingwall who later found out they had been bought by the school, and he was even more infuriated to receive a request to pay something for the plants in the headmaster's garden!

Tower became a diocesan official in London concerned with social work and was organising secretary of the Friends of London Diocese. He became rector of Much Hadham and from 1951 of Swinbrook and Widford. He was director of studies at the Church of England Education Study Centre from 1949 to 1961, and died on 21 June 1964. His memorial service was in St Paul's Cathedral on 25 July. Tower was the victim of circumstances, particularly inept financing by the Chapter and Council, and the economic depression, and he was the victim of his personality which clearly was not attractive to colleagues or impressive to boys. However, his headship provided the most sustained building programme in the College's history so far, and one which was well balanced between making the buildings attractive and providing practical facilities. With electric light came a measure of enlightenment, a move away from the Victorian ways of the early 1920s, and in much of what he did Tower was in advance of his times so that activities like foreign trips, social work, or E.S.P.U. activities had to be re-introduced at a later date. The games programme he evolved remained in place until the early 1990s. Indirectly, too, Tower made a vital contribution to the College's future. In 1933 he appointed Robert Bury and Kenneth Mason and in 1935 Robin Gregory as young masters. Together with George Lambert who arrived with Walter Dingwall, the new head, in 1937 they were to form the second group of long-serving masters who did so much to ensure Hurst's success under three headmasters.

TEN

HOME FRONT AND RECONSTRUCTION 1937-1945

Walter Dingwall and the Second World War Years

It is hoped that the German Air Force will not be imprudent enough to interrupt the Standard Sports.

The Hurst Johnian, 781/5, March 1941

I think the foundation of success for the School has been laid in the last five years, and it remains to hold on for the duration of the war, and the two post-war years, by which time with reasonable good fortune, the prosperity of the School should be assured.

Headmaster's Report to Council, Michaelmas Term, 1942

I arrived here in 1937 with the School on the verge of disaster. The present financial position is strong ... I can claim to have done what I said would take four years, and the whole position has now altered. But I cannot cope with this, I am too worn out with the struggle of war-time difficulties. My average for the last eight days of term was getting to bed between 2.30 and 3.0 a.m., finishing up with an all night show with the Home Guard just before the farming camp.

Walter Dingwall to Clifford Freeman, 1 August 1943

The clouds cleared after a windy night: there had been some rain, but not enough to make any impression on the pitch, and we lay in bed listening to the planes—some had gone over low and slowly—we wondered afterwards if they were the air-borne troops. At half past eight there were the first rumours, at nine the German reports, and for those that had a private study, first period, communiqué Number One half an hour later.

The morning of D-Day, *The Hurst Johnian*, 791/145, July 1944

The Committee [Council] approved in principle the ideas put forward by the Fleming Report ...

Committee [Council] Minutes, 13 October 1944

Dingwall's contribution to improvements in all areas at Hurst was incalculable. I became a great admirer of him, climaxed by discovering that he had paid for my education at Hurst for my last two and a half years when father lost most of his money as a result of the war.

Old Johnian in a letter, 1995

Even before he arrived the new headmaster's letters showed he was a man who combined business sense with a determined personality, and there can be no doubt that the appointment of 37-year-old Walter Spender Dingwall as Hurst's sixth headmaster was one of the most decisive events in the College's history, followed as it was by recovery and the creation of a new status for the school. Southwell, the Provost, was also chairman of the governors of St Edward's School, Oxford, and it was the warden of St Edward's together with the dean of Christ Church, Oxford and the warden of Radley College who provided Dingwall with excellent references. Dingwall was the first lay headmaster, and brought an unusual combination of experiences to his task.

Walter Dingwall was born in 1900, and went to Marlborough College, where, according to their archivist, he left no trace either as a first team player or prefect before leaving in 1918. He obtained a degree in mathematics at Christ Church, Oxford, and played hockey for the county. In 1922 he became a master, and subsequently a housemaster, at St Edward's School from where he came to Hurst. St Edward's went through a difficult patch in the 1920s, and from 1921 to 1927 was associated with the Woodard Society. In 1924 Dingwall took on the job of bursar for eight years during which time he helped to restore the school's position. In 1927 he was therefore present at the first meeting of the Public Schools Bursars Association and indeed was their secretary for six years. In 1932 he married Olive Mary Loasby (1910-1983). Unlike the Towers, Dingwall was little interested in domestic matters or even his personal finances, in part because he had private means. During his headship his salary was cut from £2,100 in 1937 to £750 by October 1940, and he also put his pension scheme in abeyance. He paid to have his house decorated and did not press his claims for the various items Tower insisted he should buy.

Wartime naturally made everyone's living conditions worse, but Dingwall made no attempt to have money spent on his own house in the way Tower had: the heating remained poor and the windows ill-fitting and on occasion unrepaired. The state of the building may be gauged by a letter Dingwall sent to the Chapter bursar in November 1944:

> This morning, in the middle of breakfast, thanks to faulty water pipes in the spare room above, a large portion of the ceiling descended and breakfast vanished. By a sheer piece of luck my wife had three minutes before gone to feed the chickens, because the bulk of it came down on her chair, and there is no doubt she would have been killed had she been there.

He went on to say it missed his father by a few feet and smashed or damaged his Venetian glass and silver spoons. 'I rather believe,' he ended, 'this is employer's liability as I have to have breakfast in a house in which, the plaster being of enormous thickness, there is more danger than from bombing.'

To others Dingwall was a generous man. He endowed a history prize and a university scholarship. He helped many boys who were in need. A typical case before the Council in 1943 concerned a boy whose father was on a low R.A.F. salary, whose mother was working as a nurse, and whose house was badly damaged by bombing. He helped with the legal costs of a boy whose parents were interned by the Japanese in Hong Kong, and in other cases like that mentioned at the start of the chapter. For the first time since Arthur and Isabel Coombes' early days, the school had an approachable and involved headmaster who combined good discipline with an easy camaradie with his sixth form and, although some of the officials and masters he dealt with found his pace too fast and his remarks too sharp, they too came to admire and like him. Dingwall was popular in the best sense of that word: indeed he stands comparison with another young headmaster of his generation, Robert Longden at Wellington College who, in David Newsome's words, 'brought with him a feeling of personal excitement and adventure which evoked from

36   Fleur de Lys day room with its new 'horse-boxes' in 1938.

the school the instant desire to share in it: it was almost as if he looked upon headmastering as fun, a thrilling experience for himself, and the community to which he had come'.

So for eight years Hurst was used to Dingwall's rapid stride along the cloisters, hair falling forward, shoulders hunched beneath his gown, and to his all-seeing eye which missed no detail. Hard working, energetic, meticulous, clever and far-sighted, he was exactly the right man to carry the double burden of securing Hurst's recovery and carrying the school through a war that had a very direct impact on everyday life. He taught economics and history. He played hockey and squash. Scott faded from sight as Dingwall was obviously his own bursar. Although Robin Gregory ran Star in its daily routine, Dingwall was involved with his house. He ran Home Guard Platoon 8, B Company for the duration, and in the holidays attended farming and forestry camps. He concerned himself with individuals, but had time to formulate plans not only for Hurst but also for reforming the Woodard Society. Indeed, perhaps towards the end of the war he was undertaking too much, putting forward too many schemes and, because he never suffered fools gladly, came to annoy some of the Chapter traditionalists.

He might say on Prize Day, 'the days of one man schools are long since past', but in fact both Dingwall and his successor Howard, in their different ways, were dominating personalities dealing with Chapter, Council, staff, parents and boys alike. But behind the public success lay the private helping hand and, when he left, the magazine after praising his work for the College said that 'as individuals there are many who owe him still more'. One example will illustrate this, and it is a good one showing as it does the impact of war on individuals.

Arthur Hodgson, housemaster of Shield, lived out, and the dormitories were run by the house prefects to whom Dingwall had given new powers. On 27 March 1939 there was ragging going on in the dormitory between three boys, Seaton Roberts, John Ascough, and Adrian Wilson who knew each other. Wilson was held down on a bed, and Ascough menaced him with the house banner pole which slipped, injuring Wilson's mouth. He went to the sanatorium and the incident was not regarded as dramatic. However, Wilson's father was in financial difficulty. He applied for a reduction in fees and, when offered only half, sued the College in April 1939 for negligence and Ascough and Roberts for assault. The case did not come before Lewes Assizes until 7 August 1940 to Dingwall's intense annoyance at the delays. By then the Battle of Britain was in full swing overhead, and the next day was to be the first major air battle over Southern England. The College won its case with costs but the assault charge was proved and fines and costs of £146 13s. 6d. incurred. Roberts paid, but Ascough's parents could not afford to do so, and the matter dragged on until January 1942 when Dingwall settled it. Ascough had been a promising boy in the first teams for rugby and hockey and Dingwall gave him every support during the rest of his school career, making him a prefect, captain of swimming, and Cadet Drum-Major. When the Ascough parents were interned in Hong Kong, Dingwall made sure the boy continued his education. Ascough joined the army in India and was killed in Burma in October 1943. The Ascough Memorial Prize was given to commemorate his parents' gratitude for all Dingwall had done.

Although the tasks facing Dingwall of restoring the school's financial and academic positions were great, he had the ability and energy to achieve them, but he would not have done so had it not been that his arrival also coincided with a period of reform in the Woodard Society. This had begun in 1934 when Southwell had replaced the 1892 statutes, but the Provost died in April 1937 after a distinguished career as acting Chaplain-General of the forces, suffragan bishop of Lewes, canon, precentor and assistant bishop of Chichester. At Hurst he was commemorated by a plaque in chapel and a portrait by P.C. Phellips (now in the archives). His successor was Kenneth Kirk, canon of Christ Church and Regius Professor of Theology at Oxford, but no sooner had he been appointed than he was made Bishop of Oxford, and it was clear he could not operate in the way previous Provosts had done. So in July 1937 it was agreed by the Chapter that, while Kirk would handle individual educational and religious matters, day-to-day administration would be in the hands of a Chapter committee.

This was to consist of the vice-provost, Hugh Hordern, Bishop of Lewes from 1929 to 1946; the custos, a post now held by Henry Pelham; the registrar, J. Millington Sing, who retired in 1942; and the secretary-bursar. Because this was a vital post a new one was appointed, Clifford Freeman, on the substantial salary of £1,000 a year. By training a solicitor, Freeman was to dominate the Chapter committee, and working with Dingwall helped him greatly with reforms and the crises of the period inseparable from wartime. In 1941 Canon A.R. Browne-Wilkinson joined the Hurst committee. A canon of Chichester, he was also an educational expert and, when Kirk gave up the Provostship in 1944, Browne-Wilkinson succeeded him, and was installed next year.

Dingwall found the administration of the school annoying, to put it mildly. He was not a fellow and therefore not entitled to attend Chapter committee meetings, and yet their decisions overrode those of the School committee. Who is the head working with, he asked on one occasion? 'Is it a body he never meets?' During 1943 matters reached a crisis when the strain of the war was starting to tell. Dingwall had set up in 1938 Hurst Johnian Trust Limited to invest all money given by way of bequests or donations after he saw how the Gorham bequest had been mishandled. By 1943 this had an income of £2,898 11s. 7d. but the Chapter committee intervened and pointed out that under the statutes this was not a Hurst trust, but a Woodard one, with the clear implication that they had a say in its dispersal. Dingwall told Freeman in the letter quoted at the start of this chapter, 'I cannot cope with this, I am too worn out with the struggle of war-time difficulties', and received a sharp letter back from Freeman saying he resented offence being taken where none was intended, and unless he was treated better 'you and Hurst will see more of what my duty demands and less of what my heart urges. Quite frankly, I'm bored with it. Now do ease up!'

In fact Dingwall and Freeman worked well together and Freeman did his best to relieve Hurst of some financial burdens. He transferred the rents of the East field to Hurst. He secured a reduction from £775 to £288 a year in Hurst's contribution to the General Purposes Fund and he modernised the Calendar so there was no 'class' difference in the presentation of the various schools. He wrote to Dingwall on another occasion, 'I am almost flattered by your suggestion that I have the ingenuity or the intelligence to dare to try to trip you up'. Dingwall continued to complain about the Woodard structure. In 1943 he said, 'I cannot cope with this out of date machinery any longer'. The next year he said, 'the machinery is breaking down' and in December put forward a formal request for reform. In fact he was pushing at an open door for both Browne-Wilkinson and Freeman wanted change, and it was one of the sad ironies of Dingwall's departure in the middle of 1945 that this coincided with the major reform of the Society introduced on 1 September that year.

The Provost of the Southern Chapter was to cease to be the overall head of the Society which would be a new office of President first filled in 1946. The four existing chapters would become divisions of the Woodard Corporation. The fellows would hold honorary positions and the business of each division would be in the hands of a Business committee chaired by the divisional bursar. Each school would have a Chairman and Council, only half of whom had to come from the Woodard Corporation, opening the way for educational experts and distinguished names to be added to the governing bodies. The school secretaries were to be bursars and also clerks to the governors and, although the boundary between division and Council responsibilities was not made clear, this all marked a considerable advance.

At Hurst Dingwall had inherited Tower's Committee [Council], and this remained unchanged until the summer of 1941 apart from the resignation of Henry Pelham in May 1940. They worked well with Dingwall and, when he received call up papers in November 1939, resolved to 'leave no stone unturned' to keep their headmaster. Canon W.H. Ferguson succeeded Pelham. The chairman, the Rev. Canon Leigh H. Nixon, was ill in 1940, and retired in June 1941 dying a few months later. His successor was a name familiar to Hurst Johnians, Sir William Campion (1870-1951). He had been M.P. for Lewes (1910-1924) and Governor of Western Australia (1924-1929) before he had joined the Council in 1931, and he was an effective chairman. A.E.C. Shippam continued to serve and was joined by A. Wigglesworth, who was keenly interested in school affairs and made several financial contributions for particular necessities, and in 1942 by Sir Noel Curtis-Bennett, whose son was at the school.

At his first Council meetings Dingwall did not mince matters, referring to the lethargic air of the school and the verge of financial disaster they were standing on. Quite clearly too his impact on the College was to disperse this as quickly as possible. 'I have been accused,' he said on Prize Day 1938, 'of breaking many traditions.' The magazine said the school had been 'rudely stirred from its apathy', and by the time the inspectors arrived in 1939 they spoke of 'considerable vitality', and said 'much has already been accomplished' towards revitalising school life and improving facilities, although they realised that financial success was still far away. In a way Dingwall began like Tower with a raft of reforms, but the reaction to Dingwall was very different. The magazine, instead of carping criticism, said most of the reforms were 'for the best', and Dingwall did as much as he could to involve everyone in what he was doing. Preparatory school heads were invited to meet him and his wife and to attend school events. Parents were sent letters explaining what was being done. He had an informal dinner with Old Johnians and welcomed their visits—there were over fifty in Lent Term 1939 alone, for example. Prize Day and Old Johnians Day were separated in 1938 to give more time to both events. Life membership was started, doubling membership with those joining after 1938.

Almost immediately financial good sense broke out in Council meetings. The rates were cut from £910 to £775 and further to £675. Dingwall was annoyed with pensions of £300 for Parham and Tower. Parham's death in 1940 ended his, and Tower's was then cut by half. The pension scheme for masters was altered although later economies prevented its full introduction. The school insurance policies were reviewed, 'some things being insured twice, others being uninsured, while even things non-existent were insured', he told Council before rationalising and reducing costs. Even a reduction of £70 in water rates was obtained. Dingwall said that Tower 'had hidden the falling numbers' behind the junior house intake, but that this house was annoying local preparatory schools and lacked proper facilities. Robert Bury transferred to Red Cross, C.W. Thomas ran it for a term, and it closed in July 1938 with boys transferring into the main school, or going to Hollingbury Court, although their fees continued to be paid to Hurst in a typically shrewd Dingwallian move.

All these moves were welcome but they did not address the fundamental financial problem— as H.M. Inspectors said, 160 boys were needed to break even and have a small surplus for investment. Astonishingly Walter Dingwall convinced Council and Chapter to go further into debt. He pointed out that the vicious circle had to be broken and it could only be done by providing good conditions, persuading boys to stay on, securing results, and so bringing in more boys. He pointed out that visiting prep school heads were critical of a 'lack of washing accommodation, and paint, and no sixth form'. Dingwall negotiated an overdraft of £4,000 and the deficit accordingly rose to £2,657 in 1938, and he used the money to transform the interior of the buildings, where again his bursarial skills enabled much to be done for what was after all not a large sum of money. He was so successful that the magazine printed a map in March 1938 for the benefit of visiting old boys: the premises, said the 1939 inspectors, 'have been made very much more attractive'. In 1938 and 1939 £1,767 was spent on repairs, and £2,912 on building.

The armoury was moved from the bottom of Chevron to the power house (Albert Hut later), and was provided with heating and a new floor. Into this space came expanded accommodation for the surgery with a doctor's room and nurses' facilities. Each house was provided with two day rooms and a house prefects' rooker even though Red Cross had to be accommodated near Shield. Chevron embellished their rooker with panelling, and furnishings were provided in this house and others by former members. Upper school was to become the lecture room and main school library, while the Randolph was to be a sixth-form library provided with newspapers. The fellows library became a Fleur day room and the contents, including much that was valuable, was relegated to the crumbling gymnasium. A school captain's room was provided near the head's study, and the rooms at the west end were set aside for hobbies. Each day room was provided with 'horse-boxes' which came originally from Winchester but were seen by Dingwall at other schools. Costing £5 each, they lasted until the mid-1990s. Hall was refloored and retabled.

37 The forestry camp at Petworth in the summer of 1942. Top right, K. Mason. Centre row, fourth from the right, Walter Spender Dingwall the headmaster from 1937 to 1945. Front row, seated third from right, R.J. Gregory, and at the end Sergeant-Major F.S. Taylor.

Upstairs the long dormitories were divided in two. Each house was provided with bathrooms containing showers, footbaths, baths, hot and cold basins, and improved toilets. Each boy was given a locker. Red blankets and rugs, curtains and floor matting made splashes of colour. Throughout the school paint and distemper were applied, doors, floors and furniture repaired. The faulty electricity supply was finally corrected after Dingwall had a voltage test done and found the company was supplying defective power! Fire bells, and escapes, and fire practice came in as part of A.R.P. precautions. Houses started providing themselves with amenities like small billiard tables and on Saturday evenings a decent film projector made its appearance. A microphone was introduced in chapel.

Dingwall wanted a new classroom block and, as this was impossible, did his best with the existing facilities. £830 of improvements took place including roofing, and repanelling of the huts which were provided with a covered way, and even beds of lupins outside. Inside blackboards, graph boards, some teaching aids, and the first single desks—100 at £1 each made their appearance. A start was made on the gymnasium with £300 of improvements including a wired glass roof, and repair of the walls.

Although no building alterations took place in chapel this was a part of the school to which he turned immediate attention. 'It cannot be said,' he told Council, 'that the general attitude towards the chapel among the boys is good.' The new chaplain reorganised services with more frequent communions, and evening rather than morning prayers on weekdays. The custom of marching into chapel ended. House prayers were encouraged. Four senior boys became sacristans to tidy up and prepare for services. A blue service book was introduced to make plain to the boys what was going on and to include special Hurst services. At the start of term he introduced a prefects' installation service; at the end, an *itinerarium* or leaving service with *Jerusalem* as the last hymn. In December 1937 a carol service based on King's College, Cambridge's Nine Lessons and Carols was started with seven of each, changed to nine by Canon Howard. Many of these changes lasted until the mid-1990s, and at the time clearly helped to make chapel more relevant. The number of boys confirmed rose from 56 in 1937 to 96 in 1939.

The changes soon began to take effect and, by 1939, in spite of ending the junior house, numbers at 159 were within one of the break-even point recommended by the inspectors. Dingwall outlined his next proposals which included the electrification of the kitchens with mixers and washing machines, and the extension of the central heating system to the sanatorium and the Coombes gallery. But the outbreak of war disrupted the programme by raising costs and reducing numbers. Boys and masters returned early to fit the blackout (costing £346 2s. 10d.) with a mixture of curtains and plywood boards and brown paper fitted in the cracks by Kenneth Mason. Only part of its cost was borne by the charge made to parents. Cadet force numbers rose but no extra money was forthcoming from the War Office for equipment and facilities. Later came a War Damage Act requiring the College to take out additional insurance policies in order to qualify, and although the Gorham bequest was used to cover the chapel, the cost of this new insurance wiped out Dingwall's previous savings in this respect. There was also inevitably a slow war-time inflation in prices although less than in the First World War.

On Prize Day 1940 Dingwall referred to the call up of 17- and 18-year-olds and, as in the previous war, leaving early to serve or leaving directly to enter the forces reduced sixth form numbers and incentive to try for university. As before, the turn over of masters became more rapid and Dingwall lost some of the key men he was relying on to raise standards. Building, of course, stopped and the contents of the fellows library found their way to the gymnasium. Moreover, Hurst was close to a war zone and inevitably suffered a drop in numbers. In 1940

Dingwall told Council that numbers 'look very bad for the next two terms' and the next year, 'I do not see how a big drop can be avoided'. He was right. By 1941 numbers were back to 137 where he started. The bank 'will not lend any more money', he told Council. With a war on economies were possible. Grants to the corps and games were cut. A large number of school servants were dismissed and Mary Dingwall was paid a wage of £60 to look after the head's house instead of employing servants. Masters' salaries were cut by ten per cent and the pension premiums paid by the College were halved. Dingwall himself accepted a cut in salary three times that of his staff.

Economies help but do not solve schools' problems: only numbers do that, and Dingwall had to find ways of raising them. In June 1940 Dingwall wrote to parents to say that, if evacuation was necessary, Hurst would go to Worksop, but as Sussex was an area to which people were being evacuated from London he saw no reason to move. On Prize Day he said 'to pack our bags and run is only going to foster disquiet and play exactly the game the Nazis want us to do'. The School would therefore stay and, because other schools like Lancing and Eastbourne were evacuated, this enabled Hurst to recruit more able boys. Moreover, a number of preparatory schools had also left the area and Dingwall therefore reversed his view on the value of a junior house. In January 1941 he had accepted a small prep school, Downsend, being evacuated from Leatherhead, to Hurst. Their head, Mr. Lindford, his staff, and 38 boys were housed in Star until March 1942 and, as well as making money for Hurst, this provided some necessary teachers.

The junior house opened in September 1941 with 12 boys and five boarders. Mr. F.N. Goodwin, formerly of Westminster Abbey Choir School, became the first headmaster, bringing with him one or two choristers. After Downsend left Mrs. Margaret Gregory and Miss Madeleine Mayo were appointed in the Summer Term of 1942. Margaret Gregory left in the summer of 1943 and was replaced by Mr J.C.C. Shrewsbury who left after having a fit in chapel, and Mr. J.A.W. Van Praagh arrived. The boys lived in Star, ate in the Coombes gallery, and were taught in the huts, Mary Dingwall helping particularly at night when the boys had to traverse the blacked-out buildings. The house turned in an instant profit. By September 1943 numbers were up to 43 and Lancaster and York houses were created. Next year there were 47 boys of whom 22 were day pupils.

As in the previous war, a wish to provide safely for children when bombing became widespread, absence of fathers from home, and the need to economise during rationing all helped to persuade parents to send their boys away. During the Second World War there was an additional bonus from the many evacuated groups of Europeans like Jews, French, Poles and Czechs in the country, and Dingwall extended his recruiting successfully in their direction. Names like Michalek, Skarznski, Axelsson, Le Fevre, Haes, Shohan, Sheinman, and Ephraimson appear in the school list, and in 1943 besides 94 confirmed Anglicans there were nine Jews, five Roman Catholics, and four Nonconformists in the school. Dingwall was proud of the way these boys far from home adapted to school life, telling the Council of their successes like that of Janouch, who spoke very little English when he came but obtained six credits in the School Certificate.

Within a comparatively short time the financial position changed as numbers rose in the senior school from 137 in 1941 to 145 in 1942, 176 in 1943, and 213 in 1944. With 260 boys in the school of whom only 38 were day boys the College was completely full, and in February 1944 a delighted Council congratulated the headmaster on the 'very pleasing' state of the 1943 accounts. Under the most difficult conditions Dingwall had succeeded in restoring the school's financial stability and indeed, as we shall see later, had done so while raising its academic reputation to its highest since the days of Edward Lowe. In common with many aspects of

English life, 1944 at Hurst was to see Dingwall embark on new financial moves and grand plans for the future.

The Revival of Hurstpierpoint under Walter Dingwall

Year	Numbers, seniors (day)		Numbers, juniors (day)		Staff i	Higher Certs	Lower Certs	Oxbridge awards
1937	137		24					
1938	129	(7)	27		12	2	15	
1939	159	(6)			15	4	23	
1940	156	(7)			10	8	20	
1941	137	(11)	ii 17	(5)	10+1	13 iii	21	2
1942	145	(16)	27	(19)	10+4	18	24 iv	
1943 v	176	(18)	43	(22)	13+4	14	25	3
1944 vi	213	(16)	47	(22)	14+3	25	24	3
1945	216	(12)	44	(19)	16+4	27	43	3

   i.   Staff total excludes Dingwall, the Sergeant-Major, and temporary staff
   ii.   Additional numbers to those in the senior school unlike those under Tower
   iii. The figure of 14 given includes an external candidate
   iv. There were 37 'very good' grades, more than any other Sussex school
   v.   Star House full with 44 boys
   vi. School completely full. More than fifty boys in the sixth form.

II

The impact of the Second World War was felt in school life even before it began because, unlike 1914, there was a lead-up period of preparation for war as articles in the *Hurst Johnian* on 'Facts About the Territorial Army', or 'R.A.F. News' indicate. Old Johnians were already stationed at aerodromes like Hornchurch or North Weald, and in 1938 two of them, R.S. James and D. Perry, were killed during training. Under Captain Kenneth Mason the corps was now 112 strong, and a third had Certificate A as training grew more purposeful and relevant. The Light Machine Gun appeared at camp in 1938. In the village A.R.P. (Air Raid Precautions) were set up but proved remarkably inefficient when a 'mock' raid tested them: it took seven minutes to clear the school buildings. In College C.W. Thomas was in charge of A.R.P., a shelter trench was dug, and blackout was installed before the term began in September 1939.

On 21 September two houses (Rigaud's and Ashburnham) from Westminster School arrived to be billeted at Hurst and in the village—the rest of the school going to Lancing. Ninety boys came, 42 of them accommodated in Red Cross and Fleur de Lys and the others billeted in the village but taking their meals at school. The boys were accompanied by six masters. The sixth form had lessons at Danny Park and the rest were taught at Hurst. There had been a trial run of this evacuation at the time of the Munich Crisis, but astonishingly the Chapter did not do any detailed planning of the operation: indeed the costing of it was done by Clifford Freeman, uncharacteristically, on a sheet of paper. Westminster was to pay £100 towards A.R.P., £105 for each boarder, £46 10s. for each out-boarder, and the latter were to pay householders 15s. a week.

Although the magazine said the evacuation, which lasted for two terms, went smoothly there is plenty of evidence that it did not. Dingwall thought Westminster's attitude to discipline 'extremely bad', and there was a particularly unpleasant row when Westminster boys booed a

Hurst team and, when the Westminster prefects investigated the matter, they claimed jurisdiction over Hurst boys: it took Dingwall two days to sort this matter out. In reports in November 1939 and May 1940 Dingwall gave detailed accounts of the impact of Westminster. He pointed out that they lived well. Billeted boys were with 'the gentry' whereas St Paul's boys had been housed in labourers' cottages miles from their evacuation school. But Westminster had shown scant regard for their fellows. Books disappeared from the library, goal posts and other property were damaged, and even the masters were not a very impressive lot, demanding more vegetables at lunch and 'moaning because they did not get chicken'.

The real problem was a financial row. Westminster made lump sum payments according to the agreed rates—Hurst received £2,400 in 1939, and £2,030 in 1940. They paid Lancing money which Hurst should have had and Frank Doherty was quick to send Walter Dingwall the £1,500 involved. The problem was that the Westminster side were unwilling to agree payment for use of or damage to amenities. Dingwall cited matters like medical expenses, haircutting, extra food like cheese or a break-time bun, telephone bills, masters using office facilities, and boys the games facilities. Failure to meet Dingwall's request 'removes much of the pleasure in welcoming Westminster as a war job'. If he had known no payment would be forthcoming, Dingwall said he would have been much stricter: 'I should never have agreed to cheese every day'. Freeman and the Westminster bursar, J.R. Turner worked out a compromise, but the Westminster governors would not agree to it. Dingwall claimed £1,500, pointing out that this would have covered the deficit for 1940-1941.

'I think', he wrote to Freeman, 'it is absolutely scandalous that we should have an overdraft at the bank because Westminster does not pay its bill.' Doherty agreed it was 'one of the biggest scandals ever known'. The dispute lasted into 1941, Dingwall asking, 'is the wear and tear on headmasters included as well?' Westminster was bombed and it became clear by October 1941 that there was 'no hope whatever of obtaining any further payment ...'. Dingwall wanted to take the matter to court but Freeman would not agree, pointing out that Westminster had access to the best legal advice and would certainly start a counter-suit. In 1942 Council decided to draw a line under the affair.

Hurst's remaining in Sussex for the war was a policy with risks, although in the end it was triumphantly successful and Hurst did not suffer more than minor bomb damage. But, as the Home Guard trained on Danny under Dingwall or the boys made their way through barbed wire to celebrate Ascension Day in 1940, they probably did not realise that the College was in the direct path of German invasion, if it had ever happened. The plans finalised on 30 August 1940 involved the 8th and 28th divisions landing between Worthing and Newhaven secured by the 6th Mountain Brigade on the Downs behind Brighton. The fortifications in the Ouse and Adur valleys and the stop line which ran close between Hayward's Heath and Horsham would have been the scene of fighting as the invaders moved inland on each side of Lewes.

It was aerial warfare, however, that was the threat. Old Johnian memoirs of the period refer to the sight of the Battle of Britain fought overhead, and later to the passage of V1s—one very close to the College—and V2s. East Sussex alone had 2,400 air-raid alerts during the war. 852 people were killed and 55,000 buildings were damaged or destroyed. 890 V1s and V2s landed in Sussex as a whole. Fortunately the only bomb damage at Hurst was sustained on 10 February 1943 on the west side of the buildings, but there was a continual threat from jettisoned bombs, falling aircraft from both sides, spent anti-aircraft shells, and a range of bombs including high explosive, incendiary, and phosphorus types as well as from parachuted land mines. There were actually 52 direct attacks on civilians by machine gun or cannon fire from planes. Putting up and putting down the black-out daily, A.R.P. and Home Guard duties for masters, firewatching, and the constant strain of alerts may have added excitement for the boys to school life, but they were an anxiety and heavy work load for Dingwall and his masters.

Curiously enough the biggest threat to the College came from the Lands Branch of the Air Ministry in August 1942. The College received a letter saying it was their intention to requisition the school grounds for the local aerodrome, demolishing outlying houses and probably the chapel tower as well as removing all the trees. This would clearly have spelled disaster, because a school near an aerodrome was unthinkable and there was nowhere for them to be evacuated to. Letters were sent including one to Richard A. Butler, then president of the Board of Education, and it turned out that the official had acted incorrectly. 'I am so sorry', A.E. Shippam wrote to Dingwall, 'you have had all this worry and anxiety' over the matter.

At first sight Dingwall's concern over extra cheese and a bun at break in the dispute with Westminster seems astonishing until it is realised that war-time shortages were a part of life for six years. Old Johnian memoirs have a good deal to say about 'ghastly' war-time food, like dried egg and the quality of what was served including liver 'suitable for resoling army boots'. By 1941 Dingwall was telling Council that there were serious difficulties in food supply. For breakfast there was sausage and bacon only once a week, corn flakes or porridge being the usual fare. At tea-time one spoonful of jam or paste was doled out on alternate days. One summer matrons were said to have 'worked heroically' making jam. One boy describes how baked beans on toast at the tuck shop became sheer delight in spartan times, and others from local farms became 'surprisingly popular' if they could provide eggs or milk.

Coal rationing and high prices recreated Victorian conditions particularly in the cold winters of 1940 and 1941 with basins frozen in the morning. Hot baths were cut to one a fortnight in 1942. Boys wore outdoor clothes in lessons. One old boy recalls icy toilets without doors or roofs—although few lingered to smoke! There were power cuts—the organ ground to a halt during the 1944 carol service—and some services unheated and unlit were distinctly forgettable. Water rationing prevented the pool from being filled, although Dingwall noticed that a local hotel filled theirs, and waxed lyrical on Prize Day 1944 when the War Office sent instructions that swimming would now be included in Certificate A tests!

In classrooms desks and chairs were in short supply. Woodwork ceased. Art materials and other teaching materials were in short supply. In sport boxing, fencing and golf were discontinued due to lack of equipment. In 1941 an appeal went out for hockey balls; in 1942 for squash balls, hockey sticks, cricket bats and socks, and in 1944 for gym shoes, cricket bats, rugby and hockey jerseys and socks, and that year cross-country had to be replaced by a six-mile walk because of lack of gym shoes. Apart from painting nothing could be done to the buildings and a backlog of repairs grew. There were domestic shortages too. Crockery began to run out in 1942, and cutlery next year. By 1945 beds and blankets were needed.

In 1939 the College had 30 domestic staff but by 1942 they had largely gone, adding to the work that needed to be done by boys and masters alike. A land girl was obtained in 1942. Masters had a hard time of it. The presence of Downsend, Westminster, and then rising numbers meant more supervision and work under crowded conditions. All but one master, said Dingwall, 'had to change into a smaller room: two had to go up to the rookeries and use old servants' bedrooms' too small for their furniture. When Kenneth Mason and Robin Gregory married this led to more problems. Margaret Gregory describes how she shared a tiny room next to Star dormitory, sat in the room at the bottom of the staircase, and took meals with the matrons. Mary Perkins produced a double bolster from the former Provost's bedroom for their bed. Dingwall continually raised the need for married quarters, and in October 1943 the west rookery was converted at a cost of £119 19s. 8d. for the Masons. To help matters Dingwall acted swiftly in June 1944 when

Highbanks in College Lane came on the market. 'I heard about it at eleven o'clock, and by twelve the house was bought', he told Campion—for £760 with his own cheque.

As in the First World War it did not prove possible to keep all the school ceremonies and traditions going although Dingwall did his best. The play lapsed from 1940 to 1943, returned in a limited way in 1944, and fully in 1945. In 1940 a small party celebrated Danny on Wolstonbury Hill, but for the rest of the war the Dole was handed out in the inner quad. The Boar's Head Feast continued although no-one seems able to say where the food came from, and one old boy refers to small boys making themselves sick at the sight of so much food once a year. Prize Day continued with A.V. Alexander, First Lord of the Admiralty, and Lord Caldecote, the Lord Chancellor, among the speakers. St Etheldreda Day continued with small attendances. The carol service continued with visitors 'braving the Blitz' to travel down in 1940, and in 1942 the College was honoured by the presence of two great reforming churchmen at the service—Bell of Chichester, and Temple of Canterbury.

But it was new duties rather than old ceremonies that occupied school time. There was a National Savings group. A.R.P. continued with fire-watching particularly important; the boys on the chapel tower one night saw the fiery tail of a V1 which later fell at Cuckfield. The Home Guard platoon commanded by Dingwall had a membership of about fifty, and the magazine described them manning road blocks, organising wireless communications, and 'learning how to deal with an enemy tank using Molotov cocktails' in 1940 and 1941. Among their last activities was to patrol the Downs the day after D-Day in case of German retaliatory measures. The corps band led the stand down parade at Hayward's Heath. Contact with the village became more frequent. The cadet force and some of the masters were involved in War Weapons Weeks, and the school supplied its corps band, a tug-of-war team, and P.T. demonstrations to help raise money.

The corps was a most important activity throughout the war, with boys expecting service on leaving. In 1941 the O.T.C. became the J.T.C. and added an Air Training Corps for three years. War-time shortages affected the corps like everyone else—there were shortages of wireless equipment and modern battledress did not arrive until 1944. In September 1941 Certificate A was divided into two parts and made harder but, of the 123 cadets in 1943, half had both parts. Hurst cadet officers helped with the local A.C.F. training and began to attend outside courses as junior leaders and in physical education. Even Kenneth Mason went on a battle training course. An assault course was created on South field, and training became realistic with field days, night operations, and patrols. Weapons training included bayonet drill, and the use of Mills bombs, grenades, mortars and L.M.Gs. There were courses in unarmed combat and knife work. With eight new sets the Signals Unit became operational in 1944. The week before D-Day cadets were involved in battle training at Newhaven with live ammunition, and John Robins describes how they could see the armada of ships in the port with barrage balloons hovering above.

Perhaps no war-time events better capture the mood of enthusiasm, hard work, and patriotism than the farming and forestry camps held in the summer holidays when it might have been thought everyone needed a rest! They were at Midhurst (1940), Withyham (1941), Bedgebury Park (1942), locally in 1943, and at Bedgebury Park in 1944. Happy and relaxed camp life, hard and healthy work, team spirit, good relations between the generations, and all members of the school give ample evidence in accounts and pictures of the frame of mind that did so much first to win the war and then to carry out social reform. It was a spirit Dingwall encouraged and harnessed, as we shall see, to everyday school life. 'Never before,' said a magazine article, 'have we been so democratic and magnanimous in spirit, and it is rumoured our interest in politics has increased in proportion.'

Of course there was hard work, and rain and wasps, but the Malcolm Saville atmosphere prevailed over local difficulties. The boys cut and sawed timber, cleared fields, copses and hedges, carted manure, weeded crops, stooked, carted and threshed wheat, and lived an open-air life in boots, funny hats, and shorts under canvas or in makeshift accommodation. They ate special issue agricultural pies and washed in cold water. Mary Dingwall, Margaret Gregory, Peggy Mason, Winifred Berry and Mary Perkins helped with cooking and medical matters, troubled though they were by a coal stove without coal and by a supply of paraffin without a paraffin stove. The boys went rabbiting and swimming, visited the cinemas and pubs of Withyham, Uckfield or Goudhurst, or on bicycles ventured further afield to Cranbrook or even Canterbury along the empty war-time lanes.

III

While it might be thought Dingwall would have had his hands full with the economic recovery of the school and coping with the problems of wartime, his headship also witnessed a remarkable academic recovery based on the creation of a large sixth form. In the main sports, too, there was by the mid-1940s a time of spectacular success, and in the life of the boys, particularly sixth formers, there was found a more intelligent and liberal approach to life and awareness of the world around than had been the case in the past. Perhaps it is no coincidence that the 1940s produced several well-known diplomats and historians educated in the kind of sixth form Dingwall created.

Academic weakness in Tower's time has already been discussed and no quick fix was possible: it takes years to turn a school round in such matters, but that such a turn round was needed was made abundantly clear in the Ministry inspectors' report in February 1939. The inspectors criticised the lack of art room, modern gymnasium, or library: indeed they said much on the shelves of the latter was 'mere junk'. They said 'teaching equipment is inadequate', and that because masters and not boys moved between rooms there were no purpose-built class-rooms. In geography, for instance, there were 'no globes, pictures or photographs'. Several masters were praised for their sixth-form teaching but 'the general standard of work ... cannot be characterised as reaching a high level'. Some masters were 'lacking in vigour and initiative' and in classics, for example, no attempt was made to widen the subject to include 'culture, history or legend'. In lower forms there was much 'drab' teaching, outdated 'chorus answering', and 'crude work' passed as acceptable by those who marked it.

The report confirmed Dingwall's own assessment to Council that 'the general standard of work is very low'. The figures confirm this. In 1939 only 36 boys were doing science in the first three years. Of 106 school leavers in Dingwall's first three years only six entered university, only three obtained Higher Certificates, and only 56 School Certificates. Had the money been available for a classroom block, highly qualified staff, and brand new equipment the solution would have been easy enough, but Walter Dingwall had to raise the results without the tools.

During his first three years things were done which together provided the basis for success. All exams were switched to the Oxford and Cambridge Board. A new scholarship exam was introduced. There were more internal exams. From 1938 Council were provided with exam results in the termly headmaster's reports. New form groupings were introduced, and the sixth form divided into history, mathematics, science, and modern divisions with the absence of a classical sixth unusual in those days. There was a new timetable and 'setting' of subjects was introduced. Dingwall made it perfectly plain that academic success was highly praiseworthy.

Prize Day was separated from St Etheldreda Day and the prizes were reorganised. Dingwall added his own history prize and sadly the war gave opportunity for the donation of other prizes, including the two Copeman geography prizes and the Verrells history and mathematics prizes among the earliest. By good fortune an exhibition at Trinity College, Cambridge donated by the Rev. Septimus Phillpotts became available. Dingwall added a further leaving exhibition: so did Broadbridge and Wigglesworth, and five scholarships were made available to help sons of serving members of the forces with their higher education. Even the school prospectus was rewritten to emphasise the academic side of life and the school calendar included a list of the year's academic honours of all kinds.

From the start Dingwall urged parents to let their sons complete a sixth-form education and he brought in the Public Schools Employment Bureau to advise boys on the need for qualifications. It was an uphill struggle made more difficult by the war but, as we shall see later, Dingwall made the sixth form distinctive, gave sixth formers privileges, and enhanced its status so that boys and parents believed that staying on helped to develop all-round character and the qualities of command and leadership. From 1941 all the changes began to work together as numbers rose and Hurst began a long period of its history as one of the best smaller academic public schools with an excellent Oxbridge record. The figures show what a turn-around was achieved. In 1938 there were two Higher and 15 School Certificates. In 1945 there were 27 Higher and 43 School Certificates. If one includes 1946 and 1947 sixth formers who received the majority of their education in Dingwall's day, between 1941 and 1947 there were 25 awards including three Oxford scholarships, 13 Oxford and Cambridge exhibitions, four state scholarships (then called bursaries), and two scholarships at Birmingham and London Universities. Among the awards were some academic guerdons at Balliol, Magdalen, Christ Church, and King's Colleges.

This success was achieved not only against the background of stern economy but that of war-time staff changes and workload. Walter Dingwall created an immensely loyal and dedicated common room: the inspectors remarked on it in 1939 and Howard did so on becoming headmaster in 1945. Kenneth Mason is not given to glowing praise for its own sake but he referred nearly fifty years later to Dingwall as 'an inspiring leader', and an old boy in his memoirs confirms the boys' view they were taught by a 'dedicated staff'. Six Hurst masters were called up—Bankes, Ronald, Coulthurst, Carrington, and the heads of classics and mathematics, Robert Bury and George Lambert, but in spite of a number of birds of passage the common room was more stable in content than it had been in the First World War.

The number of masters was 15 in 1939, fell to 10, and then rose to 16 in 1945, half of them with Oxbridge degrees. The housemasters were a particularly valuable stable group in wartime. Percy Scott and Arthur Hodgson continued in Chevron and Shield, and Robin Gregory ran Star with Dingwall. Kenneth Mason took on both Red Cross and Fleur de Lys. In September 1937 George Lambert had arrived to develop mathematics—indeed the mathematics masters were the first to attend a teaching course. The same term a new chaplain, Roy Bowyer Yin, arrived from King's College, Cambridge (his brother, incidentally, was Leslie 'Charteris', the author), and he remained throughout the war years. In music the departure of Horace Hawkins in 1938 was a blow, but he was succeeded by two distinguished musicians, R.W.S. Carrington (OJ) and Meredith Davies, and then in September 1941 by the spruce figure of Alan 'Tripper' Tregonning who was to stay for the rest of the '40s. Physical training was run by J.F. Ronald and then H.B. Coulthurst. The school sergeant, Sergeant-Major F.S. Taylor (1936-1945), was then placed in charge and senior boys attended army P.T. courses to qualify them to teach the subject.

Recruiting to teaching in wartime was difficult and there were one or two mistakes, like the master who left after 'defalcations' were found in the chapel accounts. Mrs. Zelda Crump, who came to teach biology in 1942, was the first, if temporary, woman member of the staff. We have seen already how shortages and overcrowding made everyday life difficult for masters and, as Dingwall told the Council, rising numbers and wartime imposed 'heavier and heavier burdens' on them. For a time the additional burden of falling salaries was added because in October 1940 a cut was made, and this was not made up until the end of 1943. As an indication of salaries then: after cuts Scott received £618, Pocock £431, Thomas £315, Hodgson £270, Mason £226, Bowyer Yin £203, and Gregory £164 a year in 1943. That Dingwall could secure loyalty under these circumstances shows his skill in man management: Mason indeed refers to Dingwall coming to play bridge with the younger masters and says it was a 'delight to work' in the school in those days. Among the most invigorating of the new masters was J.A.W. Van Praagh, and among those recruited who stayed some time were R.M. Farish (January 1941), T.P. Wood and R.M. Jesson (September 1943), G.K. France (September 1944), and A.J. Hill (January 1945), the last named an Old Johnian and a Cambridge history scholar.

From contemporary accounts and Old Johnian memoirs it seems clear that, apart from a small number who resented the heavy emphasis on physical education, and the degree of prefectorial power utilised by 'several natural bullies', the majority found Hurst a delight to work in as well. Perhaps one quotation might serve to illustrate this and speak for many: 'super school, marvellous education, good stern discipline, no girls, thank God, to distract, a very happy time there, all of which led to a commission in the Fleet Air Arm'. Another Old Johnian rather surprisingly says he 'never experienced nor witnessed any' bullying although elsewhere he describes a boy tied to a hot radiator or another flung naked down the stairs in a laundry basket. 'The system', says another old boy, 'was excellent' and, given the war and then conscription, no doubt the kind of life hinted at here, where the male virtues reigned supreme, was beneficial to many, even a majority then. It certainly produced boys that Howard described as 'at their ease, and yet not too much at their ease'.

Dingwall was determined to build independent-minded, self-reliant sixth formers by a combination of emphasis on physical education and posts of responsibility. By 1938 he told the Council that the boys were 'beginning to get some idea of initiative'. A school prefects induction service was begun. House prefects had extended powers of fagging—called house duties at Hurst—and corporal punishment, and were placed in charge of dormitories. House prefects were listed in the magazine and rudimentary house notes started. House books became detailed records of events. New posts of responsibility were created, like four sacristans and six librarians, and prefects took P.T. classes. It was a period in which prefects became N.C.O.s to the masters, genuinely helping to run the school, and actively consulted by Dingwall who provided the school captain with his own room. The way in which the sixth form responded is shown in the *valetes*. Instead of a brief survey of sports achievements these listed the various posts held, and boys might be, as indeed two were, music prefect and captain of shooting, or sacristan, librarian, captain of athletics and of P.T. Boys were receiving a valuable all-round education.

As numbers increased, abler boys arrived and were better educated, and a leaven of boys from many lands came into the school; the intellectual climate changed. Dissent was not stifled or regarded as disloyal, and boys and masters were encouraged to relax and enjoy activities together; Dingwall played squash and hockey with the boys in a way unseen since Coombes's early Edwardian days and not to be seen again. There are plenty of examples to show this liberal and open attitude at work. Perhaps one of the most obvious was the relaxing of uniform to blue suits and black ties on Sundays and brown sports jackets and grey flannels on week days. In chapel the rigid march in was ended. Collections were made for a wide variety of causes like Russian Aid and in 1942 the first non-Anglican preacher—a Nonconformist—

appeared. In the Michaelmas Term of 1944 both the sixth and fifth forms put on their first plays. At Christmas 1942 the school 'Pop' concerts were replaced by the first house entertainments with over twenty items ranging from Star's skit on a girl getting up in the morning to Fleur de Lys' Minstrels playing *Dark Town Strutters' Ball.*

The debating society, of course, reflected the change. In 1939, still stolidly Tory, they voted to support Chamberlain's appeasement policy but in the mid-1940s, particularly due to J.M. Caffyn and N.M. Forster, the mood was very different. A motion supporting nationalising the mines was only defeated by 52 to 41 votes, and one declaring the 'system of privileges in the school is ludicrous' was carried. Blood sports were condemned and the ugly death penalty only survived by 12 votes to eight. A motion saying Russia was a menace to world peace was defeated by 23 to 12, one speaker pointing out wisely that America was equally a threat. The Society joined the Council for Education in World Citizenship and, although these debates and some radical poetry in the magazine were the work of a minority, they clearly carried weight in the College, because the mock election in the summer of 1945 led to the victory of the Liberal, and there was even a Communist candidate.

Because of war-time activities and chores, much sport, and a good deal of hard work, school societies are less prominently reported in these years although some were clearly active. In September 1937 Bowyer Yin formed a literary society which began a tradition of reading an eclectic choice of plays, later receiving additional stimulus from A.J. Hill. Interestingly women staff members, matrons and sister attended these readings for the female rôles on some occasions. The natural history society was revived and had its first debate on conservation in 1939, while juniors had their aero, model railway and photographic clubs.

Robert Bury's last plays before the war were *Hamlet* and *Romeo and Juliet* with A.J. Hill as the outstanding actor. There were none in 1940-1943, but in 1944 Ernest Wood and E.J. Stacey put on *King John* (the School Certificate play that year), although with light and sound effects that went badly wrong. In 1945 A.J. Hill and C.W. Thomas combined to produce *Hamlet* with M.M.L. Watkins in the name part and the show was stolen by M.B.M. Devine. Music is little reported in the early war years, but in the summer of 1944 Alan Tregonning conducted Handel's *Messiah* Part 1, and thereafter some more adventurous music appeared in chapel by Allegri, Byrd and Morley. But music was revivified by two societies. In September 1941 Robin Gregory began the gramophone society which listened to something like twenty works a term and there were visits to concerts in Brighton. In September 1943 Mr. Van Praagh, a junior house master, founded in complete contrast the rhythm club, which ran into controversy, being denounced in the magazine as a group of 'devil worshippers'. However, it was extremely popular and contemporary music like Bing Crosby, Glen Miller, and Artie Shaw in the era of crooning, big bands, and Latin American rhythms was heard in the College. Warner Ottley's record collection was given to the society.

Dingwall was a keen sportsman himself and a convinced believer in shaking the school from its apathy by emphasis on physical good health and an improved sports programme. Medical facilities were improved with an expansion of the surgery and the employment of two additional nurses, and in 1942 Sister Winifrid Berry arrived to begin her masterly years in charge of the sanatorium which lasted until 1980. 'House masters,' said Dingwall, 'are now co-operating with the school doctor' on remedial health measures including correction for defective feet and poor posture. In August 1939 Dingwall first proposed the idea of a sun loggia and when this proved impossible he introduced a solar lamp.

Life was certainly tough. The pool remained unheated and only first team members wore trunks. Showers in the morning were cold. Dormitory windows were to be left open and only two blankets were allowed. Physical Training (P.T.) became an important feature of everyday life from 1939 with a master in charge and the boys, starting with H.E. Franks and T.F. Sibbald, obtaining a qualification to teach the subject. The old-fashioned army P.T. methods were used and all boys did 20 minutes a day in the open air. Senior and junior house teams were started and Chevron won the first house competition. The P.T. team soon became well-known in the area, after giving a demonstration at a Burgess Hill Tory fête, and in 1939 a large part of the College took part in the Prize Day demonstration. Also in 1938, colours and cups for sport were properly organised.

Dingwall wished to encourage athletics. There were displays by well-known athletes and special coaching on Sunday, but lack of equipment and fixtures meant there was little activity in the war years apart from a quadrangular match with Ardingly, Cranleigh and Caterham in which Hurst did not do well, and it was not until 1945 that athletics began to develop again as a major sport. However, for the ordinary boy Dingwall introduced athletics standards in 1938. There were seven timed events and boys competed for these on a form, not age, basis. A standards cup was introduced and was won first by Fleur de Lys. Within a year 60 per cent of boys reached the standards set.

Lack of facilities, equipment, and qualified staff meant that a range of sports did not attract much attention in the war years. Fives died out. There was no boxing and very little swimming—some matches, all lost, in 1943 are mentioned. Shooting declined until 1945, when Hurst came fourth in the Country Life Competition and started training for Bisley again. Tennis died out and, although squash was played by up to seventy boys, the teams did not do well. With more boys in the school staying longer and a wide pool of fitter boys, it was the three main games that benefited during these years and for the first time Hurst's record in rugby, hockey and cricket was excellent.

Rugby was run by Robin Gregory and George Lambert (until he left in 1940 for war service). In 1940 the First XV won eight of their 11 matches and entered a team for the first time at the Public Schools Sevens held at Richmond. Although the 1941 team had several bad injuries they won six and drew two of their 10 fixtures. The next two years were average ones,

38 First XV rugby, 1940. It was the first team to send a seven to the Public Schools Sevens. Seated, fourth from the left is B. Evans, and fifth, J. Ascough.

but when the 'tall, speedy and heavy Colts' reached the 1944 team captained by J.H. Neal, with its powerful forwards led by M.B.M. Devine, seven wins and two draws from 10 fixtures were recorded including victories over Cranbrook and Whitgift. The Hurst VII reached the semi-final at Richmond only to be defeated by Rugby School. Hockey was run by Kenneth Mason and Walter Dingwall. In 1939 an experienced team led by D.J. Church, including H.E. Franks and O.W.H. Berkeley Hill, won four and drew four of their nine matches and made their first visit to the Worthing hockey festival. Bad weather in 1940 and 1941 was followed in 1942 by a First XI that lost only one match. In 1944 led by P. Fawkes and 1945 led by N.M. Forster, the First XI was unbeaten.

Cricket was run by Robert Bury (until he left for war service in 1940) and Herbert Pocock, and was the sport above all other that needed to be lifted from its 1930s doldrums. From 1938 to 1941 there was an unbroken run of success: 10 wins and two draws in 1938, nine wins and four draws in 1939, eight wins and two draws in the Spitfire Summer of 1940, and 10 wins in 1941, making 45 successes and only 17 defeats in those years. The outstanding players included D.J. Church whose 621 runs in 1938 included two centuries, and whose 180 in 1939 was the highest score so far in a school match, O.W.H. Berkeley-Hill and L.C. Henwood, whose 634 runs in 1940 was a record, and who went on to score 551 next year when he and P.L. Roussell were the main bowlers. 1942 and 1943 were ordinary years followed by a return to good times in 1944 under J.M. Caffyn with six wins and two draws, and in Dingwall's last summer under J.H. Neal (who had played for Sussex) there were seven wins, three draws, and only one defeat, Neal scoring a century against the R.A.F. at Brighton and S.C. Simmons being the main wicket taker.

IV

As the clouds of war slowly parted in 1944 and 1945 reform was in the air among politicians of all parties and in every aspect of national life including education. A White Paper in July 1943 was followed by an Education Act in 1944 whose main provisions lasted until 1986. State secondary education underwent major reform. Grammar schools were divided into four groups: an expanded direct grant group, voluntary aided, voluntary controlled, and fully local authority controlled. In all of them financial help was forthcoming, and in the last three categories grammar school education was free and with maintenance grants for poorer pupils covering meals, travel and uniform. State boarding schools were set up. State bursaries or scholarships to university were sharply expanded (some counties had only one or two), and local authority grants for higher education were organised. For the first time academic education was free and available at secondary and tertiary level to a substantial number of the population.

These changes clearly affected the market for public schools, and most particularly those low fee schools like Hurst. There was no intention to abolish public schools—indeed two Labour ministers, A.V. Alexander and J. Chuter Ede, spoke in glowing terms of praise at Hurst Prize Days at this time. But in July 1944 the Fleming Report came out and Browne-Wilkinson chaired a Woodard Committee to consider a response. The Council first discussed the future of public schools as far back as May 1942 and now they seriously had to consider it. Fleming recommended up to 25 per cent of places being grant maintained at public schools, and the Council considered this and a range of other plans including parent and L.E.A. representatives on Council, state bursaries, and links between the junior house and local primary schools. In October 1944 Council approved the Fleming Report in principle and Dingwall was naturally in favour. By now recognised as a noted figure in education, he was appointed Secretary of the Southern Division of H.M.C. He went ahead with proposals to admit the first 'Fleming boys' in September 1946.

Reform usually means more expense. Clearly Hurst would have to expand its curriculum and facilities to offer something better than the local grammar schools like Haywards Heath, and this would involve building and more staff. At the same time other costs were rising. The Hetherington Committee reported on domestic servants' wages and these would clearly rise when the domestic staff returned. Ordinary wage levels for workers like builders had also risen, increasing domestic costs and any future building costs. The Burnham Committee was bound to recommend increases for schoolmasters' pay, and superannuation at a reasonable level would have to be introduced at long last. School fees were raised to £120 a year in September 1944 to help deal with this likely increase in expenditure.

The College finances were now in excellent shape. Income from fees rose from £15,702 5s. 1d. in 1937 to £25,364 18s. 9d. in 1945. The cash balance of £2,657 in 1937 had risen to £10,756 2s. 1d. during the same time. Instead of a debt at the bank there was a profit of £6,050 13s. 6d. in 1944-45. The outstanding debt was cut to less than £5,000, and £6,173 17s. was invested in a Loan Fund that replaced the Improvement Fund in January 1944. In 1943 Walter Dingwall launched a Centenary Fund because covenanted money accrued over seven years incurred no income tax. By 1945 the fund stood at £5,921 14s. 1d. cash in hand, and the covenants were rapidly approaching the appeal figure of £10,000. There was a third, Reserve, Fund totalling £5,094 in 1945 to cope with any emergencies.

Walter Dingwall was sanguine that the success would continue and he wished to seize the opportunity to expand the school to 250 boarders in the senior school and provide a large number of new buildings. A works committee was set up in December 1943 to plan these, and during 1944 and 1945 Council was literally bombarded with long memorandums from Dingwall full of glowing plans for the future. Among the projects discussed at this time were: a new heating system, new kitchens, better toilets, new servants' quarters, new married accommodation for masters, more classrooms, changing rooms for houses, a music room, an art room, an improved pool, two more squash courts, a new sanatorium, and by the summer of 1945 he was even proposing a new school hall and classroom block to complete the front quadrangle. Not all Dingwall's proposals were sound. He returned to the idea of a sun loggia for the sanatorium and spent much time on investigating an artesian well on non-water-bearing ground. The Council in June 1944 approved one new building, a sanatorium, and Stanley Roth was appointed architect.

There were three difficulties in the way of implementing a substantial part of this programme in spite of the good financial position. As we have seen, running costs, particularly wages, were due to rise sharply and by unknown amounts and for the foreseeable future. Council might also anticipate post-war inflation after the post-1918 experience. The second problem was one Dingwall did not really grapple with except to express his annoyance. Building material and planning controls were extensive. Already in April 1944 he had been turned down once by the Ministry of Education and there was no guarantee that the local council would grant planning permission for so extensive a range of buildings, or that the materials would be released. Canon Howard was to find these difficulties hard enough to cope with years later.

The third problem concerned the junior house and here, too, one feels Dingwall was trying to run before he could walk. In May 1944 he told Council that the junior house should move. This would, in his opinion, enable the senior school to rise to 250 boys. It would establish on another site a junior school of 60 boys and the combined revenues would more than cover the costs involved. Above all the space vacated would enable a good many of the new facilities to go into the existing buildings. According to Canon Howard, at least, this scheme was not properly thought through. In fact, the number of additional boys would fall well short of 250, and the costs of creating the 60 prep school places would be much higher than anticipated, only adding marginally to the total junior house revenue which could be obtained by leaving it where it was on the main site.

Dingwall pressed ahead. Negotiations were carried out to buy Belmont, a local school, and even Danny Park. Perhaps he should have taken warning from the high costs he found involved in converted Danny Park. However, he told Council he intended to try and remove the junior house by September 1945 saying, 'I am now accepting boys in the senior school on this assumption'. Council were almost pushed into buying St Peter's Court in Burgess Hill for a little over £5,000. Investigation showed it would cost at least a further £4,000 to convert the buildings, and there was as yet no planning permission and little likelihood of obtaining the necessary bricks, glass and wood.

Clearly to a cautious mind Dingwall's plans were getting out of hand. Other schools were not embarking on large-scale building at this time. The Council had been pushed rather than persuaded in a number of respects like the advance purchase of Highbanks and the swift purchase of St Peter's Court. It would be nice to know what happened next, but the Council minutes for this crucial period do not exist and Dingwall's letters cease on 26 August 1945. There were some in the common room who did not like the idea of major expansion and at least one senior figure critical of the broad tolerance extended to boys who were not Anglicans or were of other faiths. Others were a little alarmed by the radical opinions of the boys and the easy-going relations of head and senior boys. Whatever happened next did so with great speed.

The summer term of 1945 contained no hint of change. On 8 May 1945 European victory was celebrated with a service and a day off to visit Brighton or London. Mary Dingwall chaperoned girls from Burgess Hill at a dance that evening for seniors while the rest of the school watched Arthur Askey in *Ghost Train*. Fireworks and a bonfire on South field rounded off the day. Prize Day was a glitteringly successful occasion with brilliant academic and sporting results to be announced, the usual P.T. display and garden party in sunny weather, and a performance of Britten's *Te Deum*. And when the boys returned in September Dingwall was gone and a new head master was in place. The boys were told he had suffered a nervous breakdown. In October back pay and payments due to Dingwall of £1,269 3s. 4d. were agreed by Council.

Walter Dingwall became Secretary to Chichester Diocesan Fund until 1961 and retired to Woodmancote near Henfield. He returned to the College for the last time as late as 1980, when he attended George Lambert's farewell lunch, and he died in August 1990, a thanksgiving service being held in November that year. They had much to thank him for. Sometimes little things destroy great men: there is a tragic flaw in the noblest characters and when it shows itself the little people move in like the Lilliputians in Defoe's satire on power. Dingwall was only 45 when he left. If he had stayed he would no doubt have gone on to a major headship, and before that achieved great things, probably putting to flight the doubts that surrounded his 1945 plans. Walter Dingwall doubled the size and restored the fortunes of the College. He made Hurst a small, but well respected public school with excellent academic results, and he left Hurst an alive and exciting place with its main sports and its activities flourishing as never before this century. He had nearly all the great qualities needed for leadership and the mint mark of greatness was stamped upon his eight years at Hurst.

ELEVEN

AUSTERITY AND ACHIEVEMENT
1945-1956

The Second Jubilee and Ronald Howard's Early Years

The Science Block is complete and occupied; it is, I hope the Governors will agree, a handsome building, and it is the most considerable addition to the School which we have achieved over the last five years ...

> Headmaster's report to Council,
> Michaelmas Term 1950

For the first time for, I suppose, nearly a century, the School has passed the 300 mark.

> Headmaster's report to Council,
> Michaelmas Term 1953

I believe the time to expand has come, and I should be glad of some discussion on this important point.

> Headmaster's report to Council,
> Lent Term 1955

The Governors may be sure that the academic side of our work is my constant care, and I believe our prospects are getting better.

> Headmaster's report to Council,
> Summer Term 1956

We have left Tom Brown's schooldays far behind, and I have no doubt that while public schools should not be softened, they should be civilised, and it is good for the young to work and take their leisure in surroundings of good taste.

> Ronald Howard on Speech Day, June 1956
> *The Hurst Johnian*, 831/19,
> Michaelmas Term 1956

Outwardly there could hardly have been a greater contrast in appearance between Walter Dingwall and the new headmaster, Ronald Howard, appointed a few weeks before the start of term in September 1945. Howard's public manner and way of expressing himself have made it difficult in the past to make a fair judgement on the era of progress and success which lasted with few interruptions for the whole of his 19 years' headship. Much of what he stood for was the subject of attack in the 1960s and '70s, and in later years both opponents and supporters stereotyped him as the epitome of the traditional headmaster, always in cassock and clerical collar, whose often aloof and always august presence was marked by the rustle of his voluminous silk gown, as boys stood respectfully still asking, 'please may I pass, sir?'

Although this was partly true it must be obvious on reflection that there was more to Ronald Howard than first meets the eye because this and the subsequent chapter describe change and growth on an unprecedented scale, as much that Dingwall had started was carried to fruition and a school of 460 boys with a good academic reputation was created. At first he had a tough time replacing a popular head whose loss was deeply felt, and perhaps it was this experience which led him to adopt the austere and even formidable image, rising to regal heights on public occasions, of which people still speak. Certainly 'Howardisms' of manner and speech have lost nothing in the telling. But as one former member of Fleur de Lys puts it in his reminiscences, 'with hindsight we did not give Canon Howard the respect he truly merited'. 'He was', says another Old Johnian, 'indeed a great figurehead and headmaster.'

Ronald Claude Howard was born on 15 February 1902, the second son of Henry and Florence Howard of Sevenoaks. Educated privately, he went to Sidney Sussex College, Cambridge in 1921 and obtained a third-class degree in English before training for the ministry at Westcott House. He was ordained at Chichester in 1927 and was a curate at Eastbourne for two years before deciding to enter education. He was chaplain at Bradfield College for two years before becoming a master at Tonbridge School in 1930. One of his pupils there, Owen Chadwick, has recalled his spirit of fun, his kindness and his work with the scout troop during those years. In 1937 he moved to Marlborough College and a year later became their chaplain. According to *The Marlburian*, he was a popular and successful chaplain, friendly, humane and generous, whose informal discussions over cake and tea were uproarious. The boys gave him a silver inkwell when he left in 1943 for the chaplaincy of Radley College.

Moving as he was in a range of top schools, Howard was soon recognised as having headmasterly potential and was a candidate for Hurst in 1937. It was not surprising that when a new head was needed at a few weeks' notice Bishop Kirk and Canon Browne-Wilkinson both supported him. Although he met Dingwall three times and was given a memorandum of advice, Ronald Howard was thrown in at the deep end. Quite often new heads succeed when their predecessors have run their course, but in this case Howard had to follow a man who was respected and liked on a personal level, particularly by the sixth form, and who was in the midst of ambitious building plans and his proposal to move the Junior House. Clearly one of Howard's tasks was to reverse some of what Dingwall had done, and this did not make for popularity. There had to be expulsions, there were clashes with the prefects, and mutterings in the common room. During Lent Term 1946 there were several bad disciplinary incidents including the theft of four revolvers and ammunition from the armoury. Questioned, it turned out boys had been selling items on the black market in the village and at Brighton, and one said they were 'planning a hold up in London'. 'Could you,' asked Clifford Freeman, 'send me details of the miscellaneous collection of criminals under your charge!' But a new school captain worked wonders, and the main common room dissident left at the end of the year. The staff, said Howard, was now 'entirely in harmony'.

Howard's authoritarian interpretation of the headmaster's rôle differed little from that of his contemporaries. These were years when headmasters commanded rather than managed, and expected to be obeyed rather than consult masters, parents or boys. But an examination of Howard's relations with the main groups of people involved in running Hurst shows that he had the human qualities and intellectual abilities which commanded respect and even affection from those that knew him perhaps more closely than most. Throughout his headship Clifford Freeman remained divisional bursar and within a short time was writing to 'My dear Ronnie'. He had obviously great confidence in Howard and divisional interference sharply declined from what it had been in Tower's and Dingwall's times. Not until the Lent Term of 1963 did an 'apparent acceleration in borrowing money' lead to direct divisional intervention in the head's plans.

Council remained a body with a substantial clerical element. Canon A.R. Browne-Wilkinson worked well with Howard. Two successive suffragan bishops of Lewes, Geoffrey Warde (1946-1959) and James Lloyd Morrell (1959-1977) served on the Council, and it was Morrell who succeeded Browne-Wilkinson as provost in 1961. Also on the Council was the Rev. Horace Crotty, a former colonial bishop, prebendary of Chichester and vicar of Hove, who served for four years until he died in 1952, and Canon Herbert Tomkinson, vicar of Hove, who retired in 1959, and was looked after by Ronald Howard until he died four years later. To the clerical element Howard was able to add an educational one under the new rules, and by far the most important new Council member was Eric R.J. Hussey (1885-1958), a distinguished educationalist who had worked in the Sudan, Kenya, Uganda and Nigeria, and was Director of Education for the two latter countries. He had been involved with Achimota College and had been a key founder of Makerere and Yaba Colleges. When he died in 1958 his successor was Brian Thomas, formerly head of an art school. Among other academics who joined the Council were Frank Doherty and Doctors Ladborough and Kelly. Council clearly respected Howard: they voted him money for a much-needed holiday in Greece in 1951 and some years later Howard wrote: 'I should like to put on record the gratitude we all feel to the Governing Body for the immense improvements.'

The administrators who ran Howard's Hurst were a small and hard worked group. Percy Scott lingered on in a twilight zone until he retired in 1950, and Howard then appointed Major S.H. Hooker as the first official bursar in September at a salary of £133 a year. This did not work out and early in 1951 he appointed Mary Perkins, who had been school secretary since 1948, as perhaps the first lady bursar of a boys' school and as clerk to the Governors at the more reasonable salary of £300. Later, when the post of senior matron was abolished, she took over the household arrangements as well. Her work was an essential back up to Howard's, recognised by a special gift of £200 from Council when she left in 1960. In January 1961 Major R.J. Treyer-Evans was appointed bursar at £900 a year. At the same time a new post of headmaster's secretary was introduced, and in the summer a headmaster's office was created at a cost of £1,300. Until then, as Howard once remarked, 'I had either to fetch myself or telephone for any document I wanted from the office'.

Among the adverse comments made by the inspectors in 1954 was one on a matter of which Howard was only too well aware. They thought that, as far as the domestic staff were concerned, 'the living quarters both for the men and the women are very poor, and their working conditions are extremely difficult'. Their wages were low and a total annual bill of £2,440 18s. 5d. for their wages had only risen to £3,856 by 1959. Howard was a stickler for clean buildings and smart grounds, but he was also fully appreciative of the work done by those like Pacey, the carpenter, Turner, the boiler man, and the Stringers, father and son, who were electricians. But the near feudal conditions meant that as late as 1961 we find Council voting a pension of £2 a week to a retiring domestic with 38 years' service. Howard did all he could. A domestic servants' wing was built adjacent to the matrons block between August 1959 and March 1961. All non-teaching staff were enrolled from 1963 in the Social Workers Pension Fund Scheme and by the time Howard left wages had risen to £8,939 a year.

Howard's treatment of the masters, again, was very much in line with the way things were then done. There was a formal termly masters' meeting when Howard descended like a prophet from the mountain to say what would be done: on other occasions communication was by means of personal typed notes. All masters were left in no doubt what he required of them—woe betide the gownless man or the chapel absentee, and if they did not conform they had to go, as he reported to Council from time to time. One in 1954 for his 'inadequacy', another in 1959 who 'left at my instigation', and next year a man 'advised to seek fresh fields' were among them. Christopher Guise has said that when he came he was nervous of the Head, but later he came to see him differently as a 'benevolent, patriarchal, caring sort of person'. Howard's work to raise the academic standing of the common room and his care of the masters will be themes dealt with in more detail later. But here in outline it can be noticed that he provided the first common room, and that the salary bill rose from £5,165 9s. 1d. in 1945 to £49,802 when he left with a new salary scale, better allowances, and proper superannuation. He provided nine accommodation units for masters as well as the use of four houses and a flat of his own rented to them.

For himself Howard asked little and gave much. Twice in October 1948 and June 1962 he declined salary increases offered to him and during his headship his salary just doubled to £2,100 a year in September 1960. In October 1948 he was given an entertainment allowance of £100 a year and a pension designed to give him £500 a year on retirement—happily raised after the great inflation to £1,000 a year by Council in 1978. He lived in a bachelor flat on the ground floor of Star with his father and mother and later with Canon Tomkinson. Apart from fine motor cars, including a Railton and then a Rolls, and a collection of early English water colours he was a private man of quiet tastes, reading, and playing bridge, happiest when involved in school affairs, and without the school a lonely man at heart.

So seriously did he take his duties that he was ill on a number of occasions during two of which he was away long enough for Kenneth Mason to be acting-headmaster. He was away in the Summer Term of 1951 with a back complaint, had an operation in Lent Term of 1956, and was away again in May 1963 which finally decided him on his retirement. When he was ill boys, masters, and parents alike sent cards and gifts, and this was one indication of how people understood that behind the Bensonlike severity there was a genuine man, dedicated to the school, and living for the school. As early as 1949 he was said to have 'endeared himself to all' at an Old Johnian Dinner and the 1954 inspectors commented on the confidence and respect engendered by the head. 'He was fiercely proud of the College, and would allow nothing to spoil his desired image of it', says an Old Johnian in his memoirs.

II

When Howard faced his first Council meeting in October 1945 it was 15 years since an important building had been put up, and it is not surprising that after a survey he found only three out of 23 areas of building satisfactory. The age of badly maintained buildings and the lack of modern equipment in every aspect of school life from the classrooms to the kitchens meant that costly emergency repairs were increasingly needed and, although Dingwall had given a face lift to the houses, this is all it had been. Prospective parents and visiting prep school heads could see for themselves and were not impressed, and recruiting both boys and staff of all kinds was going to be difficult until living conditions had improved. From this first meeting after which he took governors to look at the facilities, Howard was determined to put matters right and it was a little ironic that a head who thought 'material things will occupy too large a space in the educational sky' became himself involved in a more or less continuous building programme and that the building which received least attention was to be the chapel.

Howard believed he could build on Dingwall's work to place Hurst 'within the category' of Tonbridge or Cranleigh and that to do this two things above all others required attention: a major building programme and a longer term programme to raise academic standards: indeed without the first there was less likelihood of the second. This of course posed the problem of where the money was to come from, and it was one of Howard's greatest achievements that he was able to finance development out of future earnings, and to persuade Council and Division to engage again in deficit financing of the kind that had helped to bring about the problems of Tower's time. However, in February 1946 Howard told Council they needed a definite development plan, as they could not 'limp along without it'. Stanley H.J. Roth was commissioned to produce plans and by 1949 a brochure appeared giving details. Proposals included a junior house, sanatorium, speech hall, laboratories, classrooms, library, and extensions southwards of Red Cross and Shield. The list itself is an indication of how much needed to be done and, although part of the plan was beyond the school's capacity, by 1956 Howard was able to tell Council they were 'moving towards the completion of the major work of rehabilitation'.

Dingwall had left behind a sound but of course limited financial position with Reserve and Development funds, and the centenary appeal almost complete: it eventually raised £11,065 2s. 7d. of its projected £12,000. But he had also left the problem of newly purchased St Peter's Court and among Howard's first strong decisions was one to reverse this proposed move of the Junior House. St Peter's Court was sold at a slight loss for £4,849 19s. 6d. at the end of 1945.

This meant the Junior House (later School) would remain on the site and, although this added to building problems, it was a wise decision. The Junior House contributed to, and shared in, the total revenue of the site, sometimes subsidising senior school development and sometimes benefiting from it. It was a guarantee of reasonable intake numbers and, as standards rose in the senior school, junior school heads were able to channel able boys to the senior school. But clearly it could not remain cramped in Star and in 1948 an important change occurred. The Junior House moved to the former sanatorium building at a cost of £16,220— followed soon afterwards with a further £1,336 for a covered way. The sanatorium was moved to the first floor of Star at a further cost of £2,378 although, as this building lacked isolation facilities, it was not ideal, nor was it big enough to cope with Lent Term influenza epidemics. Sister Winifrid Berry did wonders for 20 years in what was intended to be a temporary situation.

With the money not spent on either of two new buildings, Howard was able to start addressing the needs of the existing buildings. Two masters' houses (Coombes) costing £3,810 were the first fruits in 1946 and Mill Cottage was improved two years later for £660. Twelve bedrooms for domestic staff were provided and at a cost of £6,739 a new servery and kitchen equipment were provided. Howard was fortunate to obtain from the War Office money for a new armoury and indoor range (1951-52). He also had to spend £2,000 on a complete rewiring, and another £1,000 on defective chimneys and ailing boilers. But the most important expenditure was on a new science building. The building that opened in September 1950 cost £14,962 and, as it then appeared before any additions were made, it was 'one of the finest and most up to date in the country' in concrete, glass and steel. Unfortunately, it had from the start two defects. It was too small for the rapid rise in numbers and shift to science in the 1950s, and it was poorly equipped. Herbert Pocock, the senior science master at the time, was past his prime and neither Howard nor Council had much knowledge of scientific equipment; 'strange instruments', as the head called it. As a result a ceiling of £2,677 was placed on spending.

After the Second World War it was inevitable that a War Memorial Fund should be started and this was done in March 1946. For a time there was much interest among parents in helping the College and in providing differing forms of memorial. The Ascough, Adams, and Verrells prizes, for instance, came into existence. Some parents donated their sons' books, clothing, records, and sports gear to the College. On 17 October 1948 the memorial panel bearing the names of 79 war dead was dedicated in the Memorial Chapel. Among the names was that of Warner Ottley, who had been in the 'Dam Busters' Raid, and Mrs. Hilda Ottley wrote to Howard to offer £200 towards a memorial building. Unfortunately, many Old Johnians had covenanted with the Centenary Appeal and the War Memorial Fund did not produce as much as had been expected.

Howard was determined that the centenary year should see specific buildings. The idea of a memorial gateway modelled on that of Clifton College was replaced by two entrance pylons with eagles on top designed by Jan Rylko, a former Polish concentration camp prisoner living in the village. They cost £627. A hut designated the music school was built at a cost of £1,864 near the gymnasium. Two hard tennis courts and two hard practice wickets were laid down at a cost of £600. Lastly, the magnificence of a new pool was modified to provide an extended one capable of having a full range of diving boards. The boys did the preliminary excavation and the improved pool cost £3,178.

The Jubilee was an ideal focus for publicity and Ronald devoted intense hard work to the occasion as a bulky file on this one event indicates. Although a loss of £824 11s. 2d. was made on the day there can be no doubt that the widespread national press coverage and the image of the College portrayed that day were of immense benefit. Writing afterwards, Howard said 'it is a moving experience to be in charge of a school freighted with humanity as it crosses the line to its second century', and Hurst certainly did so with all flags flying. Howard was always the master of public occasions with his carefully honed speeches, and one is reminded of a passage in David Newsome's *History of Wellington College* describing Bertram Pollock, Wellington's bachelor Edwardian headmaster:

> towards these impressive functions the School was carefully drilled beforehand; not a gesture was left to chance. Trained to wait for guidance and to listen to orders the boys responded to their directing genius ... He was a figure of charm, dignity, and consummate grace. On a ceremonial occasion he was magnificent—reserved, polished, superbly in control.

An impressive group of guests was assembled for the great occasion. Geoffrey Fisher, formerly headmaster of Repton School and then Archbishop of Canterbury, was to preach, and royalty (albeit of the second rank)—Alexander, Earl of Athlone, Chancellor of London University, and his wife, Alice, a granddaughter of Queen Victoria, were the most prominent guests. The Corporation President, Bishop Kirk of Oxford, and the Visitor, Bishop Bell of

Chichester, would be present and some juggling had to take place as to who would be principal celebrants. Five other bishops—Rose, Greaves, Crotty, Warde and Saunders—would be present. 'Five bishops will robe in the sanatorium' went the instructions and 'albs may be borrowed from S. Bartholomew's, Brighton.' There was the Provost and the fellows, and a brace of archdeacons.

But with one possible guest Howard had considerable trouble. No invitation was sent to Dingwall, but one was to Tower. He had got on well with Howard, been back to preach, and was pleased with his portrait in hall. But he was furious to find he had no place in the procession but only a seat in the stalls. 'Am I,' enquired Tower, 'to take my place among the rank and file of your guests?' Sadly, Howard replied he had left Tower out of the procession on account of his lameness. 'I have no feelings,' replied Tower, 'about my lameness being referred to,' but as he was required to mingle with the ordinary guests, 'I feel it is no longer incumbent upon me to be present,' and he did not come.

Fifteen hundred guests enjoyed glorious weather on 23 July 1949. At 10.30 Sir William Campion met the Provost and the memorial pylons were dedicated. A procession in two halves wended its way to Star to collect the archbishop and they then returned to chapel with the masters' black, red and white, the royal blue and white of the fellows, the episcopal red, and the archbishop's cloth of gold making a brave show in the quadrangles as they entered chapel to the hymn *Thy Hand O God Hath Guided*, and the service began. It ended with a performance of Vaughan Williams *Te Deum*, and guests then left for lunch provided at a 100-yard-long buffet. The band of the Queen's Royal Regiment played. There was a cricket match with Sussex Martlets, a swimming match with Old Johnians, and tea in a marquee on East field.

By the early 1950s about £63,000 had been spent on the buildings and a debt of no more than £8,000 incurred. The inspectors later remarked on what they called 'a very remarkable achievement': that rather more than half of the improvements have been funded out of revenue, and this continued to be the case. There were bequests from time to time. The last of the Gorham Bequest went to the chapel. The Parham Bequest was incorporated in the centennial fund, and at a later date bequests from Scott and Archdeacon Weston were used to help furnish the dormitories. The Old Johnians also helped, providing, for instance, £468 for a ladies' toilet. Two Old Johnians, A.E.C. Shippam and J. Stallwood, were responsible for providing the roof shields, notice boards, and repairs to the entrance statues.

But the bulk of revenue came from increased fees and the wise investment of profits. Only twice in 1952 and 1957 was there anything like concern about the balance between income and expenditure expressed at Council meetings, and only on the first of these two occasions was it necessary to take immediate measures: in that year it meant a once-off levy of £3 on existing pupils. Because of confidence in Howard and his policies and the rising academic results, he was able to increase fees during a period of low inflation, and to persuade parents to pay the additional fees necessary because of his policy of keeping down boys for a year who did not come up to standard. Later he was also able to persuade parents to pay the extra fees involved in a third year in the sixth form. Because he was opposed to day boys in the senior school, their numbers were kept to a minimum and the number of full fee payers kept high. For all these reasons Howard was able to anticipate increased revenue, borrow, and build more. Quite often revenue rose more sharply than expected—from new houses, for example, and overdrafts could be quickly reduced, thus further encouraging banks to lend money.

39 Hurst's first modern building was the science building which opened in 1950.

Annual Boarding Fees (Senior School) and Annual Fee Income, 1945-1964

	£	£	s.	d.		£	£	s.	d.		£	£
1945	120	27,133	19	03	1953	--	61,056	02	07	1961		147,298
1946	135	27,482	12	09	1954	240	65,045	02	01	1962	429	168,502
1947	156	35,714	06	10	1955	270	67,876	05	09	1963	--	178,537
1948	165	40,417	02	11	1956	--	78,755	16	04	1964	462	185,758
1949	180	43,947	19	05	1957	300	85,539	09	04			
1950	--	46,743	17	03	1958	327	95,155			Round figures only given		
1951	208	53,315	18	00	1959	--	100,738			in accounts from 1948		
1952	225	57,198	07	05	1960		130,014					

The opening of the science block in 1950 enabled important class room changes to be made in the year G.C.E. was started. Five new classrooms were made available, and for the first time the majority of masters were given permanent rooms so that they could make them purpose-built classrooms with visual aids like charts, maps and pictures. Teaching in day rooms ceased, although prep continued to be done there by all including the sixth form. In 1951 the former crypt was divided. The eastern portion became a boot room for the four central houses, and the western half, at a cost of £750, became the masters' common room. Now hardly a month seemed to go by without some improvement. New tarmac on all paths, a new road to the armoury, flower beds and trees in the outer quad, pictures on the cloister walls, £500 on the hall staircase, and £500 more on the 25 chimneys. In the summer of 1953 a former Tonbridge county-ground groundsman was appointed (at a salary of £400 a year) and Fisons was called in to ensure the proper restoration of North field. Two more masters' houses (Lowe) were provided at a cost of £6,646.

Most important of all was the start made on improving living conditions, after a detailed report to Council by Howard in Lent Term 1952. 'I have,' he wrote, 'been ever since I came to Hurst exercised by the inadequacies of our dormitory and changing room accommodation. The necessity for drastic improvement has seldom been out of my mind,' and he asked that the problem should now be tackled. In 1952-1953 a start was made at a cost of £3,558 18s. 2d. spent on corridors, floors, walls, boot rooms, lockers and wardrobes. Cloisters were closed off to provide changing rooms and more extensive baths, showers and toilets. Star was given two day rooms instead of one, and the air of seedy decay in day rooms and dormitories was banished at long last. The necessity for these changes was made even plainer when on the night of 20 May 1954 there was a fire in Chevron House caused by towels that had dropped on an exposed heating element. By good fortune Browne-Wilkinson was staying in the College and by the end of the next day the builders had arrived. The house was repaired at a cost of £636.

40   The Chevron fire, 20 May 1954.

With so much going on it was almost inevitable that at least one mistake would be made. Far back in 1939 the inspectors had condemned the gymnasium and it was described in council minutes as an 'appalling structure'; in 1950. In Michaelmas Term 1951 it was decided on safety grounds to provide the building with a new floor but this proved an unwise move as the building continued to deteriorate, and in 1952 Howard had to tell the Council the building 'has been condemned as unsafe'. A new gymnasium was clearly needed but it was decided to use the new floor and this restricted the size of the new building. Work went ahead on Howard's 'Odeon' (a reference to the 1930s-style façade towards the North field), and it was opened in time to satisfy the 1954 inspectors and at a cost of £4,638. The building was never adequate for a school which was to rise to over five hundred boys.

Moreover, it may be recalled that in the 1949 plans a new school hall had been called for because the confusion of meals and other school activities like the play in one area was unsatisfactory. No thought was given to the idea of a hall on the gym site, large enough for exams, plays, and other functions like prize day, which could have done double duty as a gymnasium. So in July 1953 Howard launched an appeal for an Elizabethan theatre to commemorate the Coronation, and be ready for the 100th Shakespeare play due in 1956. This was a further mistake. Funds were not forthcoming, and the shape of the proposed building bore no relation to the many purposes a new hall was required for, so that a further new building would have to be constructed at a later date.

When he had first come, Howard had stated his view that the school should remain comparatively small, but as numbers mounted it became clear that this policy could not be continued. Ten years after he arrived the senior school was comparatively static, having risen from 222 to 235 boys, although only three of the latter were now day boys, but the Junior House had risen from 45 to 103 and was feeding through more boys than the senior school could cope with. There was overcrowding in the dormitories causing, as we shall see later, some return to Lent Term health problems, while five members of the Junior House had to be boarded out. By Michaelmas Term 1955 at a cost of £9,560 the first of many extensions to the Junior House was complete, and this made the accommodation problem acute.

The first meeting to discuss expansion was held by Council on 19 September 1955 and at a seminal Council meeting on 13 October that year the momentous decision was taken to expand; in 1956 no less than three important building projects were completed. To achieve this an overdraft of £20,000 was obtained but by mid-1959 this had been covered by the profits from the new house, Eagle, named after the symbolic bird of St John. First gathered at the top of Star in September 1955 under the Rev. D.N. Jenkins as tutor, a year later it entered its new building with Jenkins remaining as tutor and William Alban becoming housemaster. It began there with 29 boys, five seconded from other houses, and its first house captain was G.S.N. Cottrell, soon recording 'bags of house spirit and house pride'. Taking advantage of the nearby pool, Eagle quickly established a reputation as a swimming house, due to D. Van Weil and R.D.P. Henderson. Its Shell contained H. Bentley-Marchant, who established a record score of 255 in a house match. By 1958 a house banner was designed by D. Johnson, the art master, and that summer the house won its first trophy, receiving a letter from Star rooker hoping it would be the 'first of many eagle-ly awaited successes'. So successful was the new house that an extension was built at a cost of £2,549 as early as 1959.

Next to Eagle house was to be a theatre, said to seat 500 people, in days before fire regulations. Together the two buildings cost about £23,000, and the £1,500 collected for the Elizabethan theatre was used to equip the new building. In spite of its sloping floor Howard intended it to be used for exams, assemblies, prize day, concerts, debates, lectures, and Saturday evening films, and it was first used on Speech Day in July 1956. Superbly refurbished, the building exists today as The Bury Theatre. But Howard had more up his sleeve than relieving pressure on hall. He recognised the need for a proper school library, and it seemed to him that the new building would also free upper school and that with some alterations 'a project which is very near my heart' could be realised.

The Randolph was specifically made into a sixth form room, supplied with newspapers and magazines, and Howard always taught there. Red Cross rooker was moved into the south cloister and its former premises made the book store. Upper school was then converted, through an ingenious design by Walker Symondson, into a library, destroying in the process ancient panelling and honours boards which were not replaced. For less than £2,000 attractive shelving with concealed heating was provided in a style perhaps best described as Post Office

41   The College library, 1956-1973.

Classical. With the last of the Centenary fund money and a gift of £400 from the Old Johnians, the total cost was £2,348. Howard wished to increase the number of books to 7,000 and raised the library grant to between £200 and £300 a year, putting Horace Holloway in charge. To mark the importance of this event Howard secured the presence of royalty once again. On 1 November 1956, a sunny autumn day, Alice, Duchess of Gloucester, accompanied by the Lord Lieutenant, and the Provost presided at the opening ceremony. Centrally placed as the library was, Howard saw it as part of an academic complex with the Randolph and later a study block for university candidates. Sadly this library had a life of less than twenty years.

III

The relationship between new buildings and academic development was a symbiotic one. New buildings and facilities attracted more pupils and better quality staff. In turn they produced more revenue and better results, and these in their turn enabled more buildings to go up and attracted more pupils of a higher calibre. 'The Governors,' said Howard on one occasion, 'may be sure that the academic side of our work is my constant care.' His improvements were not to make school life easier or more pleasant for its own sake, but to enhance its prestige and augment its academic success. Dingwall had made a start from certain wartime advantages arising from lack of competition. Howard had to do what no head had done since Lowe's time: improve results and maintain the improvement over a long period of time, and that he succeeded there can be no doubt because the academic improvement lasted as long as academic O and A Level and Oxbridge entrance exams made its measurement possible. By 1957 Hurst had the best O and A Level results of any Sussex school, was well-known and regarded at Oxbridge, and throughout the country was known for having one of the best academic prep schools and being one of the best medium-sized public schools. In 1956 five per cent of boys had parents overseas, eight per cent in London, 33 per cent in Sussex, and 54 per cent in 30 other counties, a geographical spread, too, not seen since Lowe's time.

The Growth of Hurstpierpoint under Ronald Howard, 1 1945-1957

Year	Total in senior school	(day boys)	Total in Sixth Form (3rd year in brackets)	Total in junior school	(day boys)	Total in school	Masters senior junior schools	
1945	222	10		45	17	267	21	3
1946	223	8	52 (0)	43	17	266	16	4
1947	220	4		43	15	263	17	3
1948	219	1		60	19	279	17	3
1949	221	2		70	24	294	19	3
1950	226	3		67	20	293	19	4
1951	225	5		66	17	291	18	4
1952	225	8		70	17	295	18	5
1953	235	7	50 (0)	68	18	303	18	4
1954	233	5		76	26	309	19	4
1955	235	3		103	40	338	19	4
1956	257	6	89 (1)	102	39	359	19	5
1957	274	6	110 (10)	105	37	379	20	5

Numbers are taken from the headmaster's reports to Council.

Like any sensible reformer, Howard did not become complacent about the success he achieved. From time to time throughout his period of office he would remark that the School was not 'getting enough clever boys', that obvious Oxbridge candidates, like one school captain particularly, were not getting in, that Hurst was not getting its fair share of state scholarships, and that he experienced the greatest difficulty first in getting mathematics and science masters of the right calibre, and later that 'good masters are very hard to find these days'. But he need not have worried, for in these matters, as in all those concerned with academic improvement, he was uniformly successful, although what was achieved took a long time to bring to fruition in the early 1960s.

The Junior House was the educational foundation of his rehabilitation work and it remained firmly under his control even if it acquired a master and the title of Junior School in the 1960s. From the opening of the new building in 1948 progress was continuous. Next year Howard told Council that he intended to appoint only masters with degrees to the Junior House. Two masters from King's College, Cambridge and St John's College, Oxford were the first fruits of this decision, although it was not until 1954 when Russell Perry was replaced as master by Kenneth Heslop that the policy was fully implemented. Heslop with his background at Merton College, Oxford, and Magdalen College Prep School, was the ideal choice. A fine academic and an excellent disciplinarian, he soon weeded out the dead wood and began to recruit staff of the quality of Harry Maxwell from Trinity College, Dublin, and with a Blue. The Junior House staff rose to eight, five of them Oxbridge men, and included those like George Hill and Michael McAdam, whose ability took them later into the senior school.

The number of pupils passed the hundred mark in 1955, and by the time Howard left it had reached 122, of whom 43 were day boys. Fees had risen from £210 a year in 1952 to £360 in 1964. Howard rightly boasted that the Junior School was 'one of the very best prep schools in the country', and from it came an ever-increasing stream of high-calibre entrants for the senior school. Council quite naturally wanted to increase numbers whenever possible but here Howard stood firm. As early as May 1946 he told them he intended to raise the Common Entrance (C.E.) requirements and to refuse to take a substantial number of those put forward by the prep schools. Soon, he reported, 'the news [is] spreading in prep schools' with the desired result. In 1948 there was an excess of demand over supply for the first time. Howard accepted 54 boys and rejected 21 in spite of criticism and firmly told Council he would continue to raise the entrance standard 'in spite of revenue temptations'. In 1949 no boy was admitted who did not have a 'good' C.E. pass rate and Howard made it plain he would not accept other school's rejects: only two came that year. In the summer of 1954 he told Council that for three years candidates had been first rate and that from next year he would require a 50 per cent pass in all subjects; in 1958 this was raised to 58 per cent. In a typical year in the late 1950s there were 50 places and 82 candidates, and 20 good-calibre boys entered the scholarship exam. Of those accepted 22 entered the Remove straight away.

Although the traditional five years from Shell to second-year sixth was available, many boys in Howard's day pursued quite different courses through their school years. They were admitted straight into the Remove or in rare cases even into the fifth form, so that able boys might quickly reach the sixth form. In 1962 224 out of 341 boys in the school were fifteen or over. If boys did not reach the required standard they were kept down. In a typical year three were retained in the Shell, 12 in the Remove, and 11 in the fifth form. Above all Howard was determined to create a large sixth form, helped by the two years required by the new

A Level exams from 1950. The sixth form rose from 52 in 1946 to 110 in 1957 and 143 in 1964, and although this did create a substantial tail of less able boys, the overall results fully justified this substantial growth, because during the same period entrance to some form of higher education doubled from 22 to 44 per cent of the leavers. Moreover, as Oxbridge success grew a third-year sixth developed, which averaged about ten boys during Howard's last 10 years and half of them entered Oxbridge successfully. At every level from eight to eighteen quality accompanied quantity under Canon Howard.

When he arrived the public exams were the School and Higher Certificates the results of which had improved so remarkably under Walter Dingwall. With the exception of 1947, Higher results continued excellent: 1945, 27; 1946, 25; 1947, 19; 1948, 23; 1949, 21, and in the last year, 1950, 36. In School Certificate by 1950 40 out of 41 passes were secured although not all boys took the exam. But change was on the way, and change, moreover, which was of great benefit to grammar and public schools. Howard told Council in September 1950 he had appointed Robert Bury (at £10 a year) to create a timetable suitable for the new G.C.E. exams starting that year. O Level was designed for the top 20 per cent of the ability range, and appealed to the boy with good factual knowledge and a retentive memory. A Level was an academic exam designed by academics and deliberately stated to be suitable as a preparation for university entry. As only 15 per cent in Britain stayed at school in a sixth form this, too, benefited the academic minority and the depth of its approach attracted masters of high academic calibre into teaching. It was supplemented by an S Level paper, ideal as a basis for general discussion or studies in a third-year sixth, and a good preparation for Oxbridge written entrance and scholarship exams.

When the new exam started it was criticised as being easier than the old School Certificate. In fact, this was untrue at the junior level, and the sixth form actually required two rather than one year in the sixth. Howard told Council that he greatly favoured the new exam. In 1951 came the first results: at O Level 46 boys obtained 88 passes, and at A Level there were 27 subject passes. Masters applied themselves to the new exams and in a school with small classes and high calibre masters it became clear that excellent results could be obtained. By 1953, 60 per cent of O Level candidates were getting five or more passes, and this became a basic sixth-form entry qualification. By 1957, 75 per cent of boys were getting five passes or more and, as Bury skilfully manipulated the timetable, boys took an ever increasing range of subjects. By 1957, 17 A Level and 18 O Level subjects were offered, and in the early 1960s there were 20 possible A Level subjects which were accompanied in the sixth form by 13 possible subsidiary subjects. The A Level pass rate reached 80 per cent in 1962.

With such good exam results there was bound to be an improvement in university entrance, although producing precise figures is not easy. It is remarkable that no honours boards recorded open awards or state scholarships, and even the magazine's listings cannot be trusted because late entries are sometimes missed and, because of National Service, boys did not always go up in the year they are listed as entering Oxbridge. The figures given here cover the whole period from 1941 to 1964 because Dingwall's boys contributed to Howard's record for some years. They are probably incomplete, but during this period 45 open awards at Oxford and Cambridge can be traced, including 18 scholarships. One third of these were achieved by Kenneth Mason's history department, and most of the others by George Lambert's mathematicians, Wilfred Smith's musicians, and later John Peters' biologists and Christopher Dean's modern linguists. During the same period 86 boys obtained entrance to Oxbridge.

Hurstpierpoint's Oxbridge Entry Record, 1941-1964, by College

Number	College at Oxford	Number	College at Cambridge
13	St Edmund Hall	17	Jesus
4	Magdalen	9	Christ's
4	St John's	7	Trinity
4	Christ Church	6	Corpus Christi
3 each	St Peter's Hall, Queen's,	5	King's
	Lincoln and Keble	4 each	St John's & Magdalene
2 each	Oriel, Worcester & Balliol	3 each	Gonville & Caius, St Catharine's & Pembroke
1 each	Hertford, Brasenose, University,	2 each	Downing, Queens', Sidney Sussex,
	Merton, Exeter & New College		Peterhouse & Trinity Hall
1	St Catherine's Society	1	Emmanuel College
		1	Fitzwilliam House

These were times when the great public schools might get as many as sixty entrants a year to Oxbridge, but for a smaller school like Hurst this was an impressive list spread across both colleges and subjects. Howard's Hurst also sent good numbers to Trinity College, Dublin, and after 1956 to the London medical schools and colleges, particularly for science, and there was a steady stream, too, to agricultural colleges like Cirencester and Wye. Entry to Sandhurst (15), and Dartmouth (15) was also impressive. Twenty state scholarships were obtained.

Because neither house books nor magazine record many of them it is impossible to go further and discover how many went to other universities and places of higher education. Even Howard was vague about these figures, telling Council in 1962 and 1963 that there were 'about' twenty at Oxbridge, and 'about' fifty elsewhere, and whereas in 1954 only 22 per cent went on to higher education a figure of 44 per cent was given in 1963. There were signs, too, that there was widening of interest beyond the traditional 'Red Brick' universities. In 1963 A.D. Nurse and S.A. Cartwright were probably the first boys to go to technical colleges at Worthing and Brighton respectively.

Soon after he arrived Howard wanted a Ministry inspection, but one did not take place until 1954. Coming four years after the start of G.C.E. the findings of this inspection provided a focus for Howard to set about the modernisation of teaching, and the development of a high powered common room. Although the report uses measured language it is clear they found a good many defects. They were critical of the classrooms, the library, and facilities for science, geography, music and physical education, and Howard brought about improvements in all these departments' resources. Although they found excellent individual work by some masters particularly at sixth-form level and that 'the general level of teaching is distinctly good', they also commented that several masters would be hard pressed if there were substantial changes. In Howard's words to Council reviewing the report, the masters were 'lacking distinction, lacking adventure'. In some classes 'bound collections of examinations' took the place of text books and in one subject masters were requiring 'almost identical essays from all the boys in the form'. In languages there was too much translation work, and in mathematics too many repetitive examples. In English there was a 'disappointing unawareness' of literature beyond the set books and some of the science teaching was 'failing to develop methods of investigation'.

If teaching was to improve and the curriculum be widened, the common room had to improve its general calibre; another of Howard's achievements was to do this. The first requirement was to improve living conditions and salaries and, if by later standards life for masters, particularly young living-in bachelors, was spartan at times, Howard did his best to improve matters. We have seen how he provided greatly expanded living accommodation for married masters. He began to tackle salaries in 1950 with a scale on which masters began at £400 a year, and rose after 26 years to £700 a year. £120 was deducted for living-in masters, and 6¼ per cent of salary was to be deducted for superannuation. A number of allowances started with a £100 a year for the second master and the head of science, and later came departmental allowances for mathematics, history, and modern languages of £50 a year. Howard pointed out that they had lost at least two masters through their low salaries and he hoped this change would improve matters.

The new scale certainly produced an immediate improvement. Kenneth Mason went from £695 to £850, Robert Bury from £605 to £740, and George Lambert from £565 to £711 a year when all their allowances and housemasters' pay is taken into account. As the school prospered salaries, of course, could rise, and did so for the remainder of Howard's time. His last salary scale in 1962 had a starting salary of £860 which rose to £1,190 after ten years, £1,500 after 20 years, and was fixed at a maximum of £1,640 after 20 years. Residents paid £150 a year and superannuation remained at the same level. This was not riches, but it certainly helped Hurst to compete for good candidates, drawing in some heads of department from other schools; and to recruit married men in days when wives were not working, and the whole cost of a family fell on the single wage earner.

When it came to recruiting masters Howard was biased in favour of those with Oxbridge degrees. In this he was typical of his time, and it says much for the post-war status of teaching that good quality Oxbridge men were willing to teach in both senior and junior schools. Ardingly, Hurst and Lancing employed 60 Oxbridge graduates in 1964. At Hurst the staff increased in size under Howard from 17 in 1948 to 27 in 1964 and, including music masters, 23 of these had Oxbridge degrees. Junior School staff rose from three to eight in the same period, and five were Oxbridge graduates. There was obviously no direct connection between being a good master and having an Oxbridge degree: two of Hurst's finest appointments made by Howard came from Bristol and London Universities, but on the other hand it was a policy that made for homogeneity of approach in the common room. It helped to have the Oxbridge connection when placing boys there, and the combination of Oxbridge success and staff meant that, however long the academic tail, Hurst was very much an academic school. Eight of the masters had been award winners and several had top degrees, and they were able to instil academic qualities in school activities and to provide a good general studies programme for the sixth form.

There were two areas of recruitment where Howard had difficulties. The first was in obtaining mathematics and science masters of sufficient calibre also willing to take on the games, house and other duties required. On many occasions Howard told Council of this difficulty. In 1956 he told them: 'I shall go shortly to Oxford and Cambridge to seek them for myself', and as late as 1961 he remarked there was only 'limited choice' in candidates coming forward. Under George Lambert mathematics was a successful department, but he had to work with a substantial number of colleagues few of whom stayed long, including two chaplains, a junior school master, and a retired colonel with a mathematics degree. In science 1954 proved to be the decisive year when Herbert Pocock retired and G.K. France left due to illness. Ivor G.E. Wilding became head of science, and John H. Peters, head of biology. The appointment of Nicholas Heath in September 1951 had strengthened physics, and biology was strengthened further with the arrival of Jeremy B. Tatum in 1961.

The second problem area was school chaplains, where double figures were reached in appointments, possibly due to the fact that this was an area where Howard himself had a decisive voice and would accept no changes in the order of services or the performance of them. He even resented Council commenting on chapel matters, and on one occasion when he had been asked to supply information on communicants said he hoped he would not be questioned on such matters again. After Roy Bowyer Yin left in 1946 he was succeeded by Rev. John S. Ridley, who left after a year and was succeeded by the Rev. Jack H. Mills who was also a mathematician. He left in March 1952 and the Rev. Victor F. Hambling was chaplain for a term. Then came the Rev. Edwin Stark who resigned in March 1954 and the Rev. Beaumont Pierard was then chaplain for a term. In September 1954 Howard at last found a chaplain of the required ability when he appointed the Rev. David N. Jenkins who, he told Council soon, had 'the confidence of masters and boys alike'. After five years he left and Mills returned for a term. The Rev. Michael McAdam had joined the Junior House to teach languages but Howard quickly recognised his ability, and in January 1960 he became chaplain for the next eight years. The same term Howard appointed the first assistant chaplain, the Rev. Michael Tarbet (also a mathematician), but he lasted only two terms and no similar appointment was made.

These rapid chaplain changes were untypical of Howard's common room. His most important achievement, indeed, was to create a stable common room and a group of long serving masters such as Hurst had not had in the past. An examination of the other departments soon demonstrates this stability. Frank Florey arrived in September 1945 and William Alban in September 1949 and they remained the principal English masters throughout Howard's time, and for long afterwards. Reginald Ruddock arrived in September 1951 and Christopher Guise in September 1957 and they remained the principal geography masters throughout Howard's time and for long afterwards. Robert Bury remained head of classics. Kenneth Mason remained head of history and was joined by Horace Holloway in September 1946. Modern languages was less successfully run by Harry C. Packford, and it was not until the arrival of Christopher Dean in September 1960 that this department joined the ranks of the successful.

Similar success attended Howard's appointments to music and art, both of which he was determined should be an integral part of the curriculum. When Alan Tregonning left he was replaced by Wilfred Smith as the first director of music in September 1950 who for several years carried the whole musical education of the College on his shoulders. 'I think we have a first class man', said Howard to the Council, and so it proved as Smith restored and enhanced Hurst's musical reputation, assisted from 1959 by a junior school music mistress. When he left in 1962 Howard was able to attract the former director of music at Bloxham School, John E. Gardiner, and to appoint at the same time Peter A. Lattimer as assistant music master. In early years Howard could do no more than continue part-time art appointments, but in September 1957 the first full-time art master, D. Johnson, from the Byam Shaw School of Art, arrived who, in Howard's words, had good discipline 'in spite of his beard'. He was succeeded by F.M. Russell Flint, an artist in his own right, in September 1960.

By the early 1960s Hurst had a common room any school would have been proud of. Heslop ran the Junior School. Of 14 masters staffing the seven houses only two were not to give outstanding service to the College. The 12 were Mason, Bury, Ruddock, Gregory, Lambert, Bailey, Florey, Guise, Alban, Dean, Peters, and McAdam, and this ensured a high standard of discipline throughout the school. Among heads of subjects, too, there were few masters who were not excellent teachers, certainly as far as obtaining results was concerned, and the list included Mason, Bury, Lambert, Florey, Ruddock, Wilding, Dean and Peters. The following table will illustrate the careers of the most important masters appointed by Tower, Dingwall and Howard whose records of long service were an important factor in the success that Hurst achieved under Canon Howard and Roger Griffiths.

Long Serving Masters At Hurstpierpoint Appointed Before 1964

Name	Years at College	Housemasterships	Summary of other activities and posts held
Kenneth Mason	1933-1973	1933 Junior House 1934-60 Fleur de Lys (1940-45 Red Cross) 1960-67 Martlet	Acting Headmaster, Second Master Head of History, O.T.C./C.C.F., C/O hockey, squash & shooting
Robert Bury	1933-1976 (War Service)	1934-38 Junior House 1938-68 Red Cross	Second Master, Head of Classics, Producer—28 Shakespeare plays cricket
Robin Gregory	1935- d.1971	1935-65 Star	Biology Master, C.C.F. Signals, Gramophone Society rugby, squash & hockey
George Lambert	1937-1980 (War Service)	1950-69 Shield	Senior Assistant Master, Second Master Head of Mathematics C.C.F., C/O, rugby, athletics
Frank Florey	1945-1980	1950-69 Chevron	Second Master, Head of English Master i/c General Studies C.C.F., C/O Sixth Form Society
Horace Holloway	1946-1974		History master organist & librarian Editor of *The Hurst Johnian*
William Alban	1949-1982	1956-70 Eagle	Head of English Director of Drama, Debates Literary Society & tennis
Nicholas Heath	1951-1960 1974-1987	1974-79 Chevron	Head of Physics Stage Manager, astronomy, sailing & shooting
Reginald Ruddock	1951-1991	1965-80 Star	Acting Headmaster, Second Master Head of Geography, registrar Debates, cricket & hockey
John Peters	1954-1993	1959-60 Martlet 1960-77 Fleur de Lys	Second Master Director of Studies Head of Science and of Biology
Christopher Guise	1957-1988	1969-78 Shield	Geography Master C/O, C.C.C.F.
Christopher Dean	1960-1992	1968-83 Red Cross	Senior Assistant Master Head of Modern Languages, drama, author of *The Hurst Pageant*

TWELVE

A GOLDEN AGE
1957-1964

Ronald Howard's Later Years

There has been a most wearying struggle over this building, though in justice to the contractor there were from time to time shortages of both labour and materials. However, to all intents and purposes the boys' part is complete, and by the skin of our teeth we did manage to house forty-eight boys, housemaster and house tutor on the day the school opened.

> The opening of Martlet House, September 1960
> Headmaster's report to Council,
> Michaelmas Term 1960

The day ended with a grand finalé in the Inner Quad. The Hurstpierpoint Orchestra performed Suppé's *Poet and Peasant Overture*, and the *Post Horn Gallop* made extremely effective by echo from the surrounding walls. The School sang *Sussex by the Sea, The Yeomen of England*, and joined in the chorus of *'Good Night Ladies'*. Musically the performances defy comment, but marking the end of term as well as the end of the fête, they possessed a spirit akin to that engendered by the last night of the Proms.

> *The Hurst Johnian*, 846/27-29,
> Michaelmas Term 1961

It is not of course possible to produce details although I have some ideas. Still less is it possible to talk with any certainty about costs, but it looks as though we shall need at least £100,000 to do the whole thing. Stated in those terms the conception is quite fantastic for we have no money nor, so far as I can see, can we get any more, unless we have an appeal.

> Canon Howard's memorandum 'Future Needs',
> Summer Term 1962

We have a full and happy school, an established reputation, our finances are sound and we have a good waiting list. I think that we are a diligent and well-knit community coloured by a friendliness which is more easily obtained in a small school, and which has always been characteristic of Hurst.

> Canon Howard speaking on his last Speech Day, July 1964
> *The Hurst Johnian*, 855/33,
> Michaelmas Term, 1964

Old Johnians like many old boys see their own time at the School as a golden age: before them everything was prehistoric; after them, nothing was quite the same again, and much changed for the worse. The historian has to be more careful in the use of such phrases. In the course of the School's history there have clearly been periods where almost everything went well, and to which Old Johnians look back with particular pride: Lowe's time as headmaster, Cooper's middle years, just before the First World War, and Dingwall's war years were some of them. But there is only one period when all the written memoirs of old boys, and all the conversations held with those who lived at the time are unanimous; perhaps it is no co-incidence that Canon Howard's years produced more reminiscences, and more orders for this book than any other period in the School's recent history. High praise for the headmaster, admiration for many of the masters, pride in the athletic and academic achievements (often mirrored by well-known national careers later), and respect above all for the system of discipline, the traditions, and the way of doing things under Canon Howard merit the use of the phrase 'a golden age' just once in this history. Before dealing with the events of Canon Howard's later years this chapter looks at school life in the 19 years of his headship, and at the successful ethos which then existed to produce such unanimity—even if those who did not agree have perhaps kept quiet.

42   Rev. Canon Ronald C. Howard, the school's headmaster from 1945 to 1964, welcoming Lt. General Sir John Evetts to open the Schools, 25 July 1959.

Although Howard often complained about economic difficulties and on occasion about outside interference, for instance telling Council in 1958 that 'integration must come' with the state system, he was in fact a very lucky headmaster. Both Tower and Dingwall had been thrown off course by economic disaster and, in Dingwall's case, the stresses of the early war years. Griffiths had to cope with the impact of the 'public school revolution' and the changes in teenage life that went with it, and an appalling inflation. Watson had to carry out almost ceaseless change in exams and many aspects of school life required by government, and deal with the economic consequences of the worst depression in the economy since Tower's day. Howard was spared external economic difficulties except for a small amount of inflation in the early 1960s. In his first years he implemented the Fleming proposals, negotiating with and eventually taking boys from three education authorities: the L.C.C., Southend and East Sussex in 1947-48. But the scheme died out and Howard was left free from government interference.

Howard was therefore master of all he surveyed and took decisions for his school without looking over his shoulder at H.M.C., other schools, the press, parents, and health and safety legislation. He could use the cane without it being questioned and act severely if he felt it necessary. Indeed a good many of the 'Howardisms' concern his firmness of purpose, like the story of the long-haired Lancing boy halted in the cloisters and told to get his hair cut, or the boy who fainted during a collective reprimand in Howard's study, when the head paused to say 'Carry him out!', and then continued in full flow. Hurst was a hard working and somewhat isolated community during term-time which was to some extent a law unto itself. Terms were longer than nowadays—typically from 15 January to 29 March, from 30 April to 27 July, and 17 September to 17 December, and there were no half-terms. Half-days were given often on the same day to prevent any too ambitious plans for trips further afield. Few, either masters or boys, had transport and bicycles were confined to the senior boys. Motor bicycles and cars were forbidden. Many parents did not own cars and did not in those days either come at weekends or act as termly chauffeurs. Boys' luggage went by Carter Patterson and the boys themselves walked to Hassocks Station. There were radio and gramophones, strictly regulated in studies only, and television was little known—one arrived in the common room in 1961. Telephones were only for emergencies.

Lessons were 40 minutes long and there were five morning and two afternoon periods. Apart from prep on Monday to Friday evenings, there was a morning prep after breakfast of half an hour, a Saturday prep for those not in a school activity, and on Sunday a letter writing period and a further prep, all these being supervised by the prefects for all forms in day rooms. There was 20 minutes' P.T. every day. There was chapel every day and every Sunday attended by all boys and masters. Societies met on Tuesday and Thursday after games and on Saturday and Sunday, and it was virtually compulsory to join these if a boy was going to aspire to prefectship. Lights out was at 9.30 p.m. for the majority and 11.30 p.m. for the seniors, again supervised by prefects who went round to lock up.

In the first three years boys performed duties, i.e. fagging, on an extensive scale involving everything from bed making to boot and shoe cleaning, and fetching and carrying, sweeping day rooms, cleaning prefects' rookers and studies, and waiting in hall. Some boys were day room officials and house prefects, and school prefects had many duties to perform, being responsible for public good behaviour and observance of dress rules, for example. Team officials took their duties seriously and secretaries wrote detailed match reports. Each house had a house book in which every house event and honour was recorded. School societies were efficiently run by their officials who prepared meetings and wrote reports. Nearly all boys were in the corps for the duration of their school career. Training, playing and watching of sport at house level and for school teams was compulsory. Masters, too, were kept at it. Howard was unable to reach the recognised 1:13 master : boy ratio during his headship: it stayed at 1:16 with substantial junior classes and a master was lucky to have more than four 'free' periods a week. Masters ran an extensive society programme and the whole games programme. A proposal in 1962 to appoint a games master got nowhere. Nearly all masters lived on site or very close, and their lives (and their wives in many cases) were, like the boys, wholly concentrated on school during term-time.

The degree of isolation and the full programme involving virtually every master and boy left little time for contemplation of educational issues or introspective thought about what was going on. It was a working environment, somewhat regimented, highly efficient, and purpose-fully directed at all levels. Debates reflected this mood among boys. In 1952 the public school education was voted the best there was, and in 1957 the sixth-form speakers could think of few improvements, if any, in the existing system—although one suggestion was compulsory outward bound courses! In many ways Horace Holloway did a marvellous job running the magazine from 1949 to 1965, but it was not a magazine like that in Lowe's or Griffiths' time where criticism was allowed. *The Hurst Johnian* appeared to be reporting a school of 400 people all of whom seemed to agree and, moreover, to hold the same conservative views on every-thing from hair cuts to Holy Communion. 'Our doings,' said the magazine in 1953, 'do not change in any great degree.' Holloway admitted in 1963, 'we are frequently told that our pages lack the spice of novelty and change', but no attempt to start such changes occurred.

Canon Howard was exactly the right head for his time. He was a conservative and traditionalist in an age when education was set in a similar mould. 'A successful and happy society,' said Howard in 1955, was one that 'continues on an even keel.' On Prize Day 1962 the message was still the same, for during the past year 'we have largely conformed to the usual pattern', and in adopting this line Howard was undoubtedly reflecting the wishes of parents, masters, and probably a majority of the boys. Nearly all fathers of that generation had been in a uniformed service—some in two wars—and a good many of the mothers as well. Nearly all the boys would themselves be doing National Service until 1962. A majority of the masters had been officers in the war or been through National Service themselves as the years passed. The regimentation of the war years and the continued Cold War atmosphere meant that society as a whole accepted regimentation and rules, obeyed the chap in charge, and tended to value the ethos of the group above that of individuality. So there were few dissidents at any level from school traditions, house customs, initiation ceremonies, fagging, and the level of discipline imposed by head, housemasters, and prefects. A glance at house photographs shows an astonishing degree of uniformity of dress, haircuts, even expression, and the School Captain's Book compiled in 1964 outlines a mass of rules affecting every aspect of conduct and dress. Whether this way of life was beneficial, harmless or harmful was not yet considered: when boys were asked on one occasion if they approved of fagging 80 per cent said they did.

If this was the general situation in most public schools it was perhaps given an added intensification at Hurst. Once Gatwick opened in 1958 the convenience of the College for expatriates was enhanced, and at least five per cent of boys' parents were domiciled oversea; and many more had fathers whose work in the services, colonial police forces or administration meant that they, too, were overseas. Apart from the obligation on all to do National Service, a military career was still popular. Britain in Coronation Year, 1953, had an army of a million and a half, 6,000 planes in the R.A.F., and 150 capital ships in the Royal Navy. At least 15 per cent of boys took up service careers with some—like Admiral Sir Michael Boyce, Second Sea Lord, Air Marshal Sir Roy Austen-Smith, or H. Bentley-Marchant, the present, and last, Officer

Commanding in Hong Kong—rising to positions of distinction. The boys' background and their political views inclined them to an acceptance of the *status quo*, and there was a tendency to see growing up as imitating elders rather than improving on them. In a Michaelmas Term debate in 1952 masters echoed these views, with Nicholas Heath saying the leaders of the British Empire came from public schools and Edwin Stark praising corps, fagging, and prefectorial power. Boys in the audience talked about 'pukka sahibs' and the fact that 'ruling individuals were generally public school men'.

The Second World War cast a long shadow forward on social attitudes. Post-war there was a vast literature, some of an exceptionally high quality, and none of it pacificist as after the First World War, dealing with war-time experiences, and this lasted well into the 1960s from *The Wooden Horse* to *Colditz*, from *The Cruel Sea* to *The Guns of Navarone*. Boys had not read so much literature of this kind since Edwardian times. Moreover, the British cinema was flourishing in its great age and took every opportunity to turn these books into films, which Saturday by Saturday were watched in upper school, and then the theatre. Many of the actors in these films like Richard Todd, John Mills, or Jack Hawkins acted and spoke as 'public school chaps'. They were the heroes of a generation to be imitated; very different from what was to come only a few years later.

The *Hurst Johnian* continued to report military matters in a way reminiscent of the past and it was clear to boys in the school that service in the Empire or uniformed services was highly regarded. In the 1952 magazine Old Johnians were mentioned serving in nine African and eight Asian counties, and there were frequent references to Old Johnians in action in a series of colonial campaigns fought in these years. L.A. Wink, for example, was in charge of the Nairobi Police during Operation Anvil against Mau Mau terrorists, while service against Malayan terrorists by L.R. Hands, M.G. Hanney, P. Worthy, and C.A. Cherrington amongst others was described.

Hurst was very much an all-male community when it came to the collective ethos of the place. Howard certainly had no objection in principle to the employment of women. We have seen him appointing a lady bursar and he also tried unsuccessfully to appoint a lady catering manager. He continued Dingwall's employment of women as teachers in the Junior House including a Froebel mistress and two music mistresses. But women were kept in the background and by modern standards treated badly. In chapel a single pew was allocated to wives who had to turn up in their finery on the off-chance of obtaining a seat and, if the pew was full, were unable to attend the service. Housemasters' wives were confined very much to the rôle of hostess or helping with chapel flowers. The common room was barred to them until 1965.

As far as the boys were concerned Howard took a step back from the more liberal days of Dingwall with the ending in 1946 for some years of joint dances with girls' schools, although dancing lessons were allowed. In 1955 boys attended—in evening dress—a dance at St Michael's, Burton Park, and the magazine referred to dalliance on the terrace. Girls from St Michael's came to Hurst next year. The choral society continued to provide joint productions with Burgess Hill School for Girls and St Michael's, but drama did not follow their example and female parts were played by boys throughout the period. In 1957 the first mixed doubles in tennis were allowed which, according to the magazine, gave the boys 'sleepless nights'. Hurst like the majority of schools remained strongly single-sex throughout the period and co-education was not an issue, although interestingly enough a debate on the issue in 1961 was followed by a vote 101-51 in favour in a rare example of more progressive ways of thinking. Happily the boys seem to have sought out girls' company whenever they could, and on one occasion Howard expelled a boy for sleeping with a maid 'not once, not twice, but—' dramatic pause— 'six times!'

The emphasis for the majority of boys, and certainly in their pre-sixth form years, was on the cultivation of the male or military virtues: it is very reminiscent of the school as regiment as it developed in the 1890s, and it was certainly the last time the school community responded to the traditional approach to boy life without voices of dissent being heard. As an Old Johnian said in his reminiscences, life was 'Spartan,' and 'no nonsense' in 'an hierarchical society' with 'severe discipline'. A master from that period also said their conditions of living were 'pretty Spartan'. It was true in Howard's early days, although not later, that living conditions themselves were something of a test of fortitude, as his report to Council in 1951 shows. There he referred to fungoid growth on walls, accumulated dust, uneven and splintered floors, festoons of clothes, and lack of lockers in dormitories, corridors with muddy boots, and inadequate drying and washing facilities. Overcrowding, as in Lowe's day, was bound to increase the risk of infectious illness, particularly influenza, and in 1946, 1947, 1951, and 1954 there were considerable epidemics in the Lent Term. By the time Howard left these conditions, as we shall see later in this chapter, were largely transformed, as living conditions in every way were improved.

There were cold baths, an unheated swimming pool, early morning runs, outdoor P.T. and of course a substantial compulsory sports programme at house and school level. In 1949 boys attended their first Aldershot Army P.T. courses for some years and the boy rank of P.T. instructor appeared in the *valetes*. An article in the magazine in 1953 praised the strenuousness of holiday P.T. courses and in 1955 one attended by 57 boys from various schools was described in detail in the magazine: it consisted of 10 days each of 10 hours' physical training. An old boy recalls a Danish member of the Chevron Remove popular for his sporting prowess and his limited English phrase: 'me Axelsson, me strong'. In September 1956 the first lecture on outward bound at Ullswater was given and this became extremely popular, with the magazine including several articles on the various camps like that at Aberdovey where canoeing, abseiling, circuit training, and mountaineering were tried out by boys for the first time.

According to Johnian articles, at least, boys' holiday interests remained very much what they were in term-time. Their holidays often seem remarkably like endurance tests on board trawlers or in Norwegian mountains, and one boy gave details of his 530-mile cycle tour in France—although he did manage to fit in some architectural viewing. The magazine had a 'Holiday Sport' section in which it detailed how senior boys in substantial numbers spent part of their holidays playing for public school, club, and county sides. In the 1955-56 Christmas holidays 21 boys were involved in rugby and six in hockey, and a Hurst Seven played at Staines well supported on the touchline. In the Easter Holidays in 1962 eight played rugby, nine hockey, and seven squash at a good representative level.

The corps was not surprisingly a major school institution, compulsory in fact even if not legally so. There was no difficulty in staffing a large corps from a common room with plenty of former officers. Captain Mason had built up the corps under Dingwall and it was described on inspection in November 1945 as 'an outstanding unit'. Mason retired from command in early 1947, and was later awarded the M.B.E. for his corps services in wartime. His successor was Major George Lambert, a winner of the Military Cross, who was succeeded in 1952 by Major Frank Florey who had been seriously wounded in action. In September 1957 he was succeeded by Lieutenant P.J. Chambers, who had retired from the regular army and was then employed as a laboratory assistant. Three years later he was succeeded by Major Michael I. Bailey. Colour Sergeant F.S. Taylor left after 10 years, and was replaced by a former Royal Marine, Sergeant Major Upson, in 1946. He left early in 1949, and was replaced for a short time by Sergeant Major Ansell. In May 1950 Sergeant Major, later Captain, William Saunders of the Royal Army Ordnance Corps became the corps sergeant until 1976, and for many years looked after shooting and P.T. as well.

The War Office, and later the Defence Ministry, strongly backed school cadet forces in this period—the title, incidentally changing from J.T.C. to Combined Cadet Force (C.C.F.) in 1948. An armoury, subsequently enlarged, and a small-bore rifle range were provided. Modern equipment was provided and the training had a close relationship to what cadets would experience in their National Service or in the colonial wars still being fought in places like Malaya, Cyprus, or Kenya. Kit and weapons were the same as those in the adult armed services. In 1961, under Lieutenant Jeremy J. Eyre, a classics master, the corps added a naval section to its activities. Camp in the summer was attended by well over a hundred boys until the mid-1950s and substantial numbers of boys went on a wide range of military courses in the holidays. At Easter 1953, for example, there were boys at military establishments at Maidstone, Chichester, Shorncliffe, Crowborough, Ashford, Aldershot and Borden. Term-time training for Certificate A Parts I and II continued as in the past with the addition of a new assault course in 1957.

Under Lowe, it will be recalled, Hurst was one of the first school cadet forces in the country and it was particularly appropriate, therefore, at a time when it was so effective and popular, that the corps should play a key rôle in the centenary celebrations in 1960. At the College there was a special parade on 29 June with new cap badge and new colour displayed, and a good turn out by Old Johnians currently serving at Sandhurst and Dartmouth. On 22 July five members of the corps attended the march past at Buckingham Palace and the school provided the bearer and escorts for the colour party.

But there was more to Howard's Hurst than this familiar, and rather bleak, picture of life. On Prize Day in 1956 he said he believed public schools should be civilised, and there was much in school life that was academically challenging and culturally stimulating, even if these activities did not have quite such universal appeal as corps and sports. Howard encouraged art and music and fully integrated them into the curriculum. There was the annual play, an ever widening and deepening range of musical activities, and all the various activities connected with chapel. As well as writing for the *Hurst Johnian* the boys began to produce magazines of considerable quality beginning with *Counterpoint* (1960), and the *Natural History Magazine* (1961). The annual general knowledge papers in the archives would tax more than boys' brains these days. From 1948 the annual Weston speech prize revived, along with debates, public speaking and effective diction. There were seven large societies—Gramophone, Literary, Natural History, Debating, Sixth Form, Geographical and Scientific—which functioned for much of Howard's time, and over the years at least sixteen other societies had lifetimes from a few to several years and included some of real distinction like the Film and Ionian societies.

Although it is true that the boys were confined to College for the term, and under considerable pressure to join, the societies were not simply there to add weight to *valetes*. Masters were keen to give up their time to run them so that, for instance, a young master like Nicholas Heath was involved over the years in stage crew, sailing, shooting, the antiquarian society, astronomy, photography, and the Science Society. Senior masters were not busy at administration or at home and gave of their time just as freely, and most heads of department with the exception of classics and history enthusiastically ran one or more societies, and in the early 1960s Mr. Eyre and Mr. Lunn started Classical and History societies. Howard himself entertained the prefects, invited boys to meet distinguished visitors, and had chamber musicians and bridge players in his drawing room.

To a degree the societies did reflect the traditional atmosphere of the College. Some of them tended also to be repetitive and to reflect the masters' tastes. Programmes were sometimes conventional and censorship clearly operated where open criticism existed in sixth-form meetings. But by and large the societies were truly run by the boys who provided officials who planned

43 The gramophone society in session. Date unknown. On the left, by the gramophone is R.J. Gregory.

meetings, supplied refreshments, and kept records. Chairing meetings and running societies provided good training in administration, albeit unconsciously, backing up the training in leadership that more official posts gave.

Hurst genuinely functioned as a College. Masters were as strict as necessary in the classroom, and as friendly as possible in general school life, so that particularly senior boys could mix socially with masters and mature more quickly. Their minds were exposed to adult discussion as well as the racket of their peer group and, if at times this led to a certain degree of pretentiousness, it certainly helped to raise the exam results, university entrants numbers, and the quality of the best academic boys in the school. Under earlier headmasters this century Hurst had been able to produce a good list of those taking up military and colonial careers, but entrants into the professions had been few and far between even among the Oxbridge successes. Now for the first time under Canon Howard it is clear that school life provided the basics of character and the basis of knowledge for many boys to attain future distinction in many fields.

Roger Moulton's register, of course, now supplies for the first time the full details of this development. What follows illustrates why so many boys were pleased with the start they had under Dingwall and Howard and it is another measure of Howard's success as a headmaster. From the 1940s, 1950s, and early 1960s Hurst politicians included R.L. Page, M.P. for Workington and P.P.S. to John Biffen, Lord (Desmond) Plummer, Chairman of the G.L.C., and A.L. Laing, Secretary to the Hong Kong Executive Council and then Chief Clerk to the Legislative Council. Diplomats included Sir Derek Day, ambassador to Ethiopia and High Commissioner to Canada, Sir Oliver Forster, ambassador to Pakistan, Sir Bryan Cartledge, ambassador to Hungary and Russia and now master of Linacre College, and G.H. Boyce, ambassador to Quatar.

Amongst Old Johnians distinguished in the arts were Ronald Neame, a film producer and D.J. Kennard, a television producer. J.T. Sutcliffe was art editor at the *Guardian*, C. Nourse, manager at the Royal Opera House, Hugh Marchant, a fellow and professor at the Royal College of Music; Brian Primmer, an author and lecturer in music at Durham University and R.J. Steinitz, a music lecturer at Huddersfield University. In medicine P.M. Boyce was Professor of Psychiatry at Sydney University, B.P. Curwain, became a senior clinical tutor at St Mary's Hospital, G.M. Robins, a senior lecturer in veterinary science at the University of Queensland; E.J. Wood, was principal physicist and radiologist at the Royal Free Hospital and

C.E. Ackroyd, clinical surgery reader at Oxford University. There have also been several surgeons of distinction such as A.S. Chilvers and D.A. Reynolds.

In the universities important posts held by Old Johnians have included P. Benham, Professor of Aeronautical Engineering at Belfast, P.J.C. Hordern, lecturer at Saskatchewan and Brandon University, Manitoba, Rev. D.J. Lane, Oxford University history lecturer, chaplain of Pembroke College, Oxford, and assistant professor at Toronto University, T.J.T. Rooth, senior lecturer in Economic History at Portsmouth University, M.G. Macdonald, lecturer in comparative law at Kent University, C.D. Hedges, lecturer in engineering at Aston University, and Brian Manning with a distinguished career as a 17th-century historian. Among Hurst headmasters have been G. de W. Waller at Lord Wordsworth's College and now at Cranleigh School, M.I. Taylor at King's School, Tynemouth, George L. Hill at St George's School, Windsor and the Cathedral School, Llandaff, A.J. Snow at the Oratory School, and T.J.G. Marchant and P.N. Lee Smith at preparatory schools while David Hughes returned to occupy a number of positions culminating in second master at Hurst. D.M. Hart became general secretary of the National Association of Head Teachers. The Rev. D.J.C. Davies, after a period as a university chaplain, became canon and precentor of Salisbury Cathedral. Clearly what was achieved by Canon Howard and his masters left its lasting impression on hearts and minds, and showed forth in a galaxy of successful careers. Although successive heads have had their successes there was never again, in the view of those that lived through the last half century at Hurst, anything to compare with the mood of glad, confident morning that prevailed in Howard's golden age.

II

We can turn now to look in more detail at the main aspects of school life in these years starting with sport. Canon Howard was no sportsman himself. He rarely watched games and rarely referred to sport in his public speeches or reports to Council. Nevertheless he appreciated the importance of sport to the overall success of the school and he did much to improve its facilities. Under Howard came an improved pool, the first hard tennis courts, cricket hard nets and a cricket school, more squash courts, a gymnasium, and the Ruckford pitches. Sport continued to provide much of the material for *valetes*. It was a substantial section of the magazine and there can be no doubt that enthusiasm for sport at house and school level affected the vast majority of masters and boys. Results of major matches were as eagerly discussed over common room pipes as they were over rooker teas, and few boys would not have known who the leading sportsmen in the College were and how the main teams were doing.

An examination of the sports record, however, shows that in spite of the effort, interest and time devoted to sport, success only came at limited times and to a limited number of the games played. The late 1940s and the early 1960s were periods where the main sports and many of the minor ones did well, but the 1950s were, with a few exceptional teams, doldrum years for sport. Indeed the *Johnian* reports run out of excuses for the failure even of well captained sides to do well, blaming illness, weather, injury, variable team membership, pressure of fixtures, pressure of other school activities, and the state of the pitches. At first sight it is surprising that in a school which placed such emphasis on physical fitness, and the traditional respect for the games player and his games, there was not a greater list of victories. It is true that there were Lent Term epidemics in some years, and that hockey pitches, swimming pool, and tennis court facilities were not adequate, but clearly there were more complex reasons.

There was a tendency for masters to remain in charge of sports well into middle age and to become set in their ways. The games programme was loosely run by the P.G.C. but rarely the subject of general discussion. It too remained conservative. Table tennis, basket ball, and water polo, for example, made brief but unsustained appearances. Tower's games programme remained intact. There was a tendency to talk much about good sportsmanship and style, to accept defeat graciously, and not become obsessive about winning: an essentially amateur approach in a way. There was, therefore, a lack of modern coaching methods and where, in squash or cricket, they appeared occasionally results improved at once. When the swimmers went for training one year at Hove baths, it 'changed all our styles', but the training was not maintained. All-round physical fitness helps in any game, but the assault course and army-style P.T. did not necessarily create goal scorers, or track athletes. It is particularly interesting that circuit training (1958) and weight training (1962) were introduced first by the boys, and then adopted generally when their immediate impact on games was noticed. While senior teams were in the public eye junior teams had little attention paid to them in terms of proper training until Colts teams were fully organised, in several sports; and later Under-Fourteen teams, like rugby and cricket under John Peters, took on a more purposeful air. It is clear from the substantial number of boys that played representative and club sports and achieved national teams, particularly in hockey and squash, that there were many excellent games players: the difficulty always seems to have been in providing a full set of forwards or backs, or a bowling or batting order with depth.

Rugby was run by Robin Gregory, George Lambert, and George Hill. During the late 1940s the First XV did well starting in Howard's first term with seven out of ten victories, and in both 1948 and 1949 only one match was lost. White shorts made their appearance in the latter year. From 1950 to 1955 the team won only 15 out of 56 games and the reports made it clear that lack of strong forwards was the main problem. In 1955 Dudley Stratford and Jonathan Allison created a strong pack and in the next year, with Allison leading that pack, and A.J. Bradford (Wales Schools player) as captain, six out of nine fixtures were won. Poor results returned for a few years and then from 1959 to 1962 there were four good seasons. This was due in part to a group of fine sportsmen, whose names occur elsewhere in this chapter, including Jeremy Lowry, the two Snows and the two Stiffs, Keith Robinson, Nicholas Twine, Robert Wilmot, Robert Carswell and Derek Tyler. They used modern training methods and the First XV won 29 out of 44 matches in those years. In 1962 the team was unbeaten except for a penalty kick costing them one match. Hurst began to do better at Rosslyn Park Sevens, reaching the quarter finals on two occasions.

Hockey run by Kenneth Mason and Reginald Ruddock (himself a county player) was in the strange position throughout most of these years of having a national reputation, while the First XI scarcely ever won a match. Among Old Johnians who achieved prominence were Derek Day, who played for Middlesex and England, and Neil Forster who played for Surrey and England, and who both represented their country in the Olympics; R.C. Schad who played for Surrey and England; Laurence Henwood who captained Surrey, and J.A. Skues who captained Yorkshire and Gloucestershire. From 1945 to 1950 hockey continued in excellent form and during those years the astonishingly low total of only eight matches were lost. The 1948 team, captained by S.M. Pitcher, and containing Robert Schad and Geoffrey Hazzan, and the 1949 team, captained by Keith Jenkin and containing J. Skues and Roger Bartlett, were perhaps the outstanding sides.

Then from 1951 to 1963 the First XI had less than a dozen victories. The *Johnian* reports made every excuse under the sun and Ruddock called for the 'spirit of Dunkirk on the playing fields'. But poor results continued and, even when a fine captain like Brian Berks was in charge in 1959 and there was no bad weather, epidemic, or serious injuries, they still lost every match. Similarly in the next year when the group of athletes just referred to in rugby were in the team only one victory occurred. Some relief was provided by visits on occasion (1960, 1964) to the Oxford Schools hockey festival, but it was not until Howard's last year that a team, captained by Robert Hutchinson and including Geoffrey Robins, Robert Carswell, and others, won five of their seven matches, and it was not until some years later that earlier training and an all-weather pitch were to change the situation.

One of the most well-remembered sights of Howard's Hurst will always be the small, slightly stooped figure, with his pipe, of Robert Bury who ran cricket for 26 years. In 1948 he referred to 'one of the blackest months' in Hurst cricket and there were to be many of them in the coming years. Bury was a sportsman of the old school. Cricket was a game played by gentlemen in a gentlemanly way, and the interest lay in the nuances of the game not necessarily in victory. He put his finger quite correctly on the main reason for poor results in 1954 when he said that consistent and determined batting was what was needed, when clearly from *Johnian* reports this was often missing. But nothing seems to have been done to improve matters for a good many years. From 1946 to 1956 there were only 36 victories from 97 First XI matches, and only 1949, when Keith Jenkin was captain and scored a century, was a really good season. Even an effective captain like George Hill in 1950 and 1951 could not reverse the trend. From 1957 to 1960 there were only 12 victories from 54 games, and another effective captain in 1958 and 1959 did not succeed in changing matters. In those years only Malcolm Williams could be described as a top bowler and the highest individual batsman's score was sixty-six!

44   Cricket tea in the pavilion, *c.*1950. At the rear table sitting sideways is R.J. Bury.

Improvement came in the early 1960s when Ruckford pitches were in full use and in 1964 an indoor cricket area was provided for wet weather practice. Groundsmen-coaches were appointed; first, F.S. Booth, ex-Lancashire, and then J. Arnold, ex-Hampshire. Junior cricket was properly organised. In 1961 the superb batsman Howard Bentley-Marchant led a team which won six of its 15 games. He made 340 runs and a first rate batting order contained six players who made in excess of a hundred runs. Clive Stiff and Peter Green were fine bowlers, helping to dismiss Whitgift for 63 and Brighton for 64. 1963 was another good year with 'real depth' in the batting with players like Robert Carswell and John Hall, and bowling in the capable hands of Richard Smart. In 1964 came a century by Robert Hutchinson, although by this time the batting depth had gone again, and only three team members reached more than fifty runs.

In two sports Hurst went from strength to strength through the Howard years, although not always consistently. George Lambert, Christopher Wightwick, and Jonathan Pinhey ran athletics which benefited first of all by its move to the Summer Term in 1947 and secondly from its move to the East field in 1962. During the late 1940s competition centred on an annual Woodard schools fixture, starting in May 1946, and on the Milocarian Trophy for Sussex schools competed for at Withdean which Hurst won in 1947 and 1950. Under George Lambert virtually

45   The athletics team in 1947. The first winners of the Milocarian Trophy. On the right is G.E. Lambert.

every previous record was broken: 14 in 1947, six in 1948, and 10 in 1949, and athletics emerged on a new plateau of excellence and professionalism. 1954 was a particularly good year, with a very effective group of athletes including Graham Worrall and Alik Bradford and five records were broken. In 1958 Colts athletics began, and circuit training was introduced by Derek Tyler. 1960 was the next particularly good year with wins over the main rivals Cranleigh and Charterhouse by a team including Michael Boyce and Christopher Coley. In 1962 weight training was added to circuit training, and seven more records were broken. 1963 and 1964 continued the run of good seasons.

Squash remained popular as an all-year-round game and the only important indoor sport at the College. Under Keith Jenkin and Geoffrey Hazzan the 1949 and 1950 teams started the years of success with nine out of 12 victorious matches. Coaches were employed and particularly valuable were Mr. Reynolds who went on to coach at Eton College, and Michael Bickmore, a Junior School master, and later headmaster of Yardley Court Prep School. The 1960 team began the years of good results and included the Stiff brothers and John Hodgkins. In 1962 Clive Stiff won the Evans Cup at the Public Schools tournament and the next year he reached the final of the Drysdale Cup. 1963 saw Philip Ayton and Nigel Morgan in the Evans Cup, Robin Maclear and Philip Ayton playing for Sussex Schools, and Stiff and Maclear in the semi-finals of the Londonderry Cup. In Howard's last year a team including Philip Ayton and James Mason won seven victories and suitably inaugurated the new squash courts built with the Shippam Legacy. During the later 1960s Hurst's national squash reputation was to grow, spearheaded by Philip Ayton, Clive Stiff and John Richardson.

As for the other sports there is little to record until the early 1960s. With the start of a fixture list again in 1948, with good swimmers like Timothy Howard and Geoffrey Hazzan, and the extended pool the next year, it might have been thought that swimming was going to be a successful sport. It turned out not to be so. As far as the limited Johnian reports show, there were only two swimming victories over other schools, one in 1954 and one in 1959, throughout the whole decade. Swimming suffered from the pressure of being third choice after cricket and athletics. The pool was cold, even leaf strewn, and impossible to practise in during the Lent Term. Visits to neighbouring pools were rarely made and there was no expert tuition. The only really able swimmer of the decade was David Van Weil. In 1960 circuit training began, a colts team was formed, and swimming started to revive a little with boys like Ferguson and Lewis. In 1962 both senior and colts teams recorded two victories each. In 1963 Peter Nariskin's swimming and Robert Hadfield's diving brought three senior victories, and in 1964 two senior and three colts victories sustained a short-lived winning streak.

Cross-country was well patronised as an alternative to water-logged pitches in the Lent Term but it did not feature much as a sport for most of Howard's time. The Clayton and the steeplechase had gone under Dingwall and the Litter Act (1959) brought hare and hounds paper chases to an end. The races now took place on two shorter courses of three and two miles, worked out in 1947, on which the house cross-country competition was held the following year. Not until 1959 does the *Hurst Johnian* report a series of fixtures with other schools with matches against Charterhouse and Lancing. By 1961 a colts team had appeared, and the First Eight's programme had expanded to eight matches. Jonathan Pinhey was to be responsible for a short-lived revival in the 1960s.

Tennis like swimming looked in the late 1940s as if it would undergo a renaissance when it was organised by J. Harper King, two courts were built, and some thirty boys were playing it. Led by Keith Jenkin the team won six victories in 1949. Thereafter tennis is often not reported and the 1950s passed with little to notice. William Alban took over running the sport and in 1959 four wins from six matches were recorded by the First VI including F.C. and L.N. Stiff and John Waterfall. 1960 saw a colts team appear and was another good year. The P.G.C. recognised tennis as a minor sport in 1961 due to the good captaincy of William Welch, and for a time things went well. In 1964 Philip Ayton and Peter Robinson were the first Hurst Johnians to enter the public schools tennis at Wimbledon, losing to Clifton College.

Turning from the playing fields to the theatre stage the dominating event every year was a Robert Bury Shakespeare production—21 of them from 1946 to 1966. His first production on returning from the war was *The Taming of the Shrew* with Anthony Church as Petruchio, followed by an equally impressive performance next year as Falstaff in *Henry IV*—a play of Bury's devising from two Shakespeare ones. Until 1955 Bury with G.K. France and then Nicholas Heath as stage managers continued to produce plays in the hall, but in 1956 *Henry IV* was staged again with Alik Bradford as Prince Hal and John Hodgkins as Falstaff in the new theatre now renamed the Bury Theatre. Nicholas Heath continued to head the stage crew, and was joined by Christopher Dean in 1960. Wilfred Smith provided effective music and two art masters, D. Johnson and Russell Flint, the scenery.

Robert Bury did his best to present a wide selection of the plays and to include major tragedies, which was never easy given the limitations of school productions. Dialogue was described as being of a 'ponderous gait' or 'over declamatory'. *Romeo and Juliet* was performed in 1954 and 1964, *Othello* in 1948 and 1962, *Macbeth* in 1958, and *Hamlet* in 1963, three outstanding individual performances being those of Robin Courtney as Macbeth, Jeremy Davies as Hamlet, and Robert Wilmot as Othello. *Romeo and Juliet* jars on modern minds because female

46   R.H.W. Wilmot as Othello, 1962.

rôles were still played by boys—Henry Shepherd and Adrian Herring having the rôle of Juliet to play, for example, and critics had to describe how effectively young men played parts like Lady Macbeth or Queen Gertrude.

Few historical plays were produced in this period, and Bury concentrated on the lighter fare to provide the audience and players with an easier task. So there was *A Midsummer Night's Dream* in 1949, and 1957, *A Winter's Tale* in 1950 and 1959, *Twelfth Night* in 1951 and 1960, *Taming of the Shrew* in 1961 and *Much Ado About Nothing* in 1953. Bury was well aware of the limitations of his stage, his players and even the audience, and his productions aimed to be spectacles lavish in scenery, effects, and costume. He was producing plays that the First XV were going to act in, and not the members of a West End greenroom. But as the 1950s and '60s passed the English stage experienced a great renaissance and fundamental changes in production techniques, all of which passed Bury by. One began to feel that after a

Bury production hansom cabs would take you home and local newspaper comments were often much less favourable than the magazine reports of the plays. A production in 1960 was criticised for heavy scenery, numerous blackouts, hasty curtains, and intervening music necessitated by the elaborate production, and three years later *Hamlet* was criticised because costume and scenery bore little relationship to the atmosphere and theme of the play which went on until past eleven at night. By the mid-1960s change and variety were certainly needed in school drama.

Just as Robert Bury dominated the theatrical productions of these years so Wilfred Smith, Director of Music from 1950 to 1962, dominated the musical scene. Before he came Alan Tregonning ran music, with Horace Holloway as organist for many years. The choir gave its first broadcast from the chapel in December 1948, and the post-war years saw productions of Bach's *B Minor Mass* (1946) and Britten's *A Ceremony of Carols* (1948). At Lancing's centennial in 1948 Britten conducted his *St Nicolas Cantata* with the

47   D.J.C. Davies as Hamlet, 1963.

Hurst choir taking part. But it was Wilfred Smith, who with Horace Hawkins before him and Nicholas Searls later, was one of the three main figures in Hurst's music this century. After training under Harold Darke, war service in India, and a spell at Tonbridge School, Wilfred came to Hurst bringing a friendly, no-nonsense approach to music which was exactly right. Until 1957 he carried the burden of all the school's music, although with the appointment of Miss K. Laurie in the Junior House that year he began to get some assistance. When he left he had built Hurst's musical reputation so that the school could attract John Gardiner, director of music at Bloxham, and so increased musical activity that an assistant director was needed; at the same time Peter Lattimer was appointed, their first production being Brahms's *Requiem*.

It has to be said that in music as in drama there was little that was innovative and modern. With the exception of Benjamin Britten, no post-1930 American or European works were performed and the musical renaissance of the mid-century passed Hurst by at this time. There was a strong emphasis on English composers—particular favourites of Robin Gregory, who ran the Gramophone Society—and Delius, Elgar and Vaughan Williams all had their centennials celebrated at Hurst. Chapel music was equally conservative, in some ways even more so than under Hawkins. On a trip to Holland, in itself an innovation, the music offered was Howells and Vaughan Williams, and even the composers themselves expressed surprise that their music had been chosen when they were informed. Smith would have replied that Hurst was a school and not a conservatoire, and that his job was to ensure the maximum interest in music by the non-musical as well as the third of the College directly involved in playing and singing.

In this he was extremely successful. The Choral Society was reformed and their first performance in 1951 was Handel's *Messiah*. Subsequent choral works included Bach's *B Minor Mass* and *St Matthew Passion*, Rossini's *Stabat Mater*, Haydn's *Creation*, Brahms's *Requiem*, Fauré's *Requiem*, and on 25 March 1962 what was claimed to be the first school production anywhere of Elgar's *Dream of Gerontius*. The choir was affiliated to the Royal School of Church Music, and in 1952 at Canterbury and 1953 at Eton College began attending the Festival of School Choirs. The repertoire was expanded to include quite difficult pieces like Franck's setting of the 150th Psalm. In May 1957 came the first overseas visit since Hawkins' day when the choir went to The Hague and Utrecht, with van Weil as their interpreter, to sing in two churches and two schools. On 18 June 1958 the Hurst choir sang for the first time in a cathedral when they performed Evensong at Chichester where they returned in 1962 at the start of a long period of annual visits. On 27 May 1963 the choir sang at Guildford Cathedral.

An orchestra was formed. It played its first music on 28 March 1954—Elgar's *Overture in D Minor*—and gave its first concert on 21 July that year with a programme including *Peter and the Wolf* and Vaughan Williams *Folk Songs*. The orchestra gave an annual Summer Term concert, and was involved in other school events like the play and speech day. Smith did all he could to encourage interest in instrumental music. A number of distinguished performers like Robert Carrington, Leon Goossens, Meredith Davies, and Julian Bream came to the College. There were frequent chamber concerts both by the boys and by visiting groups, some held in the headmaster's house. The band was refounded in 1956. The House Music Competition was refounded in 1951 with Star's rendering of Stanford's *The Old Superb* being the winning entry just defeating Chevron's *The Yeomen of England*. At first Smith allowed these to be boisterous unison sing songs and a good many of the works given were of ancient patriotic vintage, but once the idea was established part songs came in, vocal and instrumental sections were formed, and by 1960 the competition was of sufficiently high quality to be judged by the principal of the Royal Academy of Music, Sir Thomas Armstrong.

Because concerts and public performances attract the eye it is all too easy to forget the teaching work of music departments. Here, too, Smith had a fine record. There was a goodly list of Oxbridge music awards including those to Steinitz, Hartley, Butterworth, Davies, Todd and Harling. The first music scholars' concert was given on 15 March 1957 with performances that included Steinitz playing Elgar's *Cello Concerto*, and Hartley singing Schubert. The number of visiting music teachers doubled in 10 years and by 1962 132 were learning a musical instrument in the cramped conditions of the hut by the gymnasium. Smith was a conductor of the Sussex Youth Orchestra, and it is not surprising to find that eight Hurst Johnians were playing in it in 1960. Besides choral scholars Hurst began to produce instrumentalists of quality like I.N. Murray who played in the National Youth Orchestra.

The last aspect of life in Howard's Hurst that needs some examination is the large number of societies mentioned earlier that played a key rôle in filling much leisure time with purposeful and sometimes academically beneficial activity. The Sixth Form Society run by Frank Florey and debates run by William Alban and Reginald Ruddock were the two societies where sixth formers were most free to express opinions about contemporary matters. The Sixth Form Society read papers or held discussions mainly on political matters and mainly from the conventional right wing point of view. It was perhaps not without significance that the first meeting in 1948 listened to Kenneth Mason on The Virtues of Conservatism and that in 1961 his son, James, was leading a discussion about the evils of Communism. Debates were open to the whole sixth and even the whole school at certain periods, and in a typical term like Michaelmas 1962 attendances of a hundred plus were common and term finished with one of two hundred and fifty.

School debates are quite often swayed by the personality or popularity of the speakers rather than belief in the motions, but there can be no doubt that the vast majority of debates ended in victory for a conservative or traditionalist viewpoint. In the late 1940s the British Empire was strongly supported and in one debate preferred to America by 82 to 28 votes. Thereafter Cold War mentality affected many debates. In one it was voted by a large majority that they would rather be dead than Red. Atomic weapons received full support, and C.N.D. was strongly defeated in 1961. Interestingly, though, in debates on race in 1948 and 1962 the boys strongly opposed racial discrimination (or colour bar as it was called in British colonies). Any discussion of contemporary issues is welcome in a closed community, but it is very clear that boys at Howard's Hurst were prepared to take their place in society rather than to change it. This was never entirely true. By the early 1960s the monolith was starting to crumble a little: a single Labour Party supporter and a single C.N.D. member at Oxbridge were noticed. Some boys began to take an interest in V.S.O. and among the first was David Kendrew who went to Malaya. But the narrowness of approach was to lead to future difficulties.

The same applied to discussion of school issues and life in Britain. Occasionally debates were more critically minded. They voted by 107-17 in favour of science, and by 101-51 in favour of co-education as early as 1961. Sometimes when articulate boys espoused critical causes debates were more evenly balanced. The arguments of two able boys, later Oxbridge entrants, criticising petty rules and traditions led to a close 74-62 vote for the petty rules and traditions. Other debates in which they voted themselves 'modern minded' or backed the current Conservative government were perhaps only to be expected. From time to time the routine was varied: in 1951 and 1957 by a mock trial, but inter-school debates were unfortunately not continued.

The repetitive and traditional programme of societies is very well illustrated by the records of the Literary and Gramophone Societies, the two most popular and longest lived 'arts' societies. Until 1960 William Alban's Literary Society subsisted on a diet of Noel Coward, Terence Rattigan, Emlyn Williams, and Somerset Maughan. In Michaelmas Term 1955, for instance, they read three Shaw and two Rattigan plays. Occasionally more sophisticated works were read like T.S. Eliot's *Murder in the Cathedral*, or Dylan Thomas' *Under Milk Wood*. 1959 seems to be the year when things began to change. In the Lent Term the boys put on their first one-act play—Anthony Booth's *The Sky is Overcast* and, although it was not well received, one act and other plays were now part of the society's repertoire, and by 1964 works by Chekhov and Ionescu were being performed. Strindberg's *Easter* was read in 1959, too, and 'did not appeal to all', but thereafter the society livened up—in 1961 they agreed that 'argument and criticism' of the plays should be included in their readings and works by Pinter, Osborne, Shaffer and Miller began to appear.

Robin Gregory's Gramophone Society that had started with 78s in Dingwall's day survived into the 1960s to hear Tchaikovsky on stereo sound for the first time in March 1960. Each term about twenty pieces of music were played and discussed, but it is very clear that the repertoire remained virtually unchanged for 20 years and that it was biased towards the leading English composers prior to 1939. In 1962 the Ionian Society was founded to discuss and play a much wider repertoire of music. Robin Gregory helped to launch the new society with a talk on the horn, one of the instruments about which he would later write a book. A typical programme might consist of a talk on Elgar followed by a performance of his Piano Quintet, and many of the pieces played and topics discussed revealed considerable depth of musical understanding.

Film was a major art form and a major social attraction throughout these years, particularly as British film making was in its classical era of innovation and success. Apart from the Saturday night films many societies showed an excellent range of documentaries. The boys made films. The first made in Michaelmas Term 1957 on school sport was followed by others on cross country and on Ruckford Mill. Most of the Saturday night films were inevitably of the kind thought sensible by housemasters and again it was not until the 1960s that contemporary films of a more adult nature began to appear. When *The Angry Silence* was shown in 1963 the magazine commented, 'it is significant that the School enjoyed this more than the traditional wild west or prison camp numbers'. In 1961 under Mr. Lewis a film society was started, and during its relatively short life showed an excellent programme ranging from Resnais' *Guernica* to Kazan's *Panic in the Streets.*

There were few other 'arts' societies. Robert Bury was not interested in a classical society although in the early 1960s while Jeremy Eyre was at the school an attempt was made to start one. There were visits to Classical plays at Bradfield and Cambridge, and uniquely in Hurst history in 1962 a classical play—Euripides' *Iphigenia*—was staged. In 1949 an Archaeological Society run by a variety of masters including Peter Woodard and Nicholas Heath excavated some local sites and heard lectures on a wide variety of topics like Roman Canterbury, the Sutton Hoo Ship, British Clocks, and Burial Mounds. But Kenneth Mason did not favour a history society and it was not until the arrival of Mr. Lunn in 1961 that one started and ran for some years. There were a number of good guest speakers like Roger Lockyer, and some of the members presented interesting papers like C.P. Menaul's on the International Brigades.

The more active societies were on the science side in an age when British science was at the height of its 20th-century achievements in computers, nuclear fission, jet propulsion, radio astronomy, and biological work on D.N.A. Numbers doing science rose sharply and by the late 1950s a group of talented science masters had been formed in spite of the recruitment difficulties. The Natural History Society dated from Awdry's time and in Howard's early years its activities were limited to occasional films or visits, like the annual one to Forfars to see Christmas cakes made. By the early 1960s John Peters and Jeremy Tatum had built it into the largest school society. It was announced that the Society was 'too much of a film society' and that it would concentrate on serious experimentation. Collating and experimental work was done on Sussex flora and fauna. There was a moth trap, aquaria for fresh water and tropical fish, and a bird identification project. For a time there was even a beehive in the headmaster's garden. In July 1961, edited by Christopher Luckens and Robert Ackroyd, came the first *Natural History Magazine* over fifty pages thick.

Ivor Wilding and later Alan Giles ran the Science Society started in 1955. It was stressed that it was a sixth-form society for mainly chemists and physicists and they were soon carrying out experiments in many aspects of science including weed killers, metal fatigue and fruit storage methods. Members visited Brighton College of Technology for lectures when it opened and enjoyed films and visits like those to Kemp Town Brewery or the National Physical Laboratory at Teddington. A lecture on micro-computers in 1962 was the first time this subject was discussed in the school. Nicholas Heath was involved with the Society, but his principal interest was astronomy, inevitably popular in an age of missiles and space exploration. The subject received a boost from a visit by Patrick Moore in 1955 and later from the Astronomer Royal. F.W. Bright suggested the school had its own radio telescope. One was designed by R.L. Edgar and its housing built by the boys in the summer of 1962 near the armoury. Nicholas Heath had left for New Zealand, but he donated a six-inch reflecting telescope and under Jeremy Tatum stellar observation and satellite tracking was carried out.

Over the years geography has moved from being an 'arts' to a 'science' subject, and the only rival to the Natural History Society for popularity was the Geography Society. Founded by A.J. Hill in 1946, in its early years it was mainly a meteorological society but with Reginald Ruddock's arrival it became immensely successful with well over a hundred members. Like the N.H.S. it showed too many films at first, and although it was announced in 1960 that this would stop in fact films continued to be the staple of the programme. The society compiled the annual meteorological report (often printed in the magazine), and staged a Prize Day exhibition. Soon field work began with a land use survey of the region in 1955. There were many local visits and regular ones were to Beeding Cement works and Shoreham Harbour, and one particularly interesting one was to the new town at Crawley in 1962. Farming naturally occupied a good deal of the society's time. One year regular visits were paid to Jenkin's Farm to build a picture of the agricultural year, and on another occasion Ruddock and his geographers cycled to Plumpton Agricultural College along the peaceful summer lanes of those days.

III

The 'considerable pause' in building development mentioned by Canon Howard (he became a Chichester canon in 1957) on Prize Day 1956 lasted six months. In February 1957 he told Council that the yield from new buildings had been far better than anticipated, and therefore he was proposing to renew development by enlarging the science and Junior House buildings, and completing the improvement of the houses. Sir Graham Savage of the Industrial and Scientific Fund was invited to Hurst and agreed to help with the science extension built between May and September 1957 at a cost of £5,900. Junior house improvements were carried out between June and December 1957. House improvements took much longer and were not completed until the Scott and Weston legacies made this possible in 1961. But the most important new development proposed was to build a teaching block to be called 'Schools'.

This was first discussed by Council in April 1958, but they were determined to put a ceiling on development. The foundation stone was laid in July 1958 but that autumn Council agreed to leave the single-storey art room to later and to fix a limit of about £28,000 on the proposed building. It was opened on 25 July 1959 by Lieutenant-General Sir John Evetts, although by then the building was in use. An extension to Eagle was completed in the Summer holidays. Although Howard had told Council that the Schools would complete 'the major part of the restoration' of the buildings, Council should have noticed he was already including the possibility of a block of studies in his reports. Eagle house had proved an excellent raiser of revenue— £5,000 more than the estimate in 1955 and Howard wanted another house built. During 1959 he negotiated with Horace Hawkins who wished to sell the Malt House across North field, but planning permission for a house could not be obtained. However, Ruckford House on East field came on the market instead, was bought for £8,250 in 1958, improved at a cost of £2,549, and in September 1959 opened as the nucleus of a new house under John Peters.

That term Hurst's fee income passed £100,000 for the first time and it was clear the decision was the right one. But the new house, to be called Martlet, grew very slowly as problems with the contractor and then with labour and supplies occurred and costs rose. It cost eventually £28,760 and was barely ready for occupation in September 1960. It was not until January 1961 that its full complement of boys could be admitted. But as a house it came together remarkably quickly under Peters' guidance, winning a cup while still in Ruckford and four more in its first two terms. Kenneth Mason left Fleur where Peters succeeded him, and he was helped by an excellent rooker, including David Peters, Christopher Coley, and Michael Boyce, to launch the house successfully.

No sooner were profits assured from the new house than Howard found uses for them. Now it was clear the Junior House would be permanently larger than a hundred boys a further extension was required including a classroom, dormitory, and married master's house. The work began in June 1960, but once again building delays followed which in Howard's view were 'quite scandalous' and the building was not complete until June 1961. In August 1959 a domestic servants' block was started next to the matrons' block but this was not finished until the Lent Term of 1961. Worst of all were the delays in building a study block of 26 studies with masters' accommodation above. This was started in October 1960, but not finished until September 1962, eventually costing some £16,000. Furnishings were partly provided for out of A.E.C. Shippam's legacy to the College, the rest of which went on new squash courts and indoor cricket nets. The study block, Randolph, and the library were seen by Howard as linked together as the sixth-form academic area of the school.

Ruckford House was reconverted (£1,129) into two masters' flats. A flat was made in the west wing. Two masters' houses were built across Ruckford and in January 1963 a £6,000 Colt construction house was erected in the garden of Ruckford House, so that masters' accommodation at last, even if only temporarily, was satisfactory. The art room was built. The headmaster's office and a masters' cloakroom appeared in the older buildings. £1,343 was spent reflooring and reroofing the hall, and fortunately a fire in the crypt in December 1962 was discovered by a boy before it caught hold. Some £2,000 including £400 donated by the Old Johnians was spent to turn Ruckford Fields into playing fields, and R.W. Coley (O.J.) gave the lamp standards to be seen round the buildings. The observatory appeared. The pool obtained a filtration plant. Life became rather like the Year of Victories when people woke up to ask what new building had appeared!

Not everything went according to plan. In the case of a mural planned for the west end of hall this was a good thing. In July 1960 Canon Howard said he wanted a new tuck shop which would contain a range of hobbies rooms and negotiations opened with Gorringes. They wanted a building costed at £8,000, Council would not agree, and in 1962 Howard was complaining 'still nothing has been started'. Nothing came of the idea.

What is perhaps surprising is that Canon Howard's worst proposal affected the chapel and again one can be grateful that expense got in the way and prevented it. Howard had done little for the chapel. After telling Council that on cold days 'we are conscious of no heating at all' in the building, £1,500 was spent on heating. With the last of the Gorham and Parham bequests he had extended seats to the bottom of the altar steps. But Canon Howard was of a generation that had little sympathy for Gothic revival. This was plainly shown when the eagle lectern once so admired by Lowe was removed, and a wooden lectern, donated by R.W. Elmes, took its place. Where the lectern went remains a mystery. Howard did not like Temple Moore's screen in the west arch put in by F.C. Eden, and wished to move it to the south aisle in order to extend seating through the arch. The screen in fact adjusted the proportions of the arch and the seating gain would have been minimal. S.E. Dykes Bower protested but the matter rumbled on and surfaced again under Roger Griffiths.

Chapel did, however, receive one major addition in Canon Howard's time. Between 1961 and 1964 the organ, patched together so many times since 1895, was converted into a grand instrument worthy of any major church with 51 stops and 2,000 pipes rebuilt by Degens and Rippin. At the same time S.E. Dykes Bower designed a magnificent case which was to serve as a memorial to Percy Scott (complete with wrong date!). Among Christopher Dean's earliest contributions to Hurst life was a term in the summer of 1961 devoted to the organisation of the largest fête in the College's history. There was a raffle, too, during the term, and the combined yield of £5,028 11s. 9d. covered the cost of the organ, all but £200 later subscribed by the Old Johnians.

By any standards the buildings put up between 1956 and 1962 constitute a major achievement: Eagle, Martlet, Schools, study, and domestic servants blocks, and two Junior School extensions being just the main new work. Canon Howard told Council in June 1962 he now believed Hurst was 'as well equipped as any comparable school in the country' and Council minuted that in their view the 'clever planning, budgeting, and deft administration' of the headmaster was a major reason for the success. At least £250,000 had been spent by borrowing on anticipated income and repaying quickly as fees rose in amount and numerically, and there had also been at least three useful bequests.

The Growth of Hurstpierpoint under Ronald Howard 2, 1957-1964

Year	Total in senior school	(day boys)	Total in Sixth (3rd year in brackets)		Total in junior school	(day boys)	Total in school	Masters senior junior schools	
1957	274	6	110	(10)	105	37	379	20	5
1958	280	4			107	39	387	21	6
1959	296	6			108	40	404	21	6
1960	328	9	102	(10)	111	34	439	23	6
1961	337	8			117	38	454	25	7
1962	341	7	108	(12)	119	40	460	26	7
1963	329	9	131	(08)	116	37	445	27	8
1964	340	9	143	(10)	122	43	462	27	8

In this and the previous table, (see page 222) figures are taken from the headmaster's reports, and are for the Michaelmas Term, except 1964 which are for the Summer Term.

In 1962 Canon Howard placed before the Council a long memorandum entitled 'Future Needs'. This is a crucial document and the decisions taken upon it under Canon Howard and Roger Griffiths had major consequences. The document contained much but there were four major building proposals. He wished to complete the modernisation of facilities by building new kitchens on the same level as hall and using the rest of the space for domestic quarters. Howard had fought a long battle to improve the food. In 1954 he had appointed a lady steward. A year later Practical Caterers Ltd. took over. They failed and in 1962 Gardners became the caterers. Now Howard wished to end for ever the history of poor Hurst food. Secondly, he wished to build the sanatorium proposed as long ago as 1948 and thus create space for Star studios. Thirdly he wished to build a music school with adequate practice rooms and a chamber concert hall. Lastly, and most importantly, he wished to build a new Red Cross between its present position and the Schools and to use the space to complete equipping the four central houses with studies. If this house had been built adequate dormitory and study accommodation would have been provided for all boys. The estimated cost was £100,000 which was 'fantastic' because 'we have no money'.

This last statement requires some explanation. In 1962 there was still a debt of £25,600 to the bank and this was creating some worries at divisional level where the bursar commented on 'an apparent acceleration in borrowing money'. The most recent buildings had encountered cost problems as inflation and wage rises began to squeeze ever more into the economy. It was proposed by Division and accepted by Council in October 1963 that profits should first of all be used to reduce debt—it was cut to £19,000 that year, and secondly go into a Reserve Fund started that year with £8,000. Council had good reason for their action. In the past Tower's debts had arisen from a sharply changed economic situation. Moreover, Howard pointed out to them that the end of the war-time and post-war 'baby bulge' would first reduce senior school numbers (and they did fall in 1963) and then junior school numbers in the period after 1964. There was the possibility of enlarging the College further—one Council member wanted 450 in the senior school; but Council accepted Howard's argument that this would impose strains on every facility, and that already over 500 people sat down to lunch in the College. It was resolved 'the School should remain at its present size'. Fee increases were taking place. No one objected to the 1962 rises so Council raised them again in 1963 to £462, but Howard was unhappy with this and there were limits to fee increases. Discussion took place on introducing caution money instead of raising fees again.

So all the main ways by which income had been provided for development were not available, and there was a further reason why even if income rose again most of it would have to go on current expenditure. More boys and masters, more facilities, more domestic staff, better living conditions, and new teaching methods all raised expenditure. Masters' salaries, for example, rose from £34,924 in 1960-61 to £49,802 in 1963-1964 with an addition of only three masters. A new language laboratory cost £1,447 in 1963-1964. More buildings and larger playing fields cost more to maintain at the high standard now expected, and some new charges like fire precautions began to appear. Inflation and wage costs were rising so that all the services cost more, and before long the burden of rates and taxes would start to rise as well after a long period of stable tax rates.

How then to raise the money? It was Canon Howard who suggested an appeal. There had been none since 1946 and it was clear from the experience of other schools that they could be most successful—the example of Bradfield College raising £143,000 was cited as a school of comparable size and financial position. The problem was of course that if they wanted to start building promptly they would have to have an assurance about the eventual total to be raised and it was therefore decided to approach a professional firm to organise the appeal. Again it was Canon Howard who had to hand the name of Hooker, Craigmyle and Co. Ltd. because Hooker had been a pupil of his at Marlborough. In October 1962 £900 was voted so that the firm could provide a feasibility study and this was produced in July 1963. The firm had an excellent reputation and had done work for Roedean, Brighton College and Worth locally.

The report said they could have an appeal, but recommended they try for £64,000—the firm's fee incidentally for running the appeal was to be £6,100. A development trust would be set up and the firm would handle the brochures, circulars and other matters. Council agreed to proceed and this of course had a decisive impact on Howard's plan. No part of it was officially abandoned, but it was clear that the total proposed fell far short of what Howard had estimated. Inflation would make it smaller. Announcing a sum lower than you really need is not a good idea—by October 1964 £37,561 had come in and the appeal would eventually more or less reach the target. But as Council felt they had a solid financial basis for proceeding, they started on the developments in Howard's memorandum.

They chose the kitchen development and it was estimated this would cost £36,140. Howard argued this was not new development but maintenance and should come from current expenditure, but this was not possible after the decisions of 1963. Therefore in June 1964 the kitchen improvements were given the go-ahead. It seems odd that the mention of a figure of more than half the total appeal did not alert them to the near impossibility of completing any of the other three proposals, but it did not. There was also another problem. People who give to appeals like to see buildings going up. Schools need heating systems and kitchens, but they are not the stuff of which appeal success is made. With hindsight they should have built the new Red Cross because more depended on it than on the kitchens, desirable though better food undoubtedly was, but the house was the most expensive of the four proposals. Sadly the kitchens turned out to be far more expensive than originally thought. But the decisions had now been made: an appeal, and the first priority, the kitchens, and it was this situation which faced Roger Griffiths when he arrived.

For in May 1963 Canon Howard told Council that he wished to retire. He had been in positions as chaplain and headmaster since 1937, and these jobs were and are stressful because they involve being constantly in the public eye and constantly dealing with individual problems. Howard had been ill on several occasions and perhaps his 1963 illness decided him to go. But it was in fact a fairly obvious and straightforward decision; having launched the appeal and the last building programme, he had achieved, as it is given to few heads to do, all that he had set out in his 1946 memorandum and others. No school is faultless, but we have already seen the measure of success now being achieved in every department of school life, academic, cultural, and sporting. Numbers were up and well housed. Entry standards were up, and the books full to at least 1966. Academic results were up, and the College stood well at Oxford and Cambridge. The choir was nationally known. Rugby, hockey, cricket, squash, athletics, tennis and swimming all did well in the early 1960s. A fine common room of masters had been formed. A Junior School of high reputation was completed. It was the right time to leave.

And there was, perhaps, another reason. Schools are not static—how can they be with a constant injection of young people? Howard had created a system which was conservative, conventional, and disciplined in every aspect of school life—in the houses, in chapel, in the societies, and this system was starting to show signs of cracking at the edges. 'The school,' said the magazine, 'is far from holding radical views,' but although this was true such views were starting to appear. We have seen how sportsmen were becoming more concerned about individual physical fitness and a determination to win, and less concerned about good form and sportsmanship. We have seen how the societies began to respond. The Literary Society was discussing their plays and contemporary work from the 1950s was now a part of their programme. The Film Society tried to show films above the level of Boys' Own Paper. The Shakespeare play was being criticised for outdated productions. Moreover, for the first time magazine reports noticed declines in some society numbers and this included the Sixth Form Society. It was said that the level of floor speeches at debates was starting to decline as there was less interest in this way of putting across ideas.

Howard's 'antennae' as he called them had certainly detected a change in national attitudes, and on Speech Day in 1962 and in 1964 he made one of his main points of criticism the new teenage culture, with remarks such as 'where you find trouble among the young, you nearly always find jazz'. But things were changing. Howard told Council he found younger masters more brusque and less amenable to order. The boys were starting to respond to teenage culture. In 1961 a poem 'Beatnik Poets' was the first 'modern' poem to appear in the magazine, and others followed. 'I stand lost in a lordly maze', wrote one boy. Howard was never lost in a maze of morals or thoughts. He was perfectly clear on such matters, and had he stayed on into the 'swinging' '60s there might have been very different consequences from those that did occur under a very different and young headmaster. By 1962 a Jazz Appreciation Society had appeared, something unknown since the days of Van Praagh's Rhythm Club. In 1963 there was a satirical take off of school life 'That Was the Term That Was' modelled on a contemporary television programme *That was the Week That Was*, and it was no coincidence that one of the leading lights on the jazz scene, David Kennard, was later to be a television producer. In 1963 he produced a 'beat' concert which ended with the 'shattering climax' of a group called The Layabouts.

So the end of the Summer Term came. Canon Howard was given pieces of silverware by the Old Johnians and the common room, and three 19th-century water colours by the boys, and as the shadows lengthened across the outer quad on the evening of 18 July 1964 the era of Canon Howard came to an end. He went to live in Mount Lane, Chichester where as well as his duties as a residentiary canon he was appointed communar, dealing with some financial matters and the qualifications of ordinands. But in 1967 he had to accept an honorary canonry as he decided to return to Sevenoaks to nurse his widowed mother, and after she died to return to live at Hove where he died on 15 June 1995. A bachelor and an ordained man, a believer in the Anglican Church and compulsory worship in its chapel every bit as strong as an Edward Lowe, a disciplinarian whose ultimate sanction was the cane rather than expulsion, and who disciplined masters, parents, and boys alike by his manner and his policies, always in clerical collar, cassock and gown, a man whose life was almost entirely wrapped up in the life of the College, Canon Ronald Howard was one of the last of the great headmasters, as the word 'great' was understood since the days of Arnold and Thring.

Changes in society and in the public schools created a gulf between him and his ideals, and the realities of education even by the late 1960s. Failures he had. Faults he had. But contrary to what one might expect from the picture of him just presented, he was in fact both radical and popular, words he would have scorned. But his whole 19 years saw progress and development. There was no aspect of school life, perhaps no individual, who did not quicken into life under Canon Howard out of desire or necessity. There were few buildings, classes, activities, or statistics that had not shown growth and change. And although he shunned the popular gesture or the soft soaping consultation, Howard listened very well, was kind and thoughtful, and was deeply liked by boys and masters because he did his job so clearly for others and not for himself. If Canon Howard raised himself high by modern standards he did so to raise the school high. He would have been the first to point out, bursars, second masters, governors, prefects, and many others helped to make the 1950s and early '60s so successful. When those plaudits have been given, it remains true that Howard's way was Hurst's way, and his were years in which the clouds were few and the skies often brightened by shining achievements.

THIRTEEN

EYE OF THE STORM
AND SAFE RETURN TO HARBOUR
1964-1986

The Long Headmastership of Roger Griffiths

I suppose that this is perhaps the most difficult time in the history of the public schools to try to be a headmaster.

Roger Griffiths speaking on Prize Day, 1967
The Hurst Johnian, 864/21, September 1967

The Council said that although the discipline in the School was good there was a possibility that the unrest in universities and similar bodies might spread to public schools.

Council Minutes, 12 February 1969

A community spirit is something that evolves over the years. It is not a very fashionable thing to talk of such matters in 1976 when school spirit, the honour of the school etc. seem rather outmoded. Nevertheless I feel most strongly that such emotions are worthwhile, and they are something that I would hope to engender as part of the education offered here. I am an unashamed reactionary who favours change in moderation.

Roger Griffiths Headmaster's Notes
The Hurst Johnian, 888/7-8, 1975-1976

I think that perhaps the word 'stability' is the key word here. So often in our changing and difficult world, we all need something that remains constant. So many people say to me that they like the feel of the School, that there is a good atmosphere, that they have heard that it is a caring place, that I dare to feel there is some truth in it.

Roger Griffiths Headmaster's Notes
The Hurst Johnian, 892/7 1979-1980

Hurst's next headmaster was in the earlier tradition of appointing younger men, and he was clearly intended to point a contrast with the Howard years at a time when change rather than stability was to be the principal theme in public school life. Roger Griffiths' principal achievement was to manage change with as few tears as possible, and to create an era of prosperity and stability during which much that other schools had lost during the 'public school revolution' remained at Hurst.

He was born on Christmas Day 1931 and was educated at Lancing College from 1945 to 1951 where he was a school prefect and head of Teme House. He was a librarian and a sacristan, but his main interest lay in the Modern Languages and Shakespeare Societies of which he was secretary. Roger went to King's College, Cambridge, where he was Prizeman, and obtained his degree in 1954. Two years later he went to Charterhouse as a modern languages master from where he came to Hurst eight years later. Unusually for a headmaster, he had not had experience in a senior position and he has always expressed surprise that he was appointed after an interview in which he gained the impression Council were looking for someone with different qualifications. But for the third time Council chose wisely, and George Lambert has pointed out that Walter Dingwall, Ronald Howard, and Roger Griffiths were three heads in the right place at the right time.

During his interview Roger was told that they were looking for a married man. He put this right when he married Diana Brown in the chapel in April 1966, a marriage followed in time by the birth of three daughters, Elizabeth, Helen, and Caroline. Diana Griffiths proved to be the right headmaster's wife in the right place at the right time. Hurst was more than a little misogynist in the early 1960s but no-one could maintain that attitude for long in her presence. Diana was the first head's wife since Isabel Coombes to play an important and well-liked part in school life. She was involved in chapel and school drama, and was an excellent hostess not only to distinguished guests but to the boys and masters invited to the headmaster's house. Diana clearly put the school first in her life, and helped to make it plain that the Griffiths were a husband and wife head's team.

Roger himself was not an autocrat. Virtually every photograph of him shows him smiling, and his sense of humour, his conviviality, and his obvious enjoyment of social occasions did much to make the wheels of life run smoothly. It was no coincidence that under Griffiths parents' meetings, common room guest nights, wine tastings, the leavers' lunch and Old Johnians sherry party began, and the Old Johnian Ball was held at the College. He was, said one article, 'a very cheerful and friendly person who would get on with most people', and this was vital to the school's success in years when authority was required to unbend. As well as teaching, Roger took part in school life. He produced four Shakespeare plays and compèred three Victorian evenings. He acted in common room plays and Gilbert and Sullivan. He even took part in the bizarre humour of Christmas house parties and submitted himself to a *This is Your Life* in 1984.

He was a sensitive man and diffident about making a show on great public occasions, but he never spared himself, holding frequent assemblies and masters' meetings, chairing the heads of department meeting, and preaching in chapel. Unlike previous heads he had to expose himself to public argument and never shirked this in times when he was the victim of a good deal of unpleasantness because of the division between those who thought he was too reactionary and determined to keep Hurst as he found it; and those who thought he was far too progressive and yielded to pressure too quickly. In such circumstances it is impossible to win but Roger's willingness to keep an open study door and to talk to individuals or committees like the Sixth Form Union was one of the keys to the safe voyage Hurst made through difficult times. No head could have worked harder to know all those in his kingdom and to take a genuine interest in them. He was, said one chaplain, rather like a father abbot with his flock.

Always in his study by 8.15 and rarely seen crossing the field home before 6.30, Roger Griffiths was a hard working headmaster. Quite apart from the new administrative machinery set up he was readily available to anyone, and these quick meetings instead of formally arranged interviews did much to keep things calm and sensible and engender a spirit of unity. People with a grudge did not need to go round complaining or caballing: they could take it to the headmaster. He interviewed and showed round a high percentage of prospective parents and he had no registrar. He rarely missed chapel and even during his sabbatical fiftieth term was there at the start and finish. He attended a high proportion of school matches as well as the dramatic and musical activities which were his main interest. Three times a year he visited all the houses during prep at the time of work reviews, and for many years read out full form orders in assembly. As administration became more complex he had to attend or chair many committees.

But this was only a beginning to Roger Griffiths' full educational life. He was locally governor of several prep schools and of Bishop Otter College, H.M.C.'s representative on the court of Sussex University, and from 1976 a magistrate at Hayward's Heath. He was active nationally in more positions than any head since Edward Lowe. He was on the Academic Policy Committee of H.M.C., and chaired their working party on modern language teaching. He was on the languages committee of the British Overseas Trade Board. He was deputy-chairman of the E.S.P.U. Education Committee and Hurst benefited from an excellent supply of E.S.P.U. scholars from David Holt in 1968 to Gavin Marshall in 1986. Andrew Hull in 1982 was the first Hurst boy to go the other way to the United States. In 1976 Roger Griffiths helped to found the Hurst Group of schools, and he was chairman of the Eastern Division of H.M.C. It came as no surprise that when he left he continued his educational work as membership secretary to H.M.C. for 11 years.

II

Roger Griffiths was certainly to need many of his qualities to deal with an issue which affected Hurst as it did other schools in the late 1960s and early 1970s. Jonathan Gathorne-Hardy's survey of public school history ended with two chapters 'The Monolith Starts to Crumble', and 'The End of the Monolith'. The book, published in 1977, argued that at least in the larger schools all the principal ingredients of what had until then constituted a typical public school had been abolished or seriously undermined. Later, in 1982, John Rae's *The Public School Revolution* claimed the changes began in schools like Marlborough in the mid-1960s, and had fundamentally changed the world of school—a film about Westminster, of which he had been head, certainly indicated a state of affairs that would have given Canon Howard apoplexy! Roger himself in his early years made it clear that the 'monastic community' and the 'remote' public school were no longer tenable, and he was certainly willing to embrace some change. It is less certain whether the changes of that time amounted to anything like a revolution in Hurst's case, even if various elements in the revolution played an important part in school life for a time.

The first part of the revolution was a political threat to the future of public schools. Between 1964 and 1979 there were only four years of Conservative government and during that time the Labour Party moved as far to the left as it had ever done in its history. A new educational establishment emerged with the triumph of the comprehensive principle and the enormous increase in tertiary education, with C.A.T.s, new universities, and expanded further and higher education, and this was hostile to the concept of public schools. By abolishing the direct grant and nearly all grammar schools they opened up a clear divide between the independent and state sectors, and there were those in the government who wished to abolish the charitable status Gladstone had given public schools in 1869. There were considerable discussions on this issue in Council and on Speech Day, and in the magazine frequent statements about the threat to Hurst. In fact the political element in the revolution was a damp squib. Throughout Griffiths' headship there was no government interference with the status of public schools, and no alteration in the academic exams taken by the boys: these came in the late 1980s from an unexpected source! Hurst boys themselves were rarely politically motivated: the Liberals won the 1974 mock election at the school and, apart from an angry brigade with the slogan 'Fight for a Better School' which lasted a few months, radical politics played no part in their lives. Even major youth issues like civil rights, apartheid, C.N.D., or Vietnam opposition played a small part in debates and creative writing.

Inasmuch as there was any revolution, it concerned educational and societal matters: how the school should be run and how boys should be treated. The key struggle was over sovereignty. Where did ultimate power in the school lie and how far could boys and masters share in the 'decision making process'? Hurst was an autocracy and, if formal structures were to be created, in the end these came up with 'non-negotiable' demands which in effect divided sovereignty. Roger Griffiths yielded nothing in essence on this vital point. In September 1965 a Sixth Form Union was created. Four years later a coup d'etat put radicals in charge who wished to affiliate to the N.U.S. but this was the high point of their demands. By 1972 it had become the Sixth Form Committee and its teeth were drawn.

Roger Griffiths was perfectly willing to listen and negotiate up to a point: at the crisis point in 1970 he told the masters he would discuss 'some of the more outdated regulations' with boys' representatives, but he limited discussion to practical changes. George Lambert and Frank Florey, the second masters, were adept at dealing with the S.F.U. Above all the boys themselves brought about its failure as a revolutionary junta.

Many sixth formers were uninvolved. Those that were diverted onto social changes in school life, and in the end spent most of their time on the setting up of a sixth-form common room, and later a bar, its furnishings, coffee machine, opening hours, and time allowed to drink or watch television. By a combination of boy pressure and willingness anyway on the part of the head to change, social life did change at least for the sixth form in these years although, while claiming privileges for themselves, sixth formers showed no wish to abolish duties for younger boys. Whereas in 1964 there was no television, and wirelesses, gramophones and tape recorders were almost completely banned, by the early 1970s radio, tapes, record players, and videos were all part of everyday life for many. Above all watching television had become part of school life, starting in February 1970 when the sixth form were allowed to do so on two nights a week. By 1978 the Randolph had become the television room in common parlance. An attempt to ban amplifiers failed and the quadrangles echoed to Motorhead and Status Quo.

While smoking remained banned and indeed an expellable offence after frequent repeated incidents, the rules on drinking changed. In June 1969 Roger issued regulations for masters and boys drinking together, stating that beer, wine and sherry were acceptable when with housemasters or at away matches but spirits were banned. By 1973 the sixth-form bar was being described in the magazine as 'a place where masters and boys can meet on more equal terms'. Sixth formers were no longer compelled to attend the Saturday film and the Film Society tried to put on contemporary ones although this ran into trouble due to the age range of the audience.

For those who preferred to relax by leaving the premises, school became a much more open place than in the past. All boys were allowed bicycles and a change in February 1969 brought Hassocks and Burgess Hill within bounds. Half terms began in 1965, and in 1966 sixth formers were allowed to visit London and Brighton at weekends with parents' permission. Week-end leave began to spread slowly down from the sixth form to other boys, although houses had a variety of policies. So life became more normal and relaxed and this helped to diffuse the situation.

But not entirely. In Lent Term 1969 the Headmaster's Book refers to 'destructive and irresponsible acts' and in the early 1970s there was a considerable number of these. In Lent Term 1971 there were incidents of 'extreme unpleasantness', and *The Hurst Johnian* remarked that 'the voice of complaint is rampant'. A year later things were little better for there was 'considerable unrest' in the Lent Term and later in the year 'continuous discontent and unrest' was referred to in a report on school music! That term the cane and expulsion were added to sweet reason and this really marked the peak of difficulties. Thereafter trouble was usually only to be found at the end of Summer Terms like those of 1978 and 1979. It is important, too, to remember that these difficulties in part arose not out of revolutionary principle but simple indiscipline, and pressures arising from overcrowding, which in Griffiths's words 'sometimes leads to foolish behaviour'.

Apathy can produce change just as much as agitation, and as young men's interests changed, were focused more outside school, and became more adult, there was a decline in willingness to be involved: the corollary was that idle hands soon turn to trouble. Are societies dying out, asked the magazine in September 1965? At first sight there seems to be some truth in this allegation. The Gramophone Society and some others disappeared. The Geography Society is not reported after Lent Term 1965 or the Sixth Form Society after Lent Term 1966. Robin Lunn's History Society was described as 'about to pass into history' in 1967 and two years later debates were 'moribund'. Although school societies come and go, and we shall see that school activities broadened and increased during these years, there was nevertheless a questioning of the traditional 'society' as it was run in Howard's day, which was part of a wish to opt out of school activities or use them for criticism of 'the higher authorities'. *The Hurst Johnian* described itself as a 'vehicle of a critical society' and its reports did not mince matters, describing one house captain as being 'of the right stamp of tyranny' and another house 'on the slide to depravity'. In May 1966 the magazine said sport 'was carried to absurd extremes' at the school. There were calls for an end to compulsory match watching, practices, and playing only a narrow range of sports. 'The time,' said the magazine, 'has come for a long hard look at the C.C.F.' and here too there were demands for it to be voluntary. Compulsory chapel was criticised and on one occasion in February 1972 there was a 'silent service' demonstration.

There is some evidence, too, that new members of the common room were also less than enthusiastic about what were now called 'traditional' school activities. In the Lent Term of 1967 the magazine referred to 'few enthusiastic masters and secretaries' willing to run societies, and next year Roger himself appealed in the magazine for boys to 'adopt a less apathetic approach', while he had to appeal in the common room a little later for masters to take on debates, the play and swimming among other activities.

When we come later to look at the developments in school life under Roger Griffiths we shall see that this aspect of the revolution, too, passed without doing too much damage. By the late 1970s a number of new activities occupied boys' time and a number of new societies catered for more adult interests among senior boys. Activities which had been criticised were flourishing, and with some flexibility many remained compulsory. Nor should it be forgotten that even during the short-lived age of apathy some school activities like drama and music experienced an expansion and not a decline.

The aspect of the teenage revolution which caused more time to be wasted and tempers to flare was not about fundamentals of authority or the pattern of school life. It was a battle over appearance and social behaviour. Such matters are always part of school life but undoubtedly they reached a pitch of intensity during these years, and in some cases became sufficient for boys to leave. Griffiths wittily observed on Speech Day 1966 that young men were interested in 'beer, ciggys, motor bikes, girls and A Level', and school only provided one of these. Drinking, smoking including 'pot', sex, teenage driving, raves and weekend parties, lack of censorship in speaking, reading matter, or films, and rock, punk, and metal music were not part of the majority of boys' lives, but they were certainly the main interest both of troublemakers, and at the other end of the scale, intelligent sixth formers, who were part of the swinging '60s, and not characters in a P.G. Wodehouse novel. To the older generation all this was alarming. The boys seemed to wish to grow up by being different from adults rather than conforming to the norms of the past. They were, according to their critics, badly dressed, resentful of authority, indifferent to good manners. We are faced, said Roger, with a 'radical disposal of the basic tenets by which we live'. He saw a new 'I-Society' based on 'self-centredness and complete selfishness' rather than self-fulfilment and expression. He stated that he was not going to give way, and there 'will be a basic set of disciplines and a code of behaviour' at Hurst.

Because Howard's Hurst had been so conservative it was inevitable that the contrast with new ways would create alarm, perhaps unnecessary alarm, and certainly other schools went much further than Hurst in compromising with the new mood. An advertisement for a clothing catalogue from 47A Carnaby Street in the 1967 school magazine symbolises one of the main areas of conflict—dress and hair. If one compares pictures of boys in, say, 1962 with those in 1972 it is clear that a sea change has taken place even when games or school uniform is being worn; of course, outside school normal dress and school uniform parted company whereas in the past they had been very similar. Hair in particular caused problems because a school 'cut' could not be disguised outside, making boys feel slightly ridiculous among their age-group.

But although on one occasion Griffiths remarked that 'appearance is a relatively minor point' it was not treated as such during these years. Long hair was denounced as dangerous and unhygienic and later short hair was also condemned. Crew cuts were described by Griffiths as a 'form of exhibitionism which is pointless and quite hideous'. School uniform was, however, modified considerably and the petty rules in the 1964 school captain's book largely disappeared. Grey jackets or blue blazers replaced herringbone tweed. Terylene replaced woollen trousers and in 1969, ten years after the rest of Britain, 'no turn ups' were allowed, although flares were banned. Stiff collars were replaced by soft ones, but button-down collars and colours were banned. Raincoats and duffle coats were joined by navy (but not army) greatcoats. In 1970 elastic sided shoes (but not boots) were permitted, followed by a ban on 'Doc Martens'. Scarves and track suits were allowed for all boys instead of just team members, and there was more casual wearing of sports clothes—although banned in hall in 1974. From 1978 casual dress was allowed from four o'clock on Saturdays, if boys were in school for the weekend, and it was also allowed to boys travelling to and from school and on school outings. The trouble was that this initiated a fresh battle over what 'sensible' casuals were. The Headmaster's Book in these years bears witness to the banning of item after item including moccasins, bootees, bracelets, ear-rings, fur or velvet collars, tie-pins, cutaways, and Bermuda shorts.

Having looked at some of the main aspects of the 'revolutionary' years it would appear that there was, apart from a few concessions, no revolution at Hurst. Power remained in the hands of the establishment. School life continued to revolve round the same societies and sports as in the past. The pressure for individual rights in dress, hair, participation in school life, and observance of social customs had been resisted and defeated. By 1975 Council were able to say how pleased they were with the discipline of the College, and Roger himself wrote in *The Hurst Johnian* about a more pleasant and co-operative atmosphere in the College.

But this would be too simplistic a view. Griffiths's headship spanned nearly a quarter of a century, and change was therefore inevitable and real enough. Much that had been compulsory and unquestioned was now a matter of choice and discussion. Relationships which had been formal and distant were now more fluid and friendly. Christian names, for example, were universal amongst boys and between masters instead of surnames. Photographs of houses and sports teams show a variety of dress and hair unseen since Edwardian days; and the masters, too, sported beards and sideburns in several cases. Fewer masters wore gowns and fewer went to chapel. School was therefore, firstly, a less regimented and rigid place. Secondly, the 'I-Society' of which Roger had spoken had appeared. It was no longer enough to appeal to school, house, and team spirit; to the collective virtues. Instead boys were urged to do things for their own benefit: to play sport to be fit, to join societies to enjoy themselves rather than be enlightened, and to take on positions of responsibility because they looked good on application forms. Thirdly, there was conformity but not enthusiasm by the great majority. For a nucleus of boys and masters Hurst remained the traditional boys' boarding school, but for many attendance at chapel or matches was a chore rather than a duty, and there was a steadily growing indifference to holding positions of authority, marked, for example, by the failure of secretaries to write reports of societies and sports, or houses to maintain house books in detail. There had been a change, difficult perhaps to pin down but nevertheless real for all that, and Jonathan Gathorne-Hardy's two chapter headings turn out to have been an accurate reflection of what took place: not a revolution, but a transition at the end of which the school of Cooper, Coombes and Howard no longer existed.

III

There was a much more serious issue facing Hurst in Griffiths's early years, and one which posed a genuine threat to its progress. It was inflation. From two or three per cent in the early 1960s—when we saw it having a small impact on Howard's Hurst—it rose to historic heights, reaching 25 per cent in 1975-1976. Those concerned with running the school found themselves in the strange position that annual fee income rose from £185,758 in 1964 to £1,082,970 in 1979, but throughout most of that period there was a shortage of money for long-term development, and constant annual pressure on running costs from every quarter. By 1967 the bursar was reporting 'a period of financial stringency', or 25 more boys were needed to meet rising costs. By March 1974 Roger was telling parents 'the present inflation throughout the country has hit us very hard'. In June that year Council referred to a 'serious economic situation' and 1975 was the only year in school history when fees rose twice. The bursar's report in 1976 makes grim reading, saying fees would have to rise again to meet the inevitable rises in running costs. In one year these rose 18 per cent.

Although parents were affected by rising costs and taxes on both income and business, the economic crisis facing Roger Griffiths was not one of numbers. After the predicted slight fall due to birth-rate patterns, numbers rose throughout the period apart from a fall for a time in the junior school. But taking in larger numbers created financial problems as well as solving them. Because of inflation long term planning became more or less impossible and, although there were buildings put up in this period, there was no chance of the kind of sustained development possible under Howard to cater for the increased numbers. Secondly, costs rose quantitatively just at a time when they were rising qualitatively as well. Domestic standards were rising—bed linen, for instance, was changed once a week instead of once a month. Educational facilities were becoming more complex. Nuffield Science cost £7,500 to introduce, for instance, and when a legacy was left by Mrs. Drummond Roberts of £3,000 in 1969 this was quickly used up for adding machines, overhead projectors, a record player and other such items. More masters were needed in both schools. More domestic and administrative staff were needed and they in turn required facilities. Equipment, furnishings, repairs, and main services all increased in price. The oil price-rise in 1973 was particularly unfortunate because Hurst had converted from coke to oil and now embarked on a conversion to gas in 1977. More school trips meant three mini-buses instead of one. And behind the scenes rates, insurance, and the cost of statutory requirements like fire precautions and the first Health and Safety at Work Act (1976) had to be met. Selective Employment Tax had to be paid from 1966.

The task of grappling with this new situation fell first of all, of course, on Roger himself, who had to abandon cherished schemes and put up with educational conditions of which he did not approve. Three chairmen of governors, Brian Thomas, Sir Richard Mathias, and Sir Desmond Heap span the inflationary era. Clifford Freeman survived into it and was replaced in 1966 by Ian McNeil as the divisional representative on the Council. Two bursars, Major R.J.

48 A meeting of the College Council, 10 February 1981, chaired by Sir Desmond Heap in the library. On his left the bursar, Commander Charles Bricknell, and on his right, R.N.P. Griffiths, Headmaster.

Treyer-Evans and J.F. Collins, had the unenviable task of often saying 'no' to perfectly reasonable requests because of financial restraint. In 1973 important changes took place in the way development was handled. Michael Gray was appointed Clerk of the Works to deal with the maintenance of the buildings from current income so that Council could look at longer term developments. A Development Committee, renamed House and development committee in 1977, was set up under Admiral Sir Frank Mason, and this ensured a more professional approach to future improvements. But it was not until Griffiths's later years that year-on-year improvements started, and Griffiths, his last bursar, Commander Charles Bricknell (1978-1988), and his last chairman of governors, Sir John Barnes (1983-1987) were able to enjoy the fruits of rising real income at long last and, hand in hand with Chilton, Waters and Stutchbury as architects, provide a range of high quality and long anticipated buildings.

The first effect of the great inflation was to throw Howard's plan off course. Because numbers were falling for a time fee income was not buoyant in Griffiths's early years, rising only £37,200 in his first four years. The appeal did not reach its target because the money was not being spent on a visibly interesting improvement but on the kitchen development, and this proved enormously expensive. The final cost, including the fixtures, was £59,900 and, although this enabled cafeteria service to start in September 1968 with some economies, it also put paid to any of the other three proposals in Howard's plan.

Some building and improvement was carried out during the rest of the 1960s, but much of it was necessitated by rising numbers or new school functions rather than dictated by any precise plan. The Junior School was increased in size for the third time to provide for 20 more boarders and 10 more day boys. The science building continued to send forth its unsightly pseudopodia including a projects laboratory, new physics and biology rooms, and a green house. In the main buildings a masters' dining room came into use in 1966. The music department was moved from its hut by the gymnasium to the former tuck box store, renamed the 'Albert Hut' in 1968. The same year the eastern half of the crypt became the technical activities centre. Two important developments took place. In 1968 a new sanatorium was opened and in 1969 South field became an all-weather pitch.

With the return of Conservative government in 1970 Council clearly believed that financial stability, too, might return and began once more to plan for the future. It was agreed to have an appeal, this time for £100,000. After previous experience it was decided to run the appeal internally. The Friends of Hurst were reconstituted to act as trustees and have remained in existence ever since, and in the Summer Term of 1971 the appeal was launched with a fête. Looking back now it seems strange that the appeal was still pitched at a fairly small sum particularly in view of the inflationary experience of the 1960s. Frank Florey was in charge and within four months over £40,000 had come in. Tragically in 1972 fund raising efforts led to the death of Mark Palmer returning from a sponsored walk. The appeal continued until 1976 and raised £109,957.

In February 1972 Council began discussions of long term plans. But there was a complication. Numbers had risen sharply. The total in the school had gone from 453 in 1964 to 533 in 1973, and only 79 of these were day boys. 331 were senior boarders and 140 of them in the sixth form. Accommodation was strained to breaking point with an impact on discipline and social life as each house had to find more space. Upper and lower cloisters in Chevron and Shield were taken over for accommodation, Star gained from the departure of the sanatorium, Eagle from the building of a housemaster's house, and Fleur de Lys and Red Cross took over the study block exclusively. But Red Cross with its scattered rooms was in an unsatisfactory position as a result of the non-implementation of Howard's plan for a new house.

A new house was out of the question, and it was clear that Red Cross would need to occupy the area of the new library. Council's first discussions proposed a building to include a modern library, two seminar rooms, two classrooms, book store and office which in time would have developed into an excellent resources centre. However, such a building would have taken some time to design and build, and the accommodation problem was pressing. Indeed, in one memorandum (marked confidential) it was proposed that as soon as the library was moved the area should sleep 21 boys from different houses instead of being Red Cross day rooms. Clearly this pressing problem led to a change of mind, and in October the original proposals were replaced with an ingenious scheme.

A Colt-designed headmaster's house was to be built on the far side of North field. His former house would be a new library and Red Cross would obtain its day rooms. The scheme was approved and carried out. Clearly it had unfortunate repercussions. Hurst returned to the position of having an unsatisfactory library. Too many boys remained crowded in the central buildings, preventing the modernisation of the four central houses. But it is important to bear in mind that in the 1970s inflation bit deeply into the value of the appeal and, had the bold step of a new house or the new library block been taken, it might have led to financial embarrassment. And at the time with the discipline issue uppermost in many minds it was felt essential to improve living conditions which at times resembled the lower deck of a man o'war at sea for several months. It was an unhappy decision but the inevitable one in the circumstances.

Roger told parents in 1974 that renewed inflation was preventing development. The appeal money steadily lost its value as it came in over nearly five years, and the money was mainly used for modernising parts of the older houses, setting up the projects laboratory in the science building, and extensions to the Junior School. It was not until 1978 that Council could turn to development once again, and the first project was the construction of a music school, entirely justified by the musical reputation of the College and opened by Lord Denning in 1979. The impressive design and good quality materials were in marked contrast to those used in some buildings in the past, and the building proved to be the curtain raiser to a decade when the builders were rarely absent particularly, it seemed, during exam time. Besides the music school came two new classrooms in 1979. In 1980 the art room was extended and a computer room installed in the former kitchen quarters of Star. Three new tennis courts appeared. In 1981 a covered swimming pool with changing rooms brought to an end the long period when swimming has been in the doldrums. Changing rooms were added to the squash courts. A legacy from David Wilson (OJ) was used to provide a skilfully concealed fire door in the south wall of the chapel. In 1982 an equally skilfully designed link building joined Star to the main building, providing studies for three houses, the headmaster, and second master, and enabling a careers room and library to be created. Next year the 1934 tuck shop was moved to East field as a much needed sports pavilion and a multigym was installed there in 1985. A new tuck shop and school shop were tastefully added to the north end of Star. Martlet was extended to provide more studies. Between 1981 and 1984 Red Cross and Shield were modernised in their day-room areas, and all houses were provided with separate bed units in the dormitories. A programme of re-roofing and boiler replacement spread through the buildings. A substantial legacy from Norman Cartledge (OJ) was largely used to buy 22 acres of field to the north of the College now known as Lowe fields.

Then after a pause came the most important building since the early 1960s. For years the 1950 science building had developed a bewildering variety of additions, and yet remained unsuitable on safety and teaching grounds. Designed by Chilton, Waters and Srutchbury, and built by McKellan and Westermann, an impressive building was added to the front of the old one, more or less doubling science accommodation and paving the way later for the moving of the computer and craft, design and technology departments into the same building. Sir Frank Mason was a particularly enthusiastic backer for the building and it was he who persuaded royalty to return to Hurst for the first time since 1956. On 18 May 1985 a helicopter brought Prince Philip to North field to declare the new building open.

Hurst still did not have an all-purpose hall for exams and sport and in the 1980s, as economic recovery nationally gathered strength and the College's own fee income rose from £1,082,970 to £2,378,282 between 1979 and 1986, Old Johnians, parents, and some masters met in November 1983 to start an appeal for a sports hall. A committee was set up to raise £200,000 and successively led by Roger Saxby, Brian Renn, and Malcolm Reid did much good

49 H.R.H. Prince Philip with the headmaster at the opening of the Frank Mason laboratories, 16 May 1985.

work in focusing attention on the issue and raising some money. But, although Council in February 1984 gave their blessing to the project, they were wary about committing money while the science building was the main capital expenditure—a wise decision because V.A.T. substantially increased the cost of the Frank Mason building. Delays occurred, not least when the plan to build the hall on Manyweathers pitches fell through, and by the time a building on the South Woods site had been designed the cost had risen towards £300,000. In March 1985 the sports hall appeal was launched; it was to raise about £93,000 leaving this as the first building problem to face the new headmaster.

Underpinning the fight against inflation and ensuring the successful development of the school throughout Griffiths's headship was the rise in fees and the rise in numbers. Whatever the difficulties caused by the substantial expansion of the College, including the disciplinary issue already mentioned, and the question of falling academic standards to be discussed in the next section, it has to be remembered that this expansion was economically essential and justified on those grounds alone. The fee rises during the great inflation were as follows:

Selected Years		senior school		junior school		£s p.a.
		boarding	day	boarding	day	
1968		567	408	444	294	
1974		960	750	750	480	(105, day girls)
1975	1st	1200	999	975	705	
	2nd	1350	1125	1155	825	
1976		1500	1245	1275	915	
1977		1800	1500	1500	945	
1979		2130	1755	1770	1140	

50 A Junior School tea party.

The accompanying table gives the annual details of the rise in numbers. Apart from a dip in 1964-1966 senior school numbers rose to the highest so far recorded in the school's history—421 in 1985. Similarly junior school figures rose to their highest ever at 188 in 1974. The sixth form reached 147 in 1980, exceeding its highest numbers under Canon Howard for the first time. There was only one substantial fall. In the junior school numbers declined from their peak to 112 in 1985. Throughout the period both Roger Griffiths and Robin Paul remained strong advocates of boarding education and inevitably day pupils mean smaller fees. Here the trends are interesting. In the senior school between 1978 and 1986 there was a rise and then fall in day boy numbers which peaked at 53 in 1981, and then returned to where they had been at the start of the rise, at 35, clearly reflecting the improvement in study provisions in the 1980s. In the Junior School, with an occasional slight fall, the trend was towards a day boy increase which peaked in 1982 at 76. But the important figure is that, whereas in 1964 there were 118 in the school and only 39 boarders, by 1986 of the 115 in the school 65 were day pupils. This was a significant long-term trend which would have to be addressed by the next head: should Hurst continue to remain a strong advocate of traditional boarding education at all levels?

III

Increasing numbers meant changes in admission policy. Roger obtained permission from Council to vary the number of day boys above the ceiling of 10 fixed earlier, and later to vary Common Entrance requirements. Fast stream entry into the Remove stopped and over the years the required pass mark fell; something which was admitted to parents in December 1970. By then fifty per cent was required in the main subjects, and later boys were admitted with quite low marks. With the inevitable increase in a less academically minded 'tail' of boys, discussion began on whether or not standards were falling.

For a time during the mid-1960s there was a decline in A Level results and in 1969 Griffiths introduced three work reviews a year mainly because of 'our own rather weak A Level grades'. In fact, the decline did not last. By 1971 a pass rate of 78 per cent was recorded, and this rose through the years to as high as 89 per cent in 1985, seven subjects recording 100 per cent passes that year. At O Level there was a small decline over the years in the pass rate from 82 per cent in 1971 to 77 per cent in 1985 but, as the director of studies never tired of pointing out, these were good results given the rise in numbers and the ability level of many entrants. Hurst did very well by the boys it received during Griffiths's headship. Nevertheless there was considerable criticism over the years that sixth formers in private study and prep in their studies lacked a work ethic and that the number of top grades was often low in some subjects.

Twenty-Two Years Growth Under Roger Griffiths, 1964-1986

Year	Senior School	(day pupils)	Sixth Form (3rd year in brackets)	Junior School	(day pupils)	Total in School	Sixth Form Day Girls	Staff Sen.	Jun.	Gross Fee £ Income
1964	335	7		118	39	453		28	9	185,758
1965	327	7		132	43	459		30	10	190,478
1966	307	8	123 (13)	143	45	450		30	11	198,494
1967	320	8		143	40	463		30	11	210,732
1968	310	11		163	47	473		31	12	226,958
1969	326	13	140 (16)	166	48	492	3	32	12	242,367
1970	340	18	132 (18)	166	41	506	4	34	13	261,190
1971	330	20		168	39	498	5	36	13	287,569
1972	338	17		176	49	514	6	35	12	288,647
1973	356	25		177	54	533	6	35	13	355,847
1974	358	26	141 (08)	188	63	546	5	38	13	440,246
1975	365	27		180	54	545	7	34	12	545,680
1976	380	24		180	71	560	7	34	12	701,074
1977	397	27		176	74	573	8	33	13	827,339
1978	402	35	142 (10)	178	70	580	9	38	13	970,567
1979	407	47		165	75	572	11	41	13	1,082,970
1980	407	51	147 (06)	165	72	572	9	43	13	1,791,221
1981	399	53		147	71	546	2	42	12	1,528,901
1982	396	42	143 (05)	144	76	540		42	12	1,777,799
1983	387	40	132 (02)	143	68	530		43	12	1,958,728
1984	402	40	133 (01)	130	63	532		43	12	2,084,584
1985	421	38	126	112	52	533		43	11	2,217,899
1986	418	35		115	65	533		43	12	2,378,282

The numbers are for the start of the Michaelmas Term, and vary during the year. A third year sixth ended in 1984 as Oxbridge entrance exams and scholarship exams disappeared by 1986. The girls are included in the senior school day pupil totals. Music staff are included in staff.

Throughout the period the basic form of the exams remained unchanged with O, A and S Level being taken mainly with the Oxford and Cambridge Board. There were some innovations in syllabus: Nuffield Science and SMP Mathematics, for instance, and a number of new subjects including physical science or classical civilisations. An element of project work was injected in some subjects. Teaching methods, too, showed some changes as the presence of a language laboratory, and the projects laboratory showed. Films and videos were shown more frequently in class time, overhead projectors appeared in most rooms, and the development of photocopiers released a flood of prepared material in lessons. But in spite of these modifications teaching at Hurst remained traditional in its methods, and masters and boys were comfortable with syllabuses which changed little over the 35 years of the G.C.E. examinations, and which favoured schools which had small classes, plenty of opportunity for extra work, and special repeater classes in the evenings.

Roger Griffiths wished to introduce greater flexibility through options allowing boys to drop some subjects at O Level and take a wider variety at A Level. In 1967 the number of periods per week was increased and an options scheme introduced which has formed the basis of the timetable ever since. Its introduction enabled, for example, German to be a second language, and all juniors to take biology, chemistry and physics. Very few new subjects were introduced over the years. In 1965 economics and Spanish started. Physical science and electronic systems came in on the science side, but the main change here was the start of computers. Although George Lambert introduced computing to the sixth form as early as 1971 it was in fact the arrival of Richard Hurley in 1980, soon joined by David Virgo, that established computing science as a subject. On the arts side the major change was the revival of classics under Nicolas Chisholm and then Mark Allbrook, achieved by introducing classical civilisations at O Level and ancient history at A Level. Under Norman Rechter A Level art began and his successor David Hopkins brought in the history of art and developed design. Masters for pottery (1973), woodwork (1974), and silversmithing (1979) appeared, and under James Combe woodwork flourished greatly from 1979.

In 1976 John Peters became Director of Studies, a post he held until 1992, and he was responsible for a fully professional approach to academic matters and later for the overseeing of the end of the G.C.E. era, and its replacement by G.C.S.E. and the National Curriculum. Under Roger Griffiths his main achievement was to broaden sixth-form education with a general studies programme involving exams. The programme got under way in September 1977 with subjects like Business French and German, and over the next few years added a variety of subjects including science and society and world affairs, boys taking A/O exams in many of the subjects. A fast mathematics stream was re-introduced by Keith Weber and Remove boys began to take O Levels. A system of repeating A Level internal exams to raise standards came in during the early 1980s.

Where change was most marked was in the composition and aims of the sixth form. The phenomenon of the fifth-form leaver appeared in greater numbers than in the past. Often dictated by financial reasons, leaving in the fifth form became popular as sixth form colleges and a range of other institutions began to provide alternative places to take A Level, and because of their size a range of new A Levels like business studies or law. The mood of resentment against rules was always strongest at the fifth-form stage, and some of the departures, at least, were welcomed although by no means all. By the late 1970s about twenty boys left after O Level.

Those entering the sixth form did so in an increasingly different mood from the days of Canon Howard. Then academic achievement had focused on Oxbridge, and the top 25 per cent likely to obtain places at what were then seen as the 'top' provincial universities. Hurst remained a serious contender in the Oxbridge stakes throughout Griffiths's headship although less so than under Howard. During his 22 years at least 85 boys entered Oxbridge of whom about fifty went to Cambridge. Entry varied from year to year being good to 1968, particularly good in 1971-1972 and 1976-1977, and improving during 1979 to 1986 when there were 16 successes. But here changes came from outside. Oxbridge abandoned exhibitions and scholarships except for music. They abandoned detailed written entrance examinations, and entry was to be during the second year in the sixth form largely as a result of interview and reference. This has serious consequences. It ended S Level. It ended the third year sixth by 1986. It meant that boys wishing to enter Oxbridge had to do extra work while coping with A Level, and try for entry without the advantage of a year's extra maturity. This inevitably all affected Hurst's candidates' chances adversely.

Moreover, those entering the sixth form were not, by and large, seeing themselves as potential Oxbridge candidates in academic terms. The mood of resentment against traditional institutions led able boys to look elsewhere for subjects like sociology. The pattern of higher education changed in 20 years from a small élitist group of universities into a wide range of new universities, C.A.T.s (to become polytechnics), and expanded further and higher educational institutions. It became possible to enter degree courses with two D and one E passes as well as with two As and a B, and this reduced the incentive to see A Level as the basis for wider academic enquiry. It became both fashionable and necessary to enter higher education and a wide range of new qualifications appeared. By 1976 sixth-form leavers were going to Oxbridge, traditional universities, Sandhurst, Dartmouth, agricultural colleges and medical schools as in the past, and also to polytechnics, technical colleges, and further education colleges.

This change led in turn to the development of a careers department. For Oxbridge candidates George Lambert and then Christopher Dean provided guidance, and in 1970 the first preliminary visit was held. David Hughes took charge of careers in 1968, and the first open day was held two years later. John Evans succeeded him in 1975 and became director of careers in 1991. Based on the careers room a new 'society' and a new subject joined school life with conferences, lectures, visits, interviews, seminars, films, and videos on careers. The first careers evenings were held in 1978-1979. In 1978 Challenge of Industry started which later became Understanding Industry. In 1980 came the first televised interviews and the first seminars on higher education and industry for parents and boys together. John Evans and his fellow masters produced a highly effective careers organisation which by 1982-1983 was running 32 events a year. Inside the school the Red Cross business club (1983) was the first of a number of activities designed to stimulate interest in the commercial world. Industrial sponsorships were eagerly sought, and in 1986 thirteen boys started executive shadowing courses. The Old Johnians did much to help—at one event, for example, in October 1985, 30 were present to talk about various careers. Gerald Brigg edited the first Hurst business directory in 1986.

With the rise in numbers and in the variety of subjects came a substantial increase in common room numbers: in the senior school from 28 in 1964 to 43 in 1986, and in the Junior School from nine to 13, totals which have only increased slightly since. As late as 1966 25 out of 30 senior school masters were Oxbridge and the other five were from London or Bristol. But the difficulties in recruiting increased. As tertiary education expanded and the educational establishment frowned on independent schools, there was an increasing reluctance among those from top universities or with higher degrees to enter teaching, although this was partly compensated for in public schools able to recruit discontented academic teachers from the declining grammar school sector of the state system. By 1979 the number of Oxbridge masters had fallen to 12 in the senior and one in the junior school, totals which remained more or less the same subsequently.

Although this change did not mean a fall in teaching standards it did start to break up the homogeneity of the common room and, as masters who had no experience of public or grammar schools arrived, there was an increased questioning of traditions and some reluctance to see school life as all-embracing. Teaching began to be affected by inflation, too, and by matters like equal pay for women. Masters began to join the A.M.M.A. By the early 1970s there was considerable discontent on salaries, fanned to some extent by an increase in housemasters' salaries after it was found in 1972 that Hurst lagged behind comparable schools. To meet criticism a salaries committee was established in 1975 with Hugh Thomas, Rodney Jackson, and John Peters serving on it together until 1987, and in 1981 Brian Renn became the first masters' representative on the Council. The substantial Houghton Award to teachers helped matters considerably but the rises meant that over 70 per cent of annual income was going on salaries and wages.

When Griffiths took over there were scarcely any special titles among the staff: housemaster, second master, head of science, and director of music were the only four, but with the need to keep effective masters came the creation of allowances and titles. Among those created under Griffiths were director of drama (1972), director of art (at the end of 1973), and director of studies (1976) held first of all by William Alban, Arthur Morgan, and John Peters respectively. Masters in charge of subjects became heads of department with an expanded number of allowances. There were some assistant posts, like assistant house tutor or assistant director of music. The title of senior assistant master was created and first held by George Lambert in 1969. And there were two demographic changes in the common room. By 1972 there were only eight single members of staff in the senior school, and this figure was the same in 1986 even including the younger members. Secondly, in September 1968 Dr. Rosemary Thomas was the first woman member of the common room (if temporary war-time appointments are excluded) and she was joined by Christiane Bawtree (April 1969), Joan Peters (April 1971), Mrs. M.J.W. Taylor (September 1971), and others who stayed for a short time. There were more women teachers in the common room in 1976 than in 1986, and in this context it should be remembered that day girls were admitted to the sixth form in small numbers from 1969 to 1981. Joan Peters became tutor for girls in 1972. Perhaps more surprisingly the Junior School staff still had only three women out of 13 teachers in 1986.

But if there were such changes the most important characteristic of the common room was the continued stability created by Canon Howard to which Roger Griffiths was to make considerable additions. The College continued to have the services of Ivor Wilding to 1967, Michael Bailey to 1968, Kenneth Mason to 1973, Horace Holloway to 1974, and Robert Bury to 1976, and tragically lost those of Robin Gregory by unexpected death in October 1971. Frank Florey and George Lambert continued to 1980, William Alban to 1982, and Nicholas Heath, who returned in 1974, retired in 1987. Four of the pre-Griffiths appointments went on beyond him. Christopher Guise and Reginald Ruddock retired in 1988, although the latter became the first registrar until 1991. Christopher Dean retired in 1992 and John Peters in 1993. Griffiths was well served in the senior posts where Mason, Bury, Lambert, Florey, and Ruddock succeeded as second masters, Ruddock was acting head for two terms in 1981 and 1986, and later Peters became second master under his successor, Simon Watson.

For his first 12 years Griffiths had a first-rate group of housemasters to cope with the difficulties of the 'revolutionary' years. Two, George Hill and Ronald Bawtree, went on to be headmasters, and the other five—Peters, Ruddock, Dean, Guise and Thomas—were all long-serving masters. It was unfortunate that of the two replacements for Hill and Bawtree, Nicholas Heath and David Hughes, Heath had to retire earlier than expected from his house. So too did Christopher Guise and Hugh Thomas, and among the replacements there was far less unanimity of purpose. Some favoured the cane: others did not. Some favoured relaxed dress and bounds: others did not, and it is significant that in September 1982 a new Saturday evening detention was begun so that all masters could punish boys for offences previously almost exclusively housemasters' concern. Similarly at house prefect level, while some continued excellent others neglected responsibilities and emphasised their privileges on occasion with a certain amount of bullying. The house system was less monolithic by Griffiths's last years and subject to considerable criticism by those who were not running it.

It is a truism that some masters who are only in the school for a few years make excellent contributions and move on, particularly if they are in their first post, but it is equally true that

51   The common room in 1973. Seated, from left to right: H.R. Thomas, R.T. Ruddock, H.R. Holloway, R.E. Bury, K. Mason, Roger N.P. Griffiths, headmaster from 1964-1986, G.E. Lambert, S.F. Florey, J.H. Peters, W.M. Alban and Sister Winifrid E. Berry.

without a continuing core of masters holding senior posts, aware of the school's traditions and its pitfalls and providing continuity of approach in chapel or classroom, a sense of unease spreads in a school. This was certainly true of some public schools by the 1970s but not of Hurst. The common room remained remarkably trouble free and united. It sprouted new activities like common room plays, Gilbert and Sullivan, and occasional reviews, and started regular common room guest night dinners. Masters continued to be 'all-rounders', with senior and even quite venerable looking members taking games, and there was never a lack of volunteers by the early 1980s. By and large Roger's choice of new men proved exactly right and, by the last ten years of his headship, although of course there were those that could not keep order, there was no school activity in class and out of it which was not run effectively. If one compares the 1976 and 1986 common rooms, 17 staff were still in place and many continued to be so under Simon Watson. Of the 43 staff he inherited, 21 were there when he left in 1995, although the depression years of the early 1990s had reduced movement between schools when the number of advertised posts fell sharply. In some subjects like geography, biology, history, and later classics, a decade or more passed with only one staff change. The list that follows summarises both the stability of the staff and the range of activities they ran.

Staff Appointed by Roger Griffiths Who Stayed More Than 10 Years As Heads of Department or Housemasters

Name	Year Appointed	Year Retired (compiled 1997)	Some Posts Held, and Sports Taken
David Hughes	1965		Second Master, Housemaster, Head of economics, Careers Master, i/c time table, rugby
Rodney Jackson	1967	1988	Head of Chemistry, Housemaster, salaries committee, swimming
Nicholas Searls	1967		Director of Music, Housemaster, Senior Assistant Master, cricket
Hugh Thomas	1968	1991	Head of Geography, Housemaster, salaries, fixtures, games committees, hockey
Michael Mance	1969		Head of Modern Languages, Housemaster, C/O Corps, cricket
Gerald Buss	1970	1996	Chaplain, Housemaster, general studies, history
Kenneth Ralph	1970		Head of Biology, House Tutor
Joan Peters	1971	1996	Modern Languages, Tutor for girls
David Clark	1972		Housemaster, First Housemaster of St John's House, English, rugby, athletics
Robin Perry	1972	1993	Housemaster, project work, electronic systems, librarian
Keith Grant	1973		Head of History, House Tutor, stage crew, librarian, editor of *Hurst Johnian*
John Evans	1974		Housemaster, first day Housemaster, physics, Director of Careers
Nicolas Chisholm	1976	1988	Head of Classics, Housemaster, editor of *Hurst Johnian*
Robin Williamson	1978	1997	Head of English, debates, cricket, rugby, hockey
Peter King	1979	1996	Head of History, editor of *Hurst Johnian*, cross-country, archivist
Mark Allbrook	1980	1994	Head of Classics, Housemaster, cricket
Richard Hurley	1980		Head of I.T., House Tutor, computer science
David Hopkins	1982		Director of Art, House Tutor,
Neil Morris	1983		Housemaster, Director of Drama, English, editor of *Hurst Johnian*
Martin Pulsford	1983		Director of Studies, Head of Science, Head of Physics
Christopher Gray	1985		Housemaster, history, rugby

Other long serving masters appointed by Roger Griffiths were Michael Grime (1969), Vincent Thomas (1977), Richard Cooke (1979), James Gowans (1981), Nicholas Edey (1983), and Richard Winton (1985)

IV

In spite of the provision of some new facilities, sport probably saw less change than any other school activity during this period. The P.G.C. came to the end of its long life in 1970 and was replaced by a games committee, chaired throughout its existence until 1989 by Hugh Thomas; consisting of the masters who ran the various sports. It was a conservative body which labelled rugby, hockey, cricket and later athletics as the 'major' sports and, while recognising fencing and tennis as 'minor' sports, continued to insist that they and other sports like cross country, squash and swimming had second pick of the available players. Although David Clark was appointed to run physical education in 1972, he did not fulfil this rôle and Hurst had no specific games masters under Roger Griffiths apart, of course, from a cricket coach, the most successful of whom was Derek Semmence, appointed in 1975.

At his first Council meeting Roger announced the introduction of badminton and fencing, and the latter developed as a minor sport under Keith Grant and Roger Powe. Golf (1965), judo (1966), canoeing (1971), sailing (1974)—developed under Nicholas Heath and James Gowans—and water-polo (1981) made their appearance, but none of them were more than minority interests for less than twenty boys, except for house water polo. In 1967 a school poll showed strong support for introducing football which was run by Michael McAdam and Michael Mance. By 1970 over fifty boys were opting for the sport and in 1971 a team led by D.S. Le Tocq did well, winning six matches. But those who ran other Lent Term sports objected and football disappeared from the sports curriculum before long.

Two school sports had for long been handicapped by lack of modern facilities. Hockey, run in turn by Reginald Ruddock, William Cobbett, John Horne, Vincent Thomas, and for 12 years from 1982 by Richard Crooke, needed an all-weather pitch to provide winter training. In 1968, when use was made of the new Crawley Stadium for this purpose, a team led by G. de W. Waller won eight of its 11 games, and next year the team had only one loss. The opening of the all-weather pitch was therefore a tremendous gain and hockey training began in Michaelmas Term from 1970. However, the early 1970s did not produce good seasons, and it was not until 1976 and 1977 when the First XI won nine and 10 matches that Hurst hockey showed it could win again as it had in the 1940s. A few poor years were followed by two successful teams in 1981 and 1982 led by Simon Kateley and Peter Dorwood. In 1983 came the first hockey tour which went to Barcelona, and the following year led by Augé de Rancourt the First XI was unbeaten. Bad weather increasingly affected the Lent Term so that the 1985 and 1986 teams were less successful, although doing well at the Oxford and Bath Hockey Festivals.

Swimming desperately needed a modern pool and, apart from 1969 when four victories were recorded, year followed year with poor results. In 1973 Rodney Jackson began his 15 years running swimming, and the opening of the covered pool in 1981 saw new life in school swimming with a water-polo house competition begun (the first result was a draw between Shield and Star) and a proper training programme. In 1982 led by Neil Livingston the team won seven out of eight matches and this success drew in more boys. Next year with Stephen Darch and Simon Cotton as leading lights five matches were won, and nine new school records were established. Hurst returned to the public school events at the Bath Club.

Tennis, too, received new facilities with three new courts and use of the all-weather pitch, but William Alban, Ronald Bawtree and Michael Grime always had a difficult task because cricket and athletics were recognised as major sports and swimming had revived. When Grime

52 First XI hockey team, 1984. This was an unbeaten team captained by A.J. Augé de Rancourt.

took over in 1973 there was a flurry of activity. The team led by W.L. Templar secured five wins. An open school competition and a house tennis competition started and the first Old Johnian match took place. At the end of the 1970s a good colts team emerged which stayed together and, led by Nigel Pool, won six out of 10 matches in 1980, and five out of nine in 1981. That year there was a tennis tour of Holland. Poor results then resumed until the mid-1980s when a colts team including the two Bertrams and the two Bergers won eight of their ten matches as a prelude to success as seniors.

Squash with its new courts and later its changing facilities remained popular and successful under Ronald Bawtree and John Elkins, not least because it remained the only important indoor sport, and because Philip Ayton as a national player was so well-known: he was at the 50th celebrations for squash in 1980. During 1967 and 1968 the team, led by John Richardson, did extremely well, winning the Sussex Rose Bowl for the first time, and Richardson went on to play for England. 1970 and 1971 were good years led by D.R. Watson with the Rose Bowl won again and throughout the 1970s most seasons recorded good results. The early 1980s were outstandingly good years for squash with Hugh Ruxton, Martin Rose and Martin Nichols as the top players. In 1979-1980 and in 1980-1981 there were 14 victories each year, and the Sussex Rose Bowl was won a third time. In 1980, 1981 and 1982 Hurst won the first three Woodard Schools squash tournaments. But as rugby extended into the Lent Term, and hockey back into the Michaelmas Term squash, too, began to be squeezed by major sports and also by swimming and cross country so that James Gowans had a difficult task to secure victories with constantly fluctuating teams.

Cross country and athletics to some extent go together with summer term athletes using Lent Term cross country particularly if they were long distance runners. Under Jonathan Pinhey and Mark Griffiths cross country was strong during the 1960s, appealing to boys who resented team games, and to sports loners. In 1969, for instance, the First VIII won all matches and the Colts were undefeated. After some decline in the 1970s when Epsom College organised (1970) the Hurst Penny Trophy for competition between six—later 12—schools, cross country revived in the early 1980s, and soon had over sixty boys involved in the sport as a prelude to match success later in the decade with Peter King as master in charge.

Athletics under Jonathan Pinhey, Mark Griffiths, Howard Stephens and above all David Clark from 1973 went from strength to strength and there were few years without impressive victory lists. From 1966 stretched a series of good years culminating in 1970 and 1971 when the senior athletes were unbeaten, and sustained only one defeat. In 1969 athletics 'went metric', and a number of boys such as C.J. Youngs and A.T. Russell were busy establishing a new set of records. The 1970s passed with eight or nine victories each term, and an early victory in the Sussex Championships. Junior and intermediate teams were built up by Clark and those of 1978, with E. Okezie as captain, and 1979, which lost only one match, were the fruits of this policy. 1981 saw the start of many more successful seasons with Ben Thomas, William Flood and Peter Budden among the outstanding captains. In 1981, 1982, and 1986 Hurst won the Woodard Schools Athletic Tournament. Among the distinguished athletes were Guy Williams, Mark and Alex Robinson, A.J. Augé de Rancourt, Adam Weatherley, Tamba M'Bayo, Tom Ruxton, James Gordon, Tim Herbert, Mark Corrigan, Darren Hall, and Alan Fisher.

Rugby's record was a variable one unless the first team could keep the same boys in it for two years and provide itself with a heavy, fast pack which it has not often been Hurst's lot to produce. After 1964 the rest of the 1960s and the early '70s were lean years apart from 1968 when, led by A.T. Russell, only one match was lost. It was not until the arrival of David Clark that things began to change for the better. 1975 was the 50th year of Hurst rugby and a team led by R.I. Godwin's try-scoring skills won 13 of 19 fixtures, and two sevens cups, and in December went on the first rugby tour which was to Shawnigan Lake School in Canada, where they lost three and won three matches. Next year led by Nigel Tucker another fine team won 10 and drew two of their 12 matches. Then came a lean period again in the late 1970s and early 1980s apart from the 1980 team which won six and drew one of its 12 matches and contained much talent like Steven Davenport, Simon Kateley, and Mark Speirs, and the 1982 team which won seven and drew one match with Mark and Alex Robinson, Tim Thorne, and Mark Foulds among the best players. 1984 was the best season since 1976 when, captained by Angus Turpin and including a galaxy of talent like Adam Weatherley, James Gordon, Mark Currie, Gareth Dexter, Tim Herbert, Richard Subtil, Alan Inman, Tim Perry, and Jonathan Mark, the team won 11 and lost only three matches, and at Rosslyn Park a team reached the last eight in the competition. Unusually 15 colours were awarded to a single team! The year ended with a tour to Narbonne. Sadly many of the same players were unable to sustain their form next year when an almost total reversal of fortune took place in the year David Clark was succeeded by Christopher Gray as master-in-charge.

Cricket was run by Reginald Ruddock, Nicholas Searls from 1969, Michael Mance from 1977, and Mark Allbrook from 1981 to 1994. The 1960s in cricket as in rugby were lean years except for 1968 and 1969 when the team won five and six victories respectively with G. de

53 The First XV rugby team in 1975, captained by N.C. Tucker.

54 The First XV rugby team in 1984, captained by A.R. Turpin. The whole team was uniquely awarded their colours. Amongst those who went on to play club rugby are, second row, standing, second from left, Martin R. Cass, who played for the Harlequins, Saracens and Surrey, and third from left, Timothy J. Herbert who played for West Hartlepool.

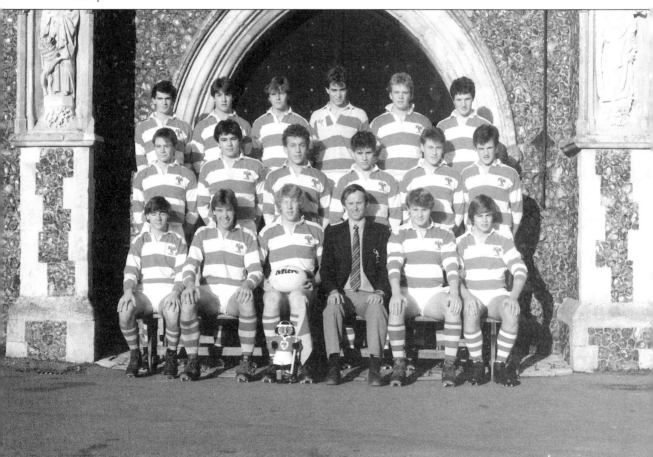

W. Waller and J.R. Blacker as leading batsmen, and Gordon Grantham as the main taker of wickets. He was tragically killed in a car accident in 1970. The early 1970s saw a series of poor years after 1971 when the First XI won eight and drew two matches with Gavin Lockhead as the leading batsman. He too was tragically killed training with the S.A.S. in 1981. From 1972 to 1975 only 12 matches were won; thereafter matters improved slightly with five victories in 1976, and four, in 1977, 1978, and 1979. Junior cricket, however, was doing well, and led by Alan Inman the Under 14s won the Lords Taverners Trophy in 1981 and did so again in 1983. The Allbrook-Semmence combination was now in full swing and the next 10 years were almost without exception excellent years for Hurst cricket and quite often at every level, too.

In 1983, captained by Tim Thorne, a team including Mark Foulds and Martin Speight as batsmen and James Lamb as bowler won eight, drew seven, and lost only four matches. They won the Woodard cricket festival at Worksop College. In 1984 captained by James Lamb the team was less successful, but Martin Speight, a future Sussex player, was showing his paces with a total of 777 runs in the season, and the team contained batsmen of the quality of Graham McMillan and bowlers like Jonathan Rose. In 1985 and 1986 Martin Speight was captain, and played for H.M.C. Schools and Sussex C.C.C. 1985 was somewhat disappointing with six wins and seven draws, indicating some weakness in bowling as the batsmen were only bowled out as a side twice. The leading batsmen were Martin Speight (556), and C.J. Davey. 1986 proved an excellent year with seven wins and seven draws in the term's matches and two further victories in the Woodard Schools festival. The team won the Simon Langdale Trophy at long last. Martin Speight completed his record-breaking years in school cricket by scoring 1,130 runs in the season. Among the batsmen C.J. Davey and A.J. Reid were the other main run scorers, and Gareth Dexter and Simon Drake polished off 59 wickets between them.

One of the most interesting, even exotic, features of Hurst cricket in these years was a series of tours of India made possible by the links between Derek Semmence and Jam Sahib of Nawanagar, and Rajkumar College. The first was in 1977-78, travelling three thousand miles. Sixteen matches were played, Hurst winning five and drawing four. As a result of this tour Chattrapal Parmar became the first Indian boy at Hurst and Damji Hodar came to help with coaching for several seasons. During the 1981-82 tour eight victories and seven draws was an excellent result as the team battled with curry and the weather. This tour was the subject of a BBC2 film in April 1982: 'The Other Tour'. In the third tour in 1985-1986 as the team lost only two matches they won the Silver Elephant Trophy. Martin Speight's 212 not out was the outstanding event on the field while the offer of a native girl for 40 rupees to the school captain was probably the most remarkable off it!

Given the mood of many boys in the 1960s, one of the most surprising features of school life to survive and indeed become more popular in the 1980s was the cadet force. Reduced to nine terms 'enlistment' by defence cuts it was now up to boys to stay on if they wished in the sixth form. As late as 1981-82 there were 265 out of 396 boys in the corps including 60 sixth formers. To some extent this was due to Hurst's 'ex-pat' and military parents and to continuing entry to Sandhurst, now supplemented by army scholarships covering the cost of university education. Perhaps, too, the Falklands War period, with its revival of flag waving and jingoism after a period of peace since 1967, played its part with several Old Johnians like J.R.M. Prime, M. Cole, J. Stone and P. Orchard involved. But more than anything else the success of the corps was achieved by its three commanders during this period: Michael Bailey to 1968, who managed to appear at his farewell parade on a horse, Christopher Guise to 1986, and Michael Mance to 1995. They were ably backed by Captain William Saunders to 1976 and Captain Thomas Bullock to 1993 as sergeant-majors, and also by the willingness of at least eight masters to serve as officers.

Change there had to be, as National Service had gone, the Army Proficiency Certificates replaced Certificate A, and training was divided into a range of skills including drill and weapons training, but also commando training, abseiling and climbing, self-defence, first aid and other courses. The assault course was developed to no less than 16 obstacles and in 1986 there was an inter-house assault course contest. The corps band revived, particularly under Christopher Moore. Shooting recovered under Nicholas Heath after he returned in 1974, and went from strength to strength under his successor in 1987, Nicholas Edey. Camps were less popular than in the past, although each year there was arduous training on Exmoor and the usual visit to army camps like Catterick and Shorncliffe. In 1971 came the first overseas camp with a visit to Malta, subsequently repeated, and during the Cold War era there was B.A.O.R. to visit for the first time in 1972 when the long-haired cadets were required to don caps in the pool. Further German visits took place in 1980 and 1986.

For those discontented in the 1960s by the traditional games, corps, and societies a range of new activities came into being, some supervised by Howard Stephens. A Service Group appeared in 1966 and was run by Christopher Dean, Michael Grime, and later Reginald Ruddock with a programme of hospital and home visits and later a Christmas tea in Red Cross. In 1967 driving lessons in school time began and by 1971 the R.A.C. Advanced Driving Test was also being taken. In 1968 motor bike lessons started in days when you could have a 125cc on provisional licence at fifteen. A motor club started in 1964 and arranged visits to places like Brands Hatch and Fords at Dagenham. In 1971 a construction group began, which did much useful small building work and repairs round the College and grounds. Other concessions were made to the real world of teenage culture. In 1967 sixth formers were no longer subjected to the Saturday night film for juniors and the Film Society returned to offer contemporary and more adult fare.

Modern music, too, gradually became acceptable and a series of groups were formed, starting with Drifting Sands in the late 1960s which actually cut a disc or two. They were followed by a considerable number including Astrakan, Disbanded, and Evil Weed in the 1970s and Rampage and Assemblage in the 1980s. Star was the first house to put on a disco in 1974 with girls from two local schools, but quite often the groups played to boys-only audiences and the theatre, in the words of a *Johnian* reporter, became 'a mass of jumping, sweating, writhing bodies'; those of earlier vintage claimed that Rodin's Gates of Hell had been opened at last.

These fresh developments were part of the changing society scene which the *Hurst Johnian* did not perhaps appreciate as much as it should have in its reporting of the 1960s and early '70s apathy. Indeed it was perhaps a little ironical that after Holloway stopped being editor in 1965 the magazine itself was not too well run. Michael Bailey took over until 1968 and deliberately altered the format. His successor to 1973 was Arthur Morgan, assisted for a time by Paul Markee. They tried to break away from the magazine as a journal of record with unfortunate results, because it could not really be Hurst's *Private Eye*. Critical and lively articles were to be welcomed, but carping criticisms did not fulfil that rôle. In 1969 *Ochre*, edited first by A. Matthews, started as a review magazine and, as no copies have survived in the archives, play reviews for the period, for instance, are non-existent. Old Johnians wanted news of school events and their own careers and so an *Old Johnian Newsletter* started, run for many years by George Lambert, and now by George Hill. Boys still felt they had no magazine for relaxed writing and so, in 1972, with R.C. Kettles as first editor, *Autolycus* appeared and raised a few eyebrows. In 1977 an attempt to be more intelligent was made by The Other Society formed by Nicholas Wermuth and Geoffrey Davey and a publication called *Animus*. Meanwhile the magazine muddled on, losing even its volume numbers, until Philip Arnold was put in charge of the first annual magazine forced on the College by the need for economy in 1975. Under Nicolas Chisholm the next four years saw the restoration of the magazine as a journal of record, which was continued by Peter King and Neil Morris.

Mention has already been made of the large growth of careers activities including visits. These added a new dimension to school activities during these years as the number of mini-buses rose to three. Several departments saw visits as a normal part of teaching, particularly classics, history and art. There were biology field weeks at Orielton and Slapton Ley and geography field work developed. Visits to the Gardner Art Centre were followed under David Hopkins by an extensive gallery visiting programme in the 1980s. There were Youth and Music visits. Drama and English substantially increased theatre visits. The Young Farmers went to the Ardingly Show and the older biologists to hospitals to see operations. With Brighton University, Technical College, and later Polytechnic, opening in the 1960s lecture visits were frequent. These visits were informal in dress and relaxed in behaviour and of real value. By the Michaelmas Term of 1972 it was calculated that there were 52 outside trips in the first half of the school year, and eventually in 1978 a fixtures committee, run by Hugh Thomas, was set up to co-ordinate activities, trips, matches and exam commitments: clear evidence again that apathy had gone and life had plenty in it for those who made the effort. Holiday visits including ski trips, classical visits, and trips to Russia with Gerald Buss showed how wide horizons were becoming.

The more traditional societies continued and reformed themselves. Throughout the 1960s and early '70s the Ionian, Science, Literary, and Jazz Societies continued, and Timothy Ganz founded a poetry society called Metre. The Natural History Society was renamed the Biology Society in 1966, and a Junior Biology Society, and a Young Farmers Club (1970) came into being. In 1967 Junior Geography, Debating, and Literary societies were set up. It was a mark of the changing world that the first junior debate was about hippies. During the period Modern Languages, Ornithology, Philatelic, and Photographic societies existed for a time and by the 1970s new ones were being formed once more. In 1971 Timothy Ganz formed the Christian Group whose activities included visits to *Godspell*, or to hear Cliff Richard speak at Lancing. Martin Williams formed an archives group, and Jonathan Howlett a war games society. Nicolas Chisholm reorganised debates, and Lilliputians and Lemuel Gulliver societies appeared to be run later by Robin Williamson. Among the last societies formed in Griffiths's day were the History and Politics in 1979 and the 1984 Society later (1992) renamed the Scholars Society. In the mid-1970s one calculation was that there were 200 meetings during one Michaelmas Term, and it should not be forgotten that art, carpentry, pottery, silver-smithing, and computing were both school subjects and societies involving boys during their leisure time. The Observatory returned in 1982. Clearly the later 1970s and early '80s were almost as fruitful in societies as Howard's era was, although they changed in character and involved fewer boys.

Drama on the other hand saw radical change and expansion in these years. The last Robert Bury productions took place in 1965 and 1966, and it then proved difficult to find a successor. From 1967 to 1971 the Shakespeare play had a variety of producers—Roger Griffiths for those of 1967, 1969, 1970, and 1971, and Arthur Morgan and Mark Griffiths in 1968. Performances of *King Lear* and *Othello* were particularly outstanding, and an opportunity arose to introduce modern lighting and staging effects. The 1967 play had three girls in it for the first time although in the 1970s the practice of boys playing girls' parts actually resumed for a time. From 1972 to 1981 William Alban was director of drama, assisted from 1974 for 10 years by Jonathan Howlett as stage manager. The play returned to November where it had first been, and Alban introduced professionalism by cutting rehearsal times and producing his Instructions to Actors. Difficulties in finding boys able to play big parts led him to avoid the major histories and tragedies, and the

1970s was marked by plays like *A Comedy of Errors* and *Measure for Measure*. A determined effort to modernise production took place. Five of the plays were in traditional mould, although even these had minimal scenery, and light and sound effects provided by a new theatre console built by the stage crew. Four were in modern dress and one in Victorian mode.

1982 saw another gap in producers into which Roger Griffiths stepped with 'Scenes from Shakespeare'. In 1983 Neil Morris produced the first of his six productions. This was a highly effective modern dress *Macbeth* accompanied by Mahler and Stockhausen's music with Richard Miller and Wendy Headwick in the lead rôles. A musical version of *A Midsummer Night's Dream* followed in 1984 with Ben Priest, Andrew Hunt, Gesine Hughes, and Elizabeth Mance as the two couples. 1985 saw a further departure from the words of the Bard with *Romeo and Juliet* transformed by break dancing, pop music, and professional choreography. Clearly Morris experienced the same problem as Alban in finding quality actors, and took the view that productions needed to be tailored to the existing talent. While some saw this production as 'polished, different and imaginative' it was also described as 'Saturday Night Shakespeare'.

But, if there was a reluctance to perform traditional Shakespeare plays, elsewhere drama flourished enormously. The common room and their wives played a part in this. Gilbert and Sullivan flourished from the *Pirates of Penzance* (1969) to *Trial by Jury* (1980) as it had not done previously at Hurst. In 1971, 1975 and 1976 Roger Griffiths compèred three Victorian evenings. There were common room reviews like 'An Evening at Hurst' (1974); the last of which was in 1983. Christopher Dean devised and produced in 1970 a pageant of the College's history, given three times in 1974 and revived thereafter on several occasions. Robin Paul, master of the Junior School from 1972 to 1985, was an enthusiastic producer of common room plays from Agatha Christie to Anton Chekhov. The houses, particularly Fleur de Lys, Red Cross and Martlet, began to produce an eclectic selection of plays. In 1977-1978, for instance, Fleur and Eagle produced two plays each, and Star their first one.

This enabled a wide variety of plays requiring smaller casts, and skilful acting to be performed from Kafka's *The Trial* (1969), Ionescu's *The Painting* (1971), Anouilh's *Ring Round the Moon* (1971) to Hall's *The Long and the Short and the Tall* (1982), Pinter's *The Birthday Party* (1982), and Stoppard's *Rosencrantz and Guildenstern are Dead* (1984). Three particularly impressive

55   The Bury Theatre opened in 1956.

56 Roger Griffiths with his wife, Diana, and his brother, Richard, at the Martlet House 'This is Your Life', 11 March 1984. The dog was called Bumble.

performances during these years were Michael Bailey's production of Christopher Fry's *A Sleep of Prisoners* (1964), and Christopher Dean's productions of Anouilh's *Becket* (1967) and Eliot's *Murder in the Cathedral* (1973). Two of these—*A Sleep* and *Becket*—were put on in the chapel.

Musical activity in the school was nothing short of remarkable during much of this period, considering that until 1979 its main centre was the 'Albert Hut'. A third of the boys studied a musical instrument, and at least a third were involved in the choir and the annual choral society performance. A Level music arrived, and there was a good record of choral and organ scholars to Oxbridge. The first music scholars concert in 1973 was described in the *Sunday Times* as 'an astonishing performance' at schoolboy level, and the house music competition left the days of patriotic choruses behind for instrumental and vocal sections at a level which did not make it incongruous to have the Director of the R.A.M. as their judge in 1979. Some figures illustrate the extent of musical activity. From 1977 to 1982 the choir sang 155 different pieces of music in addition to the service settings. In the school year 1982-83 there were 40 musical events.

It is not surprising, therefore, that Peter Lattimer, director of music from 1962 to 1971 should have moved on to be director at Bryanston School, and Neil Page, director from 1972 to 1976 to Malvern College. Nicholas Searls arrived in 1967, became the first assistant director of Music in 1972, and succeeded Neil Page at the start of 20 remarkable years as director. With Horace Hawkins and Wilfred Smith, Searls was the third great maker of Hurst music in the century. He adopted a no-nonsense, forceful approach ideally suited to the boys and, when this was combined with a similarly disciplined approach to the chapel, particularly by Gerald Buss, it produced services of a high quality in which the vast majority of masters and boys took part. Far gone indeed were the days of 'revolution' and 'God is Dead', on an evening like 8 March 1981 when the school's evening service was broadcast live by the BBC, and from choristers to tearaways the boys sang their hearts out in hymns like *Lift High the Cross* and *Thine be the Glory*. Searls was fortunate, too, to recruit an excellent succession of music masters to be assistants particularly Christopher Moore and Adrian Stark, who later became director of music at St John's, Leatherhead.

The great choral event of the year continued to be at the end of the Summer Term and the choice of works essentially conservative, although Honegger appeared on one occasion. It is always hard to single out particular performances but Elgar's *Dream of Gerontius* appeared again in 1985 as a very difficult work for school performers, and went well after only one complete rehearsal of all those involved. From 1969 to 1978 a series of remarkably varied music weeks took place at the intensely crowded end of the Summer Term, with choral and orchestral events, chapel services, organ recitals, the Ionian Society, the band, and distinguished outside soloists. Music, apart from the school orchestra and band, involved, a range of chamber groups, an *a cappella* choir, and many other groups like Close Harmony, The jazz group, wind and brass ensembles, and, of course, soloists who were heard at termly concerts and the house music competition.

But it was the chapel choir (and organists) who gave Hurst a national musical reputation by the 1980s. The music repertoire was kept conservative, and the works of S.S. Wesley, Stanford, Parry, Walmisley, Holst, Ireland, Howells, and Vaughan Williams were particularly suited to the male voice choir and the size of the chapel. Four records were made in 1974, 1976, 1978 and 1984 followed by tapes. There were fairly frequent television appearances. There were annual visits to local churches, and other visits further afield to St George's Chapel Windsor or St Mary-le-Bow. Hurst choir became a well-known part of the cathedral music scene and performed in nine cathedrals in ten years; among the most impressive occasions being visits to Canterbury and Exeter, and at the latter cathedral they gave the week's services.

In 1977 Hurst choir was chosen as the public school choir at the Schools Music Association concert at the Royal Festival Hall, and in 1983 came the greatest achievement when they won the National Schools Choir competition in a contest with many mixed choirs, singing Ireland's *Greater Love Hath No Man*. The school itself and an increasing number of parents and local visitors enjoyed magnificent set-piece services throughout the year: harvest festival amidst the foliage and marrows, St Etheldreda with the procession entering to *Jerusalem My Happy Home* as it had done in 1865, Remembrance Sunday with the full 1919 service, the corps band, the reading of names, and the Last Post lingering high in the Western arch, and at Christmas time, besides the carol services, a new candle-lit Advent service devised by Michael McAdam and Roger Griffiths in 1964. In the Summer Term came confirmation, and the Leavers' service with its banner procession. Indeed, as the magazine wisely remarked, the services were so good it was sometimes easy to forget why they were being held and just enjoy the music.

During these years there were certainly some changes in chapel. Daily services were cut to three a week, and moved to the morning. In September 1967 Junior School services were separated out. In 1974 Gerald Buss introduced morning talks by masters, the first being by George Hill, and on 4 June the first morning service given by the boys. This was followed in September 1982 by house services. The Church itself added to change by replacing first the Authorised Version of the *Bible* and then the *Book of Common Prayer* orders of service with the *New English Bible* and a series of services completed at this time with the introduction of Series III, Rite B in 1982. But the emphasis was on continuity and Hurst was fortunate to have three chaplains in succession who were good preachers, all of whom were directly involved in school life, and played a pastoral rôle with the headmaster and housemasters. Michael McAdam was involved in societies, sport and teaching. In 1970 he was succeeded by Timothy Ganz, assistant chaplain since 1965, who formed the Christian Group, was involved with other societies, and encouraged study of the architecture of the chapel. Gerald Buss arrived as assistant chaplain in 1970, became chaplain in 1974, and continued in the post until 1990. He was involved particularly in history, and Russian studies.

Roger Griffiths was absolutely firm on the position of the chapel in a Woodard school. He was broad minded: an agnostic became a housemaster and those of other faiths like Muslims entered the College, but all masters were specifically asked about their commitment to chapel at interview, and all boys, including day boys in both junior and senior schools, were

57 The choir at the Schools Music Association Concert at the Royal Festival Hall, 1977. The conductor is Nicholas Searls, director of music 1976-1996.

required to attend every Sunday service at a time convenient to the Liturgy rather than to parents. Roger and his wife set the example by their attendance, and the Head's involvement in services was both genuine and effective. But it was essentially Gerald Buss's qualities and approach that secured a general and genuine acceptance of chapel, certainly not to be seen in other schools by the mid-1980s. There were critics, perhaps more outside the College than within, who muttered about military precision, and traditional methods, but neither Roger nor Gerald had any intention of turning a High Church school into an evangelical one, or introducing parish practices into a boys' boarding school. Boys got to know the rhythm of the services from the first evening back in the darkened chapel to the last chorus of *Jerusalem* at the *itinerarium*, and acceptance of the chapel influenced the atmosphere of the College as a whole. When a new hymn book was placed alongside the Public School Hymn Book it never found favour, and in the end in later years change in the chapel had to come from outside and with the backing of the bishop and the Provost. But to have 350 confirmed boys in the College and a hundred or more receiving Communion on a regular basis showed that the impact of the services went deeper than mere enjoyment of splendid ritual.

In Michaelmas Term 1981 Council gave Roger Griffiths a sabbatical term: his 50th. With the quarter century fast approaching it was time to take stock. By then the essentials of the traditional boys' boarding school had not only been largely preserved during the difficult earlier period but were flourishing. In part this explained why certain parents and boys chose the school and regarded it with such affection and pride. It stood out from those around it. Lancing and Ardingly had passed through considerable periods of reform. All the other Sussex public schools were now at least to some extent co-educational. In most the cane, fagging, and real prefect power had gone, and the compulsory régime as regards corps, games, and boarding had been substantially modified. Yet Hurst continued and its success continued.

Roger Griffiths could by now be well pleased with what he had achieved. There was a good waiting list except in the junior school. There was a continuous building programme in operation. There were Oxbridge successes most years, rising A Level passes, and further education entries. O Level results were less impressive and there was too great a fifth form leave. But Patrick Newbery was raising junior school numbers and in the senior school day boys were actually falling in numbers in the mid-1980s. So that the figures at least indicated that Hurst was producing an education then still very much in demand. The games teams almost without exception won not only substantial numbers of school matches, but also county and national competitions. The choir was nationally known. Societies were flourishing and many new activities from careers to woodwork were running successfully.

This was pleasing to most but not to all. There were those who believed Hurst needed substantial changes if one was to look 10 years ahead or even cast an eye at neighbouring schools. Co-education had first been discussed in Council in 1976 and day boys and weekly boarding won general approval at a housemasters' meeting in 1981, but as yet there was no policy other than to continue as a boarding boys' school. With the decline of 'ex-pat' families with the end of Empire and the decline of the armed forces, to mention only two sources of new entrants, change would have to come. In the Church, services had altered fundamentally away from the traditional Prayer Book and both bishop and Provost were eager to see a more informal family form of service. John Peters wrote an article in the 1986 *Hurst Johnian* on the coming G.C.S.E. exam, and its methods would produce fundamental change in every class-room. At that time no-one knew how many other exam changes were, in fact, to come, but again the emphasis was on change not continuity.

It is harder to analyse the ethos of a school. Hurst was certainly self-sufficient and proud of itself. It produced many boys with forceful personalities, strong, and with good games records. It was a disciplined, hierarchical, and essentially conservative society in spite of all the rule changes and outward relaxations in life. But there were some who thought it was not in touch with the changing rôle of women in education and society, or with the growing classlessness of much of life, where the old school tie and attitudes long associated with it were less well regarded. Hurst was quite a shock to Shell boys joining it, and even to masters and parents coming into contact with its way of life. To embrace the changes necessary to make Hurst once more a different place was unlikely to be congenial work for someone who had subtly handled earlier change and minimised its effect. When Roger Griffiths was offered his post with H.M.C. it was therefore the right time to leave, and he did so in the Lent Term of 1986, Reginald Ruddock being acting headmaster for the next term. Roger Griffiths had managed change in such a way as to arrive at a successful compromise owing more to tradition than to change. Now the time had come to reverse these priorities.

FOURTEEN

THE LATEST AGE
1986-1995:
A FACTUAL SURVEY

Simon Watson and the End of an Era

Introduction

Writing in the *Hurst Johnian* at the end of his nine years' headship, Simon Watson said that, when he arrived, 'Hurst had a lot of catching up to do'. Speaking on another occasion to Old Johnians (1993), he referred to how 'agonizing' some of this change had been as it affected 'our hallowed traditions'. From his first term when he abolished the cane it was clear that Simon Watson had been appointed to modernise Hurst, and ensure its future by bringing it more into line with the overwhelming majority of independent schools. Change rather than stability was undoubtedly the key characteristic of Simon Watson's headship after the early years.

58 Simon A. Watson was headmaster from 1986 to 1995.

But change did not only come from the Council and the head. New examinations which themselves brought about significant changes in classroom methods and subjects taught, started with the first G.C.S.E. exams in 1987, after a period of 36 years with the same exams. Acts of parliament including an Education Act bringing in a national curriculum, a Children Act, and a Health and Safety Act in 1988-89 affected independent schools. The last two particularly, as well as other developments such as Childline, and criticisms of 'bullying' altered the ethos of boarding school life, and the internal structures of discipline and house life accepted for most of the century. As Simon Watson said himself, these changes were seen by some as 'destructive' of 'fundamental aspects' of public school life. It seemed strange to the critics that a government pledged in public to independent education, academic standards, and discipline appeared to be undermining all three.

The coincidence of these developments with changes particular to Hurst undoubtedly added to resentments and made it more difficult for Simon Watson to carry out necessary and sensible reform without encountering some bitterness. But the changes were the law and it was living in cloud-cuckoo land to imagine they could not be implemented. Changes in society lay behind them and Hurst could not opt out. It was always an unanswerable point to the critics that no other school existed by the mid-1990s in which the policies and traditions they advocated continued to any great extent. Whether the changes were right, and whether or not Hurst before them was a happier place, were irrelevant issues: they had to be carried out. It required some courage and considerable foresight to do this, given Hurst's past history.

Simon Watson was 42 when he arrived with his wife, Katey, and their two sons. He was educated at Lancing College from 1957 to 1962 where he was a prefect and head of house, played cricket and fives, and was a CCF sergeant. He went to Christ Church, Oxford where he graduated in English in 1965. He taught for a while in India before taking his P.G.C.E. at London University, and starting his teaching career at Haberdashers' Aske's, from where he moved to Abbotsholme. He then became Head of English at Haileybury College and established their first day pupil house. It is far too early to assess finally so recent a headship, and one which polarised opinions on many issues. Those who supported the changes argued they were humane, necessary and sensible, and above all inevitable, given the changes in society brought about, for instance, by the universal adoption of co-education. Perhaps in the future the changes and reforms will be seen as being fundamentally right and of crucial significance in ensuring the continued survival of the College. But this last chapter makes no judgement. It is a factual survey of the developments and school life in the last nine years.

Entry, Numbers and Economic Depression

Throughout the 1980s Hurst continued to grow. In 1987 with 422 boys the senior school reached its largest so far. In 1989 the combined numbers of junior and senior schools—573—were the second largest in the school's history. Ninety entered the Shell that year, and there were 156 boys in the sixth form—another record number. But Hurst's traditional market areas were declining and boarding education was steadily becoming less popular. So in 1988 Reginald Ruddock became the first registrar and in 1991 he was succeeded by Anthony Bennett. In 1988, also, the first three boys were taken under the Assisted Places Scheme. The real entry problem began with the onset of the most serious depression since the 1930s, one which affected actual and potential Hurst parents with unemployment, company failure, negative equity, rising taxes, and increased spending on such areas as university education of their other children. Most schools dropped their Common Entrance pass requirements at this time drawing some boys away. Recruiting of pupils now spread actively to Hong Kong, Singapore, Malaysia, Belgium and Norway, and by 1994 there was a Russian in Shield. In 1992 came the first substantial intake of overseas students and entry in all years began to grow as parents became more selective. In 1994, for example, of 85 entrants, only some 69 were in the Shell. Meanwhile junior school numbers had recovered under Patrick Newbery, and stood at 169 by 1991.

Alternatives to Full Boarding

There was a national decline in boarding education during the late 1980s. It was caused by the changing structure of family life, a narrower catchment area, less pupils whose parents had experienced public school, and economic circumstances. At Hurst the trend started in the junior school where day pupils rose from 65 in 1986 to 113 in 1995 and, once established, the trend continued upwards. Day boys in the senior school rose from 35 in 1986 to 101 in 1994, and in both cases this represented a sharp percentage rise as well as one in absolute numbers. This led to changes. In 1992 John Evans returned to housemastering to supervise the conversion of Chevron to the first day house completed in three years. It was followed in this course by Fleur de Lys. In 1987 Saturday activities had started to give a more coherent feel to the weekend, but the trend became one in which a majority of boys left the College at the weekend, and became in practice weekly boarders. Saturday games started earlier and chapel times were rearranged. Whole house weekends out began.

Co-education

By the late 1980s the overwhelming majority of European schools were co-educational, and this applied as much to boys' public schools as any other group. By 1986 Hurst was the only Sussex school exclusively for boys and at that time the Division, anxious to do all it could to preserve St Michael's girls' school, let this continue. Closer co-operation with girls schools was signalled by the Hurst-Roedean Society (1988) which held joint debates, concerts and sports fixtures. Hurst could stay exclusively male, take sixth-form girls like Lancing, or become fully co-educational like Ardingly. Influenced by the substantial change in women's rôle in society, and therefore the need for education to reflect modern society, and also by the numbers problem, Council decided on 21 March 1992 to proceed with full co-education. In September 1993 10 girls entered the Junior School. In the senior school Martlet boys moved into Star and the house was converted for girls. Deborah Treyer-Evans became head of co-education and Anita Firth arrived to take charge of girls' games. In September 1995, with Janet Watson as house-mistress, Martlet reopened with 25 girls. That term they took a house assembly and by the middle of 1996 the cadet force had its first girl N.C.O.s. The number of women teachers in the two schools rose from six in 1986 to 18 in 1995. Judith Mosley was the first woman to be a house tutor and take a senior school sport—swimming, and Helen Aubrey-Drew was the first woman   College organist.

Academic Change and Record

John Peters and Martin Pulsford, the directors of studies during these years, had an immensely difficult task in a period of unprecedented academic change or, as some had it, academic decline, affecting the whole education system and including public schools for the first time. The start of G.C.S.E. in 1987 proved to be the beginning of changes that affected every year group and every subject throughout the next eight years. The new exams had several implications for boarding schools. They increased administration. New teaching methods changed the structure of classroom teaching towards what were, in fact, methods used in state schools since the 1960s. Course work, orals and practicals all expanded and became time consuming, and these pressures meant there was less time for direct contact with pupils and, on the part of some staff, less willingness to be involved in games or at weekends. The bursar had to cope with increased costs both in paying the examination boards and in providing changes in books and equipment on an unprecedented scale. Use of photocopied material became a major expense. The Summer Term grew shorter as exams back-tracked into May, creating problems for games and house masters. As G.C.S.E. was not designed, as O Level was, to prepare for A Level, problems arose at A Level, although many exams were actually made easier in spite of government talk about A Levels being a flag ship.

A/O Levels were replaced by Mature G.C.S.E.s. A/S Levels began with conflicting university statements about their acceptability. Hurst obtained 45 passes when they were first taken in 1990 and later a pass rate of 97.8 per cent was achieved in 1994. In 1989 a National Curriculum began involving changes in G.C.S.E. syllabuses which were also being altered after criticism of course work's share in marks. The National Curriculum completed the process begun in 1988, when the Shell began computer studies, with the establishment of art, design and technology in the curriculum as well as information studies. Co-ordinated science appeared. By 1991 staff, too, were being required to be computer literate with reports, work reviews, records of achievement and pupil profiles adding to administration.

Polytechnics became universities creating a bewildering variety of choices for tertiary education. Not only the careers department was now involved. In 1992 upper sixth academic tutors to deal with work and tertiary applications made their appearance and were soon extended to the lower sixth. In 1991 the government introduced league tables and the pressure to do well in these at a time of falling pupil rolls and strong competition was considerable. In spite of all the upheavals by 1994 Hurst's results were the best of any Sussex school in percentage terms. History, ancient history, art and physics had the highest percentage passes: biology, mathematics and physics the highest number of top grades, but substantial numbers of subjects obtained 100 per cent passes at all levels. These results were particularly noted by the inspectors when the first inspection since 1954 was carried out in 1994.

House Life and St John's House

Changes in the house system were, perhaps, the most fundamental that took place in everyday school life and had the most immediate impact on the boys, particularly where boys and parents had chosen the traditional boarding boys' school, and found the situation changed. In 1986 there were seven houses, all boarding, with some day boys attached, who stayed for prep and had the same weekend obligations as boarders. In 1995 there was a girls' house, two day houses, St John's House, and four boarding houses with day boys no longer conforming to boarding hours, and being exempted from some chapel services. Ever since the College began, the sixth form as a whole was regarded as a unit, one which boys could look forward to when they were involved in running the school as house and school prefects, with privileges, and a close relationship with a housemaster who they knew for their school life. The house was the focus of deeper loyalties than the school as a whole, and while this led to introverted attitudes it also provided an emotional pull capable of inspiring effort and resolving problems.

The biggest change of all, therefore, was the creation of a house for the upper sixth, some distance away from the main building, where all the school prefects would, of course, be in

59 The common room, 1986. Seated from left to right: M.J. Mance, H.R. Thomas, D.J. Hughes, C.J. Dean. R.T. Ruddock, Headmaster, J.H Peters, C.J. Guise, R.H.T. Jackson, N.G.C. Searls and Rev. Gerald V.A. Buss.

residence. Unlike the lower sixth these boys were to have dress privileges and the sixth form bar was now restricted to them. St John's House was opened by Bishop Colin James of Winchester in a private ceremony on 5 March 1992. David Clark left Chevron to be its first housemaster, assisted by Andrew Fleck and Adrian Stark and the academic tutors. It was a well-appointed building and its common room soon became the focus of a lively social life with the foundation of Forum as a new upper sixth society.

By separating house captaincy from the school prefects the head was able to look to a different sort of leadership from his prefects. A leadership course was started and it became clear that the authoritarian and hierarchical prefects' system, which had existed for over a hundred years, was at an end. House duties substantially declined. Attendance at house matches ceased to be compulsory. House punishments were reduced to a minimum. Instead of new boys being thrown in at the deep end and given a new boys' test, they had a 'nursemaid' to look after them and had every aspect of school life explained to them. But, as Simon Watson remarked in 1988, the days of 'liking it or lumping it' were past. Attitudes at home and in the law had changed. What had been seen as 'character building' and 'toughening' was seen as bullying at worst and over-emphasis on the manly virtues at best. A family atmosphere began to spread. Rooms were provided for parents and parents were welcomed into the building. They intervened in discipline and choice of career and subject in a way quite astonishing to those brought up under what one might call 'the Howard System'. But parental 'rights' were part of government policy and educational thinking, and with the intended move to co-education the *ancien régime* had to go, whatever it meant to some or had achieved for many. Moreover, staff coming forward for house duties no longer shared the old consensus and welcomed these changes: some of them indeed found their strongest advocates at housemasters' meetings. Between 1989 and 1994 five out of seven houses changed hands, and one more not long after, and by the time Simon Watson left, the traditional house—with its housemaster in control of all aspects of a boy's life and house prefects of all aspects of house life—had ceased to exist. In the year that he left a Christian name policy for all pupils in class, reports, and elsewhere, as well as socially, marked very clearly the new kind of relations Simon Watson aimed to achieve.

Buildings

There were a number of important additions and modernisations under Simon Watson but the decline in fee income combined with a rise in V.A.T. on building improvements curbed development after 1992. Nor was it possible to complete some programmes, such as the reroofing of the main buildings after the chapel roof was completed. Changes in house function were costly in resources. After considerable debate it was decided in March 1987 to proceed with the sports hall, then called the New Hall and intended to be a multi-purpose facility for exams and assemblies. Pieters International contracted to build it in 155 days and fulfilled their contract in spite of the great storm of 16 October which brought down trees and cut off the electricity for several days. Lord Plummer of Marylebone (OJ) declared the building open in November. By then its cost had risen to £311,206 and equipping it to £30,868. For the first time in its history Hurst had a fine gymnasium. The school's classrooms were brought up to date with carpets, sound proofing, and audio-visual facilities. The masters' common room doubled in size. In 1988 the former gymnasium re-emerged as a 108-seat lecture theatre and another long felt requirement was fulfilled. The theatre was refurbished as the Bury Theatre. The area of the science building devoted to computers, design and technology was completely modernised.

Personnel

When Sir John Barnes retired in 1987 he was succeeded by Sir Derek Day (OJ) who remained Chairman of Governors throughout this period. On the retirement of Commander Charles Bricknell in 1988 he was succeeded as bursar by David Williamson who came to Hurst from East Anglia University and went on to be bursar of Marlborough College in 1994. He was succeeded by Martin Sherwin (OJ). Bishop Mark Green retired as Provost in 1988 and was succeeded by Christopher Luxmoore, canon of Chichester, and a former colonial bishop. Michael Gray the assistant bursar retired in 1992, and was succeeded by David Padgett. Mrs. Louise Louis became Financial Bursar in 1991 in succession to David James.

A Senior Management Team consisting of the two heads, the registrar and second master was created and formed a new policy-making body above the housemasters and heads of department. All the senior posts changed hands between 1989 and 1994. John Peters was succeeded as second master by David Hughes (OJ) and as director of studies by Martin Pulsford. He relinquished the title of head of science to Peter McKerchar who arrived earlier in 1988 to be head of chemistry. Martin Pulsford remained head of physics, and Kenneth Ralph succeeded John Peters as head of biology. Keith Weber, head of mathematics, left in 1988, and was succeeded by Stephen Waters who later became academic administrator. Patrick Newbery was succeeded by Adrian Gobat as Master of the Junior School in 1991.

A number of new titles appeared. Andrew Fleck who came in 1988 and was head of geography from 1991, became staff development co-ordinator. John Evans became director of careers. Martin May, who came in 1990, became head of design technology, and Richard Hurley, head of information technology and resources. Neil Morris was succeeded as director of drama by Jonathan Runswick-Cole, who also became editor of the *Hurst Johnian*. Andrew Cushing became the first director of physical education in 1987 and was succeeded in 1994 by Robert Kift who had come in 1990. Nicholas Searls remained as director of music, adding senior assistant master to his titles, and on completing 20 years in the first post became a housemaster.

As we have seen a substantial number of masters inherited from Roger Griffiths were still in place when Simon Watson left, but nevertheless the staffroom was becoming more fluid in composition, although the most to leave in any one year occurred in 1995-96. Between 1987 and 1994 half the heads of department changed hands with the departure of Nicholas Heath in 1987, Rodney Jackson, Keith Weber, and Nicolas Chisholm in 1988, Hugh Thomas in 1991, Christopher Dean and Peter King in 1992, John Peters in 1993, and Mark Allbrook in 1994. Among the new heads of department were Martin Pulsford, Peter McKerchar, Kenneth Ralph, Stephen Waters, Andrew Cushing, Martin May, Keith Grant, and Michael Mance.

The number of women in the common room increased with Judith Mosley (1986), who left in 1993, Deborah Treyer-Evans, who returned in 1992, Una Grogan, and Janet Watson among the most important. Joan Peters, the longest serving woman teacher in Hurst history so far, retired in 1996. Mention of those holding senior posts is often unfair to those who are in the school for a number of years making vital contributions of all kinds. One thinks particularly of Roger Powe, the last assistant chaplain, who left in 1989, Max Morris, who came from Burgess Hill School for Girls to enhance music, Trevor Baxter, and the growing St John Ambulance Brigade, which also had in charge of it Max Morris, and Christopher Monks, who started basketball as a school sport; Andrew Hobbs and Douglas Lang, popular young masters involved in sport, a succession of Australians who came for a year among whom Rohan Hoffman was outstanding in his contribution, Derek Semmence's contribution to sport, James Combes's to woodwork, and Thomas Bullock's as Cadet Sergeant-Major.

School Life, 1986-1987

There was no Shakespeare play this year. Instead there was a production of Christopher Hampton's *Savages*. Martlet put on *Oh What a Lovely War*, and Max Morris produced *Orpheus in the Underworld* jointly with Burgess Hill School for Girls. The choir sang at Winchester Cathedral, and the Choral Society presented Britten's *St Nicholas* cantata. A house-based charity competition raised £4,000 and Martlet won the first inter-house assault course competition.

Cross-Country Colts won the Hurst Penny for the first time, and did so again in 1988, 1990, and 1992, and were second in 1989 and 1991. Captained by Gareth Dexter the First XI won 11 and drew six matches. The two fencing teams won 11 out of 13 matches. The Under 14 cricketers won the Lords Taverners Cup. With Mark Shillaker and Matthew Priest among the leading athletes there were many victories and seven first places in the Sussex Public Schools meeting.

1987-1988

The play was *Antony and Cleopatra* with Michael Cooper and Sarah Bravo in the lead rôles. Martlet and Fleur de Lys produced plays and Shield *H.M.S. Pinafore*. The choir went to Berlin to sing at St Peter and Paul Church, and in April sang at Salisbury Cathedral; the Choral Society gave a performance of *Messiah*. Among prominent musicians at this time were Edward and Matthew Cooke and Charles Humphreys. The 900th *Hurst Johnian* was published. The first

German exchange pupils for some years arrived and there was a Shell and Remove visit to Greece.

The opening of the sports hall and the arrival of Andrew Cushing was followed by the introduction of basket- and volley-ball, trampolining and modern weight training. P.E. returned for the junior school, and the Shell. The Shooting VIII won the Staniforth trophy at the beginning of several years' substantial success in winning trophies. The athletes won 30 out of 39 matches. The First XI cricketers won five and drew six matches, and Matthew Hastwell scored a century. The Under 15s won 19 games including those for the Lords Taverners Trophy. Colts swimmers won six of their nine fixtures and, captained by Timothy Bertram, the First VI tennis won 10 out of 11 matches.

Examination Results 1987-1995

Year	A Level A-E passes	G.C.S.E. * A-C passes
1987	91	67
1988	89	73
1989	90	83
1990	91	87
1991	95	86
1992	94	83
1993	96	87
1994	98	88
1995	94	87

* O Level in the first year

1988-1989

The play was the *Comedy of Errors* using Trevor Nunn's version. Star and Fleur de Lys put on plays. The choir sang at Canterbury Cathedral in February and Chichester Cathedral in May. The Choral Society and Farlington Girls School performed Mozart's *Requiem*. The geography field work course went to Malta for the first time, and the Shell and Remove to Duisburg on exchange. The Classics visit was to Rome. Fleur de Lys started *The Grapevine* magazine. Community service, St John's Ambulance, and outdoor pursuits became more prominent school activities. Captained by Alexander Prince the First XV won 11 of their 14 matches and the Sussex Under 18s Tournament. Captained by Edward Welch the First XI hockey won 12 and drew two games. The First VI tennis won seven of nine matches. The three athletics teams won 36 of their 39 contests. Captained by Matthew Barry the First XI won seven and drew four matches. Mark Semmence and Christopher Cheshire took 59 wickets between them. On a cricket tour to Barbados Hurst won six of 10 games, and finished fourth in the English Schools.

1989-1990

Due to theatre refurbishment there was less drama this year. Fleur de Lys produced *Rosencrantz and Guildenstern are Dead*, and Martlet *Trumpets and Raspberries*. The choir sang at St Lawrence Jewry and visited Salzburg. The first Shell concert took place. Max Morris produced *The Gondoliers*, and the Choral Society performed Verdi's *Requiem*. Captained by Philip Thorne the First XV won seven matches. Colin Rhodes and Alan Checkley-Mills were in the Sussex Under

60 Cross-country First VIII, 1990. The first winners of the Hurst Penny trophy. Captain A.J. Cottle.

18s. Captained by Anthony Cottle the First VIII cross-country won the Hurst Penny Trophy for the first time. They were second in 1992. First XI cricket captained by Mark Semmence saw seven wins and six draws with Paul Wicker and Matthew King among the leading players. Hurst reached the semi-final of the Barclay's National Competition. The athletes won 31 out of their 39 matches. Captained by Alistair Brigg the Woodard Schools Trophy was won. It was won again in 1991, 1992, and 1993. Simon Leadbetter, James Hodge, Liam McCann and Ashley Gaunt were among the leading athletes. The shooting VIII won their first international trophy— the Jendeveine Cup.

1990-1991

The play, a joint venture with Varndean Sixth Form College, was *Much Ado About Nothing*. The first Shell/Remove play for many years was David Edgar's *Blood Sports With Ball Boys* with James Mount, Robert Gray, and James Hall revealing early talent. Jenz Pierce produced Red Cross's play, Peter Shaffer's *Black Comedy*; Christopher Dean's pageant was performed. The choir made two short television appearances, and sang at Chichester Cathedral. Short lunch time concerts began. The organ was reconstructed, and the summer term concert included Edward Cooke playing Handel's *Fourth Organ Concerto*; as well as Verdi's *Requiem*, and Mozart's *Vespers*.

Captained by Stuart Hall the First XI hockey won nine and drew two matches and reached the final of the Nationwide tournament. Captained by Alexander Earl, and with leading goal scorer, André Norman, the Under 16s went to Barcelona and won three of their four matches. In Mark Semmence's second year as captain First XI cricket won six and drew seven matches. In athletics Timothy Harling, Daniel Wilkins, and Liam McCann were selected for the county team and the juniors and intermediates won the mid-Sussex Trophy with Daniel Wilkins, Toby Bloomfield and Alen Smith among the leading athletes.

1991-1992

The play was the *Merchant of Venice* with Stuart Ruff, Stuart McGhie, Stuart Clark and Amy Carson in the lead rôles. *Fiddler on the Roof* was staged with Burgess Hill School for Girls. The junior forms put on Alan Ayckbourn's *A Talk in the Park*, and some seniors Tom Stoppard's *Fifteen Minute Hamlet* with James Montagu in the title rôle. A video was made of the choir visit to North Carolina and a cassette of a year in the life of the choir. The Choral Society event included Haydn's *Creation*, Christopher Burchill playing a Haydn trumpet concerto, and a *Magnificat* by Robert Woodford, a Johnian. The geography field work trip was to the Isle of Man and the classics visit to Greece. The cadet force camps were at Exmoor, Minden and Episkopi.

Captained by Keith Hoo the First XV won six and drew two matches, with Andrew Littlejohns, Ashley Rawlings, Altan Ozdemir, and Nigel MacGregor as leading players. There was a rugby tour to Singapore and Australia during which there were three wins and a draw. In spite of poor weather athletics led by Stuart Clark and Toby Bloomfield won 16 of their 26 fixtures with Daniel Wilkins in the senior, and Darryl and Mark Osman in the intermediates as the outstanding athletes. First XI cricket captained by Jack Riddy won five and drew six matches. The Under 16s attended a Public Schools Cricket tournament at Caen in Normandy. Swimming continued to improve and the Colts won four victories.

1992-1993

Drama productions began with *The Taming of the Shrew*, continued with *Burglars*, and ended with *Cahoots Macbeth*. Music began with an unusual recital by the American organist, Carlo Curley, and continued with the choir singing at St Martin-in-the-Fields, and reaching the last 16 of Sainsbury's Choir of the Year competition. There was a musical—*Annie*—with Burgess Hill School for Girls, and the year ended with Adrian Stark conducting Vivaldi's *Gloria*, and Puccini's *Messa da Gloria*. The art department visited France and made contributions to Woodard exhibitions at St Michael's and Ardingly and to the Sussex Arts Festival at East Grinstead. In chapel eastwards celebration ended with the remodelling of the east end and Rite B was replaced by Rite A.

The First XV won six and drew two matches with James Williams, Altan Ozdemir, Ashley Rawlings, and Robert Willsdon as key players. Football returned to Hurst with four matches. Under 14 rugby won six of their nine matches, and Under 14 hockey was undefeated. The Colts swimmers lost only one match. Athletics continued to do well with Toby Bloomfield, Nicholas Leathers, Daniel Wilkins and the Osman brothers as the leading lights. At the County Championships athletes had winners in five events and Paul Greenaway received a gold medal for his high jump. Cricket had a remarkable year in which only 10 matches out of 80 played by all school sides were lost. The Under 14 reached the final of the Lords Taverners, the Under 15 won the Blackshaw Bowl, and the First XI the Langdale Trophy. Eight boys played for Sussex at various age levels. The First XI won 14 and drew five matches and won the Woodard Schools Tournament. The key members of Simon Cross's team were Justin Bates, Alexander Earl, James Paterson, and Lee Atkins.

1993-1994

The play was *Twelfth Night*. A mixture of Shell, Remove and the lower sixth gave Ben Johnson's *Volpone* with James Hall and Sarah Clark in the lead rôles. The choir and orchestra performed at the British Embassy in Brussels, and *Messiah* was sung with Burgess Hill School for Girls in the summer. The College hosted the Southern Division Art Exhibition. *The Grapevine* was the regional winner of the *Daily Telegraph* School Newspaper competition.

Mark Porter captained both First XV rugby and First XI hockey. Both teams improved their record as the season progressed. The College reached the semi-final of the Sussex Sevens and the final of the Worth Sevens, and won two of their three matches at the Oxford Hockey festival. Under 15 hockey toured South Africa, and won six of their eight matches. Robert Playford, Charles Price, and James Smith were among the key players. Junior fencers won all but one of their fixtures. The shooting VIII captained by Edward Robinson won the Royal Sussex Cup at Bisley and J.J. Bowman won the Fordham and Kelly Cups.

Athletics was again spoilt by weather, but only one match was lost, and 18 medals were obtained at the Sussex A.A.A. Championships. Simon Clark in the juniors, Mark Ellis and Paul Thomas in the intermediates, Clinton Read, Darryl and Mark Osman, and R.B. Payne were among the leading athletes. First XI cricket captained by Justin Bates won seven and drew six matches. The Langdale Trophy was won for the second time. Justin Bates and Simon May scored centuries, and James Paterson, Justin Bates, and Lee Atkins accounted for the wickets. After Martin Speight, Matthew Hastwell, and Mark Semmence, Justin Bates became the fourth

61   First XI cricket, 1993, which won 14 and drew five matches. Seated, first left, D.J. Semmence, third left, J.J. Bates, fourth left, S.J. Cross, and seventh from left is M.E. Allbrook. Standing, second from right, S.P. May.

Hurst player in recent years for H.M.C. Schools. The fourth cricket tour of India unhappily did not manage to win a match in spite of the cricketing talent. Justin Bates was playing for Sussex second XI at the time and Simon Cross was captain.

1994-1995

Jonathan Runswick-Cole's last Shakespeare production was *Love's Labours Lost*, and Eagle House put on R.C. Sheriff's *Journey's End*. The choir visited Hayward's Heath twice to sing at the Methodist church and Clair Hall. The wind band performed at Chichester Cathedral and later went on tour to Holland. V.E. Day on 8 May was commemorated by a concert and a sing-song, and on Remembrance Sunday George Lambert spoke, who had served in the Second World War, and first entered the chapel as a master 57 years before in 1937. With Burgess Hill School for Girls, Adrian Stark produced *The Boyfriend*, and the summer choral event included Haydn's *Nelson Mass*, Fauré's *Requiem*, and another work by Robert Woodford, *Lo God is here*.

The Weston Speech Prize became a house event, and was won by Eagle. The geography field trip was to the Cevennes. Following the start of business studies A Level a Young Enterprise Team started to function. A charity day in March produced £2,000 for African education. Prize Day on 23 May had its guests Herr Volker Rühe and Malcolm Rifkind.

Rugby and hockey were less successful this year, but two members of the Under 16s rugby—Nicolas Lambe and Christopher Ward—were members of a Sussex Schools' team that toured Canada and won all five matches. First XI cricket won all their school matches. Simon May's batting, including two centuries, Lee Atkins bowling, and Robert Redford's batting and bowling were outstanding. With Mark Caldwell as captain, squash won the Sussex Schools' Second Division competition. In athletics the senior team won eight of their 10 fixtures with Adam Hankinson, Mark Ellis, James Hall, Christopher Charlton, and Paul Thomas among the best athletes. Simon Clark and Nicolas Lambe were winners at the Sussex A.A.A. championships. In swimming there were four senior, and five colts victories, and the senior team came eighth in the Bath Cup with George Bouras and Mark Bermingham among the leading swimmers. In hockey two teams reached the Sussex finals including the Under 16, captained by Robert Playford, who established a record by beating Lancing College 15 goals to nil.

The Changing Structure of Hurstpierpoint under Simon Watson

	Total in sen. school	(Day pupils)	Total in Jun. School	(Day pupils)	Total in VIth Form	Total in both schools	Staff Totals Senior	Junior
1986	418	35	115	65	128	533	43 (3)	12 (3)
1987	422	38	131	72	144	553	43 (4)	12 (4)
1988	412	43	147	94	154	559	44 (3)	12 (5)
1989	417	62	156	104	154	573	46 (4)	14 (6)
1990	385	61	169	122	144	554	45 (2)	14 (5)
1991	370	66	154	122	130	524	43 (2)	14 (6)
1992	360	82	147	111	132	507	45 (4)	14 (6)
1993	354	84	133 (10)	104	126	487	47 (8)	17 (9)
1994	326	101	131 (24)	101	109	455	45 (8)	18 (9)
1995	341 (25)	116	139 (27)	113	148	480	46 (11)	17 (7)

Figures in brackets are of girls and women teachers. Figures are taken from School Lists.

Bibliography and Sources

1. Original MSS

Unprinted

The College Archives at Hurstpierpoint College

The Woodard Correspondence and other materials at Lancing College

The Registry, The Sanctuary, Westminster

Printed

The Hurst Johnian May 1858—present day, and *The Hurst Johnian Newsletter*

Calendars, lists of the School, The Woodard Calendar, programmes, prospectuses, school rules, pamphlets

Press cuttings

Reports of the Schools' Inquiry Commission, Parliamentary Papers, XXXVIII, Parts I-XVIII, and Taunton Commission, Minutes of Evidence, Volume V, 45-71, Volume VII, 139-43, and Volume XI, 240-243

Statutes of the Woodard Corporation delivered in 1894

2. Secondary Sources

Previous works on Hurst history

Anon., *A Short Account of the Fabric, Reredos, and windows of St John's College Chapel*, Alabaster, Passmore and Sons, 1887.

Anon., *The History of the College Chapel at Hurstpierpoint 1861-1891*, Charles Cull and Sons, 1892.

Centenary Supplement, *The Hurst Johnian*, 1949, ed. H.R. Holloway.

Dewes, Simon (John Muriel), *When All the World Was Young*, Hutchinson, 1961.

Ganz, Rev. Timothy J., *An Historical and Descriptive Catalogue of the Chapel at Hurstpierpoint College*, privately, 1968.

Johnson, Harry L., *A Register of St John's College, Hurstpierpoint*, privately, 1914.

King, Peter, *The Climbing of Wolstonbury Hill on Ascension Day*, pamphlet, privately, 1983.

King, Peter, *The Boar's Head Feast and the Celebration of Christmas*, pamphlet, privately, 1986.

McAdam, Rev. Michael A. and Holloway, H.R., eds., *Centenary of the Chapel, 1865-1965*, pamphlet, privately, 1965.

Mitford, Bertram, *Haviland's Chum*, Chatto and Windus, 1903.

Moulton, Roger, *A History of the Junior School, Hurstpierpoint College*, privately, 1993.

Kinchin Smith, Rev. J., *Out of the Depths, A Schoolboy's Story of St Wilfrid's*, Christian Knowledge Society, 1901. There is no copy of this book in the libraries of record.

Wolseley, Faith (Stella Tower), *Which Way Came Death*, John Murray, 1936.

Woolsey, Rev. H. and Henn, Rev. P.U., eds., *Hurst Echoes*, Alabaster, Passmore and Sons, 1890.

Other Relevant Works

Baring-Gould, Sabine, *Early Reminiscences*, Vol. I, 1834-1864, John Lane, The Bodley Head, 1923.

Bryans, E., *A History of St Peter's College, Radley 1847-1924*, Basil Blackwell, Oxford, 1925.

Chandos, J., *Boys Together: English Public Schools 1800-1864*, Hutchinson, 1984.

Clarke, C.P.S., *The Oxford Movement and After*, A.R. Mowbray and Co. Ltd., 1932.

Gathorne-Hardy, Jonathan, *The Old School Tie, The Phenomenon of the English Public School*, The Viking Press, New York, 1977.

Green, V.H.H., *Oxford Common Room*, Edward Arnold, 1957.

Handford, Basil W.T., *A History of SS Mary and Nicolas College, Lancing, 1848-1930*, Basil Blackwell, Oxford, 1933, reprinted Phillimore, 1986.

Heeney, Brian, *Mission to the Middle Classes, The Woodard Schools 1848-1891*, S.P.C.K., 1969.

Henn, Wilfrid E., *A Life So Rich*, privately, Perth, Australia, 1982.

Honey, J.R. de S., *Tom Brown's Universe, The Development of The Victorian Public School*, Millington, 1977.

Hadley, Peter, ed., *Sam Brooke's Journal, The Diary of a Lower School Boy, 1860-1865*, Friends of Lancing Chapel, 1953.

Jones, Martin D.W., *Brighton College, 1845-1995*, Phillimore, 1995.

Kirk, Kenneth E., *The Story of the Woodard Schools*, Hodder and Stoughton, 1937.

Lowe, Edward Clarke, *S Nicolas College, and its Schools, A Record of Thirty Years Work* ... James Parker and Co., Oxford and London, 1878.

Meynell, Henry, *Canon Woodard's Scheme for the Education of the Middle Classes*, privately, 1881.

Mangin, J.A., *Athleticism in the Victorian and Edwardian Public School*, Cambridge University Press, 1981.

Newsome, David, *A History of Wellington College 1858-1959*, John Murray, 1959.

Otter, Sir John, *Nathaniel Woodard, A Memoir of his Life*, John Lane, The Bodley Head, 1925.

Ollard, S.L., *A Short History of the Oxford Movement*, A.R. Mowbray, 1933.

Overton, J.H., *The Anglican Revival*, Blackie and Sons, 1897.

Perry, R., *Ardingly 1858-1946, A History of the School*, Old Ardinians Association, 1951.

Victoria County History, Sussex, Vol. II (1907).

Wilson, G.H., *The History of the Universities Mission to Central Africa*, privately, 1936.

Woodard, N., *A Plea for the Middle Classes*, printed 1848, circulated privately.

Woodard, N., *The Scheme of Education of St Nicolas College with Suggestions for the Permanent Constitution of That Society*, James Parker and Co., Oxford and London, 1869.

Index